Studies in the Life of Women

AUGUST BEBEL.

"The end of social development resembles the beginning of human existence. The original equality returns. The mother-web of existence starts and rounds up the cycle of human affairs."—Bachofen.

"Since the advent of civilization, the outgrowth of property has been so immense, its forms so diversified, its uses so expanding and its management so intelligent in the interests of its owners, that it has become, on the part of the people, an unmanageable power. The human mind stands bewildered in the presence of its own creation. The time will come, nevertheless, when human intelligence will rise to the mastery over property, and define the relations of the State to the property it protects, as well as the obligations and the limits of the rights of its owners. The interests of society are paramount to individual interests, and the two must be brought into just and harmonious relations. A mere property career is not the final destiny of mankind, if progress is to be the law of the future as it has been of the past. The time which has passed away since civilization began is but a fragment of the past duration of man's existence; and but a fragment of the ages yet to come. The dissolution of society bids fair to become the termination of a career of which property is the end and aim; because such a career contains the elements of self-destruction."—Morgan.

INTRODUCTION TO THE
PAPERBACK EDITION

August Bebel's *Woman Under Socialism,* a great document of the Socialist tradition, is a most successful popularization of the essential ideas of Social-Democracy as well as of its views on the liberation of women. First published in 1883, it had reached over fifty editions in the original German at the time of the death of the author in 1913. In addition, it was translated into almost all major European languages. By the time of World War I at least fifteen foreign-language editions were in print.

The book's amazing appeal to very wide audiences is not due to its theoretical merits. Its ideas are in fact quite derivative. Rather, millions of readers found here, in a simple and earthy language, arguments and facts that helped them articulate their diffuse and inchoate yearnings for a better world to come. Bebel helped them bring into clearer focus the image of their desire. Through the prism of these pages several generations of European workers, and especially of working women, learned to perceive the social world in a new light. At least part of the book's appeal can be accounted for by the fact that August Bebel, though he was at the time of its writing already a successful Social-Democratic politician, still managed to retain a mode of exposition and a style of argumentation that he had developed in the working-class circles and debating societies where he had acquired his own education through exchanges of ideas with fellow radicals.

Modern readers, if they lack historical sense, might find much of what Bebel had to say about the role of women not only old-fashioned but obtuse. He considered a drop in the birth rate due to the use of contraceptives "a public calamity" (p. 111). He warned against the dangers of artificial abortions (pp. 110–11), and he was not above repeating contemporary clichés about the greater impulsiveness, the lesser capacity for reflection, and the more passionate nature of women (p. 121). But all this, in the last analysis, is of very little importance. What counts is that Bebel, writing in what was still the Victorian age, pleaded with conviction and sustained passion for the moral and legal equality of men and women. Bebel, the convinced democrat, could not conceive that moral and civil equality should be reserved for only half of the human race.

Bebel was deeply convinced that "the whole trend of society is to lead woman out of the narrow sphere of strictly domestic life to a full participation in the public life of the people" (p. 187). He had his sport with those who argued for the inferior intellectual endowment of women and who pointed to the relatively small number of geniuses that the female sex had so far produced. The woman, Bebel argued, from times immemorial has been crippled in her growth in a male-dominated society. "For thousands of years she has been oppressed, and she has been deprived or stunted in the opportunity and possibility to unfold her mental faculties" (p. 188). Women, just like the working class, were prevented by unjust and inhuman impediments from developing their potentialities to the full. As a consequence, "we have absolutely no measure today by which to gauge the fullness of mental powers and faculties that will develop among men and women so soon as they shall be able to unfold among natural conditions" (p. 189).

Bebel was appalled at the way in which his Germany relegated women to the kitchen and to the care of children. He wished to open for them all channels of opportunity so that they could make their contribution to the intellectual and economic tasks of the community. He wanted to demolish the walls that encased women in their dolls' houses so that they would leave the stultifying atmosphere of the private household to emerge as free and equal partners of men in the public world. He hoped that by joining the other great oppressed group, the working class, women would help tear down the house of male power in which they had been imprisoned since the beginnings of historical time.

I do not know whether Bebel knew John Stuart Mill's great essay, *The Subjection of Women*. But he would surely have endorsed Mill's view, expressed with a stylistic felicity which Bebel himself could not attain, that "We have had the morality of submission and the morality of chivalry and generosity: the time is ripe for morality of justice . . . It is totally out of keeping with modern values to have ascribed statuses: . . . human beings are no longer born to their place in life . . . individual choice is our model now."

Several generations of women of the working class, but also of the middle classes, read Bebel's book as if it were the charter of their coming emancipation. There is also little doubt that the men who read it were at least stirred into an awareness of the fact that the continued subjection of women went counter to the tenets of the ideology they professed to believe. It is much harder to know how far the actual life styles of the working class were in fact transformed by the appeals for sexual equality of Bebel and his co-thinkers. It is likely that his impact was larger in the realm of ideas than in the actual transformation of ways of acting. Life styles are hard to change. But even if many good socialists continued to practice sex discrimination at home and at their place of work, it is likely that they now did it with a measure of unease. They may often have been quite hypocritical in adhering to ideological pronouncements which they belied in their ordinary conduct. But, as the great French moralists knew well, hypocrisy is the tribute that vice pays to virtue.

August Bebel was born in 1840, the son of a petty officer in the Prussian army. His father died when Bebel was still a small child, his mother was left destitute, and the son was sent to a school for poor boys in Wetzlar. Upon completion of elementary school he was apprenticed to a turner. After his journeyman's travels he settled in Leipzig in 1860 to practice his trade. It so happened that Leipzig was at the time a center of radical activity. The young turner soon joined the newly founded *Gewerbliche Bildungsverein* (Trade Educational Association), in which many liberal and radical thinkers who had been disciplined in one way or another by the government attempted to build a bridge to artisans and handicraft workers in quest of self-improvement and political guidance. Bebel made use of the opportunity the Association provided to read voraciously on history and political economy and to fill the gaps in his formal education. In the give-and-take of the frequent discussions in this circle he gradually sharpened his dialectical skills and came to absorb much of the heritage of radical and socialist thought.

Bebel was at first attracted by the polemical writings of Ferdinand Lassalle, that erratic genius who had, almost single-handedly, created the first German labor movement, the Universal Workingmen's Association. But soon thereafter, he made the acquaintance of Wilhelm Liebknecht who had likewise joined the Leipzig association. This meeting proved decisive in determining his future career.

Liebknecht, who was almost fifteen years older than Bebel, came from a milieu very different than that of the young turner. When they met, Liebknecht already looked back on an active and militant career in the radical movement. He was the scion of a distinguished family of scholars and state officials descended from Martin Luther. Liebknecht had studied theology, philosophy, and philology at the Universities of Giessen and Berlin, from which he was dismissed on account of his socialist sympathies. He took part in the revolution of 1848 and after its collapse went into exile in London, where he made a living as a newspaper correspondent and teacher until 1862. Returning to Germany he joined the editorial staff of a Berlin paper, but resigned when he realized that the paper was in the service of Bismarck. Soon thereafter, the government expelled him from Prussia and he moved to Leipzig.

In the London years, Liebknecht had established intimate contact with Karl Marx and quickly fell under his spell. From then on, Liebknecht considered himself a Marxist, even though he differed in a number of ways from the master. Soon after his arrival in Leipzig, Liebknecht won Bebel for the cause of Marxist socialism. Henceforth Liebknecht and Bebel became an inseparable team and the nucleus of that little band of men who propagated Marx's message in his homeland.

Liebknecht, essentially a Forty-Eighter, who hated the autocratic Bismarck with all the fibers of his being, had no use for the Universal Workingmen's Association and Lassalle's attempt to create a labor movement with the blessings of the Bismarckian government. In August, 1866, Liebknecht and Bebel formulated at a congress of workers in Saxony the democratic political demands that they felt should be at the top of the agenda of working-class politics: the unrestricted right to popular self-government; universal, direct, and equal suffrage with the secret ballot; the abolition of the standing army and the constitution of a popular militia; a sovereign German Parliament; the unity of Germany as a democratic state; the abolition of all privileges of birth; and legislation for the improvement of the condition of the working class. In 1869, Bebel and Liebknecht formed the Social-Democratic Workingmen's Party at Eisenach on a program that embodied their previous demands and was roughly in tune with the general views of Marx and Engels.

When war with France broke out in 1870, Liebknecht and Bebel refused to vote for the war credits in the Diet of the North German Confederation, to which they had been elected a few years earlier. They furthermore opposed any annexation of French territory. In 1871, during the Paris uprising of the Commune, Bebel, in a memorable speech in the Reichstag, expressed his solidarity with the Paris insurgents.

Although temporarily weakened by the war and the arrest of many militants for their anti-war activities, the German Socialist movement soon regained its strength. In 1875 the Lassallean and Marxian wings of the movement united at the Gotha Congress, and from then on Bebel and Liebknecht were its recognized leaders.

By 1877 the Socialists managed to gain a half-million votes and a dozen members in the Reichstag. This alarmed Bismarck and the court. Socialist meetings were banned and the distribution of Socialist literature was halted. For years the Socialists enjoyed free speech only in the Reichstag. Despite these anti-Socialist measures, the movement continued to gain. In 1881 it had over 300,000 members, by 1890 there were nearly a million and a half. The repressive measures of the government had proved of no avail, and neither had the attempts to buy off the working class through improved social-security legislation. In 1890 the government gave up and repealed the anti-Socialist measures.

From then on, the German Social-Democratic movement grew rapidly and steadily and became the exemplar and beacon of all other socialist movements in the world. Just before World War I, the German Socialists occupied 110 seats in the Reichstag, and their vote of four-and-a-half million was about one-third of the total. The Party had by then been built into an impressive machine, manned by hundreds of functionaries, mainly, like Bebel, of working-class origin. It controlled a powerful trade-union movement and was solidly ensconced in the state parliaments and on municipal and regional levels.

The movement continued to proclaim its adherence to Marxist orthodoxy, but in fact it had mixed a good deal of water with the heady wine of the revolutionary doctrine that Marx and Engels had first elaborated in the 1840's. The apocalyptic and chiliastic vision of an imminent breakdown had quietly been replaced with a positivistic evolutionism which trusted in the benevolent effects of evolutionary trends that would "necessarily" bring about a socialist society. To be sure, full-blooded Marxist slogans would still be paraded on ceremonial occasions, but in actual political life the Party had shed its social-revolutionary husk. It still believed in the necessity of a political revolution that would sweep away the autocratic regime of the Kaiser and clear the way for full democracy, but it came to think that the further social transformation of the country would come about through parliamentary means and by a gradual transference of the means of production from private to public control. The leaders of the Party, and Bebel among them, put their trust in the benevolent course of evolutionary development and in the laws of progress which would inexorably lead the way to a good socialist society. History, they thought, was on their side.

It is faith in the benevolent course of history that radiates from the pages of Bebel's book. And it is precisely this faith that attracted so many readers. Previous socialist writers had impressed their audience with their depiction of Utopian societies of the future which they had spun out of their generous dreams. But they had failed to show in convincing detail how this earthly paradise was to be achieved. Bebel and his co-thinkers, in contrast, resting their arguments not only on Marxism but on the by then increasingly popular idea of unilinear evolution, convinced their readers that year by year, as the socialist movement grew in specific weight on the political and industrial scene, they were moving a step forward on the road to the inevitable triumph of socialism. The march of industry and science would inexorably, they said, sweep away all obstacles to progress and open the road for the emergence of just and humane social arrangements.

Such are the vagaries of social perception: Social Darwinism, which in America was perceived as a doctrine that legitimized robber barons and captains of industry as the fittest flowers of civilization, was seen by Bebel and his followers as scientific support for their socialist beliefs. "Darwinism," Bebel wrote (p. 201), "as all genuine science, is eminently democratic." Class struggles, he argued, "lead to an ever clearer understanding of the [social] situation, and finally to the recognition of the laws that govern and control . . . evolution. Man has in the end but to apply this knowledge to his social and political development, and to adapt the latter accordingly" (pp. 203–4). To Bebel, "Darwinism and Socialism are in perfect harmony," and both prove that humanity is on the march toward the good society.

The modern reader is likely to be tempted to tax Bebel and his co-thinkers with excessive naiveté and to dismiss them accordingly. Our generation, viewing history through glasses ground sharply by the horrors of two world wars and the massacres of millions of innocents in Hitler's Germany and Stalin's Russia, can hardly share Bebel's uncomplicated faith in the benevolent course of evolutionary history. Yet it would only reveal a failure of the historical imagination were we to dismiss Bebel's thought because it so patently failed to reveal the shape of things to come.

When we consider his writings within the context of his time and society, it becomes apparent that his message, despite its blemishes, performed a vital task. The socialist movement, and Bebel in particular, contributed to the moral and political self-transformation of the European working class, changing millions of workers from passive and degraded objects of history into self-conscious political subjects, autonomous actors on the political scene. Under the impact of Marxist and Social-Democratic doctrine, major portions of the European working class were transformed—to use Marx's terminology—from a class-in-itself to a class-for-itself. The Social-Democratic message penetrated to the workers' mental world and convinced them that their self-activity, rather than the actions of saviors and tribunes, would lead to their emancipation. It thus had profound democratic political results. Although Bebel and his co-thinkers spoke of the necessary sequence, the determined progression of history, they never failed to point out that the desired goals would be reached only if disciplined, methodical, and militant workers would leave aside their private passions and indulgences and lend their hands to the task of building a better future. Underneath the often platitudinous evolutionary phraseology there burned a fierce democratic and activist passion. The movement did not trust in fate but in the unfathomed potentialities inherent in all men. This is the belief that informs Bebel's view of the role of women in modern society.

At a time when, after a long period of neglect, the cause of the liberation of women is again on the agenda, a reissue of Bebel's work is most welcome. It belongs in the library of all those men or women who believe that sexual inequality, like racial inequality and class oppression, will have to give way, if we are ever to manage to build a truly humane society.

LEWIS A. COSER

State University of New York
at Stony Brook
June 1971

TRANSLATOR'S PREFACE.

Bebel's work, "Die Frau und der Socialismus," rendered in this English version with the title "Woman under Socialism," is the best-aimed shot at the existing social system, both strategically and tactically considered. It is wise tactics and strategy to attack an enemy on his weakest side. The Woman Question is the weakest link in the capitalist mail.

The workingman, we know, is a defenceless being; but it takes much sharpening of the intellect to appreciate the fact that "he cannot speak for himself." His sex is popularly coupled with the sense of strength. The illusion conceals his feebleness, and deprives him of help, often of sympathy. It is thus even with regard to the child. Proverbially weak and needing support, the child, nevertheless, is not everywhere a victim in the existing social order. Only in remote sense does the child of the ruling class suffer. The invocation of the "Rights of the Child" leaves substantially untouched the children of the rich. It is otherwise with woman. The shot that rips up the wrongs done to her touches a nerve that aches from end to end in the capitalist world. There is no woman, whatever her station, but in one way or other is a sufferer, a victim in modern society. While upon the woman of the working class the cross of capitalist society rests heaviest in all ways, not one of her sisters in all the upper ranks but bears some share of the burden, or, to be plainer, of the smudge,—and what is more to the point, they are aware of it. Accordingly, the invocation of the "Rights of Woman" not only rouses the spirit of the heaviest sufferers under capitalist society, and thereby adds swing to the blows of the male militants in their efforts to overthrow the existing order, it also lames the adversary by raising sympathizers in his own camp, and inciting sedition among his own retinue. Bebel's exhaustive work, here put in English garb, does this double work unerringly.

I might stop here. The ethic formula commands self-effacement to a translator. More so than well-brought-up children, who should be "seen and not heard," a translator should, where at all possible, be neither seen nor heard. That, however, is not always possible. In a work of this nature, which, to the extent of this one, projects itself into hypotheses of the future, and even whose premises necessarily branch off into fields that are not essentially basic to Socialism, much that is said is, as the author himself announces in his introduction, purely the personal opinion of the writer. With these a translator, however, much in general and fundamental accord, may not always agree. Not agreeing, he is in duty bound to modify the ethic formula to the extent of marking his exception, lest the general accord, implied in the act of translating, be construed into specific approval of objected to passages and views. Mindful of a translator's duties as well as rights, I have reduced to a small number, and entered in the shape of running footnotes to the text, the dissent I thought necessary to the passages that to me seemed most objectionable in matters not related to the main question; and, as to matters related to the main question, rather than enter dissent in running footnotes, I have reserved for this place a summary of my own private views on the family of the future.

It is an error to imagine that, in its spiral course, society ever returns to where it started from. The spiral never returns upon its own track. Obedient to the law of social evolution, the race often is forced, in the course of its onward march, to drop much that is good, but also much that is bad. The bad, it is hoped, is dropped for all time; but the good, when picked up again, never is picked up as originally dropped. Between the original dropping and return to its vicinity along the tracks of the spiral, fresh elements join. These new accretions so transmute whatever is re-picked up that it is essentially remodeled. The "Communism," for instance, that the race is now heading toward, is, materially, a different article from the "Communism" it once left behind. We move in an upward spiral. No doubt moral concepts are the reflex of material possibilities. But, for one thing, moral concepts are in themselves a powerful force, often hard to distinguish in their effect from material ones; and, for another, these material possibilities unfold material facts, secrets of Nature, that go to enrich the treasury of science, and quicken the moral sense. Of such material facts are the discoveries in embryology and kindred branches. They reveal the grave fact, previously reckoned with in the matter of the breeding of domestic animals, that the act of impregnation is an act of inoculation. This fact, absolutely material, furnishes a post-discovered material basis for a pre-surmised moral concept,—the "oneness of flesh" with father and mother. Thus science solidifies a poetic-moral yearning, once held imprisoned in the benumbing shell of theological dogma, and reflects its morality in the poetic expression of the monogamic family. The moral, as well as the material, accretions of the race's intellect, since it uncoiled out of early Communism, bar, to my mind, all prospect,—I would say danger, moral and hygienic,—of promiscuity, or of anything even remotely approaching that.

Modern society is in a state of decomposition. Institutions, long held as all time and for all time, are crumbling. No wonder those bodies of society that come floating down to us with the prerogatives of "teacher" are seen to-day rushing to opposite extremes. On the matter of "Woman" or "The Family" the divergence among our rulers is most marked. While both extremes cling like shipwrecked mariners to the water-logged theory of private ownership in the means of production, the one extreme, represented by the Roman Catholic church-machine, is seen to recede ever further back within the shell of orthodoxy, and the other extreme, represented by the pseudo-Darwinians, is seen to fly into ever wilder flights of heterodoxy on the matter of "Marriage and Divorce." Agreed, both, in keeping woman nailed to the cross of a now perverse social system, the former seeks to assuage her agony with the benumbing balm of resignation, the latter to relieve her torture with the blister of libertinage.

Between these two extremes stand the gathering forces of revolution that are taking shape in the militant Socialist Movement. Opinion among these forces, while it cannot be said to clash, takes on a variety of shades—as needs will happen among men, who, at one on basic principles, on the material substructure of institutional superstructure, cannot but yield to the allurements of speculative thought on matters as yet hidden in the future, and below the horizon. For one, I hold there is as little ground for rejecting monogamy, by reason of the taint that clings to its inception, as there would be ground for rejecting co-operation, by reason of the like taint that accompanied its rise, and also clings to its development. For one, I hold that the smut of capitalist conditions, that to-day clings to monogamy, is as avoidable an "incident" in the evolutionary process as are the iniquities of capitalism that to-day are found the accompaniment of co-operative labor;—and the further the parallel is pursued through the many ramifications of the subject, the closer will it be discovered to hold. For one, I hold that the monogamous family—bruised and wounded in the cruel rough-and-tumble of modern society, where, with few favored exceptions of highest type, male creation is held down, physically, mentally and morally, to the brutalizing level of the brute, forced to grub and grub for bare existence, or, which amounts to the same, to scheme and scheme in order to avoid being forced so to grub and grub—will have its wounds staunched, its bruises healed, and, ennobled by the slowly acquired moral forces of conjugal, paternal and filial affection, bloom under Socialism into a lever of mighty power for the moral and physical elevation of the race.

At any rate, however the genius of our descendants may shape matters on this head, one thing is certain: Woman—the race's mothers, wives, sisters, daughters—long sinned against through unnumbered generations—is about to be attoned to. All the moral and intellectual forces of the age are seen obviously converging to that point. It will be the crowning work of Militant Socialism, like a mightier Perseus, to strike the shackles from the chained Andromeda of modern society, Woman, and raise her to the dignity of her sex.

DANIEL DE LEON.

New York, June 21, 1903

CONTENTS

CONTENTS

Woman Under Socialism

INTRODUCTION.

We live in the age of a great social Revolution, that every day makes further progress. A growingly powerful intellectual stir and unrest is noticeable in all the layers of society; and the movement pushes towards deep-reaching changes. All feel that the ground they stand on shakes. A number of questions have risen; they occupy the attention of ever widening circles; and discussion runs high on their solution. One of the most important of these, one that pushes itself ever more to the fore, is the so-called "Woman Question."

The question concerns the position that woman should occupy in our social organism; how she may unfold her powers and faculties in all directions, to the end that she become a complete and useful member of human society, enjoying equal rights with all. From our view-point, this question coincides with that other:—what shape and organization human society must assume to the end that, in the place of oppression, exploitation, want and misery in manifold forms, there shall be physical and social health on the part of the individual and of society. To us, accordingly, the Woman Question is only one of the aspects of the general Social Question, which is now filling all heads, which is setting all minds in motion and which, consequently, can find its final solution only in the abolition of the existing social contradictions, and of the evils which flow from them.

Nevertheless, it is necessary to treat the so-called Woman Question separately. On the one hand the question, What was the former position of woman, what is it to-day, and what will it be in the future? concerns, in Europe at least, the larger section of society, seeing that here the female sex constitutes the larger part of the population. On the other hand, the prevailing notions, regarding the development that woman has undergone in the course of centuries, correspond so little with the facts, that light upon the subject becomes a necessity for the understanding of the present and of the future. Indeed, a good part of the prejudices with which the ever-growing movement is looked upon in various circles—and not last in the circle of woman herself—rests upon lack of knowledge and lack of understanding. Many are heard claiming there is no Woman Question, because the position that woman formerly occupied, occupies to-day and will in the future continue to occupy, is determined by her "natural calling," which destines her for wife and mother, and limits her to the sphere of the home.

Accordingly, whatever lies beyond her four walls, or is not closely and obviously connected with her household duties, concerns her not.

On the Woman Question, the same as on the general Social Question, in which the position of the working class in society plays the chief *role*, opposing parties stand arrayed against each other. One party, that which would leave everything as it is, have their answer ready at hand; they imagine the matter is settled with referring woman to her "natural calling." They forget that, to-day, for reasons later to be developed, millions of women are wholly unable to fill that "natural calling," so much insisted upon in their behalf, of householders, breeders and nurses of children; and that, with other millions, the "calling" has suffered extensive shipwreck—wedlock, to them, having turned into a yoke and into slavery, compelling them to drag along their lives in misery and want. Of course, this fact concerns those "wise men" as little as that other fact, that unnumbered millions of women, engaged in the several pursuits of life, are compelled, often in unnatural ways, and far beyond the measure of their strength, to wear themselves out in order to eke out a meager existence. At this unpleasant fact those "wise men" stuff their ears, and they shut their eyes with as much violence as they do before the misery of the working class, consoling themselves and others with "it has ever been, and will ever remain so." That woman has the right to share the conquests of civilization achieved in our days; to utilize these to the easing and improving of her condition; and to develop her mental and physical faculties, and turn them to advantage as well as man,—they will none of that. Are they told that woman must also be economically, in order to be physically and intellectually free, to the end that she no longer depend upon the "good-will" and the "mercy" of the other sex?—forthwith their patience is at end; their anger is kindled; and there follows a torrent of violent charges against the "craziness of the times," and the "insane emancipational efforts."

These are the Philistines of male and female sex, incapable of finding their way out of the narrow circle of their prejudices. It is the breed of the owls, to be found everywhere when day is breaking, and they cry out in affright when a ray of light falls upon their comfortable darkness.

Another element among the adversaries of the movement cannot shut its eyes before the glaring facts. This element admits that there was hardly a time when a larger number of women found themselves in so unsatisfactory a condition as to-day, relatively to the degree of general civilization; and they admit that it is therefore necessary to inquire how the condition of woman can be improved, in so far as she remains dependent upon herself. To this portion of our adversaries, the Social Question seems solved for those women who have entered the haven of matrimony.

In keeping with their views, this element demands that, to unmarried woman, at least, all fields of work, for which her strength and faculties are adequate, shall be opened, to the end that she may enter the competitive field for work with man. A small set goes even further, and demands that competition for work be not limited to the field of the lower occupations, but should also extend higher, to the professions, to the field of art and science. This set demands the admission of woman to all the higher institutions of learning, namely, the universities, which in many countries are still closed to her. Their admission is advocated to the classes of several branches of study, to the medical profession, to the civil service (the Post Office, telegraph and railroad offices), for which they consider women peculiarly adapted; and they point to the practical results that have been attained, especially in the United States, through the employment of woman. The one and the other also make the demand that political rights be conferred upon woman. Woman, they admit, is human and a member of the State, as well as man: legislation, until now in the exclusive control of man, proves that he exploited the privilege to his own exclusive benefit, and kept woman in every respect under guardianship, a thing to be henceforth prevented.

It is noteworthy that the efforts here roughly sketched, do not reach beyond the frame-work of the existing social order. The question never is put whether, these objects being attained, any real and thoroughgoing improvement in the condition of woman will have been achieved. Standing on the ground of bourgeois, that is, of the capitalist social order, the full social equality of man and woman is considered the solution of the question. These folks are not aware, or they slide over the fact that, in so far as the unrestricted admission of woman to the industrial occupations is concerned, the object has already been actually attained, and it meets with the strongest support on the part of the ruling class, who, as will be shown further on, find therein their own interest. Under existing conditions, the admission of women to all industrial occupations can have for its only effect that the competitive struggle of the working people become ever sharper, and rage ever more fiercely. Hence the inevitable result,—the lowering of incomes for female and male labor, whether this income be in the form of wage or salary.

That this solution cannot be the right one is clear. The full civic equality of woman is, however, not merely the ultimate object of the men, who, planted upon the existing social order, favor the efforts in behalf of woman. It is also recognized by the female bourgeois, active

in the Woman Movement. These, together with the males of their
mental stamp, stand, accordingly, with their demands in contrast to
the larger portion of the men, who oppose them, partly out of old-
fogy narrowness, partly also—in so far as the admission of woman to
the higher studies and the better-paid public positions is concerned—out
of mean selfishness, out of fear of competition. A difference in principle, however, a class difference, such as there is between the working
and the capitalist class, does not exist between these two sets of male
and female citizens.

Let the by no means impossible case be imagined that the representatives of the movement for the civic rights of woman carry through
all their demands for placing woman upon an equal footing with man.
What then? Neither the slavery, which modern marriage amounts to
for numberless women, nor prostitution, nor the material dependence
of the large majority of married women upon their marital lords, would
thereby be removed. For the large majority of women it is, indeed,
immaterial whether a thousand, or ten thousand, members of their own
sex, belonging to the more favored strata of society, land in the higher
branches of learning, the practice of medicine, a scientific career, or some
government office. Nothing is thereby changed in the total condition
of the sex.

The mass of the female sex suffers in two respects: On the one side
woman suffers from economic and social dependence upon man. True
enough, this dependence may be alleviated by formally placing her
upon an equality before the law, and in point of rights; but the dependence is not removed. On the other side, woman suffers from the economic dependence that woman in general, the working-woman in particular, finds herself in, along with the workingman.

Evidently, all women, without difference of social standing, have
an interest—as the sex that in the course of social development has
been oppressed, and ruled, and defiled by man—in removing such a state
of things, and must exert themselves to change it, in so far as it can
be changed by changes in the laws and institutions within the frame-
work of the present social order. But the enormous majority of
women is furthermore interested in the most lively manner in that the
existing State and social order be radically transformed, to the end
that both wage-slavery, under which the working-women deeply pine,
and sex slavery, which is intimately connected with our property and
industrial systems, be wiped out.

The larger portion by far of the women in society, engaged in the
movement for the emancipation of woman, do not see the necessity for
such a radical change. Influenced by their privileged social standing,
they see in the more far-reaching working-women's movement dangers,

not infrequently abhorrent aims, which they feel constrained to ignore, eventually even to resist. The class-antagonism, that in the general social movement rages between the capitalist and the working class, and which, with the ripening of conditions, grows sharper and more pronounced, turns up likewise on the surface of the Woman's Movement; and it finds its corresponding expression in the aims and tactics of those engaged in it.

All the same, the hostile sisters have, to a far greater extent than the male population—split up as the latter is in the class struggle—a number of points of contact, on which they can, although marching separately, strike jointly. This happens on all the fields, on which the question is the equality of woman with man, within modern society. This embraces the participation of woman in all the fields of human activity, for which her strength and faculties are fit; and also her full civil and political equality with man. These are very important, and as will be shown further on, very extensive fields. Besides all this the working woman has also a special interest in doing battle hand in hand with the male portion of the working class, for all the means and institutions that may protect the working woman from physical and moral degeneration, and which promise to secure to her the vitality and fitness necessary for motherhood and for the education of children. Furthermore, as already indicated, it is the part of the working-woman to make common cause with the male members of her class and of her lot in the struggle for a radical transformation of society, looking to the establishment of such conditions as may make possible the real economic and spiritual independence of both sexes, by means of social institutions that afford to all a full share in the enjoyment of all the conquests of civilization made by mankind.

The goal, accordingly, is not merely the realization of the equal rights of woman with man within present society, as is aimed at by the bourgeois woman emancipationists. It lies beyond,—the removal of all impediments that make man dependent upon man; and, consequently, one sex upon the other. Accordingly, this solution of the Woman Question coincides completely with the solution of the Social Question. It follows that he who aims at the solution of the Woman Question to its full extent, is necessarily bound to go hand in hand with those who have inscribed upon their banner the solution of the Social Question as a question of civilization for the whole human race. These are the Socialists, that is, the Social Democracy.

Of all existing parties in Germany, the Social Democratic Party is the only one which has placed in its programme the full equality of woman, her emancipation from all dependence and oppression. And the party has done so, not for agitational reasons, but out of necessity, out of principle. *There can be no emancipation of humanity without the social independence and equality of the sexes.*

Up to this point all Socialists are likely to agree with the presentation made of fundamental principles. But the same cannot be said on the subject of the manner in which we portray the ultimate aims to ourselves; how the measures and special institutions shall be shaped which will establish the aimed-at independence and equality of all members of the sexes, consequently that of man and woman also.

The moment the field of the known is abandoned, and one launches out into pictures of future forms, a wide field is opened for speculation. Differences of opinion start over that which is probable or not probable. That which in that direction is set forth in this book can, accordingly, be taken only as the personal opinion of the author himself; possible attacks must be directed against him only; only he is responsible.

Attacks that are objective, and are honestly meant, will be welcome to us. Attacks that violate truth in the presentation of the contents of this book, or that rest upon false premises we shall ignore. For the rest, in the following pages all conclusions, even the extremest, will be drawn, which, the facts being verified, the results attained may warrant. Freedom from prejudice is the first condition for the recognition of truth. Only the unrestricted utterance of that which is, and must be, leads to the goal.

PART I

WOMAN IN THE PAST

CHAPTER I.

Woman and the workingman have, since old, had this in common—*oppression*. The forms of oppression have suffered changes in the course of time, and in various countries. But the oppression always remained. Many a time and oft, in the course of the ages, did the oppressed become conscious of their oppression; and such conscious knowledge of their condition did bring on changes and reliefs. Nevertheless, a knowledge, that grasped the actual feature of the oppression by grasping its causes, is, with woman as with the workingman, the fruit of our own days. The actual feature of society, and of the laws that lie at the bottom of its development, had first to be known, before a general movement could take place for the removal of conditions, recognized as oppressive and unjust. The breadth and intensity of such a movement depends, however, upon the measure of the understanding prevalent among the suffering social layers and circles, and upon the measure of freedom of motion that they enjoy. In both respects, woman stands, through custom and education, as well as the freedom allowed her by law, behind the workingman. To this, another circumstance is added. Conditions, lasting through a long series of generations, finally grow into custom; heredity and education then cause such conditions to appear on both sides as "natural." Hence it comes that, even to-day, woman in particular, accepts her subordinate position as a matter of course. It is no easy matter to make her understand that that position is unworthy, and that it is her duty to endeavor to become a member of society, equal-righted with, and in every sense a peer of man.

However much in common woman may be shown to have with the workingman, she leads him in one thing:—*Woman was the first human being to come into bondage: she was a slave before the male slave existed.*

All social dependence and oppression has its roots in the *economic dependence* of the oppressed upon the oppressor. In this condition woman finds herself, from an early day down to our own. The history of the development of human society proves the fact everywhere.

The knowledge of the history of this development is, however, comparatively new. As little as the myth of the Creation of the World—as taught us by the Bible—can be upheld in sight of the investigations of geographers and scientists, grounded as these investigations are upon unquestionable and innumerable facts, just so untenable has its myth proved concerning the creation and evolution of man. True enough, as yet the veil is far from being lifted from all the sub-departments of this historical development of mankind; over many, on which already light has been shed, differences of opinion still exist among the investigators on the meaning and connection of this or that fact; nevertheless, on the whole, there is agreement and clearness. It is established that man did not, like the first human couple of the Bible, make his first appearance on earth in an advanced stage of civilization. He reached that plane only in the course of endlessly long lapses of time, after he had gradually freed himself from purely animal conditions, and had experienced long terms of development, in the course of which his social as well as his sexual relations—the relations between man and woman—had undergone a great variety of changes.

The favorite phrase—a phrase that the ignorant or impostors daily smite our ears with on the subject of the relations between man and woman, and between the poor and the rich—"it always has been so," and the conclusion drawn therefrom—"it will always be so," *is in every sense of the word false, superficial and trumped-up.*

For the purposes of this work a cursory presentation of the relations between the sexes, since primitive society, is of special importance. It is so because it can thereby be proved that, seeing that these relations have materially changed in the previous course of human development, and that the changes have taken place in even step with the existing systems of production, on the one hand, and of the distribution of the product of labor, on the other, it is natural and goes without saying that, along with further changes and revolutions in the system of production and distribution, *the relations between the sexes are bound to change again.* Nothing is "eternal," either in nature or in human life; eternal only is change and interchange.

As far back as one may go in the development of human society, the horde is found as the first human community. True enough, Honeger mentions in his "General History of Civilization" that even to-day in the little explored interior of the island of Borneo, there are wild people, living separately; and Huegel likewise maintains that, in the wild mountain regions of India, human couples have been discovered living alone, and who, ape-like, fled to the trees as soon as they were met; but there is no further knowledge on the subject. If verified, these claims would only confirm the previous superstition and hypothesis concerning the development of the human race. The probability is that, wherever human beings sprang up, there were, at first, single couples. Certain it is, however, that so soon as a larger number of beings existed, descended from a common parent stock, they held together in hordes in order that, by their joint efforts, they might, first of all, gain their still very primitive conditions of life and support, as well as to protect themselves against their common enemies, wild animals. Growing numbers and increased difficulties in securing subsistence, which originally consisted in roots, berries and fruit, first led to the splitting up or segmentation of the hordes, and to the search for new habitats.

This almost animal-like state, of which we have no further credible antiquarian proofs, undoubtedly once existed, judging from all that we have learned concerning the several grades of civilization of wild peoples still living, or known to have lived within historic times. Man did not, upon the call of a Creator, step ready-made into existence as a higher product of civilization. It was otherwise. He has had to pass through the most varied stages in an endlessly long and slow process of development. Only via ebbing and flowing periods of civilization, and in constant differentiation with his fellows in all parts of the world, and in all zones, did he gradually climb up to his present height.

Indeed, while in one section of the earth's surface great peoples and nations belong to the most advanced stages of civilization, other peoples are found in different sections standing on the greatest variety of gradations in development. They thus present to us a picture of our own past history; and they point to the road which mankind traversed in the course of its development. If but certain common and generally accepted data are established, that may serve everywhere as sign-posts to guide investigation, a mass of facts will follow, throwing a wholly new light upon the relations of man in the past and the present. A number of social phenomena—unintelligible to us to-day, and attacked by superficial judges as nonsensical, not infrequently even as "immoral"—will become clear and natural. A material lifting of the veil, formerly spread over the history of the development of our race, has been effected through the investigations made, since Bachofen, by a considerable number of scientists, like Tylor, MacLennan, Lubbock and others. Prominently among the men who joined these was Morgan, with his fundamental work, that Frederick Engels further substantiated and supplemented with a series of historical facts, economic and political in their nature, and that, more recently, has been partly confirmed and partly rectified by Cunow.[1]

[1] Bachofen's book appeared in 1861 under the title, "Das Mutterrecht" (Mother-right) "Eine Untersuchung ueber die Gynaekokratie der Alten Welt nach ihrer religioesen und rechtlichen Natur," Stuttgart, Krais & Hoffmann. Morgan's fundamental work. "Ancient Society," appeared in a German translation in 1891, J. H. W. Dietz, Stuttgart. From the same publisher there appeared in German: "The Origin of the Family, of Private Property and the State, in support of Lewis H. Morgan's Investigations," by Frederick Engels. Fourth enlarged edition, 1892. Also "Die Verwandtschafts-Organisationen der Australneger. Ein Beitrag zur Entwickelungsgeschichte der Familie," by Heinrich Cunow, 1894.

[The perspective into which the Pleiades of distinguished names are thrown in the text just above is apt to convey an incorrect impression, and the impression is not materially corrected in the subsequent references to them. Neither Bachofen, nor yet Tylor, McLennan or Lubbock contributed

By means of these expositions—especially as clearly and lucidly presented by Frederick Engels, in his support of Morgan's excellent and fundamental work,—a mass of light is shed upon hitherto unintelligible, partly seemingly contradictory phenomena in the life of the races and tribes of both high and low degree of culture. Only now do we gain an insight into the structure that human society raised in the course of time. According thereto, our former views of marriage, the family, the community, the State, rested upon notions that were wholly false; so false that they turn out to be no better than a fancy-picture, wholly devoid of foundation in fact.

to the principles that now are canons in ethnology. They were not even path-finders, valuable though their works are.

Bachofen collected, in his work entitled "Das Mutterrecht," the gleanings of vast and tireless researches among the writings of the ancients, with an eye to female authority. Subsequently, and helping themselves more particularly to the more recent contributions to archeology, that partly dealt with living aborigines, Tylor, McLennan and Lubbock produced respectively, "Early History of Mankind;" "Primitive Marriage;" and "Pre-Historic Times" and "Origin of Civilization." These works, though partly descriptive, yet are mainly descriptive. By an effort of genius—like the wood-pecker, whose instinct tells it the desired worm is beneath the bark and who pecks at and round about—all these men, Bachofen foremost, scented sense in the seeming nonsense of ancient traditions, or surmised significance in the more recently ascertained customs of living aborigines. But again, like the wood-pecker, that has struck a bark too thick for its bill, these men could not solve the problem they were at. They lacked the information to pick, and they had not, nor were they so situated as to furnish themselves with, the key to open the lock. Morgan furnished the key.

Lewis Henry Morgan, born in Aurora, N. Y., November 21, 1818, and equipped with vast scholarship and archeological information, took up his residence among the Iroquois Indians, by whom, the Hawk gens of the Seneca tribe, he was eventually adopted. The fruit of his observations there and among other Indian tribes that he visited even west of the Mississippi, together with simultaneous information sent him by the American missionaries in the Sandwich Islands, was a series of epoch-making works, "The League of the Iroquois," "Systems of Consanguinity and Affinity of the Human Family," and "Ancient Society," which appeared in 1877. A last and not least valuable work was his "Houses and Houselife of the American Aborigines." A solid foundation was now laid for the science of ethnology and anthropology. The problem was substantially solved.

The robust scientific mind of Karl Marx promptly absorbed the revelations made by Morgan, and he recast his own views accordingly. A serious ethnological error had crept into his great work, "Capital," two editions of which had been previously published in German between 1863-1873. A footnote by Frederick Engels (p. 344, Swan, Sonnenschein & Co., English edition, 1886) testifies to the revolution Morgan's works had wrought on the ethnological conceptions of the founder of Socialist economics and sociology.

Subsequently, Frederick Engels, planted squarely on the principles established by Morgan, issued a series of brilliant monographs, in which, equipped with the key furnished by Morgan and which Engels' extensive economic and sociologic knowledge enabled him to wield with deftness, he explained interesting social phenomena among the ancients, and thereby greatly enriched the literature of social science.

Finally, Heinrich Cunow, though imagining to perceive some minor flaws in some secondary parts of Morgan's theory, placed himself in absolute accord with the body of Morgan's real work, as stated later in the text in a quotation from Cunow; and, following closely in Morgan's footsteps, made and published interesting independent researches on the system of consanguinity among the Austral-Negros.—THE TRANSLATOR.]

All that is said and proved about marriage, the family, the community and the State holds good especially with regard to woman, who, in the various periods of development did likewise fill a place, that differs materially from the "eternal," imputed to her.

Morgan, whom Engels agrees with in this, divides the history of mankind into three main epochs:—savagery, barbarism and civilization. Each of the two first ones he again divides into an under, a middle and an upper period, each distinguishing itself from the other by certain innovations and improvements, predicated in each instance upon the control over subsistence. Morgan, accordingly, exactly in the sense of the materialist conception of history, as established by Karl Marx and Frederick Engels,—perceives the leading characteristics in the development of society to be the changes that, in given epochs, the conditions of life are molded into; and he perceives the changes to be due to the progress made in the process of production, that is to say, in the procurement of subsistence. Summed up in a few words, the lower period of savagery constitutes the infancy of the human race, during which the race, partly living in trees, is mainly nourished by fruits and roots, and during which articulate language takes its inception. The middle period of savagery commences with the acquisition of a fish subsistence, and the use of fire. The construction of weapons begins; at first the club and spear, fashioned out of wood and stone. Thereby also begins the chase, and probably also war with contiguous hordes for the sources of food, for domiciles and hunting grounds. At this stage appears also cannibalism, still practiced to-day by some tribes and peoples of Africa, Australia and Polynesia. The upper period of savagery is characterized by the perfection of weapons to the point of the bow and arrow; finger weaving, the making of baskets out of filaments of bark, the fashioning of sharpened stone tools have here their start, and thereby begins also the preparation of wood for the building of boats and huts. The form of life has, accordingly, become many-sided. The existing tools and implements, needed for the control of a plentiful food supply, make possible the subsistence of larger communities.

The lower period of barbarism Morgan starts with the invention of the art of pottery. The taming and domestication of animals, and, along with that, the production of meat and milk, and the preparation of hides, horns and hair for various purposes of use, have here their start. Hand in hand therewith begins the cultivation of plants,—in the West of maize, in the East of almost all known cereals, maize excepted. The middle period of barbarism shows us, in the East, the ever more extensive domestication of animals; in the West, the cultivation of maize and plants by irrigation. Here also begins the use of adobe-bricks and of stone for house-building. The domestication of animals promotes the rearing of herds, and leads to the pastoral life. The necessity of larger quantities of food for men and beasts leads to field agriculture. Along therewith, the people begin to be localized; food increases in quantity and diversity, and gradually cannibalism disappears.

The upper period of barbarism begins finally with the smelting of iron ore, and the discovery of the phonetic alphabet. The iron plow-share is invented, making possible agriculture on a larger scale; the iron axe and spade are brought into requisition, making easy the clearing of the forests. With the preparation of iron, a number of fields are opened to activity, imparting to life a new form. Iron utensils help the building of houses, vessels and weapons; with the preparation of metals arises skilled handwork, a more perfect knowledge of weapons, and the building of walled cities. Architecture, as an art, then rises; mythology, poetry and history find support and expansion in the discovery of the phonetic alphabet.

The Orient and the countries bordering on the Mediterranean, particularly Egypt, Greece and Italy, are those in which the last sketched stage of life principally unfolded; and it laid the foundation for the social transformation that in the course of time exercised a determining influence on the social development of Europe and of the whole earth.

As a matter of course, the social development of the human race through the periods of savagery and barbarism had also its peculiar sexual and social relations, differing materially from those of later days.

Bachofen and Morgan have traced these relations by means of thorough investigations. Bachofen, by studying closely all ancient and modern writings, so as to arrive at the nature of phenomena that appear singular to us in mythology, folk-lore and historic tradition, and that, nevertheless, seem to be re-echoed in incidents and events of later days, occasionally even of our own. Morgan, by spending decades of his life among the Iroquois Indians, located in the State of New York, and thereby making observations, through which he gained new and unexpected insight into the system of life, the family and the relationships of the said Indian tribe, and, based upon which, observations made elsewhere, first received their correct interpretation and explanation.

Both of them, Bachofen and Morgan, discovered, each along his own line of research, the latter, however, far more clearly than the former, that the relations of the sexes during primitive times of human development were substantially different from the relations existing in historic days, and among the modern civilized peoples. Especially did Morgan discover—thanks to his many years' sojourn among the Iroquois of North America, and grounded upon comparative studies, which he was moved to by that which he there observed,—that all the existing races, that are still materially backward, possess systems of family and consanguinity that are totally different from ours, but must be similar to those once prevalent among all races during the previous stages of civilization.

Morgan found, at the time that he lived among the Iroquois, that among them there existed a system of monogamy, easily dissolvable by both parties, and which he designated as the "pairing family." He also found that the terms for the degrees of consanguinity—father, mother, son, daughter, brother, sister—although, according to our conception, there can be no doubt as to their application, were there, nevertheless, applied in quite different sense. The Iroquois calls not only his own children "sons" and "daughters," but also the children of all his brothers; and their children call him "father." Conversely, the female Iroquois calls not only her own children "sons" and "daughters," but all those of her sisters, and likewise do their children call her "mother." On the other hand, she calls the children of her brothers "nephews" and "nieces," and these call her "aunt." The children of brothers call one another "brothers" and "sisters;" likewise the children of sisters. Finally, the children of a woman and those of her brother call one another "cousins." Accordingly, the singular spectacle is seen of the terms of relationship going, not as in our sense, by the degree of consanguinity, but by the *sex* of the relative.

This system of relationship is in full force, not only among all the American Indians, as well as among the aborigines of India, the tribes of Dekan and the Gaura tribes of Hindostan, but, according to the investigations that have taken place since Bachofen, similar conditions must have existed everywhere in primitive times, as they still exist to-day among many peoples of Upper and Further Asia, Africa and Australia. When, in connection with these investigations and established facts, the investigation will be everywhere taken up on the sex and family relations of wild and barbarous nations still living, then will the fact transpire that, what Bachofen still confusedly found among numerous peoples of antiquity, and rather surmised than otherwise; what Morgan found among the Iroquois; what Cunow found among the Austral-Negros, are but social and sexual formations, that constitute the *groundwork of human development for all the peoples of the earth.*

The investigations of Morgan bring, moreover, other interesting facts to light. Although the "pairing family" of the Iroquois starts in insolvable contradiction with the terms of consanguinity in use among them, it turns out that, as late as the first half of the 19th Century, there existed on the Sandwich Islands (Hawaii) a family-form that actually tallied with that which, among the Iroquois, existed in name only. But the system of consanquinity, in force in Hawaii, failed, in turn, to tally with the family-form actually in existence there. It referred to an older family-form, one still more primitive, but no longer extant. There, all the children of brothers and sisters, without exception, were "brothers" and "sisters." Accordingly, they were not considered the common children of their mothers and of the sisters of these, or of their fathers and of the brothers of these, but of all the brothers and sisters of their parents, without distinction. The Hawaiian system of consanquinity corresponded, accordingly, with a stage of development that was lower than the family-form still actually in existence. Hence transpires the curious fact that, in Hawaii, as with the Indians of North America, two distinct systems of consanguinity are, or rather, at a time, were in vogue, which no longer tallied with actual conditions, but were both overtaken by a higher state. On this head Morgan says: "The family represents an active principle. It is never stationary, but advances from a lower to a higher form as society advances from a lower to a higher condition, and finally passes out of one form into another of higher grade. Systems of consanguinity, on the contrary, are passive; recording the progress made by the family at long intervals apart, and only changing radically when the family has radically changed."

The theory,—even to-day generally considered conclusive, and which is stubbornly upheld as irrefutable by the representatives of the *statu quo*—to the effect that the existing family-form has existed since time immemorial, and, lest the whole social fabric be put in jeopardy, must continue to exist forever, turned out, accordingly, after these discoveries of the investigators, to be wholly false and untenable. The form, under which the relations of the sexes appear and the situation of the family is raised, depends rather upon the social conditions, upon the manner in which man controls his subsistence. The form changes with the changed degree of culture at each given period.

The study of primitive history leaves now no room for doubt that, at the lowest grades of human development, the relation of the sexes is totally different from that of latter times, and that a state of things resulted therefrom, which, looked at with modern eyes, appears as monstrous, and as a sink of immorality. Nevertheless, as each social stage of human development has its own conditions of production, so likewise has each its own code of morals, which is but the *reflection of the social condition*. That is moral which is usage; and that, in turn, is usage which corresponds with the innermost being, i. e., the needs of a given period.

Morgan reaches the conclusion that, at the lower period of savagery, there was sexual intercourse between the several grades or generations, every woman belonging to every man, and every man to every woman, —in other words, promiscuity. All men live in polygamy and all women in polyandry. There is a general community of women and of men, but also a community of children. Strabo reports (sixty-six years before our reckoning) that, among the Arabians, brothers cohabited with sisters and with their own mother. On any route other than that of incest, the increase of population is nowhere possible, if, as alleged in the Bible also, descent from one couple is granted. The Bible itself contradicts itself on this delicate point. It is stated there that Cain, after he had murdered his brother Abel, took a wife of another people. Whence came that other people? The theory of promiscuity in primitive times, that is to say, that the horde was endogamous, that sexual intercourse was indiscriminate, is furthermore supported by the Hindoo myth, according to which Brahma married his own daughter Saravasti. The same myth turns up again among the Egyptians and the northern Edda. The Egyptian god Ammon was the spouse of his own mother, and boasted of it. Odin, according to the Edda, was the mate of his own daughter Frigga.[2] Morgan proceeds from the principle that, from the state of promiscuity, soon a higher form of sexual intercourse took shape. He designates this the consanguine family. Here the groups, that stand in sexual relation, are separated by grades or generations, so that grandfathers and grandmothers, within an age group, are husbands and wives. Their children, likewise, constitute a group of common couples; likewise the children of these, so soon as they have reached the requisite age. Accordingly, in contrast with the sex relations of the rawest period, in which promiscuity of sexes exists without distinction of age, now one generation is excluded from sexual intercourse with another. Sexual intercourse, however, exists between brothers and sisters, male and female cousins of the first, second and third remove. All of these together are brothers and sisters, but towards one another, they are all husbands and wives. This family-form corresponds with the system of consanguinity that still existed in Hawaii during the first part of the 19th Century, in name only, but no longer in fact. On the other hand, according to the American Indian system of consanguinity, a brother and sister can never be the father and mother of the same child—a thing, however, permissible in the Hawaiian family system. Probably the consanguine family was the state that, at the time of Herodotus, existed among the Massagetae, on the subject of which he reports: "Each man received a wife, but all were allowed to use her." And he continues: "At any time a man desires a woman, he hangs his quiver in front of his wagon, and cohabits, unconcerned, with her. . . .

---

[2] In his book against us, Ziegler ridicules the idea of attributing to myths any significance whatever in the history of civilization. In that notion stands betrayed the superficial nature of so-called scientists. They do not recognize what they do not see. A deep significance lies at the bottom of myths. They have grown out of the people's soul; out of olden morals and customs that have gradually disappeared, and now continue to live only in the myth. When we strike facts that explain a myth we are in possession of solid ground for its interpretation.

He at the same time sticks his staff into the ground, a symbol of his
own act. . . . Cohabitation is exercised in public."[3] Similar conditions Bachofen shows have existed among the Lycians, Etruscans,
Cretans, Athenians, Lesbians and Egyptians.

According to Morgan, the consanguine family is supervened by a third
and higher form of family relationship, which he designates as the Punaluan family. *Punalua*, "dear friend," "intimate companion."

Cunow, in his above named book, takes exception with Morgan's views
that the consanguine family, which rests on the organization of marriage
classes by generations, preceded the punalua family as an original organization. Cunow does not see in the consanguine family the most primitive of all social forms, until now discovered. He sees in it merely a
middle form, that takes its origin in the generation groups; a transition
stage toward the pure gentile organization, on which, as a graft, the division in age classes, belonging to the consanguine family system, still
continues for a time in altered form, along with the division in totem-
groups.[4] Cunow explains further: The division in classes—every individual, man or woman, carries the name of his or her class and generation group totem—does not serve to exclude sexual intercourse between
collateral, but to prevent cohabitation between relatives in the ascend-
ing and descending line, between parents and children, aunts and nephews,
uncles and nieces. Terms such as "aunt," "uncle," etc., he designates as
grade-names.

Cunow furnishes the proofs for the correctness of the views in which
he differs from Morgan on some points. But, however he may differ from
Morgan in single instances, he emphatically defends him against the attacks of Westermann and others. He says:

"Although here and there a hypothesis of Morgan may have proved
itself false, and some others may be allowed only a qualified approval,
that merit none can gainsay him that he has been the first to establish
the identity of the North American totem-group with the gentile organization of the Romans; and, secondly, to demonstrate that our modern
systems of consanguinity and family-forms are the result of a long process
of development. In a measure he has thereby first made recent investigations possible; he has first built the foundation on which we may build
further." In the introduction also to his book he says expressly that his
own work is partly a supplement to Morgan's book on primitive man.

---

[3] Bachofen: "Das Mutterrecht."

[4] Totem-group means generation-group. Each grade or generation has its
own totem-animal. For instance: Opossum, emu, wolf, bear, etc., after
which the group is named. The totem-animal frequently enjoys great honor.
It is held sacred with the respective group, and its members may neither
kill the animal, nor eat its flesh. The totem-animal has a similar significance as the patron saint of the guild in the Middle Ages.

The Westermanns, the Starckes, the Zieglers—the latter of whom, in his book, criticized in the introduction to the twenty-fifth edition of this work, refers mainly to the first named, in order to attack our statements with theirs—will have to submit, with good grace or bad, to the fact that the rise and development of the family has not taken the course that fits in with their bourgeois prejudices. The refutation that, in the last part of his work, Cunow bestows upon Westermann and Starcke, Ziegler's authorities, are calculated to enlighten their most fanatic followers upon the value of their caviling criticisms of, and arguments against, Morgan.

According to Morgan, the punaluan family has its start with the exclusion of consanguineous brothers and sisters, on the mother's side. Where a woman has several husbands, the evidence of paternity is impossible. Paternity becomes a fiction. Even to-day, under the rule of strict monogamous marriage, paternity, as Goethe, in his "Apprenticeship," lets Frederick say, "rests only upon faith." If with monogamy, paternity is often doubtful, it is impossible of proof in polygamy: only descent from the mother is certain and unquestionable. Accordingly, descent from the mother afforded the only criterion. As all deep-reaching transformations in the social relations of primitive man are accomplished only slowly, the change of the so-called consanguine into the punaluan family must unquestionably have engaged vast periods of time, and been broken through by many relapses, still noticeable in much later days. The proximate external inducement for the development of the punaluan family was, possibly, the necessity of splitting up the strongly swollen membership of the family, to the end that new grounds could be ocupied for cattle ranges and agriculture. Probably, also, with the reaching of a higher grade of civilization, a sense gradually asserted itself of the harmfulness and indecorousness of sexual intercourse between brothers and sisters, and close relatives. In favor of this theory stands a pretty tradition, that, as related by Cunow, Gaston found among the Dieyeries, one of the South Australian tribes, on the rise of the "Mordu" consanguine group. He says:

"After creation, fathers, mothers, sisters, brothers and other near relatives married promiscuously among one another, until the evil effects of such connections showed themselves clearly. A conference of leaders was held, and it was considered in what way this could be avoided. The outcome of the conference was a request to the Muramura (Great Spirit); and he ordered in his answer that the tribe be divided into several branches, and that, in order to distinguish them, they be called by different names, after animate or inanimate objects. For instance: after the dingo, the mouse, the emu, the rain, the iguana-lizzard, etc. The members of one and the same group could not marry another. The son of a Dingo could not, for instance, marry the daughter of a Dingo; each of the two could, however, enter into connections with the Mouse, the Emu, the Rat, or any other family."

This tradition is more sensible and natural, by a good deal, than the Christian tradition, taught by the Bible. It shows plainly the rise of the consanguine groups. Moreover, Paul Lafargue, makes in the "Neue Zeit" the sagacious, and, we think, felicitous point, that names, such as Adam and Eve, are not names of individual persons, but the names of gentes, in which, at the time, the Jews were joined. Lafargue solves by his argument a series of otherwise obscure and contradictory passages in the first Book of Moses. Again, M. Beer calls attention, likewise in the "Neue Zeit," that, to this day, it is a conjugal custom among Jews that the bride and the bridegroom's mother *may not carry the same name*, otherwise—thus runs this belief—a misfortune will befall the family: sickness and death will pursue them. In our opinion, this is a further proof for the correctness of Lafargue's theory. The gentile organization forbids marriage between persons that descend from the same gens stock. Such a common descent must be considered to exist, according to gentile principles, between the bride, that carries the name of "Eve," and the bridegroom's mother of the same name. Modern Jews, of course, have no longer the remotest suspicion of the real connection between their prejudice and their old gentile constitution, which forbade such marriages of relatives. The old gentile order had for its object to avoid the degenerating consequences of in-breeding. Although this gentile constitution has for thousands of years been destroyed among the Jews, tradition, as we see, has continued to live in superstition.

Quite possible, the experience, made at an early day with the breeding of animals, revealed the harmfulness of in-breeding. How far this experience went transpires from the manner in which, according to the first Book of Moses, chap. 30, verse 32 and sequel, Jacob understood how to outwit his father-in-law Laban, by knowing how to encompass the birth of eanlings that were streaked and pied, and which, according to Laban's promises, were to be Jacob's. The old Israelites had, accordingly, long before Darwin, studied Darwinism.

Once upon the subject of the conditions existing among the old Jews, a few other facts are in order, clearly proving that, among them, descent in the female line was actually in force of old. True enough, on the subject of woman, I Moses, 3, 16, runs this wise: "And thy desire shall be to thy husband, and he shall rule over thee;" and the verse also undergoes the variation: "the woman shall leave father and mother, and cleave to her husband." In point of fact, however, I Moses, 2, 24, has it this way: *"Therefore shall a man leave his father and mother and shall cleave unto his wife*, and they shall be one flesh." The same language recurs in Matthew 19, 15; Mark 10, 7, and in the Epistle to the Ephesians 5, 31. The command sprang, accordingly, from the system of descent in the female line, and the exegists, at a loss what to do with it, allowed it to appear in a light that is utterly false.

Descent in female line appears clearly also in IV Moses, 32, 41. It is there said that Jair had a father, who was of the tribe of Judah, but his mother was of the tribe of Manasseh, and Jair is expressly called the *son* of Manasseh, and he inherited in that tribe. Another instance of descent in the female line among the Jews is met in Nehemiah 7, 63. There the children of a priest, who took to wife one of the daughters of Barzillai—a Jewish clan—are called children of Barzillai; they are, accordingly, not called after the father, who, moreover, as a priest occupied a privileged position, but after the mother. For the rest, already in the days of the Old Testament, accordingly, in historic times, the father-right prevailed among the Jews, and the clan and tribe organization rested on descent in the male line. Accordingly, the daughters were shut off as heirs, as may be seen in I Moses 31, 14-15, where even Leah and Rachel, the daughters of Laban, complain: "Is there yet any portion or inheritance for us in our father's house? Are we not counted of him strangers? for he has sold us, and hath quite devoured also our money."

As happened with all peoples where descent in male replaced descent in female line, woman among the Jews stood wholly bereft of rights. Wedlock was marriage by purchase. On woman the obligation was laid of the strictest chastity; on the other hand, man was not bound by the same ordinance; he, moreover, was privileged to possess several wives. Did the husband, after the bridal night, believe to have found that his wife had, before marriage, lost her maidenhood, not only had he the right to cast her off, she was stoned to death. The same punishment fell upon the adultress; upon the husband, however, only in case he committed adultery with a married Jewish woman. According to V Moses 24, 1-4, the husband had also the right to cast off his newly-married wife, if she found no favor in his eyes, even if only out of dislike. He was then to write her a bill of divorcement, give it in her hand, and let her out of the house. An expression of the low position that woman took later among the Jews is furthermore found in the circumstances that, even to this day, woman attends divine service in the synagogue, in a space strictly separated from the men, and they are not included in the prayers.[8]

The relations of the sexes in the punaluan family consisted, according to Morgan, in one or more sisters, belonging to one family group, marry-

[8] In the oldest ward of the city of Prague, there is a small synagogue that comes down from the sixth century of our reckoning, and is said to be the oldest synagogue in Germany. If the visitor steps down about seven steps into the half-dark space, he discovers in the opposite wall several target-like openings that lead into a completely dark room. To the question,

ing jointly one or more brothers of another group. The consanguine sisters, or the first, second and more remote cousins were wives in common with their husbands in common, who could not be their brothers. These consanguine brothers, or cousins of several degrees, were the husbands in common of their wives in common, who could not be their sisters. With the stopping of in-breeding, the new family-form undoubtedly contributed towards the rapid and vigorous development of the tribes, and imparted to the tribes, that had turned to this form of family connection, an advantage over those that still retained the old form of connections.

In general, the physical and intellectual differences between man and woman were vastly less in primitive days than in our society. Among all the peoples, living in the state of savagery or barbarism, the differences in the weight and size of the brain are slighter than among the peoples in civilization. Likewise, in strength of body and agility, the women among these peoples are but little behind the men. This is attested not only by the testimony of the ancient writers on the peoples who clung to the mother-right. Further testimony is furnished by the armies of women among the Ashantees and of the King of Dahomey in West Africa, who distinguished themselves by special bravery and ferocity. Likewise does the opinion of Tacitus on the women of the old Germans, and Caesar's accounts of the women of the Iberians and Scots confirm the fact. Columbus had to sustain a fight before Santa Cruz with an Indian skiff in which the women fought as bravely as the men; and we find this theory further confirmed in the passages from Havelock Ellis's work, "Man and Woman," which Dr. Hope B. Adams-Walther deals upon in Nos. 39 and 40 of the "Neue Zeit." He says:

"About the Andombis of the Congo, Johnson relates that the women work hard as carriers and in other occupations. All the same, they lead a perfectly happy life. They are often stronger and more handsomely built than the men; not a few of them have positively magnificent figures. Parke styles the Manynema of the same neighborhood 'fine animals,' and he finds the women very stately. They carry burdens as heavy as the men and with equal ease. A North American Indian chief said to Hearne: 'Women are created for labor; a woman can carry or drag as much as two men.' Schellong, who published a painstaking study on the Papuas of New Guinea in the Ethnologic Journal, issued in 1891, is of the opinion that the women are more strongly built than the men. In the interior of Australia, women are sometimes beaten by men out of jealousy; but it happens not infrequently that it is the man, who, on such occasions, receives the stronger dose. In Cuba the women fought

where these openings lead to our leader answered: "To the woman's compartment, whence they witness the service." The modern synagogues are much more cheerfully arranged, but the separation of the women from the men is preserved.

shoulder to shoulder with the men. Among some tribes in India, as well as the Pueblos of North and the Patagonians of South America, the women are as tall as the men. Even among the Arabians and Druses the difference in size is slight; and yet nearer home, among the Russians, the sexes are more alike than is the case among the western Europeans. Accordingly, in all parts of the earth there are instances of equal or approximately equal physical development."

The family relations that flow from the Punaluan family were these: The children of my mother's sisters are her children, and the children of my father's brothers are his children, and all together are my brothers and sisters. Conversely, the children of my mother's brothers are her nephews and nieces, and the children of my father's sisters are his nephews and nieces, and they, all together, are my cousins. Again, the husbands of my mother's sisters are her husbands also, and the wives of my father's brothers are also his wives; but my father's sisters and my mother's brothers are excluded from family relationship, and their children are my cousins.[6]

Along with arising civilization, sexual intercourse is proscribed between brothers and sisters, and the proscription gradually extends to the remotest collateral relatives on the mother's side. A new group of consanguinity arises, the gens, which, in its first form, is made up of a series of consanguine and more remote sisters, together with their children and their consanguine and more remote brothers on their mother's side. The gens has a common female ancestor, from whom the female successors descend in generations. The husbands of these women are not of the consanguine group, the gens, of their wives; they are of the gens of their sisters. Conversely, the children of these men belong to the family group of their, the children's mother, descent being in the female line. The mother is the head of the family; and thus arises the "mother-right," which for a long time constitutes the basis of the family and of inheritance. In keeping therewith—so long as descent was recognized in the female line—woman had a seat and voice in the councils of the gens; they voted in the election of the sachems and of the military chiefs, and deposed them.

About the Lycians, who abided by the mother-right, Herodotus says; "Their customs are partly Cretan, partly Carian. They have, however, a custom that distinguishes them from all other nations in the world. Ask a Lycian who he is, and he answers by giving you his own name, the name of his mother, and so on in the female line. Aye, if a free-born woman marries a slave, her children are citizens, but if a free man marries a stranger, or takes a concubine, even if he be the highest person in the State, his children forfeit all citizen rights."

6 Frederick Engels, "The Origin of the Family."

In those days, "matrimonium" and not "patrimonium," "mater familias" and not "pater familias" were the terms used; and the native land is called the "dear motherland." As with the previous family-forms, so did the gens rest upon the community of property, and had a communistic system of household. The woman is the real guide and leader of this family community; hence she enjoys a high degree of respect, in the house as well as in the affairs of the family community concerning the tribe. She is judge and adjuster of disputes, and frequently performs the ceremonies of religion as priestess. The frequent appearance of Queens and Princesses in antiquity, their controlling influence, even there where their sons reigned, for instance, in the history of old Egypt, are results of the mother-right. Mythology, at that epoch, assumes predominantly female characters: Astarte, Ceres, Demeter, Latona, Isis, Frigga, Freia, Gerdha, etc. Woman is considered inviolable; matricide is the blackest of all crimes: it summons all men to retribution. The blood-feud is the common concern of all the men of the tribe; each is obliged to avenge the wrong done to a member of the family community by the members of another tribe. In defence of the women the men are spurred to highest valor. Thus did the effects of the mother-right, gyneocracy, manifest themselves in all the relations of life among the peoples of antiquity—among the Babylonians, the Assyrians, the Egyptians, the Greeks, before the time of the Heroes; among the peoples of Italy, before the founding of Rome; among the Scythians, the Gauls, the Iberians and Cantabrians, the Germans of Tacitus, etc. Woman, at that time, takes in the family and in public life a position such as she has never since taken. Along these lines, says Tacitus in his "Germania": "They (the Germans) even suppose somewhat of sanctity and prescience to be inherent in the female sex; and, therefore, neither despise their counsels, nor disregard their responses;" and Diodorus, who lived at the time of Caesar, feels highly indignant over the position of women in Egypt, having learned that there, not the sons, but the daughters, supported their aging parents. He contemptuously shrugs his shoulders at the poltroons of the Nile, who relinquish household and public rights to the members of the weaker sex, and allow them privileges that must sound unheard-of to a Greek or a Roman.

Under the gyneocracy, a state of comparative peace prevailed in general. The horizon was narrow and small, life primitive. The different tribes separated themselves from one another, as best they could, and respected their mutual boundaries. Was, however, one tribe attacked by another, then the men were obliged to rush to its defence, and in this they were supported by the women in the most vigorous fashion. According to Herodotus, the women joined in battle among the Scythians: as he claims, the maid could not marry before she had slain an enemy.

What *role* women played in battle among the Germans, Iberians, Scots, etc., has already been stated. But in the gens also did they, under given circumstances, command a strong regiment:—woe to the man who was either too lazy or too unskilled to contribute his share to the common support. He was shown the door, and, either he returned to his own gens, where it was with difficulty he was again received with friendliness, or he joined another gens that was more tolerant toward him.[7]

That conjugal life still bears this character in the interior of Africa, Livingstone learned to his great surprise, as he narrates in his "Missionary Travels and Researches in Southern Africa," London, 1857. On the Zambesi he ran across the Valonda—a handsome, vigorous negro tribe, devoted to agriculture—where he found confirmed the informations received from the Portuguese, and which at first seemed incredible to him, with regard to the privileged position enjoyed by women. They sit in council; the young man who marries must move from his own, to the village of his wife: he thereby pledges himself to furnish the mother of his wife for life with kindling wood: if he divorces, the children remain the property of the mother. On the other hand, the wife must see to the sustenance of the husband. Although, occasionally, slight disagreements break out between man and wife, Livingstone found that the men did not retaliate, but he discovered that the men, who offended their wives, were punished in the most sensitive manner—through their stomachs. The husband, he says, comes home to eat, but one woman sends him off to another, and he gets nothing. Tired and hungry he climbs a tree in the most populous part of the village, and announces in woeful tones: "Hear! Hear! I thought I had married women, but they are witches to me! I am a bachelor; I have not a single wife! Is that right towards a man like me?" If a woman gives physical expression to her anger at a man, she is sentenced to carry him on her back from the court of the chieftain to her own house. While she is carrying him home, the other men scoff at and jeer her; the women, on the contrary, encourage her with all their might, calling out to her: "Treat him as he deserves; do it again!"

Similar conditions still exist in the German colony of Cameroon in West Africa. A German ship's doctor, who studied the country and its people by personal observation, writes us thus:

"With a large number of tribes, inheritance is based on maternity. Paternity is immaterial. Brothers and sisters are only the children of one mother. A man does not bequeath his property to his children, but to the children of his sister, that is to say, to his nephews and nieces, as his nearest demonstrable blood relatives. A chief of the Way people explained to me in horrible English: "My sister and I are certainly blood

[7] Frederick Engels, *ubi supra.*

relatives, consequently her son is my heir; when I die, he will be the king of my town." "And your father?" I inquired. "I don't know what that means, 'my father,'" answered he. Upon my putting to him the question whether he had no children, rolling on the ground with laughter, he answered that, with them, men have no children, only women.

"I can assure you," our informant goes on to write, "that even the heir of King Bell in Cameroon *is the King's nephew, and not one of his sons*. The so-called children of King Bell, several of whom are now going through training in German cities, are merely children of his wives, *whose fathers are unknown;* one of them I might, possibly, claim for myself."

What say the adversaries of the theory of descent in the female line to this sketch drawn from the immediate present? Our informant is a man with eyes open, who probed things to the very bottom. How many of those who live among these semi-savage races, do as much? Hence the wild accounts about the "immorality" of the natives.

Furthermore, there come to our notice the memorials of the Imperial Government, submitted to the Reichstag on the German colonies (Session of 1894-95). In the memorial on the Southwestern territory of Africa there occurs this passage, p. 239: "Without their advice—the oldest and wealthiest—he (chief of the tribe in principal village) can not render the slightest decision, and not the men only, *but quite often the women also*, even the servants, *express their opinion.*"

In the report of the Marshall Islands, p. 254 of the memorial, it runs thus: "The ruling power over all the islands of the Marshall group never rested in the hands of a single chieftain. . . . *Seeing, however, that no female member of this class (the Irody) is alive, and only the mother conveys nobility and rank to the child, the Irodies dies out with their chieftain.*" The expression used, and the descriptions made, by reporters betray what an utter blank are to them the conditions that they refer to: they can not find their bearings among them.

With an increasing population, there arise a number of sisters, which, in turn, produce daughter gentes. Over and against these, the mother gens appears as phratry. A number of phratries constitute a tribe. This social organization is so firm that it still constituted the foundation for the military organization in the old States, after the old gentile constitution had fallen to pieces. The tribe splits up into several tribes, all of which have the same constitution, and in each of which the old gentes are reproduced. However, seeing that the gentile constitution forbids the intermarriage of brothers and sisters, and of relatives on the mother's side to the furthest degree, it undermines its own foundation. Due to the evermore complicated relations of the separate gentes with one another—a condition of things that the social and economic progress promotes—the inhibition of marriage between the several gentes, that descend from the mother's side, becomes in the long run impracticable: it breaks down of itself, or is burst asunder. So long as the production of the means of subsistence was still at the lowest stages, and satisfied only simple wants, the activity of man and woman was essentially the same. Along with an increasing division of labor, there came about, not merely a division of functions, but also a division of occupations. Fishing, the hunt, cattle-raising,—demanded separate knowledge; and, to a still higher degree, the construction of tools and utensils, which became mainly the property of the men. Field agriculture expanded materially the circle of activities, and it created a supply of subsistence that satisfied the highest demands of the time. Man, whose activity stood in the foreground in the course of this development, became the real lord and owner of these sources of wealth, which, in turn, furnished the basis for commerce; and this created new relations, and social changes.

Not only did ever fresh causes of friction and conflicts arise for the possession of the best lands, due to the increase of population, and the need of wider domains for cattle-raising and agriculture, but, along with such increase of population, there arose the need of labor power to cultivate the ground. The more numerous these powers, all the greater was the wealth in products and herds. These struggles led, first, to the rape of women, later to the enslaving of conquered men. The women became laborers and objects of pleasure for the conqueror; their males became slaves. Two elements were thereby simultaneously introduced into the old gentile constitution. The two and the gentile constitution could not, in the long run, get along together.

Furthermore, hand in hand with the increasing differentiation of occupations, owing to the growing need of tools, utensils, weapons, etc., handicraft rises into existence. It follows its own course of development and separates itself from agriculture. As a consequence, a distinct population, one that plies the trades, is called into life; and it splits off from the agricultural population with entirely different interests.

According to the mother-right, i. e., so long as descent followed only in female line, the custom was that the gentile relatives inherited from the deceased gentile fellow-members on the mother's side. The property remained in the gens. The children of the deceased father did not belong to his gens, but to that of the mother: accordingly, they did not inherit from the father; at his death his property fell back to his own gens. Under the new conditions, where the father was the property-holder. i. e., the owner of herds and slaves, of weapons and utensils, and where he had become a handicraftsman, or merchant, his property, so long as he was still considered of the gens of his mother, fell after his death, not to his own children, but to his brothers and sisters, and to the children of his sisters, or to the successors of his sisters. His own children went away empty-handed. The pressure to change such a state of things was, accordingly, powerful;—and it was changed. Thereupon a condition arose that was not yet monogamy, but that approximated it; there arose the "pairing family." A certain man lived with a certain woman, and the children, born of that relation, were that couple's own children. These pairing families increased in the measure in which the marriage inhibitions, that flowed from the gentile constitution, hampered marriage, and in which the above mentioned economic grounds rendered desirable this new form of family life. Personal property accorded ill with the old condition of things, which rested upon the community of goods. Both *rank* and *occupation* now decidedly favored the necessity for the choice of a domicile. The production of merchandise begot commerce with neighboring and foreign nations; and that necessitated money. It was man who led and controlled this development. His private interests had, accordingly, no longer any real points of contact with the old gentile organization, whose interests often stood in opposition to his own. Accordingly, the importance of the gentile organization sank ever more. The gens finally became little more than the center of the religious functions for the family, its economic significance was gone. The complete dissolution of gentile organization became only a question of time.

With the dissolution of the old gentile organization, the influence and position of woman sank rapidly. The mother-right vanished; the father-right stepped into its shoes. Man now became a private property-holder: he had an interest in children, whom he could look upon as legitimate, and whom he made *the* heirs of his property: hence *he forced upon woman the command of abstinence from intercourse with other men.*

At the same time man assumed the right of taking unto himself, beside his own wife, or several of them, as many concubines as his condition allowed; and the children of these concubines were likewise treated as legitimate. On this head we find two valuable illustrations in the Bible. In I Book of Moses, chapter 16, verses 1 and 2, we read: "Now Sarai, Abram's wife, bare him no children: and she had a hand-maid, an Egyptian, whose name was Hagar. And Sarai said unto Abram, Behold now, the Lord has restrained me from bearing: I pray thee, go in unto my maid; it may be that I may obtain children by her. And Abram hearkened to the voice of Sarai." The second remarkable illustration is found in I Book of Moses 30, 1 and sequel: "And when Rachel saw that she bare Jacob no children, Rachel envied her sister; and said unto Jacob, Give me children, or else I die. And Jacob's anger was kindled against Rachel; and he said, Am I in God's stead, who hath withheld from thee the fruit of the womb? and she said, Behold my maid Bilhah, go in unto her; and she shall bear upon my knees that I may also have children by her. And she gave him Bilhah her handmaid to wife: and Jacob went in unto her."

Jacob, accordingly, had not only the daughters of Laban, two sisters, simultaneously for wives, they also helped him to their maids, all of which, according to the usage of the times, was wholly free from taint of impropriety. The two principal wives he had bought, as is well known, by serving Laban seven years for each. The purchase of a wife was at the time common among the Jews, but, along with the purchase of wives, whom they were compelled to take from among their own people, they practiced on an extensive scale the rape of women from among the peoples that they conquered. The Benjaminites raped the daughters of Silos.[8] In such wars, it was originally customary that all the men who fell into the hands of the vanquisher were killed. The captured woman became a slave, a concubine. Nevertheless, she could be raised to the dignity of a legitimate wife so soon as she had fulfilled certain conditions of the Jews: she had to cut her hair and nails; to lay off the dress she was captured in, and exchange it for another that was given her; thereupon she had to mourn a whole month for her father and mother: she was, in a manner to be dead to her own people, become estranged from them: then could she climb into the conjugal bed. The largest number of wives had King Solomon, as is known. According to Kings 1, 11, not less than 700 wives and 300 concubines are ascribed to him.

With the rule of the father-right and descent in the male line in the Jewish gentile organization, the daughters were excluded from inheritance. Later this was, however, changed, at least when a father left no sons. This appears from IV Book of Moses 27, 2-8, where it is reported that, as Zelaphehad died without sons, and his daughter complained bitterly that she was to be excluded from her father's inheritance, which was to fall back to the tribe of Joseph, Moses decided that, in that case, the daughters should inherit. But seeing that she contemplated marrying, according to custom, in another tribe, the tribe of Joseph complained that thereby the inheritance would be lost to it. Thereupon Moses decided further (4, 36) that heiresses, though free in the choice of a husband, were bound to marry in the tribe of their own father. For the sake of property, the old ordinance was overthrown. Similarly, in Athens, did Solon decree that an heiress had to marry her nearest male agnate, even though both belonged to the same gens, and, according to former law, such a marriage was forbidden. Solon ordered also that a property-holder was not compelled as thitherto, to leave his property to his own gens in case he died childless; but that he could by testament constitute any one else his heir. From all this it is obvious:—man does not rule property, property rules him, and becomes his master.

[8] Book of Judges, 20, 21 and sequel.

With the rule of private property, the subjection of woman to man, her bondage was sealed. Then came the time of disregard, even of contempt for woman.

The reign of the mother-right implied communism; equality for all; the rise of the father-right implied the reign of private property, and, with it, the oppression and enslavement of woman.

It is difficult to trace in detail the manner in which the change was achieved. A knowledge of the events is lacking. Neither did this *first great revolution* in the lap of mankind come into force simultaneously among the ancient nations; nor yet is it probable that it was accomplished everywhere in the same manner. Among the peoples of old Greece, it was Athens where the new order of things first prevailed.

Frederick Engels is of the opinion that this great revolution was accomplished peacefully, and that, after all the conditions for the new rights were at hand, it only required a simple vote in the gens in order to rear the father in the place of the mother-right. Bachofen, on the contrary, grounding his opinion upon more or less reliable information from the old writers, holds that the women offered strong resistance to this social transformation. He, for instance, sees in the legends of the Amazonian Kingdoms, which re-appear under manifold variations in the old history of Asia and the Orient, and also have turned up in South America and in China, proofs for the struggle and resistance which the women offered to the new order. We leave that as it may be.

With the rule of man, women lost their position in the community; they were excluded from the councils and from all leading influence. Man exacts conjugal fidelity from her, but claims exemption for himself. If she violates that, she is guilty of the most serious deception that can afflict the new citizen; she thereby introduces into his house stranger's children as heirs of his property. Hence, among all ancient nations, the breach of conjugal fidelity on the part of woman is punished with death or slavery.

Notwithstanding women were thus removed from their position as leaders, the customs connected with the old system of morals continued for centuries to sway the public mind, although the meaning of the surviving customs was gradually lost to the people. It is only in modern times that pains are being taken to inquire into the original meaning of these old customs. In Greece, for instance, it remained a religious practice that Greek women prayed only to goddesses for advice, help and favors. Likewise, the yearly recurring celebration of the Thesmophoria owed its origin to the days of mother-right. Even in later days, the women of Greece celebrated this festival for five days in honor of Demeter; and no man was allowed to be present. It was similarly in old Rome with a festival in honor of Ceres. Both Demeter and Ceres were considered goddesses of fertility. In Germany also such festivals, once customary in the heathen days of Frigga, were held, deep into the Middle Ages, Frigga being considered the goddess of fertility among the old Germans. According to the narratives, women gave a free reign to their frolicsomeness on the occasions of these festivals. Also here men were excluded from participation in the festival.

In Athens, where, as already stated, the mother-right made earliest room for the father-right, but, as it seems, under strong opposition from the women, the transition is portrayed touchingly and in all the fullness of its tragic import, in the "Eumenides" of Aeschylus. The story is this: Agamemnon, King of Mycene, and husband of Clytemnestra, sacrifices his daughter, Iphigenia, upon the command of the oracle on his expedition against Troy. The mother, indignant at the sacrifice of her daughter, takes, during her husband's absence, Aegysthos, for her consort. Upon Agamemnon's return to Mycene, after an absence of many years, he is murdered by Aegysthos with the connivance of Clytemnestra. Orestes, the son of Agamemnon and Clytemnestra, avenges the murder of his father, at the instigation of Apollo and Athene, by slaying his mother and Aegysthos. The Erinnyes, as representatives of the old law, pursue Orestes on acount of the murder of his mother. Apollo and Athene, the latter of whom, according to mythology, is motherless—she leaped full-armed out of the head of Jupiter—represent the new law, and defend Orestes. The issue is carried to the Areopagus, before which the following dialogue ensues. The two hostile principles come here into dramatic vividness of expression:

Erinnyes—The prophet bade thee be a matricide?
Orestes—And to this hour I am well content withal.
Erinnyes—Thoul't change that tune, when judgment seizes thee.
Orestes—My father from his tomb will take my part; I fear not.
Erinnyes—Ay, rely on dead men's aid,
When guilty of matricide!
Orestes—She, that is slain,
Was doubly tainted.
Erinnyes—How? Inform the court.
Orestes—She slew her wedded lord, and slew my sire.
Erinnyes—Death gave her quittance, then. But thou yet livest,
Orestes—And while she lived, why dids't thou not pursue her?
Erinnyes—No tie of blood bound her to whom she slew.
Orestes—But I was tied by blood-affinity
To her who bare me?
Erinnyes—Else, thou accursed one,
How nourished she thy life within her womb?
Wouldst thou renounce the holiest bond of all?

The Erinnyes, it will be noticed, recognize no rights on the part of the father and the husband; to them there exists only the right of the mother. That Clytemnestra slew her husband is indifferent to them; on the other hand, they demand punishment for the matricide, committed by Orestes: in killing his mother he had committed the worst crime imaginable under the old gentile order. Apollo, on the contrary, stands on the opposite principle. Commissioned by Zeus to avenge the murder of his father, he had led Orestes to the murder of his own mother. Apollo now defends Orestes' action before the judges, saying:

> That scruple likewise I can satisfy.
> She who is called the mother of the child
> Is not its parent, but the nurse of seed
> Implanted in begetting. He that sows
> Is author of the shoot, which she, if Heaven
> Prevent not, keeps as in a garden-ground.
> In proof whereof, to show that fatherhood
> May be without the mother, I appeal
> To Pallas, daughter of Olympian Zeus,
> In present witness here. Behold a plant,
> Not moulded in the darkness of the womb,
> Yet nobler than all scions of Heaven's stock.

According to Apollo, the act of begetting confers the superior right; whereas, according to the views in force until then, the mother, who gives to the child her blood and its life, was esteemed the sole possessor of the child, while the man, the father of her child, was regarded a stranger. Hence the Erinnyes reply to the strange notions of Apollo:

> Thou didst lead astray
> Those primal goddesses with draughts of wine,
> O'erturning ordinance.
> Young, thou wouldst override our ancient right.

The judges, thereupon, make ready for the sentence. One half stand by the old, one half by the new right; a tie is threatened; thereupon Athene seizes the ballot from the altar and dropping it in the urn, says:

> To me it falls to give my judgment last.
> Here openly I give it for Orestes.
> No mother bore me. To the masculine side
> For all save marriage my whole heart is given,—
> In all and everything the father's child.
> So little care I for a woman's death,
> That slew her lord, the guardian of her home.
> Now though the votes be even, Orestes wins.

The new right won. Marriage with the father as head, had overpowered the gyneocracy.

Another legend represents the downfall of the mother-right in Athens this way: "Under the reign of Kekrops, a double miracle happened. There broke forth simultaneously out of the earth an oil-tree, and at another place water. The frightened king sent to Delphi to interrogate the Oracle upon the meaning of these happenings. The answer was: 'The oil-tree stands for Minerva, the water for Neptune; it is now with the citizens after which of the two deities they wish to name their city.' Kekrops called together the assembly of the people in which men and women enjoyed the right of suffrage. The men voted for Neptune, the women for Minerva; and as the women had a majority of one, Minerva won. Thereupon Neptune was angered and he caused the sea to wash over the territory of the Athenians. In order to soothe the wrath of the god, the Athenians placed a threefold punishment upon their women:— *they were to forfeit the suffrage, children were no longer to carry their mother's name, and they themselves were no longer to be called Athenian women.*" [9]

As in Athens, the transition from the mother to the father-right was everywhere achieved so soon as a certain height was reached in social development. Woman is crowded into the house; she is isolated; she is assigned special quarters—the gynekonitis—, in which she lives; she is even excluded from intercourse with the male visitors of the house. That, in fact, was the principle object of her isolation.

This change finds its expression as early as the Odyssey. Telemachus forbids Penelope's, his mother's, presence among the suitors. He, the son, orders his mother:

But come now, go to thy bower, and deal with such things as ye can;
With the sock and the loom be busy, and thine handmaids order and teach,
That they speed the work and the weaving; but for men is the word and the speech;
For all, but for me the chiefest, for here am I the might and the power.

Such was the doctrine already common in Greece at that time. It went even further. Woman, even if a widow, stands so completely under the rule of the nearest male relative, that she no longer has even the choice of a husband. The suitors, tired of long waiting, due to the cunning Penelope, address themselves to Telemachus through the mouth of Antinoos, and saying:

But for thee, do we the suitors this answer to thee show,
That thou in thy soul may'st know it, and that all the folk may know,
Send thou thy mother away, and bid her a wedding to gain
With whomso her father willeth, of whomso her heart may be fain.

[9] Bachofen: "Das Mutterrecht."

It is at an end with the freedom of woman. If she leaves the house, she must veil herself not to awaken the desires of another man. In the Orient, where, due to the warm climate, sexual passion is strongest, this method of seclusion is carried even to-day to extreme lengths. Athens becomes in this a pattern for the ancient nations. Woman shares, indeed, her husband's bed, but not his table; she does not address him by name, but "Sir;" she is his maid-servant; she was allowed to appear nowhere openly; on the street she was ever veiled and clad with greatest simplicity. If she committed adultery, she paid for the trespass, according to the laws of Solon, with her life, or with her freedom. The husband could sell her for a slave.

The position of the Greek woman at the time when Greece was rushing to the zenith of her development comes into plastic expression in the "Medea" of Euripedes. She complains:

> Ay, of all living and of all reasoning things
> Are women the most miserable race:
> Who first needs buy a husband at great price,
> To take him then for owner of our lives:
> For this ill is more keen than common ills.
> And of essays most perilous is this,
> Whether one good or evil do we take.
> For evil-famed to women is divorce,
> Nor can one spurn a husband. She, so brought
> Beneath new rule and wont, had surely need
> To be a prophetess, unless at home
> She learned the likeliest prospect with her spouse.
> And if, we having aptly searched out this,
> A husband house with us not savagely
> Drawing in the yoke, ours is an envied life;
> But if not, most to be desired is death.
> And if a man grow sick to herd indoors,
> He, going forth, stays his heart's weariness,
> Turning him to some friend or natural peer;
> But we perforce to one sole being look.
> But, say they, we, while they fight with the spear,
> Lead in our homes a life undangerous:
> Judging amiss; for I would liefer thrice
> Bear brunt of arms than once bring forth a child.

Wholly otherwise stood matters for the men. Although with an eye to the begetting of legitimate heirs for his property, he imposed upon woman strict abstinence from other men, he was, nevertheless, not inclined to lay a corresponding abstinence upon himself.

Hetairism sprang up. Women distinguished for their beauty and intellect, and who, as a rule, were aliens, preferred a free life in intimate intercourse with men, to the slavery of marriage. Nothing objectionable was seen in that. The names and fame of these hetairae, who held intimate intercourse with the leading men of Greece, and participated in their learned discourses, as well as in their revels, has come down to our own days; whereas the names of the legitimate wives are mostly forgotten and lost. Thus the handsome Aspasia was the intimate friend of the celebrated Pericles, who later made her his legitimate wife; the name of Phryne became in later days the generic designation of those women that were to be had for money. Phryne held intimate relations with Hyperides, and she stood for Praxiteles, one of the first sculptors of Greece, as the model for his Aphrodite. Danae was the sweetheart of Epicurus, Archeanassa that of Plato. Other celebrated hetairae, whose names have reached our days, were Lais of Corinth, Gnathanea, etc. There is no celebrated Greek, who had no intercourse with hetairae. It belonged to the style of life of distinguished Greeks. Demosthenes, the great orator, described in his oration against Neara, the sexual life of the rich men of Athens in these words: *"We marry a woman in order to obtain legitimate children, and to have a faithful warder in the house; we keep concubines for our service and daily care; and hetairae for the enjoyment of love."* The wife was, accordingly, only an apparatus for the production of children; a faithful dog, that watched the house. The master of the house, on the contrary, lived according to his *bon plaisir*, as he willed.

In order to satisfy the demand for venal women, particularly with younger males, there arose that which was unknown under the rule of the mother-right,—*prostitution*. Prostitution distinguishes itself from the free sexual intercourse, that customs and social institutions rendered a matter of course under primitive conditions, and, accordingly, freed from objectionableness. in that the woman sells her body, either to one man or to several, for material benefit. Prostitution, therefore, exists so soon as woman makes a trade of her charms. Solon, who formulated the new law for Athens, and is, consequently, esteemed the founder of the new legal status, was also the founder of the public houses for women, the "deikterion,"—official houses of prostitution—, and the price to all the customers was the same. According to Philemon it amounted to one obolus, about four cents of our money. Like the temples with the Greeks and Romans, and the Christian churches in Middle Ages, the deikterion was inviolable: it stood under the protection of the Government. Until about a hundred and fifty years before our reckoning, the Temple of Jerusalem also was the usual place of gathering for the *filles de joie*.

For the benefit that Solon bestowed upon the Athenian male population, in founding the deikterion, he was praised in song by one of his

that is full of vigorous young men, who, in the absence of your wise institution, would give themselves over to the disturbing annoyance of the
better women." We shall see that, at the close of the nineteenth century, justification is sought for the regulation of houses of prostitution
by Government, and for the necessity of prostitution itself, upon the
identical grounds. Thus, actions, committed by men, were recognized
by legislation as a natural right, while, committed by women, were
held to be shameful, and a serious crime. As is well known, even to-day
not few are the men who prefer the company of a pretty female sinner
to that of their own wives, and who not infrequently belong to the
"Props of the State," the "Pillars of Order," and are "guardians of the
sancity of marriage and the family."

True enough, it seems, that the Greek women often revenged themselves
upon their marital-lords for the yoke placed upon them. If prostitution
is the supplement of monogamy, on the one side, adultery among women
and the cuckoldry of men is its supplement, on the other. Among the
Greek dramatic poets, Euripides is the woman-hater: he loved to make
women the object of attacks in his dramas. What all he twitted them
with appears best from the speech that a Greek woman flings at him in
the "Thesmophoria" of Aristophanes. She says among other things:

With what slandcrous dirt does not he (Euripides) besmirch us?
When does the slanderer's tongue hold its peace? In short:
Wherever there is an audience, tragedies or choruses,
There we are called corner-loafers, anglers: for men,
Fond of the wine-cup, treasonable arch-gossips,
Not a good hair is left us; we are the plague of men.
Therefore, soon as our husbands return to us home from the benches,[10]
Eyes of suspicion upon us they cast, and look about
Whether a place of concealment conceal not a rival.
Whereupon, none of the things, at first by us done,
Now is allowed us: Such stuff against us
Does he in the men's heads stick, that, if a woman
Is weaving a garland, she is held to be in love; or when,
While hustling the household to keep, something drops,
Forthwith the husband inquires: "Whom are those fragments meant for?
Plainly, they are meant for the guest from Corinthos."

We can understand that this ready-tongued Greek woman should serve
the assailer of her sex in such manner; nevertheless, Euripides could
not very well have made these accusations, nor could he have found
credence with the men, if they knew not but too well that the accusations
were justified. To judge by the concluding sentences of this address,
the custom—met later in Germany and many other countries—had not

[10] Of the theater, to which women had no access.

the custom—met later in Germany and many other countries—had not yet been naturalized in Greece, that the host placed his own wife or daughter at the disposal of his guest for the night. Murner writes on this custom, prevalent in Holland as late as the fifteenth century, in these words: "It is the custom in the Netherlands, when the host has a dear guest, that he lets his wife sleep with him on faith." [11]

The increasing struggles between the classes in the several states of Greece, and the sad state of many of the smaller communities, gave occasion for Plato to inquire into the best constitution and the best institutions for the State. In his "Republic," set up by him as ideal, he demands, at least for the first class of his citizens, the watchers, the complete equality of woman. Women are to participate in the exercises of arms, the same as the men, and are to fill the same duties as these, only they are to attend to the lighter ones, "owing to the weakness of the sex." He maintains that the natural inclinations are equally distributed among the two sexes, only that woman is in all matters weaker than man. Furthermore, the women are to be common to the men, and vice versa; likewise are the children to be common, so that neither the father may know his child, nor the child his father." [12]

Aristotle, in his "Politics," is satisfied with less. Woman should have a free hand in the selection of her husband, but she is to be subordinate to him; nevertheless, she should have the right "to give good advice." Thucydides expresses an opinion that meets with the applause of all modern Philistines. He says: "That wife deserves the highest praise of whom, outside of her home, neither good nor bad is heard."

With such views, respect for woman was bound to sink to a low level: fear of over-population even led to the avoidance of intimate intercourse with her. Unnatural means of satisfying sexual desires were resorted to. The Greek states were cities with small territories, unable to supply the usual sustenance to a population in excess of a given number. Hence the fear of over-population caused Aristotle to recommend to the men abstinence from their wives, and pederasty, instead. Before him, Socrates had praised pederasty as the sign of a higher culture. In the end, the most promising men of Greece became adherents of this unnatural passion. Regard for women sank all the deeper. There were now houses for male prostitutes, as there were for female. In such a social atmosphere, it was natural for Thucydides to utter the saying that woman was worse than the storm-lashed ocean's wave, than the fire's glow, than the cascade of the wild mountain torrent. "If it is a God that invented

---

[11] Johann Scherr, "Deutsche Kultur-und Sittengeschichte:" Leipsic, 1887. Otto Wigand. As is known, Suderman deals with the same subject in his play, "Die Ehre."

[12] Plato, "The Republic," Book V.

woman, wherever, he may be, let him know, that he is the unhallowed cause of the greatest evil." [13]

The male population of Greece having become addicted to pederasty, the female population fell into the opposite extreme: it took to the love of members of its own sex. This happened especially with the women of the island of Lesbos, whence this aberration was, and still continues to be named, "Lesbian love," for it has not yet died out: it survives among us. The poetess Sappho, "the Lesbian nightingale," who lived about six hundred years before our reckoning, is considered the leading representative of this form of love. Her passion is glowingly expressed in her hymn to Aphrodite, whom she implores:

> "Glittering-throned, undying Aphrodite,
> Wile-weaving daughter of high Zeus, I pray thee,
> Tame not my soul with heavy woe, dread mistress,
> Nay, nor with anguish."

A still more passionate sensuousness is attested in her hymn to the handsome Atthis.

While in Athens, along with the rest of Greece, the father-right ruled, Sparta, the rival for supremacy with Athens, still continued under the mother-right, a condition that had become wholly foreign to most Greeks. The story runs that one day a Greek asked a Spartan what punishment was meted out in Sparta to the adulterer. He answered: "Stranger, among us there are no adulterers." "But if there should be any?" "For punishment," the Spartan replied, sarcastically, "he must donate an ox, so large as to be able to reach over Taygetus with his head, and drink out of Eurotas." Upon the startled question, put by the stranger, "How can an ox be so large?" the Spartan answered laughing: "How is it possible that there could be an adulterer in Sparta?" At the same time the self-consciousness of the Spartan woman appears in the proud answer given a stranger by the wife of Leonidas. On his saying to her: "You female Lacedaemonians are the only women who rule over your men," she answered: "So are we the only women who bring men into the world."

The free condition of women under the mother-right promoted her beauty, raised her pride, her dignity and her self-reliance. The judgment of all ancient writers is to the effect that, during the period of the gyneocracy, these qualities were highly developed among women. The constrained condition that later supervened, necessarily had its evil effect upon them. The difference appears even in the garb of the two periods. The garb of the Doric woman hung loose from her shoulders; it left the arms free, and thighs exposed: it is the garb of Diana, who is repre-

[13] Leon Richter, "La Femme Libre."

sented as free and bold in our museums. The Ionian garb, on the contrary, concealed the body and hampered its motion. The garb of woman to-day is, far more than usually realized, a sign of her dependence and helplessness. The style of woman's dress amongst most peoples, down to our own days, renders her awkward, forces on her a sense of weakness, and makes her timid; and this, finally, finds its expression in her attitude and character. The custom among the Spartans of letting the girls go naked until marriageable age—a custom that the climate allowed—contributed considerably, in the opinion of an ancient writer, to impart to them a taste for simplicity and for attention to decency. Nor was there in the custom, according to the views of those days, aught offensive to decorum, or inciting to lust. Furthermore, the girls participated in all the bodily exercises, just as the boys, and thus there was reared a vigorous, proud, self-conscious race, a race that was conscious of its own merit, as proved by the answer of Leonidas' wife to the stranger.

In intimate connection with the mother-right, after it had ceased to be a ruling social principle, stood certain customs, which modern writers, ignorant of their meaning, designate as "prostitution." In Babylon, it was a religious duty with the maid, who had reached puberty, to appear once in the temple of Mylitta in order to offer her maidenhood as a sacrifice, by surrendering herself to some man. Similarly happened in the Serapeum of Memphis; in Armenia, in honor of the goddess Anaitis; in Cyprus; in Tyrus and Sidon, in honor of Astarte or Aphrodite. The festivals of Isis among the Egyptians served similar customs. This sacrifice of virginity was demanded in order to atone with the goddess for the exclusive surrender of woman to one man in marriage:—"Not that she may wilt in the arms of a single man is woman arrayed by nature with all the charms at its command." [14] The continued favor of the goddess had to be purchased by the sacrifice of virginity to a stranger. It was likewise in line with the old idea that the Lybian maids earned their dower by prostituting their bodies. In accord with the mother-right, these women were sexually free during their unmarried status; and the men saw so little objection in these pickings, that those were taken by them for wives who had been most in demand. It was thus also among the Thracians, in the days of Herodotus: "They do not watch the maidens, but leave them full freedom to associate with whom they please. The women, however, they watch strictly. They buy them from their parents for large sums." Celebrated were the Hierodulae of the temple of Aphrodite at Corinth, where always more than one thousand maidens were gathered, and constituted a chief point of attraction for the men of Greece. Of the daughter of King Cheops of Egypt, the legend

[14] Bachofen. "Das Mutterrecht."

relates that she had a pyramid built out of the proceeds of prostitution of her charms.

Conditions, similar to these, prevail down to now, on the Mariana, the Philippine and the Polynesian islands; according to Waitz, also among several African tribes. Another custom, prevalent till late on the Balearic islands, and indicative of the right of all men to a woman, was that, on the wedding night, the male kin had access to the bride in order of seniority. The bridegroom came last; he then took her as wife into his own possession. This custom has been changed among other people so that the priest or the tribal chiefs (kings) exercise the privilege over the bride, as representatives of the men of the tribe. On Malabar, the Caimars hire patamars (priests) to deflower their wives. . . . The chief priest (Namburi) is in duty bound to render this service to the king (Zamorin) at his wedding, and the king rewards him with fifty gold pieces.[15] In Further India, and on several islands of the great ocean, it is sometimes the priests and sometimes the tribal chiefs who undertake the function.[16] The same happens in Senegambia, where the tribal chief exercises, as a duty of his office, the deflowering of maids, and receives therefor a present. Again, with other peoples, the custom was, and continues here and yonder, that the deflowering of a maid, sometimes even of a child only a few months old, is done by means of images of deities, fashioned expressly for this purpose. It may also be accepted as certain that the "jus primae noctis" (the right of the first night), prevalent in Germany and all Europe until late in the Middle Ages, owes its origin to the same tradition, as Frederick Engels observes. The landlord, who, as master of his dependents and serfs, looked upon himself as their chief, exercised the right of the head of the tribe, a right that he considered had passed over to himself as the arbiter of their lives and existence.

Echoes of the mother-right are further detected in the singular custom among some South American tribes, that, instead of the lying-in woman, the man goes to bed, there acts like a woman in labor, and is tended by the wife. The custom implies that the father recognizes the new born child as his own. By imitating the pains of child-birth, the man fills the fiction that the birth is also his work; that he, therefore, has a right to the child, who, according to the former custom, belonged to the mother and the mother's gens, respectively. The custom is said to have also maintained itself among the Basques, who must be looked upon as a people of primitive usages and customs. Likewise is the custom said to prevail among several mountain tribes in China. It prevailed until not long since in Corsica.

[15] K. Kautsky, "Die Entstehung der Ehe und der Familie," Kosmos, 1888.
[16] Montegazza, "L'Amour dans l'Humanite."

In Greece likewise did woman become an article of purchase. So soon as she stepped into the house of her marital lord, she ceased to exist for her family. This was symbolically expressed by burning before the door the handsomely decked wagon which took her to the house of her husband. Among the Ostiaks of Siberia, to this day, the father sells his daughter: he chaffers with the representative of the bridegroom about the price to be paid. Likewise among several African tribes, the same as in the days of Jacob, the custom is that a man who courts a maid, enters in the service of his future mother-in-law. Even with us, marriage by purchase has not died out: it prevails in bourgeois society worse than ever. Marriage for money, almost everywhere customary among the ruling classes, is nothing other than marriage by purchase. Indeed, the marriage gift, which in all civilized countries the bridegroom makes to the bride, is but a symbol of the purchase of the wife as property.

Along with marriage by purchase, there was the custom of marriage by rape. The rape of women was a customary practice, not alone among the ancient Jews, but everywhere in antiquity. It is met with among almost all nations. The best known historic instance is the rape of the Sabine women by the Romans. The rape of women was an easy remedy where women ran short, as, according to the legend, happened to the early Romans; or where polygamy was the custom, as everywhere in the Orient. There it assumed large proportions during the supremacy of the Arabs, from the seventh to the twelfth century.

Symbolically, the rape of woman still occurs, for instance among the Araucans of South Chile. While the friends of the bridegroom are negotiating with the father of the bride, the bridegroom steals with his horse into the neighborhood of the house, and seeks to capture the bride. So soon as he catches her, he throws her upon his horse, and makes off with her to the woods. The men, women and children thereupon raise a great hue and cry, and seek to prevent the escape. But when the bridegroom has reached the thick of the woods, the marriage is considered consummated. This holds good also when the abduction takes place against the will of the parents. Similar customs prevail among the peoples of Australia.

Among ourselves, the custom of "wedding trips" still reminds us of the former rape of the wife: the bride is carried off from her domestic flock. On the other hand, the exchange of rings is a reminiscence of the subjection and enchainment of the woman to the man. The custom originated in Rome. The bride received an iron ring from her husband as a sign of her bondage to him. Later the ring was made of gold; much later the exchange of rings was introduced, as a sign of mutual union.

The old family ties of the gens had, accordingly, lost their foundation through the development of the conditions of production, and through the rule of private property. Upon the abolition of the gens, grounded on mother-right, the gens, grounded on the father-right first took its place, although not for long, and with materially weakened functions. Its task was mainly to attend to the common religious affairs and to the ceremonial of funerals: to safeguard the mutual obligation of protection and of help against violence: to enforce the right, and, in certain cases, the duty of marrying in the gens, in cases when rich heiresses or female orphans were concerned. The gens, furthermore, administered the still existing common property. But the segmentation of handicraft from agriculture; the ever wider expansion of commerce; the founding of cities, rendered necessary by both of these; the conquest of booty and prisoners of war, the latter of which directly affected the household,—all of these tore to shreds the conditions and bonds of eld. Handicraft had gradually subdivided itself into a larger number of separate trades— weaving, pottery, iron-forging, the preparation of arms, house and ship-building, etc. Accordingly, it pushed toward another organization. The ever further introduction of slavery, the admittance of strangers into the community,—these were all so many new and additional elements that rendered the old constitution of society ever more impossible.

Along with private property and the personal right of inheritance, class distinctions and class contrasts came into existence. Rich property-owners drew together against those who owned less, or nothing. The former sought to get into their own hands the public offices of the new commonwealth, and to make them hereditary. Money, now become necessary, created thitherto unknown forms of indebtedness. Wars against enemies from without, and conflicting interests within, as well as the various interests and relations which agriculture, handicraft and commerce mutually produced rendered necessary complicated rules of right, they demanded special organs to guard the orderly movement of the social machinery, and to settle disputes. The same held good for the relations of master and slave, creditor and debtor. A power, accordingly, became necessary to supervise, lead, regulate and harmonize all these relations, with authority to protect, and, when needed, to punish. *Thus rose the State, the product, accordingly of the conflicting interests that sprang up in the new social order.* Its administration naturally fell into the hands of those who had the liveliest interest in its establishment, and who, in virtue of their social power, possessed the greatest influence,— the rich. Aristocracy of property and democracy confronted each other, accordingly, even there where externally complete equality of political rights existed.

Under the mother-right, there was no written law. The relations were simple, and custom was held sacred. Under the new, and much more complicated order, written law was one of the most important requirements; and special organs became necessary to administer it. In the measure that the legal relations and legal conditions gained in intricacy, a special class of people gathered shape, who made the study of the law their special vocation, and who finally had a special interest in rendering the law ever more complicated. Then arose the men learned in the laws, the jurists, who, due to the importance of the statutory law to the whole of society, rose to influential social rank. The new system of rights found in the course of time its classic expression in the Roman State, whence the influence that Roman law exercises down to the present.

The institution of the State is, accordingly, the necessary result of a social order, that, standing upon the higher plane of the subdivision of labor, is broken up into a large number of occupations, animated by different, frequently conflicting, interests, and hence has the oppression of the weaker for a consequence. This fact was recognized even by an Arabian tribe, the Nabateans, who, according to Diodorus, established the regulation not to sow, not to plant, to drink no wine, and to build no houses, but to live in tents, because if those things were done, *they could be easily compelled to obey by a superior power* (the power of the State). Likewise among the Rachebites, the descendants of the father-in-law of Moses, there existed similar prescriptions.[17] Aye, the whole Mosaic system of laws is aimed at *preventing the Jews from moving out of an agricultural state, because otherwise, so the legislators feared, their democratic-communistic society would go under.* Hence the selection of the "Promised Land" in a region bounded, on one side, by a not very accessible mountain range, the Lebanon; on the other side, South and East, by but slightly fertile stretches of land, partly by deserts;— a region, accordingly, that rendered isolation possible. Hence came the keeping of the Jews away from the sea, which favored commerce, colonization and the accumulation of wealth; hence the rigid laws concerning seclusion from other peoples, the severe regulations against foreign marriages, the poor laws, the agrarian laws, the jubileum,—all of them provisions calculated to prevent the accumulation of great wealth by the individual. The Jewish people were to be kept in permanent disability ever to become the builders of a real State. Hence it happens that the tribal organization, which rested upon the gentile order, remained in force with them till its complete dissolution, and continues to affect them even now.

It seems that the Latin tribes, which took a hand in the founding of Rome, had long passed beyond the stage of the mother-right. Hence Rome was built from the start as a State. The women that they needed they captured, as the legend tells us, from the tribe of the Sabines, and

[17] Joh. David Michaelis, "Mosaisches Recht," Reutlingen, 1793.

they called themselves after their Sabine wives,—Quirites. Even in later years, the Roman citizens were addressed in the Forum as Quirites. "Populus Romanus" stood for the free population of Rome in general; but "Populus Romanus quiritium" expressed the ancestry and quality of the Roman citizen. The Roman gens was of father-right stamp. The children inherited as consanguineous heirs; if there were no children, the relatives of the male line inherited; were none of these in existence, then the property reverted to the gens. By marriage, woman lost her right to inherit her father's property and that of his brothers. She had stepped out of her gens: neither she nor her children could inherit from her father or his brothers: otherwise the inheritance would be lost to the paternal gens. The division in gentes, phratries and tribes constituted in Rome for centuries the foundation of the military organization, and also of the exercise of the rights of citizenship. But with the decay of the paternal gentes and the decline of their significance, conditions shaped themselves more favorably for woman. She could not only inherit, but had the right to administer her own fortune. She was, accordingly, far more favorably situated than her Greek sister. The freer position that, despite all legal impediments, she gradually knew how to conquer, caused the elder Cato, born 234 before our reckoning, to complain: "If, after the example of his ancestors, every head of a family kept his wife in proper subjection, we would not have so much public bother with the whole sex." [18]

So long as the father lived, he held in Rome the guardianship over his daughter, even if she were married, unless he appointed another guardian himself. When the father died, the nearest male of kin, even though declared unqualified as an agnate, came in as guardian. The guardian had the right at any time to transfer the guardianship to any third person that he pleased. Accordingly, before the law, the Roman woman had no will of her own.

The nuptial forms were various, and in the course of centuries underwent manifold alterations. The most solemn nuptials were celebrated before the High Priest, in the presence of at least ten witnesses. At the occasion, the bridal pair, in token of their union, partook together from a cake made of flour, salt and water. As will be noticed, a ceremony is here celebrated, that bears great resemblance to the breaking of the sacramental wafer at the Christian communion. A second form of nuptials consisted in possession. The marriage was considered accomplished if, with the consent of her father or guardian, a woman lived with the chosen man a whole year under one roof. A third form of nuptials was a sort of mutual purchase, both sides exchanging coins, and the promise

---

[18] Karl Heinzen, "Ueber die Rechte und Stellung der Frauen."

to be man and wife. Already at the time of Cicero,[19] free divorce for both sides was generally established; it was even debated whether the announcement of the divorce was necessary. The "lex Julia de adulteriis," however, prescribed that the divorce was to be solemnly proclaimed. This decree was made for the reason that women, who committed adultery, and were summoned to answer the charge, often claimed to have been divorced. Justinian, the Christian,[20] forbade free divorce, unless both sides desired to retire to a monastery. His successor, Justinian II, however, found himself obliged to allow it again.

With the growing power and rising wealth of Rome, mad-brained vices and excesses took the place of the former severity of manners. Rome became the center from which debauchery, riotous luxury and sensuous refinements radiated over the whole of the then civilized world. The excesses took—especially during the time of the Emperors, and, to a great extent, through the Emperors themselves—forms that only insanity could suggest. Men and women vied with one another in vice. The number of houses of prostitution became ever larger, and, hand in hand with these, the "Greek love" (pederasty) spread itself ever more among the male population. At times, the number of young men in Rome who prostituted themselves was larger than that of the female prostitutes.

"The hetairae appeared, surrounded by their admirers, in great pomp on the streets, promenades, the circus and theatres, often carried by negroes upon litters, where, holding a mirror in their hands, and sparkling with ornaments and precious stones, they lay outstretched, nude, fan-carrying slaves standing by them, and surrounded by a swarm of boys, eunuchs and flute-players; grotesque dwarfs closed the procession."

These excesses assumed such proportions in the Roman Empire that they became a danger to the Empire itself. The example of the men was followed by the women. There were women, Seneca reports, who counted the years, not as was the usage, after the consuls, but after the number of their husbands. Adultery was general; and, in order that the women might escape the severe punishments prescribed for the offense, they, and among them the leading dames of Rome, caused themselves to be entered in the registers of the Aediles as prostitutes.

Hand in hand with these excesses, civil wars and the latifundia system, celibacy and childlessness increased in such measure that the number of Roman citizens and of patricians ran down considerably. Hence in the year 16 B. C., Augustus issued the so-called Julian Law,[21] which offered prizes for the birth of children, and imposed penalties for celibacy upon

---

[19] Born 106 before our reckoning.

[20] He lived from 527 to 565 of our reckoning.

[21] Augustus, the son of Caesar by adoption, was of the Julian gens, hence the title "Julian" law.

the Roman citizens and patricians. He who had children had precedence in rank over the childless and unmarried. Bachelors could accept no inheritance, except from their own nearest kin. The childless could only inherit one-half; the rest fell to the State. Women, who could be taxed with adultery, had to surrender one-half of their dower to the abused husband. Thereupon there were men who married out of speculation on the adultery of their wives. This caused Plutarch to observe: "The Romans marry, not to obtain heirs, but to inherit."

Still later the Julian Law was made severer. Tiberius decreed that no woman, whose grandfather, father or husband had been or still was a Roman Knight, could prostitute herself for money. Married women, who caused themselves to be entered in the registers of prostitutes, were condemned to banishment from Italy as adulteresses. Of course, there were no such punishments for the men. Moreover, as Juvenal reports, even the murder of husbands by poison was a frequent occurrence in the Rome of his day—the first half of the first century before Christ.

CHAPTER II.

UNDER CHRISTIANITY.

The opposite of polygamy,—as we have learned to know it among Oriental peoples, and as it still exists among them, but owing to the number of available women and the cost of their support, can be indulged in only by the privileged and the rich—is polyandry. The latter exists mainly among the highland people of Thibet, among the Garras on the Hindoo-Chinese frontier, among the Baigas in Godwana, the Nairs in the southern extremity of India; it is said to be found also among the Eskimos and Aleutians. Heredity is determined in the only way possible,—after the mother: the children belong to her. The husbands of a woman are usually brothers. When the elder brother marries, the other brothers likewise become the husbands of the woman; the woman, however, preserves the right to take other men besides. Conversely, the men also are said to have the right of taking a second, third, fourth, or more wives. To what circumstances polyandry owes its origin is not yet clear. Seeing that the polyandrous nations, without exception, live either on high mountain regions, or in the cold zone, polyandry probably owes its existence to a phenomenon that Tarnowsky comments on.[1] He learned from reliable travelers that a long sojourn at high elevations lowers the sensuous pleasures, and weakens erection, both of which return with new vigor by re-descension to lower altitudes. This lowering of the sexual powers, Tarnowsky is of the opinion, might partly account for the comparative slight increase of population on highland regions; and he is of the opinion that, when the debility is transmitted, it may become a source of degeneration that operates upon the perversity of the sexual sense.

We may also add that a protracted domicile, together with the habits of life contracted on very high or cold regions, may have for a further result that polyandry lays no excessive demands upon a woman. The women themselves are correspondingly affected in their nature. That they are so is rendered probable by the circumstance that, among the Eskimo girls, menstruation sets in only with the nineteenth year, whereas in the warm zones it sets in as early as the tenth or eleventh, and in the temperate latitudes between the fourteenth and the sixteenth year. In view of the fact that warm climates, as universally recognized, exercise a strongly stimulating influence upon the sexual instinct,—whence polygamy finds its widest diffusion in warm countries—it is quite likely that cold regions—to which high mountains and plateaus belong, and

[1] Tarnowsky. "Die krankhaften Erscheinungen des Geschlechtsinnes." Berlin, August Hirschwald.

where the thinner air may also contribute its share—may exercise materially a restringent effect upon the sexual instinct. It must, moreover, be noted that experience shows conception occurs rarer with women who cohabit with several men. The increase of population is, accordingly, slight under polyandry; and it fits in with the difficulty of securing subsistence, encountered in cold lands and mountain regions;—whereby additional proof is furnished that also, in this, to us so seemingly strange phenomenon of polyandry, production has its determining influence upon the relations of the sexes. Finally, it is to be ascertained whether among these peoples, who live on high mountains or in cold zones, the killing of girl babies is not a frequent practice, as is oft reported of the Mongolian tribes, on the highlands of China.

Exactly the reverse of the custom among the Romans during the Empire, of allowing celibacy and childlessness to gain the upper hand, was the custom prevalent among the Jews. True enough, the Jewish woman had no right to choose; her father fixed upon the husband she was to wed; but marriage was a duty, that they religiously followed. The Talmud advises: "When your daughter is of marriageable age, give his freedom to one of your slaves and engage her to him." In the same sense the Jews followed strictly the command of their God: "Increase and multiply." Due to this, and despite all persecutions and oppression, they have diligently increased their numbers. The Jew is the sworn enemy of Malthusianism.

Already Tacitus says of them: "Among themselves there is a stubborn holding together, and ready open-handedness; but, for all others, hostile hatred. Never do they eat, never do they sleep with foes; and, although greatly inclined to sensuousness, they abstain from procreation with foreign women. Nevertheless they strive to increase their people. Infanticide is held a sin with them; and the souls of those who die in battle or by execution they consider immortal. Hence the love of procreation beside their contempt of death." Tacitus hated and abhorred the Jews, because, in contempt of the religion of their fathers, they heaped up wealth and treasures. He called them the "worst set of people," an "ugly race."[2]

Under the over-lordship of the Romans, the Jews drew ever closer together. Under the long period of sufferings, which, from that time on, they had to endure, almost throughout the whole of the Christian Middle Ages, grew that intimate family life that is to-day considered a sort of pattern by the modern bourgeois *regime*. On the other side, Roman society underwent the process of disintegration and dissolution, which led the Empire to its destruction. Upon the excesses, bordering on in-

[2] Tacitus, "Histories," Book I.

sanity, followed the other extreme,—the most rigid abstinence. As excess, in former days, now asceticism assumed religious forms. A dreamland-fanaticism made propaganda for it. The unbounded gluttony and luxury of the ruling classes stood in glaring contrast with the want and misery of the millions upon millions that conquering Rome dragged, from all the then known countries of the world, into Italy and slavery. Among these were also numberless women, who, separated from their domestic hearths, from their parents or their husbands, and torn from their children, felt their misery most keenly, and yearned for deliverance. A large number of Roman women, disgusted at that which happened all around them, found themselves in similar frame of mind; any change in their condition seemed to them a relief. A deep longing for a change, for deliverance, took possession of extensive social layers;— and the deliverer seemed to approach. The conquest of Jerusalem and of the Jewish kingdom by the Romans had for its consequence the destruction of all national independence, and begot among the ascetic sects of that country, dreamers, who announced the birth of a new kingdom, that was to bring freedom and happiness to all.

Christ came, and Christianity arose. It embodied the opposition to the bestial materialism that reigned among the great and the rich of the Roman Empire; it represented the revolt against the contempt for and oppression of the masses. But originating in Judaism, which knew woman only as a being bereft of all rights, and biased by the Biblical conception which saw in her the source of all evil, Christianity preached contempt for woman. It also preached abstinence, the mortification of the flesh, then so sinful, and it pointed with its ambiguous phrases to a prospective kingdom, which some interpreted as of heaven, others as of earth, and which was to bring freedom and justice to all. With these doctrines it found fertile ground in the submerged bottom of the Roman Empire. Woman, hoping, along with all the miserable, for freedom and deliverance from her condition, joined readily and zealously. Down to our own days, never yet was a great and important movement achieved in the world without women also having been conspicuously active as combatants and martyrs. Those who praise Christianity as a great achievement of civilization should not forget that it was woman in particular to whom Christianity owes a great part of its success. Her proselyting zeal played a weighty *role* in the Roman Empire, as well as among the barbarous peoples of the Middle Ages. The mightiest were by her converted to Christianity. It was Clotilde, for instance, who moved Clovis, the King of the Franks, to accept Christianity; it was, again, Bertha, Queen of Kent, and Gisela, Queen of Hungary, who introduced Christianity in their countries. To the influence of the women is due the conversion of many of the great. But Christianity, requited woman ill. Its tenets breathe the same contempt for woman that is breathed in all the religions of the East. It orders her to be the obedient servant of her husband, and the vow of obedience she must, to this day, make to him at the altar.

Let us hear the Bible and Christianity speak of woman and marriage. The ten commandments are addressed only to the men; in the tenth commandment woman is bracketed with servants and domestic animals. Man is warned not to covet his neighbor's wife, nor his manservant, nor his maid-servant, nor his ox, nor his ass, nor anything that is his. Woman, accordingly, appears as an object, as a piece of property, that the man may not hanker after, if in another's possession. Jesus, who belonged to a sect—the sect which imposed upon itself strict asceticism and even self-emasculation[3]—being asked by his disciples whether it is good to marry, answers: "All men cannot receive this saying, save they to whom it is given. For there are some eunuchs, which were so born from their mother's womb; and there are some eunuchs, which were made eunuchs of men; and there be eunuchs, *which have made themselves eunuchs for the kingdom of heaven's sake.*" [4] Emasculation is, according hereto, an act hallowed by God, and the renunciation of love and marriage a good deed.

Paul, who, in a higher degree than even Jesus himself, may be called the founder of the Christian religion; Paul, who first impressed an international character upon this creed, and tore it away from the narrow sectarianism of the Jews, writes to the Corinthians: "Now concerning the things whereof ye wrote unto me: "It is good for a man not to touch a woman;" "he that giveth her in marriage doeth well; but he that giveth her not in marriage doeth better."[5] "Walk in the Spirit and fulfil not the lust of the flesh, for the flesh lusteth against the Spirit and the Spirit against the flesh;" "they that are Christ's have crucified the flesh, with the affections and lusts." He followed his own precepts, and did not marry. This hatred of the flesh *is the hatred of woman, but also the fear of woman,* who—see the scene in Paradise—is represented as the seducer of man. In this spirit did the Apostles and the Fathers of the Church preach; in this spirit did the Church work throughout the whole of the Middle Ages, when it reared its cloisters, and introduced celibacy among the priesthood;—and to this day it works in the same spirit.

According to Christianity, woman is the *unclean being;* the seducer, who introduced sin into the world and ruined man. Hence Apostles,

[3] Montegazza "L'Amour dans l'Humanite."
[4] Matthew, ch. 19; 11 and 12.
[5] I. Corinthians, ch. 7; 1 and 38.

and Fathers of the Church alike, have ever looked upon marriage as a necessary evil,—the same as is said to-day of prostitution. Tertulian exclaims: "Woman, thou should ever walk in mourning and rags, thy eyes full of tears, present the aspect of repentance to induce orgetfulness of your having ruined the human race. Woman, thou art the Gate of Hell!" Hieronymus says: "Marriage always is a vice; all that we can do is to excuse and cleanse it," hence it was made a sacrament of the Church. Origenes declares: "Marriage is something unholy and unclean, a means for sensuality," and, in order to resist the temptation, he emasculated himself. Tertulian declares: "Celibacy is preferable, even if the human race goes to ground." Augustine teaches: "The celibates will shine in heaven like brilliant stars, while their parents (who brought them forth) are like dark stars." Eusebius and Hieronymus agree that the Biblical command, "Increase and multiply," no longer fits the times, and does not concern the Christians. Hundreds of other quotations from the most influential Fathers of the Church could be cited, all of which tend in the same direction. By means of their continuous teaching and preaching, they have spread those unnatural views touching sexual matters, and the intercourse of the sexes, *the latter of which, nevertheless, remains a commandment of nature, and obedience to which is one of the most important duties in the mission of life.* Modern society is still severely ailing from these teachings, and it is recovering but slowly.

Peter calls out emphatically to women: "Ye wives, be in subjection to your own husbands."[6] Paul writes to the Ephesians: "The husband is the head of the wife, even as Christ is the head of the Church;"[7] and in Corinthians: "Man is the image and glory of God; but the woman is the glory of the man."[8] According to which every sot of a man may hold himself better than the most distinguished woman;—indeed, it is so in practice to-day. Also against the higher education of women does Paul raise his weighty voice: "Let the woman learn in silence with all *subjection. But I suffer not a woman to teach, nor to usurp authority over the man, but to be in silence;"*[9] and again: "Let your women *keep silence* in the churches; *for it is not permitted unto them to speak; but they are commanded to be under obedience,* as also saith the law. And if they will learn anything, *let them ask their husbands at home; for it is a shame for women to speak in the church.*"[10]

Such doctrines are not peculiar to Christianity only. Christianity being a mixture of Judaism and Greek philosophy, and seeing that these,

[6] Peter I., ch. 3 ; 1.
[7] Paul : Ephesians, ch. 5 ; 23.
[8] Paul : I. Corinthians, ch. 11 ; 7.
[9] I. Timothy, ch. 2 ; 11 and 12.
[10] I. Corinthians, ch. 14 ; 34 and 35.

in turn, have their roots in the older civilization of the Egyptians, Babylonians, and Hindoos, the subordinate position that Christianity assigned to woman was one common in antiquity. In the Hindoo laws
of Manu it is said regarding woman: "The source of dishonor is woman;
the source of strife is woman; the source of earthly existence is woman;
therefore avoid woman." Beside this degradation of woman, fear of her
ever and anon reappears naively. Manu further sets forth: "Woman is
by nature ever inclined to tempt man; hence a man should not sit in a
secluded place even with his nearest female relative." Woman, accordingly, is, according to the Hindoo as well as the Old Testament and
Christian view, everywhere the tempter. All masterhood implies the
degradation of the mastered. The subordinate position of woman continues, to this day, even more in force in the backward civilization of
the East than among the nations that enjoy a so-called Christian view-
point. That which, in the so-called Christian world, gradually improved
the situation of woman was, not Christianity, but *the advanced culture
of the West struggling against the Christian doctrine.*

Christianity is guiltless of woman's present improved position to what
it was at the start of the era. Only reluctantly, and forced thereto, did
Christianity become untrue to its true spirit with regard to woman.
Those who rave about "the mission of Christianity to emancipate mankind," differ from us in this, as in other respects. They claim that
Christianity freed woman from her previous low position, and they
ground themselves upon the worship of Maria, the "mother of God,"—
a cult, however, that sprang up only later in Christendom, but which
they point to as a sign of regard for the whole sex. The Roman Catholic Church, which celebrates this cult, should be the last to lay claim
to such a doctrine. The Saints and Fathers of the Church, cited above,
and whose utterances could be easily multiplied—and they are the leading Church authorities—express themselves separately and collectively
hostile to woman and to marriage. The Council of Macon, which, in
the sixteenth century, discussed the question whether woman had a soul,
and which decided with a majority of but one vote, that she had, likewise argues against the theory of such a friendly posture towards woman.
The introduction of celibacy by Gregory VII[11]—although resorted to
first of all and mainly with the end in view of holding in the unmarried
priesthood a power that could not be alienated from the service of the
Church through any family interests—was, nevertheless, possible only

[11] This was a move that the parish priests of the diocese of Mainz, among
others, complained against, expressing themselves this wise: "You Bishops
and Abbots possess great wealth, a kingly table, and rich hunting equipages;
we, poor, plain priests have for our comfort only a wife. Abstinence may be
a handsome virtue, but, in point of fact, it is hard and difficult."—Yves-
Guyot: "Les Theories Sociales du Christianisme."

with such fundamental doctrines as the Church held touching the sinfulness of the lusts of the flesh; and it goes to confirm our theory.

Neither did the Reformers, especially Calvin and the Scotch ministers, with their wrath at the "lusts of the flesh," entertain any doubt touching the hostile posture of Christianity towards woman.[12]

By the introduction of the cult of Maria, the Roman Catholic Church shrewdly placed the worship of Mary in the place of that of the heathen goddesses, in vogue among *all* the people over whom Christianity was then extending itself. *Maria* took the place of the Cybele, the Mylitta, the Aphrodite, the Venus, the Ceres, etc., of the southern races; of the Freia, the Frigga, etc., of the Germanian tribes. She was a mere spiritually-Christian idealization.

The primeval, physically robust, though rude yet uncorrupted races, that, during the first centuries of our reckoning, crowded down from the North and East like a gigantic ocean wave, and swamped the worn-out universal Empire of Rome, where Christianity had gradually been superimposing itself as master, resisted with all their might the ascetic doctrines of the Christian preachers. With good grace or bad, the latter were forced to reckon with these robust natures. With astonishment did the Romans perceive that the customs of those peoples were quite different from their own. Tacitus rendered to this fact the tribute of his acknowledgement, which, with regard to the Germans, he expressed in these words: "The matrimonial bond is, nevertheless, strict and severe among them; nor is there anything in their manners more commendable than this. Almost singly among the barbarians, they content themselves with one wife. Adultery is extremely rare among so numerous a people. Its punishment is instant, and at the pleasure of the husband. He cuts off the hair of the offender, strips her, and in the presence of her relations expels her from his house, and pursues her with stripes through the whole village. Nor is any indulgence shown to a prostitute. Neither beauty, youth, nor riches can procure her a husband; for none there looks on vice with a smile, or calls mutual seduction the way of the world. The youths partake late of the pleasures of love, and hence pass the age of puberty unexhausted; nor are the virgins hurried into marriage; the same maturity, the same full growth is required; the sexes unite equally matched, and robust; and the children inherit the vigor of their parents."

With the object in view of holding up a pattern to the Romans, Tacitus painted the conjugal conditions of the old Germans with rather too rosy a hue. No doubt, the adulteress was severely punished among them; but the same did not hold good with regard to the adulterer. At

[12] Buckle, in his "History of Civilization in England," furnishes a large number of illustrations on this head.

the time of Tacitus, the gens was still in bloom among the Germans. He, to whom, living under the advanced Roman conditions, the old gentile constitution, together with its principles, was bound to seem strange and incomprehensible, narrates with astonishment that, with the Germans, the mother's brother, considered his nephew as an own son; aye, some looked upon the bond of consanguinity between the uncle on the mother's side and his nephew as more sacred and closer than that between father and son. So that, when hostages were demanded, the 'sister's son was considered a better guarantee than an own son. Engels adds hereto: "If an own son was given by the members of such a gens as a pledge for a treaty, and he fell a sacrifice through his own father's violation of the treaty, the latter had to settle accounts for himself. If, however, it was a sister's son who was sacrificed, then the old gentile right was violated. The nearest gentile relative, held before all others to safeguard the boy or lad, had caused his death; he either had no right to offer him as a pledge, or he was bound to observe the treaty."[13]

For the rest, as Engels shows, the mother-right had already yielded to the father-right among the Germans, at the time of Tacitus. The children inherited from their father; in the absence of these, then the brothers and the uncle of the father on the mother's side. The admission of the mother's brother as an heir, although descent from the father determined the line of inheritance, is explained with the theory that the old right had only recently died away. It was only reminiscences of the old right that furnished the conditions, which enabled Tacitus to find a, to the Romans, incomprehensible regard for the female sex among the Germans. He also found that their courage was pricked to the utmost by the women. The thought that their women might fall into captivity or slavery was the most horrible that the old German could conceive of; it spurred him to utmost resistance. But the women also were animated by the spirit that possessed the men. When Marius refused the captured women of the Teutons to dedicate themselves as priestesses to Vesta (the goddess of maidenly chastity) they committed suicide.

In the time of Tacitus, the Germans already acquired settled habitations. Yearly the division of land by lots took place. Besides that, there was common property in the woods, water and pasture grounds. Their lives were yet simple; their wealth principally cattle; their dress consisted of coarse woolen mantles, or skins of animals. Neither women nor chiefs wore under-clothing. The working of metals was in practice only among those tribes located too far away for the introduction of

---

[13] Engel's "Der Ursprung der Familie."

Roman products of industry. Justice was administered in minor affairs by the council of elders; on more important matters, by the assembly of the people. The chiefs were elected, generally out of the same family, but the transition of the father-right favored the heredity of office, and led finally to the establishment of a hereditary nobility, from which later sprang the kingdom. As in Greece and Rome, the German gens went to pieces with the rise of private property and the development of industries and trade, and through the commingling with members of strange tribes and peoples. The place of the gens was taken by the community, the mark, the democratic organization of free peasants, the latter of which, in the course of many centuries, constituted a firm bulwark in the struggles against the nobility, the Church and the Princes,—a bulwark that broke down by little and little, but that did not wholly crumble even after the feudal State had come to power, and the one-time free peasants were in droves reduced to the condition of serfs and dependents.

The confederation of marks was represented by the heads of the families. Married women, daughters, daughters-in-law were excluded from council and administration. The time when women were conspicuous in the conduct of the affairs of the tribe—a circumstance that likewise astonished Tacitus in the highest degree, and which he reports in terms of contempt—were gone. The Salic law abolished in the fifth century of our reckoning the succession of the female sex to hereditary domains.

Soon as he married, every member of a mark was entitled to a share in the common lands. As a rule, grand-parents, parents and children lived under one roof, in communal household. Hence, with a view of being allotted a further share, under-aged or unripe sons were not infrequently married by their father to some marriageable maiden; the father then filled the duties of husband, in the stead of his son.[14] Young married couples received a cart-load of beechwood, and timber for a block-house. If a daughter was born to the couple, they received one load of wood; if a son, two loads.[15] The female sex was considered worth only one-half.

Marriage was simple. A religious formality was unknown. Mutual declarations sufficed. As soon as a couple mounted the nuptial bed, the marriage was consummated. The custom that marriage needs an act

[14] The same thing happened under the rule of the muir in Russia. See Lavelaye: "Original Property."

[15] "Eyn iglich gefurster man, der ein kindbette hat, ist sin kint eyn dochter, so mag eer eyn wagen vol bornholzes von urholz verkaufen of den samstag. Ist iz eyn sone, so mag he iz tun of den dinstag und of den samtsag von ligenden holz oder von urholz und sal der frauwen davon kaufen, win und schon brod dyeweile sie kintes june lit."—G. L. v. Maurer: "Geschichte der Markenverfassung in Deutschland."

of the Church for its validity, came in only in the ninth century. Only in the sixteenth century, on decree of the Council of Trent, was marriage declared a sacrament of the Roman Catholic Church.

With the rise of feudalism, the condition of a large number of the members of the free communities declined. The victorious army-commanders utilized their power to appropriate large territories unto themselves; they considered themselves masters of the common property, which they distributed among their devoted retinue—slaves, serfs, freedmen, generally of foreign descent,—for a term of years, or with the right of inheritance. They thus furnished themselves with a court and military nobility, in all things devoted to their will. The establishment of the large Empire of the Franks finally put an end to the last vestiges of the old gentile constitution. In the place of the former councils of chiefs, now stood the lieutenants of the army and of the newly formed nobility.

Gradually, the mass of the freemen, members of the once free communities, lapsed into exhaustion and poverty, due to the continuous wars of conquest and the strifes among the great, whose burdens they had to bear. They could no longer meet the obligation of furnishing the army requisitions. In lieu thereof, Princes and high nobility secured servants, while the peasants placed themselves and their property under the protection of some temporal or spiritual lord—the Church had managed, within but few centuries, to become a great power—wherefor they paid rent and tribute. Thus the thitherto free peasant's estate was transformed into hired property; and this, with time, was burdened with ever more obligations. Once landed in this state of dependence, it was not long before the peasant lost his personal freedom also. In this way dependence and serfdown spread ever more.

The landlord possessed the almost absolute right of disposal over his serfs and dependents. He had the right, as soon as a male reached his eighteenth year, or the female her fourteenth, to compel their marriage. He could assign a woman to a man, and a man to a woman. He enjoyed the same right over widows and widowers. In his attribute of lord over his subjects, he also considered the sexual use of his female serfs and dependents to be at his own disposal,—a power that finds its expression in the "jus primae noctis" (the right of the first night). This right also belonged to his representative, the stewart, unless, upon the payment of a tribute, the exercise of the right was renounced. The very names of the tribute betray its nature.[16]

It is extensively disputed that this "right of the first night" ever existed. The "right of the first night" is quite a thorn in the side of

[16] "Bettmund," "Jungfernzins," "Hemdschilling," "Schuerzenzins," "Bunzengroschen,"

certain folks, for the reason that the right was still exercised at an age, that they love to hold up as a model,—a genuine model of morality and piety. It has been pointed out how this "right of the first night" was the rudiment of a custom, that hung together with the age of the mother-right, when all the women were the wives of all the men of a class. With the disappearance of the old family organization, the custom survived in the surrender of the bride, on the wedding night, to the men of her own community. But, in the course of time, the right is ever more restricted, and finally falls to the chief of the tribe, or to the priest, as a religious act, to be exercised by them alone. The feudal lord assumes the right as a consequence of his power over the person who belongs to the land, and which is his property; and he exercises the right if he wills, or relinquishes it in lieu of a tribute in products or money. How real was the "right of the first night" appears from Jacob Grimm's "Weisthumer."[17]

Sugenheim[18] says the "jus primae noctis," as a right appertaining to the landlords, originates in that his consent to marriage was necessary. Out of this right there arose in Bearn the usage that all the first-born of marriages, in which the "jus primae noctis" was exercised, were of free rank. Later, the right was generally redeemable by a tribute. According to Sugenheim, those who held most stubbornly to the right were the Bishops of Ameins; it lasted with them till the beginning of the fifteenth century. In Scotland the right was declared redeemable by King Malcolm III, towards the end of the eleventh century; in Germany, however, it continued in force much longer. According to the archives of a Swabian cloister, Adelberg, for the year 1496, the serfs, located at Boertlingen, had to redeem the right by the bridegroom's giving a cake of salt,' and the bride paying one pound seven shillings, or with a pan, "in which she can sit with her buttocks." In other places the bridegrooms had to deliver to the landlord for ransom as much cheese or butter "as their buttocks were thick and heavy." In still other places they had to give a handsome cordovan tarbouret "that they could just fill."[19] According to the accounts given by the Bavarian Judge of the Supreme Court of Appeals, Welsch, the obligation to redeem the "jus primae noctis" existed in Bavaria as late as

[17] "Aber sprechend die Holfüt, weller hie zu der helgen see kumbt, der sol einen meyer (Gutsverwalter) laden und ouch sin frowen, da sol der meyer lien dem brütigan ein haffen, da er wol mag ein schaff in geseyden, ouch sol der meyer bringen ein fuder holtz an das hochtzit, ouch sol ein meyer und sin frow bringen ein viertenteyl eines schwynsbachen, und so die hochtzit vergat, so sol der brütigan den meyer by sim wib lassen ligen die ersten nacht, oder er sol sy lösen mit 5 schilling 4 pfenning."—I., p. 43.

[18] "History of the Abolition of Serfdom in Europe to the Middle of the 19th Century." St. Petersburg, 1861.

[19] Memminger, Staelin and others. "Beschreibung der Wuertembergischen Aemter." Hormayr. "Die Bayern im Morgenlande." Also Sugenheim.

the eighteenth century.[20] Furthermore, Engels reports that, among the
Welsh and the Scots, the "right of the first night" prevailed throughout
the whole of the Middle Ages, with the difference only that, due to the
continuance of the gentile organization, it was not the landlord, or his
representative, but the chief of the clan, as the last representative of
the one-time husbands in common, who exercised the right, in so far as
it was not redeemed.

There is, accordingly, no doubt whatever that the so-called "right of
the first night" existed, not only during the whole of the Middle Ages,
but continued even down to modern days, and played its *role* under the
code of feudalism.   In Poland, the noblemen arrogated the right to
deflower any maid they pleased, and a hundred lashes were given him
who complained. That the sacrifice of maidenly honor seems even to-
day a matter of course to landlords and their officials in the country,
transpires, not only in Germany, oftener than one imagines, but it is
a frequent occurrence all over the East and South of Europe, as is
asserted by experts in countries and the peoples.

In the days of feudalism, marriage was a matter of interest to the
landlord. The children that sprang therefrom entered into the same
relation of subjection to him as their parents; the labor-power at his
disposal increased in numbers, his income rose. Hence *spiritual* and
temporal landlords favored marriage among their vassals. The matter
lay otherwise, particularly for the Church, if, by the prevention of marriage, the prospect existed of bringing land into the possession of the
Church by testamentary bequests. This, however, occurred only with
the lower ranks of freemen, whose condition, due to the circumstances
already mentioned, became ever more precarious, and who, listening to
religious suggestions and superstition, relinquished their property to
the Church in order to find protection and peace behind the walls of a
cloister. Others, again, placed themselves under the protection of the
Church, in consideration of the payment of duties, and the rendering of
services. Frequently their descendants fell on this route a prey to the
very fate which their ancestors had sought to escape. They either
gradually became Church dependents, or were turned into novices for
the cloisters.

The towns, which, since the eleventh century were springing up, then
had at that time a lively interest in promoting the increase of population; settlement in them and marriage were made as easy as possible.
The towns became especially asylums for countrymen, fleeing from unbearable oppression, and for fugitive serfs and dependents. Later, how-

[20] "Ueber Stetigung und Abloesung der baeuerlichen Grundlasten mit beson-
derer Ruecksicht auf Bayern, Wuertemberg, Baden, Hessen, Preussen und
Oesterreich." Landshut, 1848.

ever, matters changed. So soon as the towns had acquired power, and contained a well-organized body of the trades, hostility arose against new immigrants, mostly propertyless peasants, who wanted to settle as handicraftsmen. Inconvenient competitors were scented in these. The barriers raised against immigration were multiplied. High settlement fees, expensive examinations, limitations of a trade to a certain number of masters and apprentices,—all this condemned thousands to pauperism, to a life of celibacy, and to vagabondage. When, in the course of the sixteenth century, and for reasons to be mentioned later, the flower-time of the towns was passing away, and their decline had set in, the narrow horizon of the time caused the impediments to settlement and independence to increase still more. Other circumstances also contributed their demoralizing effect.

The tyranny of the landlords increased so mightily from decade to decade that many of the vassals preferred to exchange their sorrowful life for the trade of the tramp or the highwayman,—an occupation that was greatly aided by the thick woods and the poor condition of the roads. Or, invited by the many violent disturbances of the time, they became soldiers, who sold themselves where the sold was highest, or the booty seemed most promising. An extensive male and female slum-proletariat came into existence, and became a plague to the land. The Church contributed faithfully to the general depravity. Already, in the celibatic state of the priesthood there was a main-spring for the fostering of sexual excesses; these were still further promoted through the continuous intercourse kept up with Italy and Rome.

Rome was not merely the capital of Christendom, as the residence of the Papacy. True to its antecedents during the heathen days of the Empire, Rome had become the new Babel, the European High School of immorality; and the Papal court was its principal seat. With its downfall, the Roman Empire had bequeathed all its vices to Christian Europe. These vices were particularly nursed in Italy, whence, materially aided by the intercourse of the priesthood with Rome, they crowded into Germany. The uncommonly large number of priests, to a great extent vigorous men, whose sexual wants were intensified by a lazy and luxurious life, and who, through compulsory celibacy, were left to illegitimate or unnatural means of gratification, carried immorality into all circles of society. This priesthood became a sort of pest-like danger to the morals of the female sex in the towns and villages. Monasteries and nunneries—and their number was legion—were not infrequently distinguishable from public houses only in that the life led in them was more unbridled and lascivious, and in that numerous crimes, especially infanticide, could be more easily concealed, seeing that in the cloisters only they exercised the administration of justice who led in the wrong-doing. Often did peasants seek to safe-guard wife and daughter from priestly seduction by accepting none as a spiritual shepherd who did not bind himself to keep a concubine;—a circumstance that led a Bishop of Constance to impose a "concubine tax" upon the priests of his diocese. Such a condition of things explains the historically attested fact, that during the Middle Ages—pictured to us by silly romanticists as so pious and moral—not less than 1500 strolling women turned up in 1414, at the Council of Constance.

But these conditions came in by no means with the decline of the Middle Ages. They began early, and gave continuous occasion for complaints and decrees. In 802 Charles the Great issued one of these, which ran this wise: "The cloisters of nuns shall be strictly watched; the nuns may not roam about; they shall be kept with great diligence; neither shall they live in strife and quarrel with one another; they shall in no wise be disobedient to their Superiors or Abbesses, or cross the will of these. Wherever they are placed under the rules of a cloister they are to observe them throughout. Not whoring, not drunkenness, not covetuousness shall they be the ministrants of, but in all ways lead just and sober lives. Neither shall any man enter their cloisters, except to attend mass, and he shall immediately depart." A regulation of the year 869 provided: "If priests keep several women, or shed the blood of Christians or heathens, or break the canonical law, they shall be deprived of their priesthood, because they are worse than laymen." The fact that the possession of several women was forbidden in those days only to the priests, indicates that marriage with several wives was no rare occurrence in the ninth century. In fact, there were no laws forbidding it.

Aye, and even later, at the time of the Minnesaenger, during the twelfth and thirteenth centuries, the possession of several wives was considered in order.[21]

The position of woman was aggravated still more by the circumstance that, along with all the impediments which gradually made marriage and settlement harder, their number materially exceeded that of the men. As special reasons herefor are to be considered the numerous wars and feuds, together with the perilousness of commercial voyages

---

[21] A poem of Albrecht von Johansdorf, in the collection of "Minnesang-Fruehling" (Collection of Lachman and Moritz Haupt; Leipsic, 1857; S. Hirtel), has this passage:
"waere ez niht unstaete
"der Zwein wiben wolte sin fur eigen jehen,
"bei diu tougenliche? sprechet, herre, wurre ez iht?
"(man sol ez den man erlouben und den vrouwen nicht.)"
The openness, with which two distinct rights, according to sex, are here considered a matter of course, corresponds with views that are found in force even to this day.

of those days.   Furthermore, mortality among men was higher, as the
result of habitual excesses and drunkenness.   The predisposition to
sickness and death that flowed from such habits of life, manifested itself
strongly in the numerous pest-like diseases that raged during the Middle
Ages.   In the interval between 1326 to 1400, there were thirty-two; from
1400 to 1500, forty-one; and from 1500 to 1600, thirty years of pesti-
lence.[22]

Swarms of women roamed along the highways as jugglers, singers and
players in the company of strolling students and clericals; they flooded
the fairs and markets; they were to be found wherever large crowds
gathered, or festivals were celebrated.   In the regiments of foot-soldiers
they constituted separate divisions, with their own sergeants.   There, and
quite in keeping with the guild character of the age, they were assigned
to different duties, according to looks and age; and, under severe penalties, were not allowed to prostitute themselves to any man outside of
their own branch.   In the camps, they had to fetch hay, straw and
wood; fill up trenches and ponds; and attend to the cleaning of the
place along with the baggage lads.   In sieges, they had to fill up the
ditches with brushwood, lumber and faggots in order to help the storming of the place.   They assisted in placing the field pieces in position;
and when these stuck in the bottomless roads, they had to give a hand
in pulling them out again.[23]

In order to counteract somewhat the misery of this crowd of helpless
women, so-called "Bettinen houses" were instituted in many cities, and
placed under municipal supervision.   Sheltered in these establishments,
the women were held to the observance of a decent life.   But neither
these establishments, nor the numerous nunneries, were able to receive
all that applied for succor.

The difficulties in the way of marriage; the tours undertaken by
Princes, and by temporal and spiritual magnates, who with their ret-
inues of knights and bondmen, visited the cities; even the male youth
of the cities themselves, the married men not excluded, who, buoyant
with life and unaffected by scruples, sought change in pleasures;—all
this produced as early as in the Middle Ages the demand for prostitution.   As every trade was in those days organized and regulated, and
could not exist without a guild, it so was with prostitution also.   In
all large cities there were "houses of women"—municipal, prince or
Church regalities—the net profits of which flowed into the corresponding
treasuries.   The women in these houses had a "head-mistress," elected
by themselves, who was to keep discipline and order, and whose special

[22] Dr. Karl Buecher, "Die Frauenfrage im Mittelalter," Tuebingen.
[23] Dr. Karl Buecher.

duty it was to diligently watch that non-guild competitors, the "inter-
lopers," did not injure the legitimate trade. When caught, these were
condignly punished. The inmates of one of these houses for women,
located in Nuerenberg, complained with the Magistrate, that "other
inn-keepers also kept women, who walked the streets at night, and took
in married and other men, and that these plied (the trade) to such an
extent, and so much more brazenly, than they did themselves in the
municipal (guild) girls-house, that it was a pity and a shame to see
such things happen in this worthy city."[24] These "houses for women"
enjoyed special protection; disturbances of the peace in their neighborhood were fined twice as heavily. The female guild members also
had the right to take their place in the processions and festivals, at
which, as is known, the guilds always assisted. Not infrequently were
they also drawn in as guests at the tables of Princes and Municipal
Councilmen. The "houses of women" were considered serviceable for
the "protection of marriage and of the honor of the maidens,"—the
identical reasoning with which State brothels were justified in Athens,
and even to-day prostitution is excused. All the same, there were not
wanting violent persecutions of the *filles de joie*, proceeding from the
identical male circles who supported them with their custom and their
money. The Emperor Charlemagne decreed that prostitutes shall be
dragged naked to the market place and there whipped; and yet, he
himself, "the Most Christian King and Emperor," had not less than six
wives at a time; and neither were his daughters, who followed their
father's example, by any means paragons of virtue. They prepared for
him in the course of their lives many an unpleasant hour, and brought
him home several illegitimate children. Alkuin, the friend and adviser
of Charlemagne, warned his pupils against "the crowned doves, who
flew at night over the palatinate," and he meant thereby the daughters
of the Emperor.

The identical communities, that officially organized the brothel system, that took it under their protection, and that granted all manner
of privileges to the "priestesses of Venus," had the hardest and most
cruel punishment in reserve for the poor and forsaken Magdalen. The
female infanticide, who, driven by desperation, killed the fruit of her
womb, was, as a rule, sentenced to suffer the most cruel death penalty;
nobody bothered about the unconscionable seducer himself. Perchance
he even sat on the Judge's bench, which decreed the sentence of death
upon the poor victim. The same happens to-day.[25] Likewise was adul-

---

[24] Joh. Scherr, "Geschichte der Deutschen Frauenwelt," Leipsic, 1879.

[25] Leon Richter reports in "La Femme Libre" the case of a servant girl in
Paris who was convicted of infanticide *by the father of the child himself*, a
respected and religious lawyer, who sat on the jury. Aye, worse: *the lawyer*

tery by the wife punished most severely; she was certain of the pillory, at least; but over the adultery of the husband the mantle of Christian charity was thrown.

In Wuerzburg, during the Middle Ages, the keeper of women swore before the Magistrate: "To be true and good to the city, and to procure women." Similarly in Nuerenberg, Ulm, Leipsic, Cologne, Frankfurt and elsewhere. In Ulm, where the "houses of women" were abolished in 1537, the guilds moved in 1551 that they be restored "in order to avoid worse disorders." Distinguished foreigners were provided with *filles de joie* at the expense of the city. When King Ladislaus entered Vienna in 1452, the Magistrate sent to meet him a deputation of public girls, who, clad only in light gauze, revealed the handsomest shapes. At his entry into Brugges, the Emperor Charles V was likewise greeted by a deputation of naked girls. Such occurrences met not with objection in those days.

Imaginative romancers, together with calculating people, have endeavored to represent the Middle Ages as particularly "moral," and animated with a veritable worship for woman. The period of the Minnesangers—from the twelfth to the fourteenth century—contributed in giving a color to the pretence. The knightly "Minnedienst" (service of love) which the French, Italian and German knights first became acquainted with among the Moriscos of Spain, is cited as evidence concerning the high degree of respect in which woman was held at that time. But there are several things to be kept in mind. In the first place, the knights constituted but a trifling percentage of the population, and, proportionately, the knights' women of the women in general; in the second place, only a very small portion of the knights exercised the so-called "Minnedienst;" thirdly, the true nature of this service is grossly misunderstood, or has been intentionally misrepresented. The age in which the "Minnedienst" flourished was at the same time the age of the grossest right-of-the-fist in Germany,—an age when all bonds of order were dissolved; and the knights indulged themselves without restraint in waylaying of travelers, robbery and incendiarism. Such days of brutal force are not the days in which mild and poetic sentiments are likely to prevail to any perceptible extent. The contrary is true. This period contributed to destroy whatever regard possibly existed for the female sex. The knights, both of country and town, consisted mainly of rough, dissolute fellows, whose principal passion, besides feuds and guzzling, was the unbridled gratification of sexual cravings. The chronicles of the time do not tire of telling about the deeds of rapine and

in question was himself the murderer, and the mother was entirely guiltless, as, after her conviction, she herself declared in court.

violence, that the nobility was guilty of, particularly in the country, but in the cities also, where, appearing in patrician *role*, the nobility held in its hands the city regiment, down to the thirteenth, and partly even in the fourteenth and fifteenth centuries. Nor did the wronged have any means of redress; in the city, the squires (yunker) controlled the judges' bench; in the country, the landlord, invested with criminal jurisdiction, was the knight, the Abbot or the Bishop. Accordingly, it is a violent exaggeration that, amid such morals and customs, the nobility and rulers had a particular respect for their wives and daughters, and carried them on their hands as a sort of higher beings, let alone that they cultivated such respect for the wives and daughters of the townsmen and peasants, for whom both the temporal and the spiritual masters entertained and proclaimed contempt only.

A very small minority of knights consisted of sincere worshippers of female beauty, but their worship was by no means Platonic; it pursued quite material ends. And these material ends were pursued by those also with whom Christian mysticism, coupled with natural sensuousness, made a unique combination. Even that harlequin among the worshippers of "lovely women," Ulrich von Lichtenstein, of laughable memory, remained Platonic only so long as he had to. At bottom the "Minnedienst" was the apotheosis of the best beloved—at the expense of the own wife; *a sort of hetairism, carried over into Middle Age Christianity*, as it existed in Greece at the time of Pericles. In point of fact, during the Middle Ages, the mutual seduction of one another's wives was a "Minnedienst" strongly in vogue among the knights, just the same as, in certain circles of our own bourgeoise, similar performances are now repeated. That much for the romanticism of the Middle Ages and their regard for women.

There can be no doubt that, in the open recognition of the pleasures of the senses, there lay in that age the acknowledgement that the natural impulses, implanted in every healthy and ripe human being, are entitled to be satisfied. In so far there lay in the demonstration a victory of vigorous nature over the asceticism of Christianity. On the other hand, it must be noted that the recognition and satisfaction fell to the share of only one sex, while the other sex, on the contrary, was treated as if it could not and should not have the same impulses; the slightest transgression of the laws of morality prescribed by man, was severely punished. The narrow and limited horizon, within which moved the citizen of the Middle Ages, caused him to adopt narrow and limited measures also with respect to the position of woman. And, as a consequence of continued oppression and peculiar education, woman herself has so completely adapted herself to her master's habits and system of thought, that she finds her condition natural and proper.

Do we not know that there have been millions of slaves who found slavery natural, and never would have freed themselves, had their liberators not risen from the midst of the class of the slave-holders? Did not Prussian peasants, when, as a result of the Stein laws, they were to be freed from serfdom, petition to be left as they were, "because who was to take care of them when they fell sick?" And is it not similarly with the modern Labor Movement? How many workingmen do not allow themselves to be influenced and led without a will of their own?

The oppressed needs the stimulator and firer, because he lacks the independence and faculty for initiative. It was so with the modern proletarian movement; it is so also in the struggle for the emancipation of woman, which is intimately connected with that of the proletariat. Even in the instance of the comparatively favorably situated bourgeois of old, noble and clerical advocates broke the way open for him to conduct his battle for freedom.

However numerous the shortcomings of the Middle Ages, there was then a healthy sensualism, that sprang from a rugged and happy native disposition among the people, and that Christianity was unable to suppress. The hypocritical prudery and bashfulness; the secret lustfulness, prevalent to-day, that hesitates and balks at calling things by their right name, and to speak about natural things in a natural way;—all that was foreign to the Middle Ages. Neither was that age familiar with the piquant double sense, in which, out of defective naturalness and out of a prudery that has become morality, things that may not be clearly uttered, are veiled, and are thereby rendered all the more harmful; such a language incites but does not satisfy; it suggests but does not speak out. Our social conversation, our novels and our theatres are full of these piquant equivoques,—and their effect is visible. This spiritualism, which is not the spiritualism of the transcendental philosopher, but that of the roue, and that hides itself behind the spiritualism of religion, has great power to-day.

The healthy sensualism of the Middle Ages found in Luther its classic interpreter. We have here to do, not so much with the religious reformer, as with Luther the man. On the human side, Luther's robust primeval nature stepped forward unadulterated; it compelled him to express his appetite for love and enjoyment forcibly and without reserve. His position, as former Roman Catholic clergyman, had opened his eyes. By personal practice, so to speak, had he learned the unnaturalness of the life led by the monks and nuns. Hence the warmth with which he warred against clerical and monastic celibacy. His words hold good to this day, for all those who believe they may sin against nature, and imagine they can reconcile with their conceptions of morality and propriety, governmental and social institutions that prevent millions from fulfilling their natural mission. Luther says: "Woman, except as high and rare grace, can dispense with man as little as she can with food, sleep, water and other natural wants. Conversely, also, neither can man dispense with woman. The reason is this: It is as deeply implanted in nature to beget children as to eat and drink. Therefore did God furnish the body with members, veins, discharges and all that is needed therefor. He who will resist this, and prevent its going as Nature wills, what else does he but endeavor to resist Nature's being Nature, that fire burn, water wet, that man eat, drink or sleep?" And in his sermon on married life he says: "As little as it is in my power that I be not a man, just so little is it in your power to be without a man. For it is not a matter of free will or deliberation, but a necessary, natural matter that all that is male must have a wife, and what is female must have a husband." Luther did not speak in this energetic manner in behalf of married life and the necessity of sexual intercourse only; he also turns against the idea that marriage and Church have anything in common. In this he stood squarely on the ground of the olden days, which considered marriage an act of free will on the part of those who engaged in it, and that did not concern the Church. On this head he said: "Know, therefore, that marriage is an outside affair, as any other earthly act. The same as I am free to eat, drink, sleep, walk, ride, deal, speak and trade with a heathen, a Jew, a Turk or a heretic, *likewise am I free to enter into and remain in wedlock with one of them. Turn your back upon the fool laws that forbid such a thing.* . . . A heathen is a man and woman, created by God in perfect form, as well as St. Peter and St. Paul and St. Luke; be then silent for a loose and false Christian that you are." Luther, like other Reformers, pronounced himself against all limitation of marriage, and he was for also allowing the re-union of divorced couples, against which the Church was up in arms. He said: "As to the manner in which marriage and divorce are to be conducted among us, I claim that it should be made the business of the jurists, and placed under the jurisdiction of earthly concerns, because marriage is but an earthly and outside matter." It was in keeping with this view that, not until the close of the seventeenth century, was marriage by the Church made obligatory under Protestantism. Until then so-called "conscience marriage" held good, i. e., the simple mutual obligation to consider each other man and wife, and to mean to live in wedlock. Such a marriage was considered by German law to be legally entered into. Luther even went so far that he conceded to the unsatisfied party—even if that be the woman—the right to seek satisfaction outside of the marriage bonds "in order to satisfy nature, which cannot be crossed."[20] This

[20] Dr. Karl Hagen, "Deutschlands Literarische und Religloese Verhaelt-

conception of marriage is the same that prevailed in antiquity, and that came up later during the French Revolution. Luther here set up maxims that will arouse the strongest indignation of a large portion of our "respectable men and women," who, in their religious zeal, are so fond of appealing to him. In his treatise "On Married Life,"[27] he says: "If an impotent man falls to the lot of a hearty woman, and she still cannot openly take another, and does not wish to marry again, she shall say unto her husband: 'Lo, dear husband, thou shalt not be wronged by me. Thou hast deceived me and my young body, and hast therefore brought my honor and salvation into danger. There is no glory to God between us two. Grant me to cohabit secretly with thy brother or nearest friend, and thou shalt have the name, *so that thy property come not to strange heirs; and allow thyself to be, in turn, willingly deceived by me, as thou did deceive me without thy will.*" The husband, Luther goes on to show, is in duty bound to grant the request. "If he declines, then has she the right to run away from him to another, and to woo elsewhere. Conversely, if a woman declines to exercise the conjugal duty, her husband has the right to cohabit with another, only he should tell her so beforehand."[28] It will be seen that these are wonderfully radical, and, in the eyes of our days, so rich in hypocritical prudery, even downright "immoral" views, that the great Reformer develops. Luther, however, expressed only that which, at the time, was the popular view.[29]

The passages quoted from the writings and addresses of Luther on marriage, are of special importance for the reason that these views are in strong contradiction with those that prevail to-day in the Church. In the struggle that it latterly has had to conduct with the clerical fraternity, the Social Democracy can appeal with full right to Luther,

nisse im Reformationszeitalter." Frankfort-on-the-Main, 1868.

[27] II., 146, Jena, 1522.

[28] Dr. Karl Hagen.

[29] Jacob Grimm informs us ("Deutsche Rechtsalterthuemer. Weisthum aus dem Amte Blankenburg") :

"Daer ein Man were, der sinen echten wive ver frowelik recht niet gedoin konde, der sall si sachtelik op sinen ruggen setten und draegen sie over negen erstnine und setten sie sachtelik neder sonder stoeten, slaen und werpen und sonder enig quaed woerd of oevel sehen, und rolpen dae sine naebur aen, dat sie inne sines wives lives noet helpen weren, und of sine naebur dat niet doen wolden of kunden, so sall he si senden up die neiste kermisse daerbi gelegen und dat sie sik süverlik toe make und verzere und hangen ör einen buidel wail mit golde bestikt up die side, dat sie selft wat gewerven kunde ; kumpt sie dannoch wider ungeholpen, so help ör dar der duifel."

As appears from Grimm, the German peasant of the Middle Ages looked in marriage, first of all, for *heirs*. If he was unable himself to beget these, he then, as a practical man, left the pleasure, without special scruples, to some one else. The main thing was to gain his object. We repeat it : Man does not rule property, property rules him.

who takes on the question of marriage a stand free from all prejudice.

Luther and all the Reformers went even further in the marriage question, true enough, only for opportunist reasons, and out of complaisance towards the Princes whose strong support and permanent friendship they sought to secure and keep to the Reformation. The friendly Duke of Hessen, Philip I, had, besides his legitimate wife, a sweetheart, willing to yield to his wishes, but only under the condition that he marry her. It was a thorny problem. A divorce from the wife, in the absence of convincing reasons, would give great scandal; on the other hand, a marriage with two women at a time was an unheard of thing with a Christian Prince of modern days; it would give rise to no less a scandal. All this notwithstanding, Philip, in his passion, decided in favor of the latter step. The point was now to establish that the act did no violence to the Bible, and to secure the approval of the Reformers, especially of Luther and Melanchthon. The negotiations, set on foot by the Duke, began first with Butzer, who declared himself in favor of the plan, and promised to win over Luther and Melanchthon. Butzer justified his opinion with the argument: To possess several wives at once was not against the evangelium. St. Paul, who said much upon the subject of who was not to inherit the kingdom of God, made no mention of those who had two wives. St. Paul, on the contrary, said "that a Bishop was to have but one wife, the same with his servants; hence, if it had been compulsory that every man have but one wife he would have so ordered, and forbidden a plurality of wives." Luther and Melanchthon joined this reasoning, and gave their assent to double marriages, after the Duke's wife herself had consented to the marriage with the second wife under the condition "that he was to fulfil his marital duties towards her more than ever before."[30] The question of the justification of bigamy had before then—at the time when the issue was the consenting to the double marriage of Henry VIII of England—caused many a headache to Luther, as appears from a letter to the Chancellor of Saxony, Brink, dated January, 1524. Luther wrote to him that, *in point of principle, he could not reject bigamy* because it ran not counter to Holy Writ;[31] but that he held it scandalous when the same happened among Christians, who should leave alone even things that are permissible." After the wedding of the Duke, which actually took place in March, 1540, and in answer to a letter of acknowledgement from him, Luther wrote (April 10): "That your Grace is happy on

---

[30] Johann Jansen, "Geschichte des Deutschen Volkes," 1525-1555, Freiburg.

[31] Which is perfectly correct, and also explainable, seeing that the Bible appeared at a time when polygamy extended far and wide among the peoples of the Orient and the Occident. In the sixteenth century, however, it was in strong contradiction with the standard of morality.

the score of our opinion, *which we fain would see kept secret; else, even
the rude peasants* (in imitation of the Duke's example) might finally
produce as strong, if not stronger, reasons, whereby we might then have
much trouble on our hands."

Upon Melanchthon, the consent to the double .marriage of the Duke
must have been less hard. Before that, he had written to Henry VIII
"every Prince has the right to introduce polygamy in his domains."
But the double marriage of the Duke made such a great and unpleasant
sensation, that, in 1541, he circulated a treatise in which polygamy is
defended as no transgression against Holy Writ.[32] People were not then
living in the ninth or twelfth century, when polygamy was tolerated
without shocking society. Social conditions had very materially changed
in the meantime; in a great measure the mark had had to yield to the
power of the nobility and the clergy; it had even extensively disappeared,
and was further uprooted after the unhappy issue of the Peasant Wars.
Private property had become the general foundation of society. Beside
the rural population, that cultivated the soil, a strong, self-conscious
handicraft element had arisen, and was dominated by the interests of
its own station. Commerce had assumed large dimensions, and had produced a merchant class, which, what with the splendor of its outward
position and its wealth, awoke the envy and hostility of a nobility that
was sinking ever deeper into poverty and licentiousness. The burghers'
system of private property had triumphed everywhere, as was evidenced
by the then universal introduction of the Roman law; the contrasts between the classes were palpable, and everywhere did they bump against
one another. Monogamy became, under such conditions, the natural
basis for the sexual relations; a step such as taken by the Duke of
Hessen now did violence to the ruling morals and customs, which, after
all, are but the form of expression of the economic conditions that happen at the time to prevail. On the other hand, society came to terms
with prostitution, as a necessary accompaniment of monogamy, and
an institution supplemental thereto;—and tolerated it.

In recognizing the gratification of the sexual impulses as a law of
Nature, Luther but uttered what the whole male population thought,
and openly claimed for itself. He, however, also contributed—through
the Reformation, which carried through the abolition of celibacy among
the clergy, and the removal of the cloisters from Protestant territories—
that to hundreds of thousands the opportunity was offered to do justice
to nature's impulses under legitimate forms. True again,—due to the
existing order of property, and to the legislation that flowed therefrom,—hundreds of thousands of others continued to remain excluded.
The Reformation was the first protest of the large-propertied bourgeoise

[32] Johann Janssen.

or capitalist class, then rising into being, against the restrictions imposed by feudalism in Church, State and society. It strove after freedom from the narrow bonds of the guild, the court and the judiciary; it strove after the centralization of the State, after the abolition of the numerous seats of idlers, the monasteries; and it demanded their use for practical production. The movement aimed at the abolition of the feudal form of property and production; it aimed at placing in its stead the free property of the capitalist, i. e., in the stead of the existing system of mutual protection in small and disconnected circles, there was to be unchained the free individual struggle of individual efforts in the competition for property.

On the religious field, Luther was the representative of these bourgeois aspirations. When he took a stand for the freedom of marriage, the question could not be simply about civic marriage, which was realized in Germany only in our own age through the civil laws and the legislation therewith connected,—freedom to move, freedom of pursuit, and freedom of domicile. In how far the position of woman was thereby improved will be shown later. Meanwhile things had not matured so far at the time of the Reformation. If, through the regulations of the Reformation many were afforded the possibility to marry, the severe persecutions that followed later hampered the freedom of sexual intercourse. The Roman Catholic clergy having in its time displayed a certain degree of tolerance, and even laxity, towards sexual excesses, now the Protestant clergy, once itself was provided for, raged all the more violently against the practice. War was declared upon the public "houses of women;" they were closed as "Holes of Satan;" the prostitutes were persecuted as "daughters of the devil;" and every woman who slipped was placed on the pillory as a specimen of all sinfulness.

Out of the once hearty small property-holding bourgeois of the Middle Ages, who lived and let live, now became a bigoted, straight-laced, dark-browed maw-worm, who "saved-up," to the end that his large property-holding bourgeois successor might live all the more lustily in the nineteenth century, and might be able to dissipate all the more. The respectable citizen, with his stiff necktie, his narrow horizon and his severe code of morals, was the prototype of society. The legitimate wife, who had not been particularly edified by the sensuality of the Middle Ages, tolerated in Roman Catholic days, was quite at one with the Puritanical spirit of Protestantism. But other circumstances supervened, that, affecting, as they did, unfavorably the general condition of things in Germany, joined in exercising in general an unfavorable influence upon the position of woman.

The revolution—effected in production, money and trade, particularly as regarded Germany,—due to the discovery of America and the sea-route to the East Indies, produced, first of all, a great reaction on the social domain. Germany ceased to be the center of European traffic and commerce. Spain, Portugal, Holland, England, took successively the leadership, the latter keeping it until our own days. German industry and German commerce began to decline. At the same time, the religious Reformation had destroyed the political unity of the nation. The Reformation became the cloak under which the German principalities sought to emancipate themselves from the Imperial power. In their turn, the Princes brought the power of the nobility under their own control, and, in order to reach this end all the more easily, favored the cities, not a few of which, in sight of the ever more troubled times, placed themselves, of their own free will, under the rule of the Princes. The final effect was that the bourgeois or capitalist class, alarmed at the financial decline of its trade, raised ever higher barriers to protect itself against unpleasant competition. The ossification of conditions gained ground; and with it the impoverishment of the masses.

Later, the Reformation had for a consequence the calling forth of the religious wars and persecutions—always, of course, as cloaks for the political and economic purposes of the Princes—that, with short interruptions, raged throughout Germany for over a century, and ended with the country's complete exhaustion, at the close of the Thirty Years' War in 1648. Germany had become an immense field of corpses and ruins; whole territories and provinces lay waste; hundreds of cities, thousands of villages had been partially or wholly burnt down; many of them have since disappeared forever from the face of the earth. In other places the population had sunk to a third, a fourth, a fifth, even to an eighth and tenth part. Such was the case, for instance, with cities like Neurenberg, and with the whole of Franconia. And now, at the hour of extreme need, and with the end in view of providing the depopulated cities and villages as quickly as possible with an increased number of people, the drastic measure was resorted to of "raising the law," and *allowing a man two wives.* The wars had carried off the men; of women there was an excess. On February 14, 1650, the Congress of Franconia, held in Nuerenberg, adopted the resolution that "men under sixty years of age shall not be admitted to the monasteries;" furthermore, it ordered "the priests and curates, if not ordained, and the canons of religious establishments, shall marry;" "moreover every male shall be allowed to marry two wives; and all and each males are earnestly reminded, and shall be often warned, *from the pulpit* also, to so comport themselves in this matter; and care shall be taken that he shall fully and with becoming discretion diligently endeavor, so that, as a married man, to whom is granted that he take two wives, he not only take proper care of both wives, but avoid all misunderstanding among them." At that time, we see, matters, that are to-day kept under strictest secrecy, were often discussed as of course from the pulpit itself.

But not commerce alone was at a standstill. Traffic and industry had been extensively ruined during this protracted period; they could recover only by little and little. A large part of the population had become wild and demoralized, disused to all orderly occupations. During the wars, it was the robbing, plundering, despoiling and murdering armies of mercenaries, which crossed Germany from one end to the other, that burned and knocked down friend and foe alike; after the wars, it was countless robbers, beggars and swarms of vagabonds that threw the population into fear and terror, and impeded and destroyed commerce and traffic. For the female sex, in particular, a period of deep suffering had broken. Contempt for woman had made great progress during the times of license. The general lack of work weighed heaviest on their shoulders; by the thousands did these women, like the male vagabonds, infest the roads and woods, and filled the poorhouses and prisons of the Princes and the cities. On top of all these sufferings came the forcible ejectment of numerous peasant families by a land-hungry nobility.

Compelled, since the Reformation, ever more to bend before the might of the Princes, and rendered ever more dependent upon these through court offices and military posts, the nobility now sought to recoup itself double and threefold with the robbery of peasant estates for the injury it had sustained at the hand of the Princes. The Reformation offered the Princes the desired pretext to appropriate the rich Church estates, which they swallowed in innumerable acres of land. The Elector August of Saxony, for instance, had turned not less than three hundred clergy estates from their original purpose, up to the close of the sixteenth century.[33] Similarly did his brothers and cousins, the other Protestant Princes, and, above all, the Princes of Brandenburg. The nobility only imitated the example by bagging peasant estates, that had lost their owners, by ejecting free as well as serf peasants from house and home, and enriching themselves with the goods of these. To this particular end, the miscarried peasant revolts of the sixteenth century furnished the best pretext. After the first attempts had succeeded, never after were reasons wanting to proceed further in equally violent style. With the aid of all manner of chicaneries, vexations and twistings of the law—whereto the in-the-meantime naturalized Roman law lent a convenient handle—the peasants were bought out at the lowest prices, or they were driven from their property in order to round up the estates of noblemen. Whole villages, the peasant homes of as much as half a province, were in this way wiped out. Thus—so as to give a few illustrations—out of 12,543 peasant

[33] Johann Jansen. Vol. III.

homestead appanages of knightly houses, which Mecklenburg still possessed at the time of the Thirty Years' War, there were, in 1848, only 1,213 left. In Pommerania, since 1628, not less than 12,000 peasant homesteads disappeared. The change in peasant economy, that took place in the course of the seventeenth century, was a further incentive for the expropriation of the peasant homesteads, especially to turn the last rests of the commons into the property of the nobility. The system of rotation of crops was introduced. It provided for a rotation in cultivation within given spaces of time. Corn lands were periodically turned into meadows. This favored the raising of cattle, and made possible the reduction of the number of farm-hands. The crowd of beggars and tramps grew ever larger, and thus one decree followed close upon the heels of another to reduce, by the application of the severest punishments, the number of beggars and vagabonds.

In the cities matters lay no better than in the country districts. Before then, women were active in very many trades in the capacity of working women as well as of employers. There were, for instance, female furriers in Frankfurt and in the cities of Sleswig; bakers, in the cities of the middle Rhine; embroiderers of coats of arms and beltmakers, in Cologne and Strassburg; strap-cutters, in Bremen; clothing-cutters in Frankfurt; tanners in Nuerenberg; gold spinners and beaters in Cologne.[84] Women were now crowded back. The abandonment of the pompous Roman Catholic worship alone, due to the Protestantizing of a large portion of Germany, either injured severely a number of trades, especially the artistic ones, or destroyed them altogether; and it was in just these trades that many working women were occupied. As, moreover, it ever happens when a social state of things is moving to its downfall, the wrongest methods are resorted to, and the evil is thereby aggravated. The sad economic condition of most of the German nations caused the decimated population to appear as *overpopulation*, and contributed greatly towards rendering a livelihood harder to earn, and towards prohibitions of marriage.

Not until the eighteenth century did a slow improvement of matters set in. The absolute Princes had the liveliest interest, with the view of raising the standard abroad of their rule, to increase the population of their territories. They needed this, partly in order to obtain soldiers for their wars, partly also to gain taxpayers, who were to raise the sums needed either for the army, or for the extravagant indulgences of the court, or for both. Following the example of Louis XIV of France, the majority of the then extraordinarily numerous princely courts of Germany displayed great lavishness in all manner of show and tinsel. This

---

[84] Dr. Karl Buecher, "Die Frauenfrage im Mittelalter."

was especially the case in the matter of the keeping of mistresses, which stood in inverse ratio to the size and capabilities of the realms and realmlets. The history of these courts during the eighteenth century belongs to the ugliest chapters of history. Libraries are filled with the chronicles of the scandals of that era. One potentate sought to surpass the other in hollow pretentiousness, insane lavishness and expensive military fooleries. Above all, the most incredible was achieved in the way of female excesses. It is hard to determine which of the many German courts the palm should be assigned to for extravagance and for a life that vitiated public morals. To-day it was this, to-morrow that court; no German State escaped the plague. The nobility aped the Princes, and the citizens in the residence cities aped the nobility. If the daughter of a citizen's family had the luck to please a gentleman high at court, perchance the Serenissimus himself, in nineteen cases out of twenty she felt highly blessed by such favor, and her family was ready to hand her over for a mistress to the nobleman or the Prince. The same was the case with most of the noble families if one of their daughters found favor with the Prince. Characterlessness and shamelessness ruled over wide circles.

As bad as the worst stood matters in the two German capitals, Vienna and Berlin. In the Capua of Germany, Vienna, true enough, the strict Maria Theresa reigned through a large portion of the century, but she was impotent against the doings of a rich nobility, steeped in sensuous pleasures, and of the citizen circles that emulated the nobility. With the Chastity Commissions that she established, and in the aid of which an extensive spy-system was organized, she partly provoked bitterness, and partly made herself laughaḅle. The success was zero. In frivolous Vienna, sayings like these made the rounds during the second half of the eighteenth century: "You must love your neighbor like yourself, that is to say, you must love your neighbor's wife as much as your own;" or "If the wife goes to the right, the husband may go to the left: if she takes an attendant, he takes a lady friend." In how frivolous a vein marriage and adultery were then taken, transpires from a letter of the poet Ew. Chr. von Kleist, addressed in 1751 to his friend Gleim. Among other things he there says: "You are already informed on the adventure of the Mark-Graf Heinrich. He sent his wife to his country seat and intends to divorce her because he found the Prince of Holstein in bed with her. . . . The Mark-Graf might have done better had he kept quiet about the affair, instead of now causing half Berlin and all the world to talk about him. Moreover, *such a natural thing should not be taken so ill*, all the more when, like the Mark-Graf, one is not so waterproof himself. Mutual repulsion, we all know, is unavoidable in married life: all husbands and wives are perforce unfaithful, due *to their illusions concerning other estimable persons. How can that be punished that one is forced to?"* On Berlin conditions, the English Ambassador, Lord Malmsbury, wrote in 1772: "Total corruption of morals pervades both sexes of all classes, whereto must be added the indigence, caused, partly through the taxes imposed by the present King, partly through the love of luxury that they took from his grandfather. The men lead a life of excesses with limited means, while the women are harpies, wholly bereft of shame. They yield themselves to him who pays best. Tenderness and true love are things unknown to them." [35]

Things were at their worst in Berlin under Frederick II, who reigned from 1786 to 1796. He led with the worst example; and his court chaplain, Zoellner, even lowered himself to the point of marrying the King to the latter's mistress, Julie von Boss, as a second wife, and as she soon thereupon died in childbed, Zoellner again consented to marry the King to the Duchess Sophie of Doenhoff as a second wife by the side of the Queen.

More soldiers and more taxpayers was the leading desire of the Princes. Louis XIV, after whose death France was entirely impoverished in money and men, set up pensions for parents who had ten children, and the pension was raised when they reached twelve children. His General, the Marshal of Saxony, even made to him the proposition to *allow marriages only for the term of five years.* Fifty years later, in 1741, Frederick the Great wrote, "I look upon men as a herd of deer in the zoological garden of a great lord, their only duty is to populate and fill the park." [36]

Later, he extensively depopulated his "deer park" with his wars, and then took pains to "populate" it again with foreign immigration.

The German multiplicity of States, that was in fullest bloom in the eighteenth century, presented a piebald map of the most different social conditions and legislative codes. While in the minority of the States efforts were made to improve the economic situation by promoting new industries, by making settlement easier and by changing the marriage laws in the direction of facilitating wedlock, the majority of the States and statelets remained true to their backward views, and intensified the unfavorable conditions of marriage and settlement for both men and women. Seeing, however, that human nature will not allow itself to be suppressed, all impediments and vexations notwithstanding, concubinage sprang up in large quantity, and the number of illegitimate children was at no time as large as in these days when the "paternal regiment" of the absolute Princes reigned in "Christian simplicity."

The married woman of citizen rank lived in strict seclusion. The number of her tasks and occupations was so large that, as a conscientious

---

[35] Johann Scherr: "Geschichte der Deutschen Frauenwelt."
[36] Karl Kautsky, "Ueber den Einfluss der Volksvermehrung auf den Fortschritt der Gesellschaft." Vienna, 1880.

housewife, she had to be at her post early and late in order to fulfil her duties, and even that was possible to her only with the aid of her daughters. Not only were there to be filled those daily household duties which to-day, too, the small middle class housewife has to attend to, but a number of others also, which the housewife of to-day is freed from through modern development. She had to spin, weave, bleach and sew the linen and clothes, prepare soap and candles, brew beer,—in short, she was the veriest Cinderella: her only recreation was Sunday's church. Marriage was contracted only within the same social circles; the strongest and most ludicrous spirit of caste dominated all relations, and tolerated no transgression. The daughters were brought up in the same spirit; they were held under strict home seclusion; their mental education did not go beyond the bounds of the narrowest home relations. On top of this, an empty and hollow formality, meant as a substitute for education and culture, turned existence, that of woman in particular, into a veritable treadmill. Thus the spirit of the Reformation degenerated into the worst pedantry, that sought to smother the natural desires of man, together with his pleasures in life under a confused mass of rules and usages that affected to be "worthy," but that benumbed the soul.

Gradually, however, an economic change took place, that first seized Western Europe and then reached into Germany also. The discovery of America, the doubling of the Cape of Good Hope, the opening of the sea route of the East Indies, the further discoveries that hinged on these, and finally, the circumnavigation of the earth, revolutionized the life and views of the most advanced nations of Europe. The unthought-of rapid expansion of the world's commerce, called to life through the opening of ever newer markets for European industry and products, revolutionized the old system of handicraft. Manufacture arose, and thence flowed large production. Germany—so long held back in her material development by her religious wars and her political disintegration, which religious differences promoted,—was finally dragged into the stream of the general progress. In several quarters, large production developed under the form of manufacture: flax and wool-spinning and weaving, the manufacture of cloth, mining, the manufacture of iron, glass and porcelain, transportation, etc. Fresh labor power, female included, came into demand. But this newly rising form of industry met with the most violent opposition on the part of the craftsmen, ossified in the guild and medieval corporation system, who furiously fought every change in the method of production, and saw therein a mortal enemy. The French Revolution supervened. While casting aside the older order in France, the Revolution also carried into Germany a fresh current of air, which the old order could not for long resist. The French invasion hastened the downfall,—this side of the Rhine also—of the old, worn-out system.

Whatever attempt was made, during the period of re-action after 1815, to turn back the wheels of time, the New had grown too strong, it finally remained victorious.

The rise of machinery, the application of the natural sciences to the process of production, the new roads of commerce and traffic burst asunder the last vestiges of the old system. The guild privileges, the personal restrictions, the mark and jurisdictional rights, together with all that thereby hung, walked into the lumber room. The strongly increased need of labor-power did not rest content with the men, it demanded woman also as a cheaper article. The conditions that had become untenable, had to fall; and they fell. The time thereto,—long wished-for by the newly risen class, the bourgeoisie or capitalist class—arrived the moment Germany gained her political unity. The capitalist class demanded imperiously the unhampered development of all the social forces; it demanded this for the benefit of its own capitalist interests, that, at that time, and, to a certain degree, were also the interests of the large majority. Thus came about the liberty of trade, the liberty of emigration, the removal of the barriers to marriage.—in short, that whole system of legislation that designates itself "liberal." The old-time reactionists expected from these measures the smash-up of morality. The late Adolph Ketteler of Mainz moaned, already in 1865, accordingly, before the new social legislation had become general, "that the tearing down of the existing barriers to matrimony meant the dissolution of wedlock, it being now possible for the married to run away from each other at will." A pretty admission that the moral bonds of modern marriage are so weak, that only *compulsion* can be relied on to hold the couple together.

The circumstance, on the one hand, that the now naturally more numerous marriages effected a rapid increase of population, and, on the other, that the gigantically developing industry of the new era brought on many ills, never known of before, caused the spectre of "overpopulation" to rise anew. Conservative and liberal economists pull since then the same string. We shall show what this fear of so-called overpopulation means; we shall trace the feared phenomenon back to its legitimate source. Among those who suffer of the overpopulation fear, and who demand the restriction of freedom to marry, especially for workingmen, belong particularly Prof. Ad. Wagner. According to him, workingmen marry too early, in comparison with the middle class. He, along with others of this opinion, forget that the male members of the higher class, marry later only in order to wed "according to their station in life," a thing they can not do before they have obtained a certain position. For this abstinence, the males of the higher classes indemnify themselves with prostitution. Accordingly, it is to prostitution that the working class are referred, the moment marriage is made difficult for, or, under certain

circumstances, is wholly forbidden to, them. But, then, let none wonder
at the results, and let him not raise an outcry at the "decline of morality," if the women also, who have the same desires as the men, seek to
satisfy in illegitimate relations the promptings of the strongest impulse
of nature. Moreover, the views of Wagner are at fisticuffs with the
interests of the capitalist class, which, oddly enough, shares his views:
it needs many "hands," so as to own cheap labor-power that may
fit it out for competition in the world's market. With such petty notions
and measures, born of a near-sighted philistinism, the gigantic growing
ills of the day are not to be healed.

PART II

WOMAN IN THE PRESENT

CHAPTER I.

SEXUAL INSTINCTS, WEDLOCK, CHECKS AND OBSTRUCTIONS TO MARRIAGE.

Plato thanked the gods for eight favors bestowed upon him. As the first, he took it that they had granted him to be born a freeman, and not a slave; the second was that he was created a man, and not a woman. A similar thought finds utterance in the morning prayer of the Jews. They pray: "Blessed be Thou, our God and Lord of Hosts, *who hast not created me a woman;*" the Jewish women, on the other hand, pray at the corresponding place: *"who hast created me after thy will."* The contrast in the position of the sexes can find no more forcible expression than it does in the saying of Plato, and in the different wording of the prayer among the Jews. The male is the real being, the master of the female. With the views of Plato and the Jews, the larger part of men agree, and many a woman also wishes that she had been born a man and not a woman. In this view lies reflected the condition of the female sex.

Wholly irrespective of the question whether woman is oppressed as a female proletarian, as sex she is oppressed in the modern world of private property. A number of checks and obstructions, unknown to man, exist for her, and hem her in at every step. Much that is allowed to man is forbidden to her; a number of social rights and privileges, enjoyed by the former, are, if exercised by her, a blot or a crime. She suffers both as a social and a sex entity, and it is hard to say in which of the two respects she suffers more.

Of all the natural impulses human beings are instinct with, along with that of eating and drinking, the sexual impulse is the strongest. The impulse to procreate the species is the most powerful expression of the "Will to Live." It is implanted most strongly in every normally developed human being. Upon maturity, its satisfaction is an actual necessity for man's physical and mental health. Luther was perfectly right when he said: "He who would resist the promptings of Nature, and prevent their going as Nature wills and must, *what else does he but endeavor to resist Nature's being Nature, that fire burn, water wet, that man eat, drink or sleep?*" These are words that should be graven in granite over the doors of our churches, in which the "sinful flesh" is so diligently preached against. More strikingly no physician or physiologist can describe the necessity for the satisfaction of the craving for love on the part of a healthy being,—a craving that finds its expression in sexual intercourse.

It is a commandment of the human being to itself—a commandment that it must obey if it wishes to develop normally and in health—that it neglect the exercise of no member of its body, deny gratification to no natural impulse. Each member must fill the function, that it is intended for by Nature, on penalty of atrophy and disease. The laws of the physical development of man must be studied and observed, the same as those of mental development. The mental activity of the human being is the expression of the physiologic composition of its organs. The complete health of the former is intimately connected with the health of the latter. A disturbance of the one inevitably has a disturbing effect upon the other. Nor do the so-called animal desires take lower rank than the so-called mental ones. One set and the other are effects of the identical combined organism: the influence of the two upon each other is mutual and continuous. This holds good for man as for woman.

It follows that, the knowledge of the properties of the sexual organs is just as needful as that of the organs which generate mental activity; and that man should bestow upon the cultivation of both an equal share of care. He should realize that organs and impulses, found implanted in every human being, and that constitute a very essential part of his nature, aye, that, at certain periods of his life control him absolutely, must not be objects of secrecy, of false shame and utter ignorance. It follows, furthermore, that a knowledge of the physiology and anatomy of the sexual organs, together with their functions, should be as general among men and women as any other branch of knowledge. Equipped with an accurate knowledge of our physical make-up, we would look upon many a condition in life with eyes different from those we now do. The question of removing existing evils would then, of itself, force itself upon those before whom society, to-day, passes by in silence and solemn bashfulness, notwithstanding these evils command attention within the precincts of every family. In all other matters, knowledge is held a virtue, the worthiest and most beautiful aim of human endeavor—only not knowledge in such matters that are in closest relation with the essence and health of our own *Ego*, as well as the basis of all social development.

Kant says: "Man and woman only jointly constitute the complete being: one sex supplements the other." Schopenhauer declares: "The sexual impulse is the fullest utterance of the will to live, hence it is the concentration of all will-power;" again: "The affirmative declaration of the will in favor of life is concentrated in the act of generation, and that is its most decisive expression." In accord therewith says Mainlaender: "The center of gravity of human life lies in the sexual instinct: it alone secures life to the individual, which is that which above all else it wants. . . . To nothing else does man devote greater earnestness than to the work of procreation, and for the care of none other does he compress and concentrate the intensity of his will so demonstratively as for the act of procreation." Finally, and before all of these, Buddha said: "The sexual instinct is sharper than the hook wild elephants are tamed with; it is hotter than flames; it is like an arrow, shot into the spirit of man."[1]

Such being the intensity of the sexual impulse, it is no wonder that sexual abstinence at the age of maturity affects the nervous system and the whole organism of man, with one sex as well as the other, in such a manner that it often leads to serious disturbances and manias; under certain conditions even to insanity and death. True enough, the sexual instinct does not assert itself with equal violence in all natures, and much can be done towards curbing it by education and self-control, especially by avoiding the excitation resulting upon certain conversations and reading. It is thought that, in general, the impulse manifests itself lighter with women than with men, and that the irritation is less potent with the former. It is even claimed that, with woman, there is a certain repugnance for the sexual act. The minority is small of those with whom physiologic and psychologic dispositions and conditions engender such a difference. "The union of the sexes is one of the great laws of living Nature; man and woman are subject to it the same as all other creatures, and can not transgress it, especially at a ripe age, without their organism suffering more or less in consequence."[2] Debay quotes among the diseases, caused by the inactivity of the sexual organs, satyriasis, nymphomania and hysteria; and he adds that celibacy exercises upon the intellectual powers, especially with woman, a highly injurious effect. On the subject of the harmfulness of sexual abstinence by woman, Busch says:[3] "Abstinence has in all ages been considered particularly harmful to woman; indeed it is a fact that excess, as well as abstinence, affects the female organism equally harmfully, and the effects show themselves more pronouncedly and intensively than with the male organism."

It may, accordingly, be said that man—be the being male or female— is complete in the measure in which, both as to organic and spiritual culture, the impulses and manifestations of life utter themselves in the sexes, and in the measure that they assume character and expression. Each sex of itself reached its highest development. "With civilized man," says Klenke in his work "Woman as Wife," "the compulsion of

[1] Mainlaender, "Philosophie der Erlösung," Frankfort-on-the-Main, 1886, E. Koenitzer.
[2] D. A. Debay, "Hygiene et Physiologue du Marriage," Paris, 1884. Quoted in "Im Freien Reich" by Ioma v. Troll-Borostyani, Zurich, 1884.
[3] "Das Geschlechtsleben des Weibes, in physiologischer, pathologischer und therapeutischer Hinsicht dargestellt."

procreation is placed under the direction of the moral principle, and that is guided by reason. This is true. Nevertheless, it were an impossible task, even with the highest degree of freedom, wholly to silence the imperative command for the preservation of the species,—a command that Nature planted in the normal, organic expression of the both sexes. Where healthy individuals, male or female, have failed in their life-time to honor this duty towards Nature, *it is not with them an instance of the free exercise of the will*, even when so given out, or when, in self-deception, it is believed to be such. *It is the result of social obstacles, together with the consequences which follow in their wake; they restricted the right of Nature;* they allowed the organs to wilt; allowed the stamp of decay and of sexual vexation—both in point of appearance and of character—to be placed upon the whole organism; and, finally, brought on—through nervous distempers—diseased inclinations and conditions both of body and of mind. The man becomes feminine, the woman masculine in shape and character. The sexual contrast not having reached realization in the plan of Nature, each human being *remained one-sided, never reached its supplement, never touched the acme of its existence.*" In her work, "The Moral Education of the Young in Relation to Sex," Dr. Elizabeth Blackwell says: "The sexual impulse exists as an indispensable condition of life, and as the basis of society. It is the greatest force in human nature. Often undeveloped, not even an object of thought, but none the less the *central fire of life,* this inevitable instinct is the natural protector against any possibility of extinction."

Science agrees, accordingly, with the opinion of the philosophers, and with Luther's healthy common sense. It follows that every human being has, not merely the right, but also the duty to satisfy the instincts, that are intimately connected with its inmost being, that, in fact, imply existence itself. Hindered therein, rendered impossible to him through social institutions or prejudices, the consequence is that man is checked in the development of his being, is left to a stunted life and retrogression. What the consequences thereof are, our physicians, hospitals, insane asylums and prisons can tell,—to say nothing of the thousands of tortured family lives. In a book that appeared in Leipsic, the author is of the opinion: "The sexual impulse is neither moral nor immoral; it is merely natural, like hunger and thirst: Nature knows nothing of morals;"[4] nevertheless bourgeois society is far from a general acceptance of this maxim.

The opinion finds wide acceptance among physicians and physiologists that even a defectively equipped marriage is better than celibacy. Experience agrees therewith. In Bavaria there were, in 1858, not less

[4] "Die Prostitution vor dem Gesetz," by Veritas. Leipsic, 1893.

than 4,899 lunatics, 2,576 (53 per cent.) of them men, 2,323 (47 per cent.) women. The men were, accordingly, more strongly represented than the women. Of the whole number, however, the *unmarried* of both sexes ran up to 81 per cent., the married only to 17 per cent., while of 2 per cent. the conjugal status was unknown. As a mitigation of the shocking disproportion between the unmarried and the married, the circumstance may be taken into consideration that a not small number of the unmarried were insane from early childhood. In Hanover, in the year 1856, there was one lunatic to every 457 unmarried, 564 widowed, 1,316 married people. Most strikingly is the effect of unsatisfied sexual relations shown in the number of suicides among men and women. In general, the number of suicides is in all countries considerably higher among men than among women. To every 1,000 female suicides there were in:[5]

England	from	1872-76	2,861	men
Sweden	"	1870-74	3,310	"
France	"	1871-76	3,695	"
Italy	"	1872-77	4,000	"
Prussia	"	1871-78	4,239	"
Austria	"	1873-78	4,586	"

But between the ages of 21 and 30, the figures for *female suicides is in all European countries higher than for males*, due, as Oettingen assumes, to sexual causes. In Prussia the percentages of suicides between the ages of 21 to 30 were on an average:

Years.	Males.	Females.
1869-72	15.8	21.4
1873-78	15.7	21.5

In Saxony there were to every 1,000 suicides between the ages of 21 to 30 these averages:

Years.	Males.	Females.
1854	14.95	18.64
1868	14.71	18.79

For widowed and divorced people also the percentage of suicides is larger than the average. In Saxony there are seven times as many suicides among divorced males, and three times as many among divorced females, as the average of suicides for males and females respectively. Again, suicide is more frequent among divorced and widowed men and women when they are childless. Of 491 widowed suicides in Prussia (119 males and 372 females) 353 were childless.

Taking into further consideration that, among the unmarried women,

[5] V. Oettingen, "Moralstatistik." Erlangen, 1882.

who are driven to suicide between the ages of 21 and 30, many a one is to be found, who takes her life by reason of being betrayed, or because she can not bear the consequences of a "slip," the fact remains that sexual reasons play a decided *role* in suicide at this age. Among female suicides, the figure is large also for those between the ages of 16 to 20, and the fact is probably likewise traceable to unsatisfied sexual instinct, disappointment in love, secret pregnancy, or betrayal. On the subject of the women of our days as sexual beings, Professor V. Krafft-Ebing expresses himself: "A not-to-be-underrated source of insanity with woman lies in her social position. Woman, by nature more prone than man to sexual needs, at least in the ideal sense of the term, knows no honorable means of gratifying the need other than marriage. At the same time marriage offers her the only support. Through unnumbered generations her character has been built in this direction. Already the little girl plays mother with her doll. Modern life, with its demands upon culture, offers ever slighter prospects of gratification through marriage. This holds especially with the upper classes, among whom marriage is contracted later and more rarely. While man—as the stronger, and thanks to his greater intellectual and physical powers, together with his social position—supplies himself easily with sexual gratification, or, taken up with some occupation, that engages all his energies, easily finds an equivalent, these paths are closed to single women. This leads, in the first place, consciously or unconsciously, to dissatisfaction with herself and the world, to morbid brooding. For a while, perhaps, relief is sought in religion; but in vain. Out of religious enthusiasm, there spring with or without masturbation, a host of nervous diseases, among which hysteria and insanity are not rare. Only thus is the fact explainable that insanity among single women occurs with greatest frequency between the ages of 25 and 35, that is to say, the time when the bloom of youth, and, along therewith, hope vanishes; while with men, insanity occurs generally between the ages of 35 and 50, the season of the strongest efforts in the struggle for existence.

"It certainly is no accident that, hand in hand with increasing celibacy, the question of the emancipation of woman has come ever more on the order of the day. I would have the question looked upon as a danger signal, set up by the social position of woman in modern society —a position that grows ever more unbearable, due to increasing celibacy; I would have it looked upon as the danger signal of a justified demand, made upon modern society, to furnish woman some equivalent for that to which she is assigned by Nature, and which modern social conditions partly deny her."[6]

[6] "Lehrbuch der Psychiatrie," Vol. I, Stuttgart, 1883.

And Dr. H. Plotz, in his work, "Woman in Nature and Ethnography,"[7] says in the course of his explanation of the results of ungratified sexual instincts upon unmarried women: "It is in the highest degree note-worthy, not for the physician only, but also for the anthropologist, that there is an effective and never-failing means to check this process of decay (with old maids), but even to cause the lost bloom to return, if not in all its former splendor yet in a not insignificant degree,— *pity only that our social conditions allow, or make its application possible only in rare instances.* The means consist in regular and systematic sexual intercourse. The sight is not infrequent with girls, who lost their bloom, or were not far from the withering point, yet, the opportunity to marry having been offered them, that, shortly after marriage, their shape began to round up again, the roses to return to their cheeks, and their eyes to recover their one-time brightness. *Marriage is, accordingly, the true fountain of youth for the female sex.* Thus Nature has her firm laws, that implacably demand their dues. No 'vita praeter naturam,' no unnatural life, no attempt at accommodation to incompatible conditions of life, passes without leaving noticeable traces of degeneration, upon the animal, as well as upon the human organism."

As to the effect that marriage and celibacy exercise upon the mind, the following figures furnish testimony. In 1882, there were in Prussia, per 10,000 inhabitants of the same conjugal status, 33.2 unmarried male and 29.3 female lunatics, while the percentage of the married ones was 9.5 for men, and 9.5 for females, and of the widowed, 32.1 males, and 25.6 females. Social conditions can not be considered healthy, that hinder a normal satisfaction of the natural instincts, and lead to evils like those just mentioned.

The question then rises: Has modern society met the demands for a natural life, especially as concerns the female sex? If the question is answered in the negative, this other rises: Can modern society meet the demands? If both questions must be answered in the negative, then this third arises: How can these demands be met?

"Marriage and the family are the foundation of the State; consequently, he who attacks marriage and the family attacks society and the State, and undermines both"—thus cry the defenders of the present order. Unquestionably, monogamous marriage, which flows from the bourgeois system of production and property, is one of the most important cornerstones of bourgeois or capitalist society; whether, however, such marriage is in accord with natural wants and with a healthy development of human society, is another question. We shall prove that the marriage, founded upon bourgeois property relations, is more or less a marriage by compulsion, which leads numerous ills in its train,

[7] Vol. II. Leipsic, 1887.

and which fails in its purpose quite extensively, if not altogether. We shall show, furthermore, that it is a social institution, beyond the reach of millions, and is by no means that marriage based upon love, which alone corresponds with the natural purpose, as its praise-singers maintain.

With regard to modern marriage, John Stuart Mill exclaims: *"Marriage is the only form of slavery that the law recognizes."* In the opinion of Kant, man and woman constitute only jointly the full being. Upon the normal union of the sexes rests the healthy development of the human race. The natural gratification of the sexual instinct is a necessity for the thorough physical and mental development of both man and woman. But man is no animal. Mere physical satisfaction does not suffice for the full gratification of his energetic and vehement instinct. He requires also spiritual affinity and oneness with the being that he couples with. Is that not the case, then the blending of the sexes is a purely mechanical act: such a marriage is immoral. It does not answer the higher human demands. Only in the mutual attachment of two beings of opposite sexes can be conceived the spiritual ennobling of relations that rest upon purely physical laws. Civilized man demands that the mutual attraction continue beyond the accomplishment of the sexual act, and *that it prolong its purifying influence upon the home that flows from the mutual union.*[8] The fact that these demands can not be made upon numberless marriages in modern society is what led Barnhagen von Ense to say: "That which we saw with our own eyes, both with regard to contracted marriages and marriages yet to be contracted, was not calculated to give us a good opinion of such unions. On the contrary, the whole institution, which was to have only love and respect for its foundation, and which in all these instances (in Berlin) we saw founded on everything but that, seemed to us mean and contemptible, and we loudly joined in the saying of Frederick Schlegel which we read in the fragments of the 'Atheneum': Almost all marriages are concubinages, left-handed unions, or rather provisional attempts and distant resemblances at and of a true marriage, whose real feature consists, according to all spiritual and temporal laws, in that two persons become one."[9] Which is completely in the sense of Kant.

The duty towards and pleasure in posterity make permanent the love relations of two persons, when such really exists. A couple that wishes to enter into matrimonial relations must, therefore, be first clear

[8] "The moods and feelings in and which husband and wife approach each other, exercise, without a doubt, a definite influence upon the result of the sexual act, and transmit certain characteristics to the fruit." Dr. Elizabeth Blackwell, "The Moral Education of the Young in Relation to Sex." See also Goethe's "Elective Affinities," where he sketches clearly the influence exerted by the feelings of two beings who approach each other for intimate intercourse.
[9] "Denkwuerdigkeiten," Vol. I, p. 239, Leipsic, F. A. Brockhaus.

whether the physical and moral qualities of the two are fit for such a union. The answer should be arrived at uninfluenced; and that can happen only, first, *by keeping away all other interests*, that have nothing to do with the real object of the union,—the gratification of the natural instinct, and the transmission of one's being in the propagation of the race; secondly, by a certain degree of insight that curbs blind passion. Seeing, however, as we shall show, that *both conditions are, in innumerable cases, absent in modern society, it follows that modern marriage is frequently far from fulfilling its true purpose; hence that it is not just to represent it, as is done, in the light of an ideal institution.*

How large the number is of the marriages, contracted with views wholly different from these, can, naturally, not be statistically given. The parties concerned are interested in having their marriage appear to the world different from what it is in fact. There is on this field a state of hypocrisy peculiar to no earlier social period. And the State, the political representative of this society, has no interest, for the sake of curiosity, in initiating inquiries, the result of which would be to place in dubious light the social system that is its very foundation. The maxims, which the State observes with respect to the marrying of large divisions of its own officials and servants, *do not suffer the principle to be applied that, ostensibly, is the basis of marriage.*

Marriage—and herewith the bourgeois idealists also agree—should be a union that two persons enter into only out of mutual love, in order to accomplish their natural mission. This motive is, however, only rarely present in all its purity. With the large majority of women, matrimony is looked upon as a species of institution for support, which they must enter into at any price. Conversely, a large portion of the men look upon marriage from a purely business standpoint, and from material view-points all the advantages and disadvantages are accurately calculated. Even with those marriages, in which low egotistical motives did not turn the scales, raw reality brings along so much that disturbs and dissolves, that only in rare instances are the expectations verified which, in their youthful enthusiasm and ardor, the couple had looked forward to.

And quite naturally. If wedlock is to offer the spouses a contented connubial life, it demands, together with mutual love and respect, *the assurance of material existence, the supply of that measure of the necessaries of life and comfort which the two consider requisite for themselves and their children.* The weight of cares, the hard struggle for existence—these are the first nails in the coffin of conjugal content and happiness. The cares become heavier the more fruitful the marriage proves itself, i. e., *in the measure in which the marriage fulfils its purpose.* The peasant, for instance, is pleased at every calf that his cow brings him; he counts with delight the number of young that his sow litters; and he communicates the event with pleasure to his neighbors. But the same peasant looks gloomy when his wife presents him with an increase to his own brood—and large this may never be—which he believes to be able to bring up without too much worry. His gloom is all the thicker if the new-born child is a *girl*.

We shall now show how, everywhere, marriages and births are completely controlled by the economic conditions. This is most classically exemplified in France. There, the allotment system prevails generally in the country districts. Land, broken up beyond a certain limit, ceases to nourish a family. The unlimited division of land, legally permissible, the French peasant counteracts by his rarely giving life to more than two children,—hence the celebrated and notorious "two child system," that has grown into a social institution in France, and that, to the alarm of her statesmen, keeps the population stationery, in some provinces even registering considerable retrogression. The number of births is steadily on the decline in France; but not in France only, also in most of the civilized lands. Therein is found expressed a development in our social conditions, that should give the ruling classes cause to ponder. In 1881 there were 937,057 children born in France; in 1890, however, only 838,059; accordingly, the births in 1890 fell 98,998 behind the year 1881. Characteristic, however, is the circumstance that the number of *illegitimate* births in France was 70,079 for the year 1881; that, during the period between 1881 and 1890, the number reached high-water mark in 1884, with 75,754; and that the number was still 71,086 strong in 1890. Accordingly, the whole of the decline of births fell exclusively upon the legitimate births. This decline in births, and, we may add, in marriages also, is, as will be shown, a characteristic feature, noticeable throughout the century. To every 10,000 French population, there were births in the years:

1801......333	1841......282	1868......269
1821......307	1851......270	1886......230
1831......303	1856......261	1890......219

This amounts to a decline of births in 1890, as against 1801, of 114 to every 10,000 inhabitants. It is imaginable that such figures cause serious headaches to the French statesmen and politicians. But France does not stand alone in this. For a long time Germany has been presenting a similar phenomenon. In Germany, to every 10,000 population there were births in the years:

1869..........406	1883..........358
1876..........403	1887..........369.4
1880..........390	1890..........357.6

Accordingly, Germany too reveals, in the space of only 21 years, a decline of 49 births to every 10,000 inhabitants. Similarly with the other States of Europe. To every 10,000 population there were live births:

States.	From 1865-1867.	From 1886-1888.	Decrease.	Increase.
Ireland	262	231	31	..
Scotland	353	313	40	..
England and Wales	353	314	39	..
Holland	388	344	44	..
Belgium	320	293	27	..
Switzerland	320	278	42	••
Austria	374	380	..	6
Hungary	399	445	..	46
Italy	378	371	7	..
Sweden	320	297	23	..
Norway	344	308	36	..

The decline in births is, accordingly, pretty general, only that, of all European States, it is strongest in France. Between 1886 and 1888, France had, to every 1,000 inhabitants, an average of 23.9 births, England 32.9, Prussia 41.27, and Russia 48.8.

These facts show that the birth of a human being, the "image of God," as religious people express it, ranks generally much cheaper than new-born domestic animals. What this fact does reveal is the *unworthy* condition that we find ourselves in,—and it is mainly the female sex which suffers thereunder. In many respects, modern views distinguish themselves but little from those of barbarous nations. Among the latter, new-born babes were frequently killed, and such a fate fell to the lot of girls mainly; many a half-wild race does so to this day. We no longer kill the girls; we are too civilized for that; but they are only too often treated like pariahs by society and the family. The stronger man crowds them everywhere back in the struggle for existence; and if, driven by the love for life, they still take up the battle, they are visited with hatred by the stronger sex, as unwelcome competitors. It is especially the men in the higher ranks of society who are bitterest against female competition, and oppose it most fiercely. That working-men demand the exclusion of female labor on principle happens but rarely. A motion to that effect being made in 1877, at a French Labor Convention, the large majority declared against it. Since then, it is just with the class-conscious workingmen of all countries, that the principle, that working-women are beings with equal rights as themselves, makes immense progress. This was shown especially by the resolutions of the International Labor Congress of Paris in 1889. The class-conscious workingman knows that the modern economic development forces woman to set herself up as a competitor with man; but he also knows that, to prohibit female labor, would be as senseless an act as the prohibition of the use of machinery.   Hence he strives to enlighten woman on her position in society, and *to educate her into a fellow combatant in the struggle for the emancipation of the proletariat from capitalism.* True enough,—due to the ever more widespread employment of female labor in agriculture, industry, commerce and the trades—the family life of the workingman is destroyed, and the degenerating effects of the double yoke of work for a living, and of household duties, makes rapid progress in the female sex.   Hence the endeavor to keep women by legislative enactments, from occupations that are especially injurious to the female organism, and by means of protective laws to safeguard her as a mother and rearer of children.   On the other hand, the struggle for existence forces women to turn in ever larger numbers to industrial occupations.   It is *married woman*, more particularly, who is called upon to increase the meager earnings of her husband with her work,—and she is particularly welcome to the employer.[10]

Modern society is without doubt more cultured than any previous one, and woman stands correspondingly higher.   Nevertheless, the views concerning the relations of the two sexes have remained at bottom the same.   Professor L. von Stein published a book,[11]—a work, be it said in passing, that corresponds ill with its title—in which he gives a poetically colored picture of modern marriage, as it supposedly is.   Even in this picture the subaltern position of woman towards the "lion" man is made manifest.   Stein says among other things: "Man deserves a being that not only loves, but also understands him.   He deserves a person with whom not only the heart beats for him, but whose hand may also smooth his forehead, and whose presence radiates peace, rest, order, a quiet command over herself and the thousand and one things upon which he daily reverts: he wants someone who spreads over all these things that indescribable aroma of womanhood, one who is the life-giving warmth to the life of the house."

In this song of praise of woman lies concealed her own degradation, and along therewith, the low egotism of man.   The professor depicts woman as a vaporous being, that, nevertheless, shall be equipped with

[10] Mr. E., a manufacturer .   . informed me that he employed females exclusively, at his power-looms .   . gives a decided preference to married females, especially those who have families at home dependent on them for support; they are attentive, docile, more so than unmarried females, and are compelled to use their utmost exertions to procure the necessties of life. Thus are the virtues, the peculiar virtues of the female character to be perverted to her injury—thus all that is most dutiful and tender in her nature is made a means of her bondage and suffering. Speech of Lord Ashley, March 15, 1884, on the Ten Hour Factory Bill. Marx's "Capital."

[11] "Die Frau auf dem Gebiete der Nationaloekonomie."

the necessary knowledge of practical arithmetic; know how to keep the balance between "must" and "can" in the household; and, for the rest, float zephyr-fashion, like sweet spring-tide, about the master of the house, the sovereign lion, in order to spy every wish from his eyes, and with her little soft hand unwrinkle the forehead, that he, "the master of the house," perchance himself crumpled, while brooding over his own stupidity. In short, the professor pictures a woman and a marriage such as, out of a hundred, hardly one is to be found, or, for that matter, can exist. Of the many thousand unhappy marriages; of the large number of women who never get so far as to wed; and also of the millions, who, like beasts of burden beside their husbands, have to drudge and wear themselves out from early morn till late to earn a bit of bread for the current day,—of all of these the learned gentleman knows nothing. With all these wretched beings, hard, raw reality wipes off the poetic coloring more easily than does the hand the colored dust of the wings of a butterfly. One look, cast by the professor at those unnumbered female sufferers, would have seriously disturbed his poetically colored picture, and spoiled his concept. The women, whom he sees, make up but a trifling minority, and that these stand upon the plane of our times is to be doubted.

An oft-quoted sentence runs: "The best gauge of the culture of a people is the position which woman occupies." We grant that; but it will be shown that our so much vaunted culture has little to brag about. In his work, "The Subjection of Woman,"—the title is typical of the opinion that the author holds regarding the modern position of woman —John Stuart Mill says: "The lives of men have become more domestic, growing civilization lays them under more obligations towards women." This is only partly true. In so far as honorable conjugal relations may exist between husband and wife, Mill's statement is true; but it is doubtful whether the statement applies to even a strong minority. Every sensible man will consider it an advantage to himself if woman step forward into life out of the narrow circle of domestic activities, and become familiar with the currents of the times. The "chains" he thereby lays upon himself do not press him. On the other hand, the question arises whether modern life does not introduce into married life factors, that, to a higher degree than formerly, act destructively upon marriage.

Monogamous marriage became, from the start, an object of material speculation. The man who marries endeavors to wed property, along with a wife, and this was one of the principal reasons why daughters, after being at first excluded from the right to inherit, when descent in the male line prevailed, soon again reacquired the right. But never in earlier days was marriage so cynically, in open market, so to speak, an object of speculation; a money transaction, as it is to-day. To-day trading in marriage is frequently conducted among the property classes —among the propertyless the practice has no sense—with such shamelessness, that the oft-repeated phrase concerning the "sanctity" of marriage is the merest mockery. This phenomenon, as everything else, has its ample foundation. At no previous period was it, as it is to-day, hard for the large majority of people to raise themselves into a condition of well-being, corresponding to the then general conceptions; nor was at any time the justified striving for an existence worthy of human beings so general as it is to-day. He who does not reach the goal, feels his failure all the more keenly, just because all believe to have an equal right to enjoyment. *Formally*, there are *no* rank or class distinctions. Each wishes to obtain that which, according to his station, he considers a goal worth striving for, in order to come at fruition. But many are called and few are chosen. In order that one may live comfortably in capitalist society, twenty others must pine; and in order that one may wallow in all manner of enjoyment, hundreds, if not thousands, of others must renounce the happiness of life. But each wishes to be of that minority of favored ones, and seizes every means, that promise to take him to the desired goal, provided he does not compromise himself too deeply. One of the most convenient means, and, withal, nearest at hand, to reach the privileged social station, is the *money-marriage*. The desire, on the one hand, to obtain as much money as possible, and, on the other, the aspiration after rank, titles and honor thus find their mutual satisfaction in the so-called upper classes of society. There, marriage is generally considered a business transaction; it is a purely conventional bond, which both parties respect externally, while, for the rest, each often acts according to his or her own inclination. Marriage for political reasons, practiced in the higher classes, need here to be mentioned only for the sake of completeness. With these marriages also, as a rule, the privilege has tacitly existed—of course, again, for the husband to a much higher degree than for the wife—that the parties keep themselves scathless, *outside of the bonds of wedlock*, according as their whims may point, or their needs dictate. There have been periods in history when it was part of the *bon ton* with a Prince to keep mistresses: it was one of the princely attributes. Thus, according to Scherr, did Frederick William I. of Prussia (1713-1740), otherwise with a reputation for steadiness, keep up, at least for the sake of appearances, relations with a General's wife. On the other hand, it is a matter of public notoriety that, for instance, August the Strong, King of Poland and Saxony, gave life to 300 illegitimate children; and Victor Emanuel of Italy, the *re galantuomo*, left behind 32 illegitimate children. There is still extant a romantically located little German residence city, in which are at least a dozen charming villas, that the corresponding "father of his country" had built as places of recreation for his resigned mistresses. On this head thick books could be written: as is well known, there is an extensive library on these piquant matters.

The inside history of most of the German princely courts and noble families is to the informed an almost uninterrupted *chronique scandaleuse*, and not infrequently has it been stained with crimes of blackest dye. In sight of these facts, it certainly is imperative upon the sycophantic painters of history, not only to leave untouched the question of the "legitimacy" of the several successive "fathers and mothers of their country," but also to take pains to represent them as patterns of all virtues, as faithful husbands and good mothers. Not yet has the breed of the augurs died out; they still live, as did their Roman prototypes, on the ignorance of the masses.

In every large town, there are certain places and days when the higher classes meet, mainly for the purpose of match-making. These gatherings are, accordingly, quite fitly termed "marriage exchanges." Just as on the exchanges, speculation and chaffer play here the leading *role*, nor are deception and swindle left out. Officers, loaded with debts, but who can hold out an old title of nobility; *roues*, broken down with debauchery, who seek to restore their ruined health in the haven of wedlock, and need a nurse; manufacturers, merchants, bankers, who face bankruptcy, not infrequently the penitentiary also, and wish to be saved; finally, all those who are after money and wealth, or a larger quantity thereof, government office-holders among them, with prospects of promotion, but meanwhile in financial straits;—all turn up as customers at these exchanges, and ply the matrimonial trade. Quite often, at such transactions, it is all one whether the prospective wife be young or old, handsome or ugly, straight or bent, educated or ignorant, religious or frivolous, Christian or Jew. Was it not a saying of a celebrated statesman: "The marriage of a Christian stallion with a Jewish mare is to be highly recommended"?[12] The figure, characteristically borrowed from the horse-fair, meets, as experience teaches, with loud applause from the higher circles of our society. Money makes up for all defects, and outweighs all vices. The German penal code punishes[13] the coupler with long terms of imprisonment; when, however, parents, guardians and relatives couple their children, wards or kin to a hated man or woman only for the sake of money, of profit, of rank, in short, for the sake of external benefits, there is no District Attorney ready to take charge, and yet a crime has been committed. There are numerous well organized matrimonial bureaus, with male and female panders of all degrees, out for prey, in search of the male and female candidates for the "holy bonds of matrimony." Such business is especially profitable when the

[12] See "Fuerst Bismarck und seine Leute," Von Busch.
[13] Sections 180 and 181.

"work" is done for the members of the upper classes. In 1878 there was a criminal trial in Vienna of a female pander on the charge of poisoning, and ended with her being sentenced to fifteen years in the penitentiary. At the trial it was established that the French Ambassador in Vienna, Count Bonneville, had paid the pander 12,000 florins for procuring his own wife. Other members of the high aristocracy were likewise highly compromised through the trial. Evidently, certain Government officials had left the woman to pursue her dark and criminal practices for many years. The "why" thereof is surely no secret. Similar stories are told from the capital of the German Empire. During recent years, it is the daughters and heirs of the rich American capitalist class, who, on their side, aspire after rank and honors, not to be had in their own American home, that have become a special subject of matrimonial trading for the needy noblemen of Europe. Upon these particular practices characteristic light is thrown by a series of articles that appeared in the fall of 1889 in a portion of the German press. According thereto, a *chevalier d'industry* nobleman, domiciled in California, had recommended himself as a matrimonial agent in German and Austrian papers. The offers that he received amply betray the conception concerning the sanctity of marriage and its "ethical" side prevalent in the corresponding circles. Two Prussian officers of the Guards, both, as they say themselves, belonging to the oldest nobility of Prussia, declared that they were ready to enter into negotiations for marriage because, as they frankly confessed, they owed together 60,000 marks. In their letter to the pander they say literally: "It is understood that we shall pay no money in advance. You will receive your remuneration after the wedding trip. Recommend us only to ladies against whose families no objections can be raised. It is also very desirable to be introduced to ladies of attractive appearance. If demanded, we shall furnish, for discreet use, our own pictures to your agent, after he shall have given us the details, and shown us the pictures, etc. We consider the whole affair strictly confidential and as a matter of honor (?), and, of course, demand the same from you. We expect a speedy answer through your agent in this place, if you have one. Berlin, Friedrichstrasse 107, December 15, 1889. Baron v. M——, Arthur v. W——."

An Austrian nobleman also, Karl Freiherr v. M—— of Goeding in Moravia, seized the opportunity to angle for a rich American bride, and to this end sent to the swindle-bureau the following letter:

"According to a notice in the papers of this place, you are acquainted with American ladies who wish to marry. In this connection I place myself at your service, but must inform you that I have no fortune whatever. I am of very old noble stock (Baron), 34 years old, single, was a cavalry officer and am at present engaged in building railroads. I should be pleased to inspect one or more pictures, which, upon my word of honor, I shall return. Should you require my picture, I shall forward same to you. I also request you to give me fuller information. Expecting a speedy answer in this matter, I remain, very respectfully, your Karl Freiherr v. M——, Goeding, Moravia, Austria, November 29, 1889."

A young German nobleman, Hans v. H——, wrote from London that he was 5 feet 10 tall, of an old noble family, and employed in the diplomatic service. He made the confession that his fortune had been greatly reduced through unsuccessful betting at the horse races, and hence found himself obliged to be on the lookout for a rich bride, so as to be able to cover his deficit. He was, furthermore, ready to undertake a trip to the United States forthwith.

The *chevalier d'industry* in question claimed that, besides several counts, barons, etc., three Princes and sixteen dukes had reported to him as candidates for marriage. But not noblemen only, bourgeois also longed for rich American women. An architect, Max W—— of Leipsic, demanded a bride who should possess not only money, but beauty and culture also. From Kehl on the Rhine, a young mill-owner, Robert D——, wrote that he would be satisfied with a bride who had but 400,000 marks, and he promised in advance to make her happy.

But why look so far, when at hand the quarry is rich! A very patriotic-conservative Leipsic paper, which plumes itself very particularly upon its Christianity, contained in the spring of 1894 an advertisement, that ran thus: "A cavalry officer of the Guards, of large, handsome build, noble, 27 years of age, desires a financial marriage. Please address, Count v. W. I., Post Office General Delivery, Dresden." In comparison with the fellow who makes so cynical an offer, the street-walker, who, out of bitter necessity, plies her trade, is a paragon of decency and virtue. Similar advertisements are found almost every day in the papers of *all* political parties—*except the Social Democratic.* A Social Democratic editor or manager, who would accept such or similar advertisements for his paper, would be expelled from his party as dishonorable. The capitalist press is not troubled at such advertisements: they bring in money: and it is of the mind of the Emperor Vespasian,— *non olet*, it does not smell. Yet all that does not hinder that same press from going rabid mad at "the marriage-undermining tendencies of Socialism." Never yet was there an age more hypocritical than the one we are living in. With the view to demonstrate the fact once more, the above instances were cited.

Bureaus of information for marriage,—that's what the advertisement pages of most of the newspapers of our day are. Whosoever, be it

male or female, finds near at hand nothing desirable, entrusts his or her
heart's wants to the pious-conservative or moral-liberal press, that, in
consideration of cash and without coaxing, sees to it that the kindred
souls meet.   With illustrations, taken on any one day from a number
of large newspapers, whole pages could be filled.   Off and on the interesting fact also crops out that even clergymen are sought for husbands,
and, *vice versa*, clergymen angle for wives, with the aid of advertisements.   Occasionally, the suitors also offer to overlook a *slip*, provided
the looked-for woman be rich.   In short, the moral turpitude of certain
social circles of our society can be pilloried no better than by this sort
of courtship.

State and Church play in such "holy matrimony" a by no means handsome *role*.   Whether the civil magistrate or clergyman, on whom may
devolve the duty to celebrate the marriage, be convinced that the bridal
couple before him has been brought together by the vilest of practices;
whether it be manifest that, neither in point of age nor that of bodily
or mental qualities, the two are compatible with each other; whether,
for instance, the bride be twenty and the bridegroom seventy years old,
or the reverse; whether the bride be young, handsome and joyful, and
the bridegroom old, ridden with disease and crabbed;—whatever the
case, it concerns not the representative of the State or the Church; it
is not for them to look into that.   The marriage bond is "blessed,"—as
a rule, blessed with all the greater solemnity in proportion to the size
of the fee for the "holy office."

When, later, such a marriage proves a most unfortunate one—as
foreseen by everybody, by the ill-starred victim, in most instances the
woman, herself,—and either party decides to separate, then, State and
Church,—who never first inquire whether real love and natural, moral
impulses, or only naked, obscene egotism tie the knot—now raise the
greatest difficulties.   At present, moral repulsion is but rarely recognized a sufficient ground for separation; at present, only palpable proofs,
proofs that always dishonor or lower one of the parties in public
esteem, are, as a rule, demanded; separation is not otherwise granted.
That the Roman Catholic Church does not allow divorces,—except by
special dispensation of the Pope, which is hard to obtain, and, at best,
only from board and bed—only renders all the worse the conditions,
under which all Catholic countries are suffering.   Germany has the
prospect of receiving, in the not too far distant future, a civil code that
shall embrace the whole Empire.   It is, therefore, a side-light upon
our times that, although even the superficial observer must reach the
conclusion that at no previous period have unhappy marriages been so
numerous as now—a natural consequence of our whole social development—the new draft for a civil code still renders divorce materially

difficult.   It is but a fresh instance of the old experience,—a social
system, in the throes of dissolution, seeks to keep itself up by artificial
means and compulsion, and to deceive itself upon its actual state.   In
declining Rome, marriage and births were sought to be promoted by
premiums: in the German Empire, whose social order stands under a
constellation similar with that of the decaying Empire of the Caesars,
it is now sought to prevent the ever more frequent desire for the dissolution of marriage by means of forcible constraints.

Thus people remain against their will chained to each other through
life.   One party becomes the slave of the other, compelled to submit out
of "conjugal duty" to that other's most intimate embraces, which, perhaps, it abhors worse than insult or ill-treatment.   Fully justified is
Montegazza's dictum:[14] "There is probably no worse torture than that
which compels a human being to put up with the caresses of a person it
does not love."

We ask, Is such a marriage—and their number is infinite—not worse
than prostitution?   The prostitute has, to a certain degree, the freedom
to withdraw from her disgraceful pursuit; moreover, she enjoys the
privilege, if she does not live in a public house, to reject the purchase
of the embraces of him who, for whatever reason, may be distasteful
to her.   But a sold married woman must submit to the embraces of her
husband, even though she have a hundred reasons to hate and despise
him.

When in advance, and with the knowledge of both parties, marriage
is contracted as a marriage for money or rank, then, as a rule, matters
lie more favorably.   The two accommodate themselves mutually, and a
modus vivendi is established.   They want no scandal, and regard for
their children compels them to avoid any, although it is the children
who suffer most under a cold, loveless life on the part of their parents,
even if such a life does not develop into enmity, quarrel and dissension.
Often accommodation is reached in order to avoid material loss.   As a
rule it is the husband, whose conduct is the rock against which marriage
is dashed.   This appears from the actions for divorce.   In virtue of his
dominant position, he can indemnify himself elsewhere when the marriage is not pleasing to him, and he can not find satisfaction in it.   The
wife is not so free to step on side-roads, partly because, as the receiving
sex, such action is, for physiologic reasons, a much more risky one on
her part; then, also, because every infraction of conjugal fidelity is imputed a crime to her, which neither the husband nor society pardons.
Woman alone makes a "slip"—be she wife, widow or maid; man, at
worst, has acted "incorrectly."   One and the same act is judged by
society with wholly different standards, according as it be committed by

[14] "The Physiology of Love."

a man or a woman.   And, as a rule, women themselves judge a "fallen"
sister most severely and pitilessly.[15]

As a rule, only in cases of crassest infidelity or maltreatment, does
the wife decide upon divorce. She is generally in a materially dependent
position, and compelled to look upon marriage as a means of support:
moreover, as a divorced wife, she finds herself socially in no enviable
situation: unless special reasons render intercourse with her desirable,
she is considered and treated by society as a neuter, so to speak. When,
despite all this, most actions for divorce proceed from wives, the circumstance is an evidence of the heavy moral torture that they lie under.
In France, even before the new divorce law came into effect (1884), by
far the more numerous actions for separation from bed and board came
from women. For an absolute divorce they could apply only if the
husband took his concubine into the married home, against the will of
his wife. Actions for separations from bed and board occurred:[16]

Years.	Average Per Year by Wives.	Average Per Year by Husbands.
1856-1861	1729	184
1861-1866	2135	260
1866-1871	2591	330

But not only did women institute by far the larger number of actions;
the figures show that these increased from period to period. Furthermore, so far as reliable information before us goes, it appears that
actions for absolute divorce also proceed preponderatingly from wives.
In the Kingdom of Saxony, during the period of 1860-1868, there were
instituted, all told, 8,402 actions for divorce; of these, 3,537 (42 per
cent.) were by men, 4,865 (58 per cent.) by wives.

In the period from 1871 to 1878, there were actions for divorce in
Saxony[17]:

Year.	By Husbands.	By Wives.
1871	475	574
1872	576	698
1873	553	673
1874	643	697
1875	717	752
1876	722	839
1877	746	951
1878	754	994
Total	5,186	6,158

[15] Alexander Dumas says rightly, in "Monsieur Alfonse:" "Man has built
two sorts of morals; one for himself, one for his wife; one that permits him
love with all women, and one that, as indemnity for the liberty she has forfeited forever, permits her love with one man only."
[16] L. Bridel, "La Puissance Maritale." Lausanne, 1879.
[17] v. Oettingen, "Moralstatistik," Erlangen, 1882.

The fact that divorce, as a rule, hurts women more, did not restrain them in Saxony either from instituting most of the actions. The total actions for divorce increased, however, in Saxony, as in France, much faster than population. In Switzerland, during the year 1892, there were granted 1,036 applications for divorce. Of these, wives had instituted 493, husbands 229, and both parties 314.

Statistics teach us, however, not alone that wives institute the larger number of actions for divorce; they also teach us that the number of divorces is in rapid increase. In France, divorce has been regulated anew by law since 1884. Since then, divorces have greatly increased from year to year. The number of divorces, and years they fell in, were as follows:

1884..........1,657		1887..........3,636
1885..........2,477		1888..........4,708
1886..........2.950		1889..........4,786
		1890..........5,457

In Vienna there were, from 1870 to 1871, 148 divorces; they increased from year to year; from 1878 to 1879 they ran up to 319 cases.[16] But in Vienna, being a preponderatingly Catholic city, divorce is hard to obtain. That notwithstanding, about the year 1885 a Vienna Judge made the remark: "Complaints on the ground of broken marriage vows are as frequent as complaints for broken window-panes." In England and Wales there was, in 1867, 1 divorce to every 1,378 marriages, but in 1877 there was 1 to every 652 marriages; and in 1886, 1 to as few as 527. In the United States the number of divorces for 1867 was 9,937, and for 1886 as many as 25,535. The total number of divorces in the United States between 1867 and 1886 was 328,716, and the fault fell in 216,176 cases upon the husband, in 112,540 upon the wife.

Relatively speaking, the largest number of divorces occurs in the United States. The proportion between marriages and divorces during the period of 1867 to 1886 stood for those States in which an accurate record is kept:

States.	Marriages.	Divorces.	Marriages to Every One Divorce.
Connecticut	96,737	8,542	11.32
Columbia	24,065	1,105	21.77
Massachusetts	308,195	9,853	31.28
Ohio	544,362	26,367	20.65
Rhode Island	49,593	4,462	11.10
Vermont	54,913	3,238	19.95

[16] v. Oettingen, "Moralstatistik."

In the other States of the Union, from which less accurate returns are at hand, the proportion seems to be the same. The reasons why in the United States divorces are more frequent than in any other country, may be sought in the circumstance, first, that divorce is there more easily obtained than elsewhere; secondly, that *women occupy in the United States a far freer position than in any other country, hence are less inclined to allow themselves to be tyrannized by their martial lords.*[19]

In Germany there was, by judicial decision, 1 dissolution of marriage—

In the Years	To Population.	To Mariages.
1881-1885	8,410	1,430
1886	7,585	1,283
1887	7,261	1,237
1888	6,966	1,179
1889	7,155	1,211

According to Dr. S. Wernicke, there were to every 1,000 marriages, divorces in:

Years.	Belgium.	Sweden.	France.
1841-1845	0.7	4.2	2.7
1846-1850	0.9	4.4	2.8
1851-1855	1.0	4.4	4.0
1856-1860	1.4	4.3	4.9
1861-1865	1.6	4.8	6.0
1866-1870	1.9	5.0	7.6
1871-1875	2.8	5.8	6.5
1876-1880	4.2	7.1	9.0

It would be an error to attempt to arrive at any conclusion touching the different conditions of morality, by deductions from the large discrepancy between the figures for the different countries cited above. No one will dare assert that the population of Sweden has more inclination or cause for divorce than that of Belgium. First of all must the legislation on the subject be kept in mind, which in one country makes divorce difficult, in another easier, more so in some, less in others. Only in the second instance does the condition of morality come into consideration, i. e., the average reasons that, now the husbands, then the wives, consider determining factors in applying for separation. But all these figures combine in establishing that divorces increase much

---

[19] [According to the census of 1900, there were in the United States 198,914 divorced persons: males 84,237, females 114,677. The percentage of divorced to married persons was 0.7. The census warns, however, that "divorced persons are apt to be reported as single, and so the census returns in this respect should not be accepted as a correct measure of the prevalence of divorce throughout the country."—THE TRANSLATOR.]

faster than population; and that they *increase* while marriages *decline*. About this, more later.

On the question how the actions for divorce distribute themselves among the several strata of society, there is only one computation at our disposal, from Saxony, but which is from the year 1851.[20] At that time, to each 100,000 marriages, there were actions for divorce from the stratum of

Domestic servants ....289 or 1 application to 346 marriages
Day laborers ....324 or 1 application to 309 marriages
Government employes ....337 or 1 application to 289 marriages
Craftsmen and merchants........354 or 1 application to 283 marriages
Artists and scientists............485 or 1 application to 206 marriages

Accordingly, the actions for divorce were at that period in Saxony 50 per cent. more frequent in the *higher* than in the *lower* social strata.

The increasing number of divorces signifies that, in general, the marriage relations are becoming ever more unfavorable, and that the factors multiply which destroy marriage. On the other hand, they also furnish evidence that an ever larger number of spouses, women in particular, decide to shake off the unbearable oppressing yoke.

But the evils of matrimony increase, and the corruption of marriage gains ground in the same measure as the struggle for existence waxes sharper, and marriage becomes ever more a money-match, or be it, marriage by purchase. The increasing difficulty, moreover, of supporting a family determines many to renounce marriage altogether; and thus the saying that woman's activity should be limited to the house, and that she should fill her calling as housewife and mother, becomes ever more *a senseless phrase*. On the other hand, the conditions can not choose but favor the gratification of sexual intercourse outside of wedlock. Hence the number of prostitutes increases, while the number of marriages decreases. Besides that, the number increases of those who suffer from unnatural gratification of the sexual instinct.

Among the property classes, not infrequently the wife sinks, just as in old Greece, to the level of a mere apparatus for the procreation of legitimate offspring, of warder of the house, or of nurse to a husband, wrecked by debauchery. The husbands keep for their pleasure and physical desires hetairae—styled among us courtesans or mistresses—who live in elegant abodes, in the handsomest quarters of the city. Others, whose means do not allow them to keep mistresses, disport themselves, after marriage as before, with Phrynes, for whom their hearts beat stronger than for their own wives. With the Phrynes they amuse themselves; and quite a number of the husbands among the "property

[20] v. Oettingen, "Moralstatistik."

and cultured classes" is so corrupt that it considers these entertainments in order.[21]

In the upper and middle classes of society, the money matches and matches for social position are the mainspring of the evils of married life; but, over and above that, marriage is made rank by the lives these classes lead. This holds good particularly with regard to the women, who frequently give themselves over to idleness or to corrupting pursuits. Their intellectual food often consists in the reading of equivocal romances and obscene literature, in seeing and hearing frivolous theatrical performances, and the fruition of sensuous music; in exhilarating nervous stimulants; in conversations on the pettiest subjects, or scandals about the dear fellow mortals. Along therewith, they rush from one enjoyment into another, from one banquet to another, and hasten in summer to the baths and summer retreats to recover from the excesses of the winter, and to find fresh subjects for talk. The *chronique scandaleuse* recruits itself from this style of life: people seduce and are seduced.

In the lower classes money-matches are unknown, as a rule, although they occasionally do play a role. No one can wholly withdraw himself from the influence of the society he lives in,—and the existing social conditions exercise a particularly depressing influence upon the circumstances of the lower classes. As a rule, the workingman weds out of inclination, but there is no lack of causes to disturb his marriage. A rich blessing of children brings on cares and troubles; but too often want sets in. Sickness and death are frequent guests in the workingman's family. Lack of work drives misery to its height. Many a circumstance pares off the worker's earnings, or temporarily robs him wholly of it. Commercial and industrial crises throw him out of work; the introduction of new machinery, or methods of work, casts him as superfluous on the sidewalk; wars, unfavorable tariffs and commercial treaties, the introduction of the new indirect taxes, disciplinary acts on the part of the employer in punishment for the exercise of his convictions, etc., destroy his existence, or seriously injure it. Now one thing, then another happens, whereby, sometimes for a shorter, sometimes for a longer

[21] In his work frequently cited by us, "Die Frauenfrage im Mittelalter," Buecher laments the decay of marriage and of family life; he condemns the increasing female labor in industry, and demands a "return" to the "real domain of woman," where she alone produces "values" in the house and the family. The endeavors of the modern friends of woman appear to him as "dilettanteism" and he hopes finally "that the movement may be switched on the right track," but he is obviously unable to point to a successful road. Neither is that possible from the bourgeois standpoint. The marriage conditions, like the condition of woman in general, have not been brought about arbitrarily. They are the natural product of our social development. But the social development of peoples does not cut capers, nor does it perpetrate any such false reasonings in a circle; it takes its course obedient to imminent laws. It is the mission of the student of civilization to discover these laws, and, planted upon them, to show the way for the removal of existing evils.

period, he becomes an unemployed, i. e., a starving being. Uncertainty is the badge of his existence. When such blows of fortune happen, they at first produce dissatisfaction and bitterness, and in the home life this mood finds its first expression when daily, every hour, demands are made by wife and children for the most pressing needs, needs that the husband can not satisfy. Out of despair, he visits the saloon, and seeks comfort in bad liquor. The last penny is spent. Quarrel and dissension break out. The ruin of both marriage and the family is accomplished.

Let us take up another picture. Both—husband and wife—go to work. The little ones are left to themselves, or to the care of older brothers and sisters, themselves in need of care and education. At noon, the so-called lunch is swallowed down in hot haste,—supposing that the parents have at all time to rush home, which, in thousands of cases is impossible, owing to the shortness of the hour of recess, and the distance of the shop from the home. Tired out and unstrung, both return home in the evening. Instead of a friendly, cheerful home, they find a narrow, unhealthy habitation, often lacking in light and air, generally also in the most necessary comforts. The increasing tenement plague, together with the horrible improprieties that flow therefrom, is one of the darkest sides of our social order, and leads to numerous evils, vices and crimes. Yet the plague increases from year to year in all cities and industrial regions, and it draws within the vortex of its evils ever new strata of society: small producers, public employes, teachers, small traders, etc. The workingman's wife, who reaches home in the evening tired and harassed, has now again her hands full. She must bestir herself at breakneck speed in order but to get ready the most necessary things in the household. The crying and noisy children are hurried off to bed; the wife sits up, and sews, and patches deep into the night. The so-much-needed mental intercourse and encouragement are absent. The husband is often uneducated and knows little, the wife still less; the little they have to say to each other is soon got through with. The husband goes to the saloon, and seeks there the entertainment that he lacks at home; he drinks; however little that be that he spends, for his means it is too much. At times he falls a prey to gambling, which, in the upper circles of society also, claims many victims, and he loses more than he spends in drink. The wife, in the meantime, sits at home and grumbles; she must work like a dray-horse; for her there is no rest or recreation; the husband avails himself of the freedom that accident gives him, of having been born a man. Thus disharmony arises. If, however, the wife is less true to duty, she seeks in the evening, after she has returned home tired, the rest she is entitled to; but then the household goes back, and misery is twice as great. Indeed, we live "in the best world possible."

Through these and similar circumstances, marriage is shattered ever more among the working class also. Even favorable seasons of work exert their destructive influence: they compel him to work Sundays and overtime: they take from him the hours he still had left for his family. In many instances he has to travel hours to reach the shop; to utilize the noon recess for going home is an impossibility; he is up in the morning at the very earliest, when the children are still sound asleep, and returns home late, when they are again in the same condition. Thousands, especially those engaged in the building trades in the cities, remain away from home all week, owing to the vastness of the distance, and return only on Saturdays to their family. And yet it is expected of family life that it thrive under such circumstances. Moreover, female labor is ever on the increase, especially in the textile industry, whose thousands of steam weaving and spinning looms are served by cheap woman and children's hands. Here the relations of sex and age has been reversed. Wife and child go into the mill, the now breadless husband sits at home and attends to household duties. In the United States, that, due to its rapid large-capitalist development, produces all the evils of European industrial States in much larger dimensions, a characteristic name has been invented for the state of things brought on by such conditions. Industrial places that employ women mainly, while the husbands sit at home, are called "she-towns."

The admission of women to all the manual trades is to-day conceded on all hands. Capitalist society, ever on the hunt for profit and gain, has long since recognized what an excellent subject for exploitation is woman—more docile and submissive, and less exacting woman—in comparison with man. Hence the number of trades and occupations, in which women are finding employment increases yearly. The extension and improvement of machinery, the simplification of the process of production through the ever minuter subdivision of labor, the intenser competition of capitalists among themselves, together with the competitive battle in the world's market among rival industrial countries,— all these continue to favor the ever further application of female labor. It is a phenomenon noticeable in all industrial countries alike. But in the same measure that the number of working-women increases, competition among the workingmen is thereby intensified. One branch of industry after another, one branch of work after the other, is being taken by working-women, who are ever more displacing the men. Numerous passages in the reports of factory inspectors, as well as in the statistical figures on the occupation of working-women, go to confirm the fact.

The condition of the women is worst in the industrial branches in which they preponderate, for instance, the clothing and underwear industry, those branches, in general, in which work can be done at home. The inquiry into the condition of the working-women in the underwear and confectionery industries, ordered in 1886 by the Bundesrath, has revealed the fact that the wages of these working-women are often so miserable that they are compelled to prostitute their bodies for a side-source of income. A large number of the prostitutes are recruited from the strata of ill-paid working-women.

Our "Christian" Government, whose Christianity, as a rule, is looked for in vain there where it should be applied, and is found where the same is superfluous and harmful,—this Christian Government acts exactly like the Christian capitalists, a fact that does not astonish him who knows that the Christian Government is but the agent of our Christian capitalists. The Government only with difficulty decides in favor of laws to limit woman-labor to a normal measure, or to wholly forbid child-labor;—on the same principle that that Government denies many of its own employes both the requisite Sunday rest and normal hours of work, and in that way materially disturbs their family life. Post Office, railroad, penitentiary and other Government employes often must perform their functions far beyond the time limit, and their salaries stand in inverse ratio to their work. That, however, is, to-day, the normal condition of things, still considered quite in order by the majority.

Seeing, furthermore, that rent, in comparison to the wages and earnings of the workingmen, the lower Government employes and the small men included, is much too high, these must exert themselves to the utmost. Lodgers are taken into these homes, only males in some, females in others, often both. The young and the old live together in narrow quarters, without separating the sexes, and are crowded together even during the most private acts. How the sense of shame, or morality fares thereby, horrifying facts proclaim. The increasing brutalization of the youth, so extensively discussed, is due mainly to the conditions prevalent in our industrial system, with which the wretchedness of the home is closely connected. And, as to the children, what must be upon them the effect of industrial labor! The very worst imaginable, both physically and morally.

The ever increasing industrial occupation of married women also is accompanied with fatal results. Especially is this the case in connection with pregnancy and child-birth, as also during the early life of the child when it depends upon the nourishment of the mother. A number of ailments arise during pregnancy that affect destructively both the fruit and the organism of the woman, and cause premature and still-born births, upon all of which more later. After the child is born, the mother is compelled to return as quickly as possible to the factory, lest her place be taken by a competitor. The inevitable results to the little ones are: neglected care, improper or total lack of nourishment. They are drugged with opiates to keep them quiet. The further results are: a vast mortality, or stunted development; in short, the degeneration of the race. The children often grow up without having enjoyed true motherly and fatherly love, or having on their part, felt filial affection. Thus is the proletariat born, thus does it live and die. And the "Christian" Government, this "Christian" society wonders that rudeness, immorality and crime cumulate.

When. in the early sixties of last century, due to the American Civil War for the emancipation of the negroes, many thousands of workingmen in the English cotton industries were out of work, physicians made the remarkable discovery that, despite great want among the population, mortality among children had *declined*. The cause was simple. The children now enjoyed the mother's nourishment and better care than they had ever had during the best seasons of work. The same fact was attested by physicians during the crisis of the seventies in the United States, especially in New York and Massachusetts. The general lack of employment compelled the women to rest from labor, and left them time for the care of their children. Similar observations were also made by Dr. v. Recherberg during the inquiry into the condition of the weavers of the region of Zittau in Saxony, as shown by him in a work that he wrote during the summer of 1890.

In the home-industries, which romantic economists love to represent as idyllic, conditions are no better. Here the wife is chained to her husband, at work early and late into the night, and the children are from an early age hitched on. Crowded into the narrowest space imaginable, husband, wife and family, boys and girls, live together, along with the waste of materials, amidst the most disagreeable dusts and odors, and without the necessary cleanliness. The bedrooms are of a piece with the sitting and working rooms: generally dark holes and without ventilation, they would be sufficiently unsanitary if they housed but a part of the people huddled into them. In short, the conditions of these places are such as to cause the skin to creep of anyone accustomed to a life worthy of a human being.

The ever harder struggle for existence often also compels women and men to commit actions and tolerate indignities that, under other circumstances, would fill them with disgust. In 1877 it was authentically established in Munich that, among the prostitutes, registered by and under the surveillance of the police, there were not less than 203 wives of workingmen and artisans. And how many are not the married women, who, out of distress, prostitute themselves without submitting to a police control that deeply lacerates the sense of shame and dignity!

But we have wandered somewhat from our subject. It was shown that the number of actions for divorce is on the increase in all countries of civilization, and that the majority of these actions proceed from wives. This steadily rising figure of actions for divorce is a sign of *the decay of bourgeois marriage, which is answering its purpose ever less*. But a still much worse sign of its decay is the circumstance that, simultaneously, the number of marriages is in almost all these countries steadily on the decline. Experience tells that high prices for corn in one single year have an unfavorable effect both upon the number of marriages and that of births. Long industrial crises, and increasing deterioration of the general economic condition must, accordingly, have a lasting evil effect. This is confirmed by the statistics of marriages for almost all countries in civilization.

In France, marriages between 1881-1890 cast the following picture on the canvas. Marriages were contracted in—

1881	282,079	1886	283,208
1882	281,060	1887	277,060
1883	284,519	1888	276,848
1884	289,555	1889	272,934
1885	283,170	1890	269,332

There is, accordingly, a considerable decrease of marriages.

In the German Empire, the number of marriages was highest after the close of the war between Germany and France, during which they had stood still. In 1872 there were 423,900 marriages contracted, but in 1876 they numbered only 366,912, and during the worst year of the crisis, the year 1879, they dropped to 335,113. They have since risen again slowly, and numbered in

1882	350,457	1889	389,339
1886	372,326	1892	398,775

Although in the year 1892 the population of Germany was larger by 8,000,000 heads than in 1872, the number of marriages was not even as large as in 1874 when it amounted to 400,282. In the period between 1871-1880, there were, to an average of 1,000 inhabitants in Germany, 8.6 marriages; in the period between 1881-1888, only 7.8.

In Prussia, to the average 10,000 inhabitants, there married—

Between 1831-35	1,849
Between 1866-70	1,605
Between 1871-75	1,896
Between 1881-85	1,529
And in 1888	1,624

A similar, partly even more unfavorable picture than in Germany, is furnished by the statistical tables for other European countries.

Out of every 10,000 persons, there married—

Year	Holland	Switzerland	Austria	France	Italy	Belgium	England	Scotland	Ireland	Denmark	Norway	Sweden	Hungary
1873	171	152	188	178	159	156	176	155	96	162	145	146	223
1874	168	166	181	167	153	152	170	152	92	164	153	145	214
1875	167	179	171	164	168	145	167	148	91	170	157	140	218
1876	165	162	165	158	163	142	166	150	99	171	154	141	198
1877	162	157	150	150	154	149	157	144	93	161	151	137	182
1878	155	147	152	151	142	135	152	134	95	148	146	129	187
1879	153	138	155	152	150	136	144	128	87	147	135	126	205
1880	150	137	152	149	140	141	149	132	78	152	133	126	182
1881	146	136	160	150	162	142	151	139	85	156	128	124	198
1882	143	135	164	149	157	140	155	140	86	154	134	127	203
1883	142	136	157	150	161	136	154	140	85	154	132	128	205
1884	144	136	157	153	164	136	151	135	91	156	137	131	201
1885	139	138	152	149	158	136	144	129	86	151	133	133	...
1886	139	137	155	149	158	134	141	124	84	142	131	...	...
Average	153	147	161	155	156	141	156	139	89	156	141	133	202

These figuures are interesting in more respects than one. In the first place, they prove that, in all the countries named, the number of marriages *declines*. Like Germany, all these countries show the highest frequency of marriage in the beginning of 1872, and then follows a drop in most of them. Hungary comes out best; Ireland, on the contrary, worst, showing the smallest figures of all. The ejectment of the Irish population from their lands, and the ever greater concentration of the same in the hands of the large landlords, express themselves clearly in the figures given.[22]

Industrial conditions have a marked effect upon the number of marriages. As the former has, on an average, become ever more unfavorable since the middle of the seventies, the decline in marriages is not astonishing. But not the industrial conditions only, also the manner in which the property relations develop affects marriages in a high degree, as just seen in Ireland. The Year-Book of Schmoller for 1885, section 1, gives information on the statistics of population of the Kingdom of Wuertemberg, from which it appears strikingly that with the increase of large

[22] "Neue Zeit," **Jahrgang 1888,** p. 239.

landed estates, the number of *married* males between 25 and 30 years of age *declines*, while the number of *unmarried* men between the ages of 40 and 50 *rises*:

Districts.	Up to 5.	Percentage of Landed Property by Hectares. 5-20.	Over 20.	Percentage of Males. Married of the Age of 25-30.	Un-married of the Age of 40-50.
Upper Neuenburg 79.6		20.4	0.0	63.6	4.4
East of Stuttgart 78.9		17.7	3.4	51.3	8.1
South of Stuttgart 67.6		24.8	7.6	48.6	8.7
North of Stuttgart 56.5		34.8	8.8	50.0	10.0
Schwarzwald 50.2		42.2	7.6	48.6	10.1
Upper Neckar 43.6		40.3	16.1	44.3	10.8
Eastward 39.5		47.6	12.8	48.7	10.0
Northeast, except north of Hall 22.2		50.1	27.7	38.8	10.6
Swabian Alb 20.3		40.8	38.3	38.8	7.5
North Upper Swabia.......19.7		48.0	32.3	32.5	9.7
From Hall eastward.......15.5		50.0	34.5	32.5	13.8
Bodensee district 14.2		61.4	24.4	23.5	26.4
Middle and South Upper Swabia 12.6		41.1	46.3	30.0	19.1

There can be no doubt: small landed property favors marriages: it makes a living possible for a larger number of families, although the living be modest. Large landed property, on the contrary, works directly against marriage, and promotes celibacy. All the figures here quoted prove, accordingly, that, not *morals*, but purely *material* causes are the determining factor. *The number of marriages, like the moral conditions of a commonwealth, depends upon its material foundations.*

The fear of want, the mental worry lest the children be not educated up to their station,—these are further causes that drive the wives, in particular, of all ranks to actions that are out of keeping with nature, and still more so with the criminal code. Under this head belong the various means for the prevention of pregnancy, or, when, despite all care, this does set in, then the removal of the unripe fruit—*abortion*. It were an error to claim that these measures are resorted to only by heedless, unconscionable women. Often, rather, it is conscientious women, who wish to limit the number of children, in order to escape the dilemma of either having to deny themselves their husbands, or of driving them to paths that they are naturally inclined to. It often is such women who prefer to undergo the dangers of abortion. Besides these, there are other women, especially in the higher walks of life, who, in order to conceal a "slip," or out of aversion for the inconveniences of pregnancy, of child-birth and of nursing, perhaps, out of fear of sooner losing their charms, and then forfeiting their standing with either husband or male friends, incur such criminal acts, and, for hard cash, find ready medical and midwife support.

To conclude from diverse indications, artificial abortion is coming ever more into practice; nor is the practice new. Artificial abortion was in frequent use among the ancient peoples, and is, to this day, from the most civilized down to the barbarous. According to Jules Roget,[23] the women of Rome took recourse to abortion for several reasons: They either sought to destroy the evidence of illicit relations—a reason that even to-day is often at its bottom; or they wished to be able to indulge their excesses without interruption. There were also other reasons: they wished to avoid the changes that pregnancy and child-birth work upon woman's physique. Among the Romans, a woman was old from twenty-five years to thirty. Accordingly, she sought to avoid all that might impair her charms. In the Middle Ages, abortion was punishable with severe bodily chastisement, often even with death; the free woman, guilty thereof, became a serf. At present, abortion is especially in use in the United States. In all large cities of the Union, there are institutions in which girls and women are prematurely delivered: many American papers contain the advertisements of such places: abortion is talked of there almost as freely as of a regular birth. In Germany and Europe, opinion on the subject is different: the German criminal code, for instance, makes the act of both the principal and the accessory a penitentiary offense.[24]

Abortion is, in many cases, accompanied by the most serious results. The operation is dangerous; death not infrequently occurs; often the result is a permanent impairment of health. "The troubles of troublesome pregnancy and child-birth are infinitely less than the sufferings

---

[23] "Etudes Medicales sur l'Ancienne Rome," Paris, 1859.

[24] The above account of the United States, concerning the contrast between it and Europe, is incorrect. At the time in the nation's history when material conditions were easy, theoretically, the thought of abortion, let alone its execution, could not spring up; and it did not. All the reports of that time, not forgetting Washington Irving's humorous account of the custom of "bundling," confirm the fact. Births were numerous, families large.

Subsequently, when conditions became less easy, and in the measure that the country entered increasingly into the sphere of the material hardships implied in advancing capitalism, theoretically, again, the thought of abortion, and, along with it, the deed, must be expected to have sprung up; and so they did. But the same development that carried the country into the material sphere of capitalism, also, and at the same time, carried its people into the sphere of capitalist affectation of morality and measuredness of language; in short, of hypocrisy. The being, that will commit the crimes of a higher civilization with the plain-spokenness of the barbarian, is a monstrosity. Capitalist United States is abreast of, and moves in even step with, capitalist Europe, not in the practice only of crime, but in the pharisaism of its condemnation and the severity of its punishment also.—THE TRANSLATOR.

consequent upon artificial abortion."[25] Barrenness is one of its most common consequences. All that, notwithstanding, abortion is practiced also in Germany, ever more frequently, and for the reasons given. Between 1882-1888, the number of cases in Berlin, of which the criminal courts took cognizance, rose 155 per cent. The *chronique scandaleuse* of the last years dealt frequently with cases of abortion, that caused great sensation, due to the circumstance that reputable physicians and women, prominent in society, played a *role* in them. Furthermore, to judge from the rising number of announcements in our newspapers, the institutions and places increase in which married and unmarried women of the property class are offered an opportunity to await the results of a "slip" in perfect secrecy.

The dread of a large increase of children—due to the smallness of means, and the cost of bringing up—has, among all classes and even peoples, developed the use of preventatives into a system, that here and yonder has grown into a public calamity. It is a generally known fact that, in all strata of French society, the "two-child system" is in force. In few countries of civilization are marriages relatively as numerous as in France, and in no country is the average number of children so small, and the increase of population so slow. The French capitalist, like the small-holder and allotment peasant, pursues the system; the French workingman follows suit. In many sections of Germany the special situation of the peasants seem to have led to similar conditions. We know a charming region in Southwest Germany, where, in the garden of every peasant, there stands the so-called "Sevenbaum," whose properties are applied to abortive purposes: In another district of the same country the regular two-child system prevails among the peasants: they do not wish to divide the places. Moreover, striking is the measure in which literature, that treats with and recommends the means of "facultative sterility," increases in Germany both in volume and demand,—of course, always under the colors of science, and in allusion to the alleged threatening danger of over-population.

Along with abortion and the artificial prevention of conception, crime plays its *role*. In France, the murder of children and their exposure is perceptibly on the increase, both promoted by the provision of the French civil code that forbids all inquiry after the paternity of the child. Section 340 of the *Code Civil* decrees: *"La recherche de la paternite est interdite;"* on the other hand, Section 314 provides: *"La recherche de la maternite est admise."* To inquire after the paternity of a child is forbidden, but is allowed after its maternity,—a law that glaringly brings out the injustice contemplated towards the seduced woman. The men of France are free to seduce as many women and

[25] "Geschichte und Gefahren der Fruchtabtreibung," Dr. Ed. Reich, Leipsic, 1893.

girls as they are able to; they are free from all responsibility; they owe no support to the child. These provisions were instituted under the pretext that the female sex should be frightened against seducing the men. As you see, everywhere it is the weak man, this limb of the stronger sex, who is seduced, but never seduces. The result of Section 340 of the *Code Civil* was Section 312, which provides: "*L'enfant conçupendant le marriage a pour pere le mari.*"[26] Inquiry after the paternity being forbidden, it is logical that the husband, crowned with horns, rest content with having the child, that his wife received from another, considered his own. Inconsistency, at any rate, can not be charged to the French capitalist class. All attempts to amend Section 340 have so far failed. Lately, February, 1895, the Socialist deputies in the French Chamber of Deputies presented a bill intended to put an end to the disfranchised position of the seduced or betrayed woman. Whether the attempt will be crowned with success is doubtful.

On the other hand, the French capitalist class—sensible of the cruelty it committed in so framing the law as to make it impossible for the deceived woman to turn for support to the father of her child—sought to make up for its sins by establishing foundling asylums. According to our famous "morals," there is no paternal feeling towards the illegitimate child; that exists only for "legitimate heirs." Through the foundlings' asylums the mother also is taken from the new-born child. According to the French fiction, foundlings are orphans. In this way, the French capitalist class has its illegitimate children brought up, *at the expense of the State,* as "children of the fatherland." A charming arrangement. In Germany, things bid fair to be switched on the French track. The provisions in the bill for a civil code for the German Empire contain maxims on the legal status of illegitimate children, strongly in contrast with the humane law still in force.

According to the bill, a dishonored girl—even if blameless, or seduced with the promise of subsequent marriage, or induced to consent to coition through some criminal act—has no claim against the seducer except as indemnity for the costs of delivery, and for support during the first six weeks after the birth of the child, and then only within the bounds of what is strictly necessary. Only in some of the cases of the worst crimes against morality, can a slight money indemnity be granted to the seduced girl, at the discretion of the court, and without the necessity of proving actual damages. The illegitimate child has no claim upon the seducer of his mother, except for the merest necessaries of life, and then only until its fourteenth year. All claims of the child on its father are, however, barred if, within pregnancy, any other man cohabit with its mother. The plaintiff child has, moreover, to prove that its mother has not accepted the embraces of any other man.

[26] "The child conceived during marriage has the husband for father."

Menger, the expositions in whose treatise[27] we here follow, justly raises against the bill the serious charge that it only accrues to the advantage of the well-to-do, immoral men, seducers of ignorant girls, often girls who sin through poverty, but leaves these fallen girls, together with their wholly guiltless children, entirely unprotected, aye, pushes them only deeper into misery and crime. Menger cites, in this connection, the provisions of the Prussian law. According thereto, an unmarried woman or widow of good character, who is made pregnant, is to be indemnified by the man according to his means. The indemnity shall, however, not exceed one-fourth of his property. An illegitimate child has a claim upon its father for support and education, regardless of whether his mother is a person of good character: the expenditure, however, shall be no higher than the education of a legitimate child would cost to·people of the peasant or of ordinary citizen walks of life. If the illicit intercourse occurred under promise of future marriage, then, according to the further provisions of Prussian law, the Judge is duly to award the woman, pronounced innocent and a wife, the name, standing and rank of the man, together with all the rights of a divorced woman. The illegitimate child has, in such cases, all the rights of children born in wedlock. We may await with curiosity to see whether the provisions of this bill, so hostile to woman, will acquire the force of a civil code of law in Germany. But retrogression is the key-note in our legislation.

Between the years of 1830-1880, there were 8,563 cases of infanticide before the French court of assizes, the figures rising from 471 in 1831, to 980 in 1880. During the same period, 1,032 cases of abortion were tried, 41 in 1831, and in 1880 over 100. Of course, only a small part of the abortions came to the knowledge of the criminal court; as a rule, only when followed by serious illness or death. In the cases of infanticide, the country population contributed 75 per cent., in the cases of abortion the cities 65 per cent. In the city, the women have more means at command to prevent normal birth; hence, the many cases of abortion and the small number of infanticides. It is the reverse in the country.

Such is the composition of the picture presented by modern society in respect to its most intimate relations. The picture differs wide from that that poets and poetically doused phantasts love to paint it. Our picture, however, has this advantage,—it is true. And yet the picture still calls for several strokes of the brush to bring out its character in full.

In general, there can be no difference of opinion touching the present and average mental inferiority of the female sex to the male. True enough, Balzac, by no means a woman-lover, claims: "The woman, who has received a male education, possesses in fact the most brilliant and

[27] "Das buergerliche Recht und die besitzlosen Klassen," Tuebingen, 1890.

fruitful qualities for the building of her own happiness and that of her husband;" and Goethe, who knew well both the men and women of his times, expresses himself in Wilhelm Meister's Apprenticeship (confessions of a pure soul): "Learned women were ridiculed, and also the educated ones were disliked, probably because it was considered impolite to put so many ignorant men to shame." We agree with both. Nevertheless, the fact is no wise altered that, in general, women stand intellectually behind the men. This difference is compulsory, because *woman is that which man, as her master, has made her*. The education of woman, more so than that of the working class, has been neglected since time immemorial; nor are latter-day improvements adequate. We live in days when the aspiration after exchange of thought grows in all circles, in the family also; and there the neglected education of woman is felt as a serious fault, and it avenges itself upon the husband.

The object of the education of man—at least it is so claimed, although due to the mistaken methods, the object is often missed, perchance, also, is not meant to be reached—aims at the development of the intellect, the sharpening of the powers of thought, the broadening of the field of practical knowledge, and the invigoration of the will-power, in short, at the cultivation of the functions of the mind. With woman, on the contrary, education, so far as at all attended to in a higher degree, is mainly aimed at the intensification of her feelings, at formality and polite culture—music, belles-lettres, art, poetry—all of which only screw her nervous sensitiveness and phantasy up to a higher pitch. This is a mistaken and unhealthy policy. In it the fact transpires that the powers, which determine the measure of woman's education, are guided only by their ingrained prejudices regarding the nature of the female character, and also by the cramped position of woman. The object must not be to develop still further the sentimental and imaginative side of woman, which would only tend to heighten her natural inclination to nervousness; neither should her education be limited to etiquette and polite literature. The object, with regard to her as to man, should be to develop their intellectual activity and acquaint them with the phenomena of practical life. It would be of greatest benefit to both sexes if, in lieu of a superfluity of sentiment, that often becomes positively uncanny, woman possessed a good share of sharpened wit and power for exact reasoning; if, in lieu of excessive nervous excitation and timidity, she possessed firmness of character and physical courage; in lieu of conventional, literary refinement, in so far as she at all has any, she had a knowledge of the world, of men and of the powers of Nature.

Generally speaking, what is termed the feeling and spirituality of woman has hitherto been nurtured without stint, while her intellectual development has, on the contrary, been grossly neglected and kept under.

As a consequence, she suffers of hypertrophy of feeling and spirituality, hence is prone to superstition and miracles,—a more than grateful soil for religious and other charlataneries, a pliant tool for all reaction. Blockish men often complain when she is thus affected, but they bring no relief, because often they are themselves steeped up to the ears in prejudices.

By reason of woman's being almost generally as here sketched, she looks upon the world differently from man. Hence, again, a strong source of contrariety between the two sexes.

Participation in public life is to-day one of the most essential duties of a man; that many men do not yet understand this does not alter the fact. Nevertheless, the number of those is ever increasing who realize that public institutions stand in intimate connection with the private lot of the individual; that his success or failure, together with that of his family, depend infinitely more upon the condition of public affairs than upon his own personal qualities and actions. The fact is beginning to receive recognition that the greatest efforts of the individual are powerless against evils that lie in the very condition of things, and that determine his state. On the other hand, the struggle for existence now requires much greater efforts than before. Demands are now made upon man that engage ever more his time and strength. The ignorant, indifferent wife stands dumb before him, and feels herself neglected. It may be even said that, the mental difference between man and woman is to-day greater than formerly, when the opportunities for both were slight and limited, and lay more within the reach of her restricted intellect. Furthermore, the handling of public affairs occupies to-day a large number of men to a degree before unknown; this widens their horizon; but it also withdraws them ever more from the mental sphere of their homes. The wife deems herself set back, and thus another source of friction is started. Only rarely does the husband know how to pacify his wife and convince her. When he does that, he has escaped a dangerous rock. As a rule the husband is of the opinion that what he wants does not concern his wife, she does not understand it. He takes no pains to enlighten her. "You don't understand such matters," is his stereotyped answer, the moment the wife complains that she is neglected. Lack of information on the part of wives is promoted by lack of sense on the part of most husbands. More favorable relations between husband and wife spring up in the rank of the working class in the measure that both realize they are tugging at the same rope, and that there is but one means towards satisfactory conditions for themselves and their family,—the radical reformation of society that shall make human beings of them all. In the measure that such insight gains ground among the wives of the proletariat, then, despite want and misery, their married life is *idealized*: both now have a common aim, after which they strive; and they have an inexhaustible source of mutual encouragement in the mutual interchange of views, whereto their joint battle leads them. The number of proletarian women who reach this insight is every year larger. Herein lies a movement, that is in process of development, and that is fraught with decisive significance for the future of mankind.

In other social strata, the differences in education and views—easily overlooked at the beginning of married life, when passion still predominates—are felt ever more with ripening years. Sexual passion cools off, and its substitution with harmony of thought is all the more needful. But, leaving aside whether the husband has any idea of civic duties and attends to the same, he, at any rate, thanks to his occupation and constant intercourse with the outer world, comes into continuous touch with different elements and opinions, on all sorts of occasions, and thus floats into an intellectual atmosphere that broadens his horizon. As a rule, and in contrast with his wife, he finds himself in a state of intellectual molting, while she, on the contrary, due to her household duties, which engage her early and late, is robbed of leisure for further education, and, accordingly, becomes mentally stunted and soured.

The domestic wretchedness in which the majority of wives live today, is correctly depicted by the bourgeois-minded Gerhard von Amyntor in his "Marginal Notes to the Book of Life."[23] In the chapter entitled "Deadly Gnat-bites" he says among other things:

"Not the shocking events, that none remain unvisited by, and that bring, here the death of a husband, yonder the moral downfall of a beloved child; that lie, here in a long and serious illness, yonder in the wrecking of a warmly nursed plan;—not these undermine her (the housewife's) freshness and strength. It is the small, daily-recurring marrow and bone-gnawing cares. . . . How many millions of brave little house-mothers cook and scour away their vigor of life, their very cheeks and roguish dimples, in attending to domestic cares until they become crumpled, dried and broke-up mummies. The ever-recurring question, what shall be cooked to-day? the ever-recurring necessity of sweeping, and beating, and brushing, and dusting is the continuously falling drop that slowly, but surely, wears away mind and body. The kitchen-hearth is the place where the saddest balances are drawn up between income and expense, where the most depressing observations are forced upon the mind on the rising dearness of the necessaries of life, and on the ever increasing difficulty to earn the needed cash. On the flaming altar, where the soup kettle bubbles, youth and mental ease, beauty and good humor are sacrificed; and who recognizes in the old care-bent

[23] Sam. Lucas, Elberfeld.

cook, the one-time blooming, overbearing, coy-coquette bride in the array of her myrtle crown? Already in antiquity the hearth was sacred, near it were placed the Lares and patron dieties. Let us also hold sacred the hearth at which the dutiful German bourgeois house-wife dies a slow death, in order to keep the house comfortable, the table covered and the family in health." Such is the consolation offered in bourgeois society to the wife, who, under the present order of society, is miserably going to pieces.

Those women, who, thanks to their social condition, find themselves in a freer state, have, as a rule, a one-sided, superficial education, that, combined with inherited female characteristics, manifests itself with force. They generally have a taste for mere superficialities; they think only about gew-gaws and dress; and thus they seek their mission in the satisfaction of a spoiled taste, and the indulgence of passions that demand their pay with usury. In their children and the education of these they have hardly any interest: they give them too much trouble and annoyance, hence are left to the nurses and servants, and are later passed on to the boarding-schools. At any rate their principal task is to raise their daughters as show-dolls, and their sons as pupils for the *jeunesse dore* (gilded youth) out of which dudedom recruits its ranks—that despicable class of men that may be fairly put upon a level with procurers. This *jeunesse dore* furnishes the chief contingent to the seducers of the daughters of the working class. They look upon idleness and squandering as a profession.

CHAPTER II.

Cast in the mold of the conditions above described, many a feature of woman's character took shape, and they reached ever fuller development from generation to generation. Of these features men love to dwell with predeliction, but they forget that they are themselves the cause thereof, and have promoted with their conduct the defects they now make merry about, or censure. Among these widely censured female qualities, belong her dreaded readiness of tongue, and passion for gossip; her inclination to endless talk over trifles and unimportant things; her mental bent for purely external matters, such as dress, and her desire to please, together with a resulting proneness to all the follies of fashion; lastly, her easily arousable envy and jealousy of the other members of her sex.

These qualities, though in different degrees, manifest themselves generally in the female sex from early childhood. They are qualities that are born under the pressure of social conditions, and are further developed by heredity, example and education. A being irrationally brought up, can not bring up others rationally.

In order to be clear on the causes and development of good or bad qualities, whether with the sexes or with whole peoples, the same methods must be pursued that modern natural science applies in order to ascertain the formation and development of life according to genus and species, and to determine their qualities. They are the laws that flow from the material conditions for life, laws that life demands, that adapt themselves to it, and finally became its nature.

Man forms no exception to that which holds good in Nature for all animate creation. Man does not stand outside of Nature: looked at physiologically, he is the most highly developed animal,—a fact, however, that some would deny. Thousands of years ago, although wholly ignorant of modern science, the ancients had on many matters affecting man, more rational views than the moderns; above all, they gave practical application to the views founded on experience. We praise with enthusiastic admiration the beauty and strength of the men and women of Greece; but the fact is overlooked that, not the happy climate, nor the bewitching nature of a territory that stretched along the bay-indented sea, but the physical culture and maxims of education, consistently enforced by the State, thus affected both the being and the development of the population. These measures were calculated to combine beauty, strength and suppleness of body with wit and elasticity of mind, both of which were transmitted to the descendants. True enough, even then, in comparison with man, woman was neglected in point of mental, but not of corporal culture.[1] In Sparta, that went furthest in the corporal culture of the two sexes, boys and girls went naked until the age of puberty, and participated in common in the exercises of the body, in games and in wrestling. The naked exposure of the human body, together with the natural treatment of natural things, had the advantage that sensuous excitement—to-day artificially cultivated by the separation of the sexes from early childhood—was then prevented. The corporal make-up of one sex, together with its distinctive organs, was no secret to the other. There, no play of equivocal words could arise. Nature was Nature. The one sex rejoiced at the beauty of the other. Mankind will have to return to Nature and to the natural intercourse of the sexes; it must cast off the now-ruling and unhealthy spiritual notions concerning man; it must do that by setting up methods of education that fit in with our own state of culture, and that may bring on the physical and mental regeneration of the race.

Among us, and especially on the subject of female education, seriously erroneous conceptions are still prevalent. That woman also should have strength, courage and resolution, is considered heretical, "unwomanly," although none would dare deny that, equipped with such qualities, woman could protect herself against many ills and inconveniences. Conversely, woman is cramped in her physical, exactly as in her intellectual development. The irrationalness of her dress plays an important *role* herein. It not only, unconscionably hampers her in her physique, it directly ruins her;—and yet, but few physicians dare take a stand against the abuse, accurately informed though they are on the injuriousness of her dress. The fear of displeasing the patient often causes them to hold their tongues, if they do not even flatter her insane notions. Modern dress hinders woman in the free use of her limbs, it injures her physical growth, and awakens in her a sense of impotence and weakness. Moreover, modern dress is a positive danger to her own and the health of those who surround her: in the house and on the street, woman is a walking raiser of dust. And likewise is the development of woman hampered by the strict separation of the sexes,

[1] Plato requires in his "Republic" that "the women be educated like the men," and he demands careful selection in breeding. He, accordingly, was thoroughly familiar with the effect of a careful selection on the development of man. Aristotle lays it down as a maxim of education that "First the body, then the mind must be built up," Aristotle's "Politics." With us, when thought is at all bestowed upon the matter, the body, the scaffolding for the intellect, is considered last.

both in social intercourse and at school—a method of education wholly in keeping with the spiritual ideas that Christianity has deeply implanted in us on all matters that regard the nature of man.

The woman who does not reach the development of her faculties, who is crippled in her powers, who is held imprisoned in the narrowest circle of thought, and who comes into contact with hardly any but her own female relatives,—such a woman can not possibly raise herself above the routine of daily life and habits. Her intellectual horizon revolves only around the happenings in her own immediate surroundings, family affairs and what thereby hangs. Extensive conversations on utter trifles, the bent for gossip, are promoted with all might; of course her latent intellectual qualities strain after activity and exercise;— whereupon the husband, often involved thereby in trouble, and driven to desperation, utters imprecations upon qualities that he, the "chief of creation," has mainly upon his own conscience.

With woman—whose face all our social and sexual relations turn toward marriage with every fibre of her being—marriage and matrimonial matters constitute, quite naturally, a leading portion of her conversation and aspirations. Moreover, to the physically weaker woman, subjected as she is to man by custom and laws, the tongue is her principal weapon against him, and, as a matter of course, she makes use thereof. Similarly with regard to her severely censured passion for dress and desire to please, which reach their frightful acme in the insanities of fashion, and often throw fathers and husbands into great straits and embarrassments. The explanation lies at hand. To man, woman is, first of all, an object of enjoyment. Economically and socially unfree, she is bound to see in marriage her means of support; accordingly, she depends upon man and becomes a piece of property to him. As a rule, her position is rendered still more unfavorable through the general excess of women over men,—a subject that will be treated more closely. The disparity intensifies the competition of women among themselves; and it is sharpened still more because, for a great variety of reasons, a number of men do not marry at all. Woman is, accordingly, forced to enter into competition for a husband with the members of her own sex, by means of the most favorable external presentation of her person possible.

Let the long duration, through many generations, of these evils be taken into account. The wonder will cease that these manifestations, sprung from equally lasting causes, have reached their present extreme form. Furthermore, perhaps in no age was the competition of women for husbands as sharp as it is in this, due partly to reasons already given, and partly to others yet to be discussed. Finally, the difficulties of obtaining a competent livelihood, as well as the demands made by society, combine, more than ever before, to turn woman's face towards matrimony as an "institute for support."

Men gladly accept such a state of things: they are its beneficiaries. It flatters their pride, their vanity, their interest to play the *role* of the stronger and the master; and, like all other rulers, they are, in their *role* of masters, difficult to reach by reason. It is, therefore, all the more in the interest of woman to warm towards the establishment of conditions that shall free her from so unworthy a position. Women should expect as little help from the men as workingmen do from the capitalist class.

Observe the characteristics, developed in the struggle for the coveted place, on other fields, on the industrial field, for instance, so soon as the capitalists face each other. What despicable, even scampish, means of warfare are not resorted to! What hatred, envy and passion for calumny are not awakened!—observe that, and the explanation stands out why similar features turn up in the competition of women for a husband. Hence it happens that women, on the average, do not get along among themselves as well as men; that even the best female friends lightly fall out, if the question is their standing in a man's eye, or pleasingness of appearance. Hence also the observation that wherever women meet, be they ever such utter strangers, they usually look at one another as enemies. With one look they make the mutual discovery of ill-matched colors, or wrongly-pinned bows, or any other similar cardinal sin. In the look that they greet each other with, the judgment can be readily read that each has passed upon the other. It is as if each wished to inform the other: "I know better than you how to dress, and draw attention upon myself."

On the other hand, woman is by nature more impulsive than man; she reflects less than he; she has more abnegation, is naiver, and hence is governed by stronger passions, as revealed by the truly heroic self-sacrifice with which she protects her child, or cares for relatives, and nurses them in sickness. In the fury, however, this passionateness finds its ugly expression. But the good as well as the bad sides, with man as well as woman, are influenced, first of all, by their social position; favored, or checked, or transfigured. The same impulse, that, under unfavorable circumstances, appears as a blemish, is, under favorable circumstances, a source of happiness for oneself and others. Fourier has the credit of having brilliantly demonstrated how the identical impulses of man produce, under different conditions, wholly opposite results.

Running parallel with the effects of mistaken education, are the no less serious effects of mistaken or imperfect physical culture upon the purpose of Nature. All physicians are agreed that the preparation of woman for her calling as mother and rearer of children leaves almost everything to be wished. "Man exercises the soldier in the use of his weapons, and the artisan in the handling of his tools; every office requires special studies; even the monk has his novitiate. Woman alone is not trained for her serious duties of mother."[2] Nine-tenths of the maidens who marry enter matrimony with almost utter ignorance about motherhood and the duties of wedlock. The inexcusable shyness, even on the part of mothers, to speak with a grown-up daughter of such important sexual duties, leaves the latter in the greatest darkness touching her duties towards herself and her future husband. With her entrance upon married life, woman enters a territory that is wholly strange to her. She has drawn to herself a fancy-picture thereof— generally from novels that are not particularly to be commended—that does not accord with reality.[3] Her defective household knowledge, that, as things are to-day, is inevitable, even though many a function, formerly naturally belonging to the wife, has been removed from her, also furnishes many a cause for friction. Some know nothing whatever of household matters: They consider themselves too good to bother about them, and look upon them as matters that concern the servant girl; numerous others, from the ranks of the masses, are prevented, by the struggle for existence, from cultivating themselves for their calling as householders: they must be in the factory and at work early and late. It is becoming evident that, due to the development of social conditions, the separate household system is losing ground every day; and that it can be kept up only at the sacrifice of money and time, neither of which the great majority is able to expend.

Yet another cause that destroys the object of marriage to not a few men is to be found in the physical debility of many women. Our food, housing, methods of work and support, in short, our whole form of life, affects us in more ways than one rather harmfully than otherwise. We can speak with perfect right of a "nervous age." Now, then, this nervousness goes hand in hand with physical degeneration. Anaemia and nervousness are spread to an enormous degree among the female sex: They are assuming the aspect of a social calamity, that, if it

[2] "Die Mission unseres Jahrhunderts. Eine Studie zur Frauenfrage," Irma v. Troll-Borostyani; Pressburg and Leipsic.

[3] In "Les Femmes Qui Tuent et les Femmes Qui Votent," Alexander Dumas, son, narrates: "A Catholic clergyman of high standing stated in the course of a conversation that, out of a hundred of his former female pupils, who married, after a month at least eighty came to him and said they were disillusioned and regretted having married." This sounds very probable. The Voltarian French bourgeoisie reconcile it with their conscience to allow their daughters to be educated in the cloisters. They proceed from the premises that an ignorant woman is more easy to lead than one who is posted. Conflicts and disappointment are inevitable. Laboulaye gives the flat-footed advice to keep woman in moderate ignorance, because "notre empire est detruit, si l'homine est reconnu" (our empire is over if the man is found out).

continue a few generations longer, as at present, and we fail to place our social organization on a normal footing, is urging the race towards its destruction.[4]

With an eye to its sexual mission, the female organism requires particular care,—good food, and, at certain periods, the requisite rest. Both of these are lacking to the great majority of the female sex, at least in the cities and industrial neighborhoods, nor are they to be had under modern industrial conditions. Moreover, woman has so habituated herself to privation that, for instance, numberless women hold it a conjugal duty to keep the tid-bits for the man, and satisfy themselves with insufficient nourishment. Likewise are boys frequently given the preference over girls in matters of food. The opinion is general that woman can accommodate herself, not with less food only, but also with food of poorer quality. Hence the sad picture that our female youth, in particular, presents to the eyes of the expert. A large portion of our young women are bodily weak, anaemic, hypernervous. The consequences are difficulties in menstruation, and disease of the organs connected with the sexual purpose, the disease often assuming the magnitude of incapacity to give birth and to nurse the child, even of danger to life itself. "Should this degeneration of our women continue to increase in the same measure as before, the time may not be far away when it will become doubtful whether man is to be counted among the mammals or not."[5] Instead of a healthy, joyful companion, of a capable mother, of a wife attentive to her household duties, the husband has on his hands a sick, nervous wife, whose house the physician never quits, who can stand no draft, and can not bear the least noise. We shall not expatiate further on this subject. Every reader—and as often as in this book we speak of "reader," we mean, of course, the female as well as the male—can himself further fill the picture: he has illustrations enough among his own relatives and acquaintances.

Experienced physicians maintain that the larger part of married women, in the cities especially, are in a more or less abnormal condition. According to the degree of the evil and the character of the couple, such unions can not choose but be unhappy, and, they give the husband the right, in public opinion, to allow himself freedoms outside of the mar-

---

[4] According to observations made in the psychiatric clinic at Vienna, paralysis (softening of the brain) is making by far greater progress among women than among men. To 100 patients taken in, there were in the years:
  1873-77 : 15.7 male and 4.4 female paralytics.
  1888-92 : 19.7 male and 10.0 female paralytics.
During the sixties there was, on the average, 1 female paralytic to 8 males; now there is 1 female paralytic to 3.49 males in Denmark, to 3.22 in middle and upper Italy, 2.89 in England, 2.77 in Belgium, and 2.40 in France.—"Wiener Arbeiter Zeitung," January 31, 1895.

[5] Dr. F. B. Simon: "Die Gesundheitspflege des Weibes," Stuttgart, 1893, F. J. Dietz.

riage bed, the knowledge of which throws the wife into the most wretched of moods. Furthermore the, at times, very different sexual demands of one party or the other give occasion to serious friction, without the so much wished-for separation being possible. A great variety of considerations render that, in most cases, out of all question.

Under this head the fact may not be suppressed that a *considerable number of husbands are themselves responsible for certain serious physical ailments of their wives, ailments that these are not infrequently smitten with in marriage.* As consequences of the excesses indulged in during bachelorship, a considerable number of men suffer of chronic séxual diseases, which, seeing these cause them no serious inconvenience, are taken lightly. Nevertheless, through sexual intercourse with the wife, these diseases bring upon her disagreeable, even fatal troubles of the womb, that set in, soon after marriage, and often develop to the point of rendering her unable to conceive or to give birth. The wretched woman usually has no idea of the cause of the sickness, that depresses her spirits, embitters her life, and uproots the purpose of marriage. She blames herself, and accepts blame for a condition, that the other party is alone responsible for. Thus many a blooming wife falls, barely married, a prey to chronic malady, unaccountable to either herself or her family.

"As recent investigations have proved, this circumstance—that, as a result of gonorrhea, the male sperm no longer contains any seed-cells, and the man is, consequently, incapacitated for life from begetting children—*is a comparatively frequent cause of matrimonial barrenness, in contradiction to the old and convenient tradition of the lords of creation, who are ever ready to shift to the shoulder of the wife the responsibility for the absence of the blessing of children.*"[6]

Accordingly, a large number of causes are operative in preventing modern married life, in the large majority of instances, from being that which it should be:—a union of two beings of opposite sexes, who, out of mutual love and esteem, wish to belong to each other, and, in the striking sentence of Kant, mean, jointly, to constitute the complete human being. It is, therefore, a suggestion of doubtful value—made even by learned folks, who imagine thereby to dispose of woman's endeavors after emancipation—that she look to domestic duties, to marriage,—to marriage, that our economic conditions are ever turning into a viler caricature, and that answers its purpose ever less!

The advice to woman that she seek her salvation in marriage, this being her real calling,—an advice that is thoughtlessly applauded by the majority of men—sounds like the merest mockery, when both the advisers and their *claqueuers* do the opposite. Schopenhauer, the phil-

[6] Dr. F. B. Simon. Simon devotes extensive consideration to this theme, together with that akin thereto,—why so many married women take sick shortly after marriage without knowing why; and he holds up the mirror to the men.

osopher, has of woman only the conception of the philistine. He says: "Woman is not meant for much work. Her characteristicon is not action but *suffering*. She pays the debt of life with the pains of travail, anxiety for the child, *subjection to man*. The strongest utterances of life and sentiment are denied her. Her life is meant to be quieter and less important than man's. Woman is destined for nurse and educator of infancy, *being herself infant-like, and an infant for life*, a sort of intermediate stage between the child and the man, *who is the real being . . .* Girls should be trained for domesticity and *subjection. . . Women are the most thorough-paced and incurable Philistines.*"

In the same spirit as Schopenhauer, who, of course, is greatly quoted, is cast Lombroso and Ferrerro's work, "Woman as a Criminal and a Prostitute." We know no scientific work of equal size—it contains 590 pages—with such a dearth of valid evidence on the theme therein treated. The statistical matter, from which the bold conclusions are drawn, is mostly meager. Often a dozen instances suffice the joint authors to draw the weightiest deductions. The matter that may be considered the most valuable in the work is, typically enough, furnished by a woman,—Dr. Tarnowskaja. The influence of social conditions, of cultural development, is left almost wholly on one side. Everything is judged exclusively from the physiologico-psychologic view-point, while a large quantity of ethnographic items of information on various peoples is woven into the argument, without submitting these items to closer scrutiny. According to the authors, just as with Schopenhauer, woman is a grown child, a liar *par excellence*, weak of judgment, fickle in love, incapable of any deed truly heroic. They claim the inferiority of woman to man is manifest from a large number of bodily differences. "Love, with woman, is as a rule nothing but a secondary feature of maternity,—all the feelings of attachment that bind woman to man arise, not from sexual impulses, but from the instincts of subjection and resignation, acquired through habits of conformancy." How these "instincts" were acquired and "conformed" themselves, the joint authors fail to inquire into. They would then have had to inquire into the social position of woman in the course of thousands of years, and would have been compelled to find that it is that that made her what she now is. It is true, the joint authors describe partly the enslaved and dependent position of woman among the several peoples and under the several periods of civilization; but as Darwinians, with blinkers to their eyes, they draw all that from physiologic and psychologic, not from social and economic reasons, which affected in strongest manner the physiologic and psychologic development of woman.

The joint authors also touch upon the vanity of woman, and set up the opinion that, among the peoples who stand on a lower stage of civilization, man is the vain sex, as is noticeable to-day in the New Hebrides and Madagascar, among the peoples of the Orinoco, and on many islands of the Polynesian archipelago, as also among a number of African peoples of the South Sea. With peoples standing on a higher plane, however, woman is the vain sex. But why and wherefor? To us the answer seems plain. Among the peoples of a lower civilization, mother-right conditions prevail generally, or have not yet been long overcome. The *role* that woman there plays raises her above the necessity of seeking for the man, the man seeks her, and to this end, ornaments himself and grows vain. With the people of a higher grade, especially with all the nations of civilization, excepting here and there, not the man seeks the woman, but the woman him. It happens rarely that a woman openly takes the initiative, and offers herself to the man; so-called propriety forbids that. In point of fact, however, the offering is done by the manner of her appearance; by means of the beauty of dress and luxury, that she displays; by the manner in which she ornaments herself, and presents herself, and coquets in society. The excess of women, together with the social necessity of looking upon matrimony as an institute for support, or as an institution through which alone she can satisfy her sexual impulse and gain a standing in society, forces such conduct upon her. Here also, we notice again, it is purely economic and social causes that call forth, one time with man, another with woman, a quality that, until now, it was customary to look upon as wholly independent of social and economic causes. Hence the conclusion is justified, that so soon as society shall arrive at social conditions, under which all dependence of one sex upon another shall have ceased, and both are equally free, *ridiculous vanity and the folly of fashion will vanish, just as so many other vices that we consider to-day uneradicable, as supposedly inherent in man.* Schopenhauer, as a philosopher, judges woman as one-sidedly as most of our anthropologists and physicians, who see in her only the sexual, never the social, being. Schopenhauer was never married. He, accordingly, has not, on his part, contributed towards having one more woman pay the "debt of life" that he debits woman with. And this brings us to the other side of the medal, which is far from being the handsomer.

Many women do not marry, simply because they cannot. Everybody knows that usage forbids woman to offer herself. She must allow herself to be wooed, i. e., chosen. She herself may not woo. Is there no wooer to be had, then she enters the large army of those poor beings who have missed the purpose of life, and, in view of the lack of safe material foundation, generally fall a prey to want and misery, and but too often to ridicule also. But few know what the discrepancy in numbers between the two sexes is due to; many are ready with the hasty answer: "There are too many girls born." Those who make the claim are

wrongly informed, as will be shown. Others, again, who admit the unnaturalness of celibacy, conclude from the fact that women are more numerous than men in most countries of civilization, that polygamy should
be allowed. But not only does polygamy do violence to our customs,
it, moreover, degrades woman, a circumstance that, of course, does not
restrain Schopenhauer, with his underestimation of and contempt for
women, from declaring: "For the female sex, as a whole, polygamy is
a benefit."

Many men do not marry because they think they cannot support a
wife, and the children that may come, according to their station. To
support *two* wives is, however, possible to a small minority only, and
among these are many who now have two or more wives,—one legitimate and several illegitimate. These few, privileged by wealth, are not
held back by anything from doing what they please. Even in the Orient,
where polygamy exists for thousands of years by law and custom, comparatively few men have more than one wife. People talk of the demoralizing influence of Turkish harem life; but the fact is overlooked
that this harem life is possible only to an insignificant fraction of the
men, and then only in the ruling class, while the majority of the men
live in monogamy. In the city of Algiers, there were, at the close of the
sixties, out of 18,282 marriages, not less than 17,319 with one wife only;
888 were with two; and only 75 with more than two. Constantinople,
the capital of the Turkish Empire, would show no materially different
result. Among the country population in the Orient, the proportion is
still more pronouncedly in favor of single marriages. In the Orient, exactly as with us, the most important factor in the calculation are the
material conditions, and these compel most men to limit themselves to
but one wife. If, on the other hand, material conditions were equally
favorable to all men, polygamy would still not be practicable,—for want
of women. *The almost equal number of the two sexes, prevalent under
normal conditions, points everywhere to monogamy.*

As proof of these statements, we cite the following tables, that Buecher
published in an essay.[7]

In these tables the distinction must be kept in mind between the
enumerated and the estimated populations. In so far as the population
was enumerated, the fact is expressly stated in the summary for the
separate main divisions of the earth. The sexes divide themselves in the
population of several divisions and countries as follows:

---

[7] Karl Buecher: "Ueber die Vertheilung der beiden Geschlechter auf der
Erde," "Allgemeines Statistisches Archiv," Tuebingen, 1892.

1. EUROPE.

Countries.	Census Year.	Males.	Females.	Population.	Females for Every 1,000 Men.
Great Britain and Ireland	1891	18,388,756	19,499,397	37,888,153	1,060
Denmark and Faror..	1890	1,065,447	1,119,712	2,185,159	1,052
Norway	1891	951,496	1,037,501	1,988,997	1,090
Sweden	1890	2,317,105	2,467,570	4,784,675	1,065
Finland	1889	1,152,111	1,186,293	2,338,404	1,030
Russia	1886	42,499,324	42,895,885	85,395,209	1,009
Poland	1886	3,977,406	4,279,156	8,256,562	1,076
German Empire	1890	24,231,832	25,189,232	49,421,064	1,039
Austria	1880	10,819,737	11,324,507	22,144,244	1,047
Hungary	1880	7,799,276	7,939,192	15,738,468	1,019
Liechtenstein	1886	4,897	4,696	9,593	959
Luxemburg	1890	105,419	105,669	211,088	1,002
Holland	1889	2,228,487	2,282,925	4,511,415	1,024
Belgium	1890	3,062,656	3,084,385	6,147,041	1,007
Switzerland	1888	1,427,377	1,506,680	2,934,057	1,055
France	1886	18,900,312	19,030,447	37,930,759	1,007
Spain and the Canary Islands	1887	8,608,532	8,950,776	17,559,308	1,039
Gibraltar (Civil population)	1890	9,201	9,326	18,527	1,013
Portugal	1878	2,175,829	2,374,870	4,550,699	1,091
Italy	1881	14,265,383	14,194,245	28,459,628	995
Bosnia and Herzegovina	1885	705,025	631,066	1,336,091	895
Servia	1890	1,110,731	1,052,028	2,162,759	947
Bulgaria	1881	1,519,953	1,462,996	2,982,949	962
Roumania	1860	2,276,558	2,148,403	4,424,961	944
Greece	1889	1,133,625	1,053,583	2,187,208	929
Malta	1890	82,086	83,576	165,662	1,018
Total		170,818,561	174,914,119	345,732,680	1,024

2. AMERICA.

Countries.	Census Year.	Males.	Females.	Population.	Females for Every 1,000 Men.
Danish Greenland 1888		4,838	5,383	10,221	1,112
British North America.1881		2,288,196	2,229,735	4,517,931	974
United States of North America 1880		25,518,820	24,636,963	50,155,783	965
Bermuda Islands 1890		7,767	8,117	15,884	1,046
Mexico 1882		5,072,054	5,375,920	10,447,974	1,060
North America and Islands		32,891,675	32,256,118	65,147,793	981
Nicaragua 1883		136,249	146,591	282,845	1,076
British Honduras 1881		14,108	13,344	27,452	946
Cuba 1877		850,520	671,164	1,521,684	789
Porto Rico 1877		369,054	362,594	731,648	983
British West Indies...1881		589,012	624,132	1,213,144	1,060
French West Indies...1885		176,364	180,266	356,630	1,022
Danish Possessions ...1880		14,889	18,874	33,763	1,263
Dutch Colony Curacao.1889		20,234	25,565	45,799	1,263
Central America and the West Indies....		2,170,430	2,042,535	4,212,965	941
British Guiana 1891		151,759	126,569	278,328	834
French Guiana 1885		15,767	10,735	26,502	681
Dutch Guiana 1889		30,187	28,764	58,951	953
Brazil 1872		5,123,869	4,806,609	9,930,478	938
Chili 1885		1,258,616	1,268,353	2,526,969	1,008
Falkland Islands 1890		1,086	703	1,789	647
South America total..		6,581,284	6,241,733	12,823,017	949
Population of America		41,643,389	40,540,386	82,183,775	973

3. ASIA.

Countries.	Census Year.	Males.	Females.	Population.	Females for Every 1,000 Men.
Russian Caucasia	1885	3,876,868	3,407,699	7,284,567	879
Siberia, minus Amur and Sachalin	1885	2,146,411	2,002,879	4,149,290	933
Province Uralsk	1885	263,915	263,686	527,601	999
General Province of the Prairies	1885	926,246	781,626	1,707,872	844
Province Fergana	1885	365,461	350,672	716,133	959
Province Samarkand ..	1885	335,530	305,616	641,146	911
Russian Possessions, total		7,914,431	7,112,178	15,026,609	899
British India (immediate possessions)	1891	112,150,120	108,313,980	220,464,100	966
Tributary States (so far known)	1891	31,725,910	29,675,150	61,401,060	935
Hong Kong	1889	138,033	56,449	194,482	409
Ceylon	1881	1,473,515	1,290,469	2,763,984	876
Of the French Possessions:					
Cambodscha	?	392,383	422,371	814,754	1,076
Cochinchina	1889	944,146	932,543	1,876,689	988
Philippines (partly) ..	1877	2,796,174	2,762,846	5,559,020	988
Japan .... ,......	1888	20,008,445	19,598,789	39,607,234	979
Cyprus	1891	104,887	104,404	209,291	995
Total population in Asia		177,648,044	170,269,179	347,917,223	**958**

4. AUSTRALIA AND POLYNESIA.

Countries.	Census Year.	Males.	Females.	Population.	Females for Every 1,000 men.
Australia, New Zealand (1890) and Tasmania	1891	2,059,594	1,772,472	3,832,066	861
Fiji Islands	1890	67,902	57,780	125,682	851
French Possessions (Tahiti, Marquesas, etc.).	1889	11,589	10,293	21,882	888
Hawaii	1890	58,714	31,276	89,990	533
Total		2,197,799	1,871,821	4,069,620	852

5. AFRICA.

Countries.	Census Year.	Males.	Females.	Population.	Females for Every 1,000 Men.
Egypt	1882	3,401,498	3,415,767	6,817,265	1,004
Algeria (minus Sahara)	1886	2,014,013	1,791,671	3,805,684	889
Senegal	1889	70,504	76,014	146,518	1,078
Gambia	1881	7,215	6,935	14,150	961
Sierra Leone	1881	31,201	29,345	60,546	940
Lagos	1881	37,665	39,605	75,270	998
St. Helena	1890	2,020	2,202	4,222	1,090
Capeland	1890	766,598	759,141	1,525,739	990
Natal	1890	268,062	275,851	543,913	1,029
Orange Free State:					
White	1890	40,571	37,145	77,716	915
Black	1890	67,791	61,996	129,787	914
Republic:					
White	1890	66,498	52,630	119,128	791
Black	1890	115,589	144,045	259,634	1,246
Reunion	1889	94,430	71,485	165,915	757
Mayotte	1889	6,761	5,509	12,270	815
St. Marie de Madagaskar	1888	3,648	4,019	7,667	1,102
Total		6,994,064	6,771,360	13,765,424[a]	968

[a] Besides 550,430 children without specification of sex.

Probably the result of this presentation will be astonishing to many. With the exception of Europe, where, on an average, there are 1,024 women to every 1,000 men, the reverse is the case everywhere else. If it is further considered that in the foreign divisions of the earth, and even there where actual enumeration was had, information upon the female sex is particularly defective—a fact that must be presumed with regard to all the countries of Mohammedan population, where the figures for the female population are probably below the reality—it stands pat that, apart from a few European nations, the female sex nowhere tangibly exceeds the male. It is otherwise in Europe, the country that interests us most. Here, with the exception of Italy and the southeast territories of Bosnia, Herzogovinia, Servia, Bulgaria, Roumania and Greece, the female population is everywhere more strongly represented than the male. Of the large European countries, the disproportion is slightest in France—1,002 females to every 1,000 males; next in order is Russia, with 1,009 females to every 1,000 males. On the other hand, Portugal, Norway and Poland, with 1,076 females to every 1,000 males, present the strongest disproportion. Next to these stands Great Britain,—1,060 females to every 1,000 males. Germany and Austria lie in the middle: they have, respectively, 1,039 and 1,047 females to every 1,000 males.

In the German Empire, the excess of the female over the male population, according to the census of December 1, 1890, was 957,400, against 988,376, according to the census of December 1, 1885. A principal cause of this disproportion is emigration, inasmuch as by far more men emigrate than women. This is clearly brought out by the opposite pole of Germany, the North American Union, which has about as large a deficit in women as Germany has a surplus. The United States is the principal country for European emigration, and this is mainly made up of males. A second cause is the larger number of accidents to men than to women in agriculture, the trades, the industries and transportation. Furthermore, there are more males than females temporarily abroad,—merchants, seamen, marines, etc. All this transpires clearly from the figures on the conjugal status. In 1890 there were 8,372,486 married men to 8,398,607 married women in Germany, i. e., 26,121 more of the latter. Another phenomenon, that statistics establish and that weigh heavily in the scales, is that, on an average, women reach a higher age than men: at the more advanced ages there are more women than men. According to the census of 1890 the relation of ages among the two sexes were these:

	Males.	Females.	Excess of Males.	Excess of Females.
Below ten years...	5,993,681	5,966,226	27,455	......
10 to 20 years.....	5,104,751	5,110,093	.....	5,342
20 to 30 years.....	3,947,324	4,055,321	.....	107,997
30 to 40 years.....	3,090,174	3,216,704	.....	126,530
40 to 50 years.....	2,471,617	2,659,609	.....	187,992
50 to 60 years.....	1,826,951	2,041,377	.....	214,426
60 to 70 years.....	1,177,142	1,391,227	.....	214,085
70 and up.........	619,192	757,081	.....	137,889
	24,230,832	25,197,638	27,455	994,261

This table shows that, up to the tenth year, the number of boys exceeds that of girls, due merely to the disproportion in births. Everywhere, there are more boys born than girls. In the German Empire, for instance,[9] there were born:—

In the year 1872 to 100 girls 106.2 boys
In the year 1878 to 100 girls 105.9 boys
In the year 1884 to 100 girls 106.2 boys
In the year 1888 to 100 girls 106.0 boys
In the year 1891 to 100 girls 106.2 boys

But the male sex dies earlier than the female, and from early childhood more boys die than girls. Accordingly, the table shows that, between the ages of 10 to 20 the female sex exceeds the male.

To each 100 females, there died, males:—[10].

In 1872.........107.0   In 1884.........109.2
In 1878.........110.5   In 1888.........107.9
                        In 1891.........107.5

The table shows, furthermore, that at the matrimonial age, proper, between the ages of 20 and 50, the female sex exceeds the male by 422,519, and that at the age from 50 to 70 and above, it exceeds the male by 566,400. A very strong disproportion between the sexes appears, furthermore, among the widowed.

According to the census of 1890, there were:—

Widowers 774,967
Widows 2,154,870

Excess of widows over widowers.........1,382,903

Of these widowed people, according to age, there were:—

Age.	Males.	Females.
40-60	222,286	842,920
60 and over...............	506,319	1,158,712

[9] "Statistisches Jahrbuch fuer das Deutsche Reich." Jahrgang 1893.
[10] Ibidem.

The number of divorced persons was, in 1890: Males, 25,271; females, 49,601. According to age, they were distributed:—

Age.	Males.	Females.
40-60	13,825	24,842
60 and over...............	4,917	7,244

These figures tell us that *widows and divorced women are excluded from remarriage*, and at the fittest age for matrimony, at that; there being of the age of 15-40, 46,362 widowers and 156,235 widows, 6,519 divorced men and 17,515 divorced women. These figures furnish further proof of the injury that divorce entails to married women.

In 1890, there were unmarried:—[11]

Age.	Males.	Females.
15-40 5,845,933		5,191,453
40-60	375,881	503,406
60 and over...............	130,154	230,966

Accordingly, among the unmarried population between the ages of 15 and 40, the male sex is stronger by 654,480 than the female. This circumstance would seem to be favorable for the latter. But males between the ages of 15 and 21 are, with few exceptions, not in condition to marry. Of that age there were 3,590,622 males to 3,774,025 females. Likewise with the males of the age of 21-25, a large number are not in a position to start a family: we have but to keep in mind the males in the army, students, etc. On the other side, all women of this age period are marriageable. Taking further into consideration that for a great variety of reasons, many men do not marry at all— the number of unmarried males of 40 years of age and over alone amounted to 506,035, to which must be added also the widowed and divorced males, more than two million strong—it follows that the situation of the female sex with regard to marriage is decidedly unfavorable. Accordingly, a large number of women are, under present circumstances, forced to renounce the legitimate gratification of their sexual instincts, while the males seek and find solace in prostitution. The situation would instantaneously change for women with the removal of the obstacles that keep to-day many hundreds of thousands of men from setting up a married home, and from doing justice to their natural instincts in a legitimate manner. For that the existing social system must be upturned.

As already observed, emigration across the seas is, in great part, responsible for the disproportion in the number of the sexes. In the years 1872-1886, on an average, more than 10,000 males left the country in excess of females. For a period of fifteen years, that runs up to 150,000 males, most of them in the very vigor of life. Military duties

[11] "Statistik des Deutschen Reichs," 1890.

also drive abroad many young men, and the most vigorous, at that. In 1893, according to the report officially submitted to the Reichstag on the subject of substitutes in the army, 25,851 men were sentenced for emigrating without leave, and 14,522 more cases were under investigation on the same charge. Similar figures recur from year to year. The loss in men that Germany sustains from this unlawful emigration is considerable in the course of a century. Especially strong is emigration during the years that follow upon great wars. That appears from the figures after 1866 and between 1871 and 1874. We sustain, moreover, severe losses in male life from accidents. In the course of the years 1887 to 1892, the number of persons killed in the trades, agriculture, State and municipal undertakings, ran up to 30,568,[12] of whom only a small fraction were women. Furthermore, another and considerable number of persons engaged in these occupations are crippled for life by accidents, and are disabled from starting a family; others die early and leave their families behind in want and misery. Great loss in male life is also connected with navigation. In the period between 1882-1891, 1,485 ships were lost on the high seas, whereby 2,436 members of crews—with few exceptions males—and 747 passengers perished.

Once the right appreciation of life is had, society will prevent the large majority of accidents, particularly in navigation; and such appreciation will touch its highest point under Socialist order. In numberless instances human life, or the safety of limb, is sacrificed to misplaced economy on the part of employers, who recoil before any outlay for protection; in many others the tired condition of the workman, or the hurry he must work in, is the cause. Human life is cheap; if one workingman goes to pieces, three others are at hand to take his place.

On the domain of navigation especially, and aided by the difficulty of control, many unpardonable wrongs are committed. Through the revelations made during the seventies by Plimsoll in the British Parliament, the fact has become notorious that many shipowners, yielding to criminal greed, take out high insurances for vessels that are not seaworthy, and unconscionably expose them, together with their crews, to the slightest weather at sea,—all for the sake of the high insurance. These are the so-called "coffin-ships," not unknown in Germany, either. The steamer "Braunschweig," for instance, that sank in 1881 near Helgoland, and belonged to the firm Rocholl & Co., of Bremen, proved to have been put to sea in a wholly unseaworthy condition. The same fate befell, in 1889, the steamer "Leda" of the same firm; hardly out at sea, she went to the bottom. The boat was insured with the Russian Lloyd for 55,000 rubles; the prospect of 8,500 rubles were held out to the captain, if he took her safe to Odessa; and the captain, in turn, paid

[12] "Statistisches Jahrbuch für das Deutsche Reich," 1889-1894.

the pilot the comparatively high wage of 180 rubles a month. The verdict of the Court of Admiralty was that *the accident was due to the fact that the "Leda" was unseaworthy and unfit to be taken to Odessa.* The license was withdrawn from the captain. According to existing laws, the real guilty parties could not be reached. No year goes by without our Court of Admiralty having to pass upon a larger number of accidents at sea, to the effect that the accident was due to vessels being too old, or too heavily loaded, or in defective condition, or insufficiently equipped; sometimes to several of these causes combined. With a good many of the lost ships, the cause of accident can not be established: they have gone down in midocean, and no survivor remains to tell the tale. Likewise are the coast provisions for the saving of shipwrecked lives both defective and insufficient; they are dependent mainly upon private charity. The case is even more disconsolate along distant and foreign coasts. A commonwealth that makes the promotion of the well-being of all its highest mission will not fail to so improve navigation, and provide it with protective measures that these accidents would be of rare occurrence. But the modern economic system of rapine, that weighs men as it weighs figures, to the end of whacking the largest possible amount of profit, not infrequently destroys a human life if thereby there be in it but the profit of a dollar. With the change of society in the Socialist sense, immigration, in its present shape, also would drop; the flight from military service would cease: suicide in the Army would be no more.

The picture drawn from our political and economic life shows that woman also is deeply interested therein. Whether the period of military service be shortened or not; whether the Army be increased or not; whether the country pursues a policy of peace or one of war; whether the treatment allotted to the soldier be worthy or unworthy of human beings; and whether as a result thereof the number of suicides and desertions rise or drop;—*all of these are questions that concern woman as much as man.* Likewise with the economic and industrial conditions and in transportation, in all of which branches the female sex, furthermore, steps from year to year more numerously as working-women. Bad conditions and unfavorable circumstances injure woman as a social and as a sexual being; favorable conditions and satisfactory circumstances benefit her.

But there are still other momenta that go to make marriage difficult or impossible. A considerable number of men are kept from marriage by the State itself. People pucker up their brows at the celibacy imposed upon Roman Catholic clergymen; but these same people have not a word of condemnation for the much larger number of soldiers who also are condemned thereto. The officers not only require the

consent of their superiors, they are also limited in the choice of a wife:
the regulation prescribes that she shall have property to a certain, and
not insignificant, amount. In this way the Austrian corps of officers,
for instance, obtained a social "improvement" at the cost of the female
sex. Captains rose by fully 8,000 guilders, if above thirty years of age,
while the captains under thirty years of age were thenceforth hard to
be had, in no case for a smaller dower than 30,000. "Now, a 'Mrs.
Captain,'" it was thus reported in the "Koelnische Zeitung" from
Vienna, "who until now was often a subject of pity for her female
colleagues in the administrative departments, can hold her head higher
by a good deal; everybody now knows that she has wherewith to
live. Despite the greatly increased requirements of personal excellence, culture and rank, the social status of the Austrian officer was
until then rather indefinite, partly because very prominent gentlemen
stuck fast to the Emperor's coat pocket; partly because many poor
officers could not make a shift to live without humiliation, and many families of poor officers often played a pitiful *role*. Until then, the officer who
wished to marry had, if the thirty-year line was crossed, to qualify in
joint property to the amount of 12,000 guilders, or in a 600-guilder side
income, and even at this insignificant income, hardly enough for decency,
the magistrates often shut their eyes, and granted relief. The new
marriage regulations are savagely severe, though the heart break. The
captain under thirty must forthwith deposit 30,000 guilders; over
thirty years of age, 20,000 guilders; from staff officers up to colonels,
16,000 guilders. Over and above this, only one-fourth of the officers may
marry without special grace, while a spotless record and corresponding
rank is demanded of the bride. This all holds good for officers of the
line and army surgeons. For other military officials with the rank of
officer, the new marriage regulations are milder; but for officers of
the general staff still severer. The officer who is detailed to the captain of the general staff may not thereafter marry; the actual captain
of the staff, if below thirty, is required to give security in 36,000
guilders, and later 24,000 more." In Germany and elsewhere, there are
similar regulations. Also the corps of under-officers is subject to
hampering regulations with regard to marriage, and require besides the
consent of their superior officers. These are very drastic proofs of
the *purely materialistic conception* that the State has of marriage.

In general, public opinion is agreed that marriage is not advisable for
men under twenty-four or twenty-five years of age. Twenty-five is
the marriageable age for men fixed by the civil code, with an eye to
the civic independence that, as a rule, is not gained before that age.
Only with persons who are in the agreeable position of not having to
first conquer independence—with people of princely rank—does public

opinion consider it proper when occasionally the men marry at the
age of eighteen or nineteen, the girls at that of fifteen or sixteen. The
Prince is declared of age with his eighteenth year, and considered
capable to govern a vast empire and numerous people. Common mortals
acquire the right to govern their possible property only at the age of
twenty-one.

The difference of opinion as to the age when marriage is desirable
shows that public opinion judges by the social standing of the bride
and bridegroom. Its reasons have nothing to do with the human being
as a natural entity, or with its natural instincts. It happens, however,
that Nature's impulses do not yoke themselves to social conditions,
nor to the views and prejudices that spring from them. So soon as
man has reached maturity, the sexual instincts assert themselves with
force; indeed, they are the incarnation of the human being, and they
demand satisfaction from the mature being, at the peril of severe
physical and mental suffering.

The age of sexual ripeness differs according to individuals, climate
and habits of life. In the warm zone it sets in with the female sex, as
a rule, at the age of eleven to twelve years, and not infrequently are
women met with there, who, already at that age, carry offspring on
their arms; but at their twenty-fifth or thirtieth year, these have lost
their bloom. In the temperate zone, the rule with the female sex is
from the fourteenth to the sixteenth year, in some cases later. Likewise is the age of puberty different between country and city women.
With healthy, robust country girls, who move much in the open air
and work vigorously, menstruation sets in later, on the average, than
with our badly nourished, weak, hypernervous, ethereal city young
ladies. Yonder, sexual maturity develops normally, with rare disturbances; here a normal development is the exception: all manner of ill-
nesses set in, often driving the physician to desperation. How often
are not physicians compelled to declare that, along with a change of life,
the most radical cure is marriage. But how apply such a cure? In-
superable obstacles rise against the proposition.

All this goes to show where the change must be looked for. In the
first place, the point is to make possible a totally different education, one that takes into consideration the physical as well as the
mental being; in the second place, to establish a wholly different system
of life and of work. But both of these are, without exception, possible for all only under *wholly different social conditions*.

Our social conditions have raised a violent contradiction between
man, as a natural and sexual being, on the one hand, and man as a social
being on the other. The contradiction has made itself felt at no period
as strongly as at this; and it produces a number of diseases into whose

nature we will go no further, but that affect mainly the female sex: in the first place, her organism depends, in much higher degree than that of man, upon her sexual mission, and is influenced thereby, as shown by the regular recurrence of her periods; in the second place, most of the obstacles to marriage lie in the way of women, preventing her from satisfying her strongest natural impulse in a natural manner. The contradiction between natural want and social compulsion goes against the grain of Nature; it leads to secret vices and excesses that undermine every organism but the strongest.

Unnatural gratification, especially with the female sex, is often most shamelessly promoted. More or less underhandedly, certain preparations are praised, and they are recommended especially in the advertisements of most of the papers that penetrate into the family circle as especially devoted to its entertainment. These puffs are addressed mainly to the better situated portion of society, seeing the prices of the preparations are so high that a family of small means can hardly come by them. Side by side with these shameless advertisements are found the puffs— meant for the eyes of both sexes—of obscene pictures, especially of whole series of photographs, of poems and prose works of similar stripe, aimed at sexual incitation, and that call for the action of police and District Attorneys. But these gentlemen are too busy with the "civilization, marriage and family-destroying" Socialist movement to be able to devote full attention to such machinations. A part of our works of fiction labors in the same direction. The wonder would be if sexual excesses, artificially incited, besides, failed to manifest themselves in unhealthy and harmful ways, and to assume the proportions of a social disease.

The idle, voluptuous life of many women in the property classes; their refined measures of nervous stimulants; their overfeeding with a certain kind of artificial sensation, cultivated in certain lines on the hot-house plan, and often considered the principal topic of conversation and sign of culture by that portion of the female sex that suffers of hypersensitiveness and nervous excitement;—all this incites still more the sexual senses, and naturally leads to excesses.

Among the poor, it is certain exhausting occupations, especially of a sedentary nature, that promotes congestion of blood in the abdominal organs, and promotes sexual excitation. One of the most dangerous occupations in this direction is connected with the, at present, widely spread sewing machine. This occupation works such havoc that, with ten or twelve hours' daily work, the strongest organism is ruined within a few years. Excessive sexual excitement is also promoted by long hours of work in a steady high temperature, for instance, sugar refineries, bleacheries, cloth-pressing establishments, night work by gaslight in overcrowded rooms, especially when both sexes work together.

A succession of further phenomena has been here unfolded, sharply illustrative of the irrationableness and unhealthiness of modern conditions. These are evils deeply rooted in our social state of things, and removable neither by the moral sermonizings nor the palliatives that religious quacks of the male and female sexes have so readily at hand. The axe must be laid to the root of the evil. The question is to bring about a natural system of education, together with healthy conditions of life and work, and to do this in amplest manner, to the end that the normal gratification of natural and healthy instincts be made possible for all.

As to the male sex, a number of considerations are absent that are present with the female sex. Due to his position as master, and in so far as social barriers do not hinder him, there is on the side of man the free choice of love. On the other hand, the character of marriage as an institution for support, the excess of women, custom;—all these circumstances conspire to prevent woman from manifesting her will; they force her to wait till she is wanted. As a rule, she seizes gladly the opportunity, soon as offered, to reach the hand to the man who redeems her from the social ostracism and neglect, that is the lot of that poor waif, the "old maid." Often she looks down with contempt upon those of her sisters who have yet preserved their self-respect, and have not sold themselves into mental prostitution to the first comer, preferring to tread single the thorny path of life.

On the other hand, social considerations tie down the man, who desires to reach by marriage the gratification of his life's requirements. He must put himself the question: Can you support a wife, and the children that may come, so that pressing cares, the destroyers of your happiness, may be kept away? The better his marital intentions are, the more ideally he conceives them, the more he is resolved to wed only out of love, all the more earnestly must he put the question to himself. To many, the affirmative answer is, under the present economic conditions, a matter of impossibility: they prefer to remain single. With other and less conscientious men, another set of considerations crowd upon the mind. Thousands of men reach an independent position, one in accord with their wants, only comparatively late. But they can keep a wife in a style suitable to their station only if she has large wealth. True enough, many young men have exaggerated notions on the requirements of a so-called life "suitable to one's station." Nevertheless, they can not be blamed—as a result of the false education above described, and of the social habits of a large number of women,—for guarding against demands from that quarter that are far beyond their powers. Good women, modest in their demands, these men often never come to know. These women are retiring; they are not to be found there where such men have acquired the habit of looking for a wife; while those whom they meet are not infrequently such as seek to win a husband by means of their looks, and are intent, by external means, by show, to deceive him regarding their personal qualities and material conditions. The means of seduction of all sorts are plied all the more diligently in the measure that these ladies come on in years, when marriage becomes a matter of hot haste. Does any of these succeed in conquering a husband, she has become so habituated to show, jewelry, finery and expensive pleasures, that she is not inclined to forego them in marriage. The superficial nature of her being crops up in all directions, and therein an abyss is opened for the husband. Hence many prefer to leave alone the flower that blooms on the edge of the precipice, and that can be plucked only at the risk of breaking their necks. They go their ways alone, and seek company and pleasure under the protection of their freedom. Deception and swindle are practices everywhere in full swing in the business life of capitalist society: no wonder they are applied also in contracting marriage, and that, when they succeed, both parties are drawn into common sorrows.

According to E. Ansell, the age of marriage among the cultured and independent males of England was, between 1840-1871, on an average 29.25 years. Since then the average has risen for many classes, by at least one year. For the different occupations, the average age of marriage, between 1880-1885, was as follows:—

Occupations.	Age.
Miners	23.56
Textile workers	23.88
Shoemakers and tailors	24.42
Skilled laborers	24.85
Day laborers	25.06
Clerks	25.75
Retailers	26.17
Farmers and their sons	28.73
Men of culture and men of independent means	30.72

These figures give striking proof of how social conditions and standing affect marriage.

The number of men who, for several reasons, are kept from marrying is ever on the increase. It is especially in the so-called upper ranks and occupations that the men often do not marry, partly because the demands upon them are too great, partly because it is just the men of these social strata who seek and find pleasure and company elsewhere. On the other hand, conditions are particularly unfavorable to women in places where many pensionaries and their families, but few young men, have their homes. In such places, the number of women who cannot marry rises to 20 or 30 out of every 100. The deficit of candidates for marriage affects strongest those female strata that, through education and social position, make greater pretensions, and yet, outside of their persons, have nothing to offer the man who is looking for wealth. This concerns especially the female members of those numerous families that live upon fixed salaries, are considered socially "respectable," but are without means. The life of the female being in this stratum of society is, comparatively speaking, the saddest of all those of her fellow-sufferers. It is out of these strata that is mainly recruited the most dangerous competition for the working-women in the embroidering, seamstress, flower-making, millinery, glove and straw hat sewing; in short, all the branches of industry that the employer prefers to have carried on at the homes of the working-women. These ladies work for the lowest wages, seeing that, in many cases, the question with them is not to earn a full livelihood, but only something over and above that, or to earn the outlay for a better wardrobe and for luxury. Employers have a predilection for the competition of these ladies, so as to lower the earnings of the poor working-woman and squeeze the last drop of blood from her veins: it drives her to exert herself to the point of exhaustion. Also not a few wives of government employes, whose husbands are badly paid, and can not afford them a "life suitable to their rank," utilize their leisure moments in this vile competition that presses so heavily upon wide strata of the female working class.

The activity on the part of the bourgeois associations of women for the abolition of female labor and for the admission of women to the higher professions, at present mainly, if not exclusively, appropriated by men, aims principally at procuring a position in life for women from the social circles just sketched. In order to secure for their efforts greater prospects of success, these associations have loved to place themselves under the protectorate of higher and leading ladies. The bourgeois females imitate herein the example of the bourgeois males, who likewise love such protectorates, and exert themselves in directions that can bring only *small*, never *large results*. A Sisyphus work is thus done with as much noise as possible, to the end of deceiving oneself and others on the score of the necessity for a radical change. The necessity is also felt to do all that is possible in order to suppress all doubts regarding the wisdom of the foundations of our social and political organization, and to prescribe them as treasonable. The conservative nature of these endeavors prevents bourgeois associations of women from being seized with so-called destructive tendencies. When, accordingly, at the Women's Convention of Berlin, in 1894, the opinion was

expressed by a minority that the bourgeois women should go hand and
hand with the working-women, i. e., with their Socialist citizens, a
storm of indignation went up from the majority. But the bourgeois
women will not succeed in pulling themselves out of the quagmire by
their own topknots.

How large the number is of women who, by reason of the causes
herein cited, must renounce married life, is not accurately ascertainable. In Scotland, the number of unmarried women of the age of
twenty years and over was, towards the close of the sixties, 43 per
cent. of the female population, and there were 110 women to every 100
men. In England, outside of Wales, there lived at that time 1,407,228
more women than men of the age of 20 to 40, and 359,966 single women
of over forty years of age. Of each 100 women 42 were unmarried.

The surplus of women that Germany owns is very unevenly distributed in point of territories and age. According to the census of 1890,
it stood:—[13]

Divisions.	Under 15.	15-40.	40-60.	Over 60.
To Every 1,000 Males, Females of the Age of				
Berlin	1,014	1,056	1,108	1,666
Kingdom of Saxony	1,020	1,032	1,112	1,326
Kingdom of Bavaria, on the right of the Rhine	1,022	1,040	1,081	1,155
On the left of the Rhine	986	1,024	1,065	1,175
Wurtemberg	1,021	1,076	1,135	1,158
Baden	1,006	1,027	1,099	1,175
Hamburg	1,003	967	1,042	1,522
Province of Brandenburg	986	981	1,085	1,261
Province of Pommern	984	1,053	1,126	1,191
Province of Rhineland	984	990	1,010	1,087
German Empire	995	1,027	1,094	1,196

Accordingly, of marriageable age proper, 15-40, the surplus of women
in the German Empire amounts to 27 women to every 1,000 men. Seeing
that, within these age periods, there are 9,429,720 male to 9,682,454
female inhabitants, there is a total female surplus of 252,734. In the
same four age periods, the proportion of the sexes in other countries of
Europe and outside of Europe stood as follows:—[14]

[13] "Statistik des Deutschen Reiches."
[14] "Statistik des Deutschen Reiches."

	To Every 1,000 Males, Females of the Age of			
Countries.	Under 15.	15-40.	40-60.	60 and Over.
Belgium (1890)	992	984	1,018	1,117
Bulgaria (1888)	950	1,068	837	947
Denmark(1890)	978	1,080	1,073	1,179
France (1886)	989	1,003	1,006	1,063
England and Wales (1891) .	1,006	1,075	1,096	1,227
Scotland (1891)	973	1,073	1,165	1,389
Ireland (1891)	966	1,036	1,109	1,068
Italy (1881)	963	1,021	1,005	980
Luxemburg (1891)	996	997	1,004	1,042
Holland (1889)	990	1,022	1,035	1,154
Austria (1890)	1,005	1,046	1,079	1,130
Hungary (1890)	1,001	1,040	996	1,000
Sweden (1890)	975	1,062	1,140	1,242
Switzerland (1888)	999	1,059	1,103	1,148
Japan (1891)	978	962	951	1,146
Cape of Good Hope (1891).	989	1,008	939	1,019

It is seen that all countries of the same or similar economic structure reveal the identical conditions with regard to the distribution of the sexes according to ages. According thereto, and apart from all other causes already mentioned, a considerable number of women have in such countries no prospect of entering wedded life. The number of unmarried women is even still larger, because a large number of men prefer, for all sorts of reasons, to remain single. What say hereto those superficial folks, who oppose the endeavor of women after a more independent, equal-righted position in life, and who refer them to marriage and domestic life? The blame does not lie with the women that so many of them do not marry; and how matters stand with "conjugal happiness" has been sufficiently depicted.

What becomes of the victims of our social conditions? The resentment of insulted and injured Nature expresses itself in the peculiar facial lines and characteristics whereby so-called old maids, the same as old ascetic bachelors, stamp themselves different from other human beings in all countries and all climates; and it gives testimony of the mighty and harmful effect of suppressed natural love. Nymphomania with women, and numerous kinds of hysteria, have their origin in that source; and also discontent in married life produces attacks of hysteria, and is responsible for barrenness.

Such, in main outlines, is our modern married life and its effects. The conclusion is: *Modern marriage is an institution that is closely connected with the existing social condition, and stands or falls with it. But this marriage is in the course of dissolution and decay, exactly as capitalist society itself,*—because, as demonstrated under the several heads on the subject of marriage:

1. Relatively, the number of births declines, although population increases on the whole,—showing that the condition of the family deteriorates.

2. Actions for divorce increase in numbers, considerably more than does population, and, in the majority of cases, the plaintiffs are women, although, both economically and socially, they are the greatest sufferers thereunder,—showing that the unfavorable factors, that operate upon marriage, are on the increase, and marriage, accordingly, is dissolving and falling to pieces.

3. Relatively, the number of marriages is on the decline, although population increases,—showing again that marriage, in the eyes of many, no longer answers its social and moral purposes, and is considered worthless, or dangerous.

4. In almost all the countries of civilization there is a disproportion between the number of the sexes, and to the disadvantage of the female sex, and the disproportion is not caused by births—there are, on the average, more boys born than girls,—but is due to unfavorable social and political causes, that lie in the political and economic conditions.

Seeing that all these unnatural conditions, harmful to woman in particular, are grounded in the nature of capitalist society, and grow worse as this social system continues, the same proves itself unable to end the evil and emancipate woman. Another social order is, accordingly, requisite thereto.

CHAPTER III.

Marriage presents one side of the sexual life of the capitalist or bourgeois world; prostitution presents the other. Marriage is the obverse, prostitution the reverse of the medal. If men find no satisfaction in wedlock, then they usually seek the same in prostitution. Those men, who, for whatever reason, renounce married life, also usually seek satisfaction in prostitution. To those men, accordingly, who, whether out of their free will or out of compulsion, live in celibacy, as well as to those whom marriage does not offer what was expected of it, conditions are more favorable for the gratification of the sexual impulse than to women.

Man ever has looked upon the use of prostitution as a privilege due him of right. All the harder and severer does he keep guard and pass sentence when a woman, who is no prostitute, commits a "slip." That woman is instinct with the same impulses as man, aye, that at given periods of her life (at menstruation) these impulses assert themselves more vehemently than at others,—that does not trouble him. In virtue of his position as master, he compels her to violently suppress her most powerful impulses, and he conditions both her character in society and her marriage upon her chastity. Nothing illustrates more drastically, and also revoltingly, the dependence of woman upon man than this radically different conception regarding the gratification of the identical natural impulse, and the radically different measure by which it is judged.

To man, circumstances are particularly favorable. Nature has devolved upon woman the consequences of the act of generation: outside of the enjoyment, man has neither trouble nor responsibility. This advantageous position over against woman has promoted that unbridled license in sexual indulgence wherein a considerable part of men distinguish themselves. Seeing, however, that, as has been shown, a hundred causes lie in the way of the legitimate gratification of the sexual instinct, or prevent its full satisfaction, the consequence is frequent gratification, like beasts in the woods.

Prostitution thus becomes a social institution in the capitalist world, the same as the police, standing armies, the Church, and wage-mastership.

Nor is this an exaggeration. We shall prove it.

We have told how the ancient world looked upon prostitution, and considered it necessary, aye, had it organized by the State, as well in Greece as in Rome. What views existed on the subject during the Middle Ages has likewise been described. Even St. Augustine, who, next to St. Paul, must be looked upon as the most important prop of Christendom, and who diligently preached asceticism, could not refrain from exclaiming: "Suppress the public girls, and the violence of passion will knock everything of a heap." The provincial Council of Milan, in 1665, expressed itself in similar sense.

Let us hear the moderns:

Dr. F. S. Huegel says:[1] "Advancing civilization will gradually drape prostitution in more pleasing forms, but only with the end of the world will it be wiped off the globe." A bold assertion; yet he who is not able to project himself beyond the capitalist form of society, he who does not realize that society will change so as to arrive at healthy and natural social conditions,—he must agree with Dr. Huegel.

Hence also did Dr. Wichern, the late pious Director of the Rauhen House near Hamburg, Dr. Patton of Lyon, Dr. William Tait of Edinburg, and Dr. Parent-Duchatelet of Paris, celebrated through his investigations of the sexual diseases and prostitution, agree in declaring: "Prostitution is ineradicable *because it hangs together with the social institutions,*" and all of them demanded its regulation by the State. Also Schmoelder writes: "Immorality as a trade has existed at all times and in all places, and, so far as the human eye can see, *it will remain a constant companion* of the human race." [2] Seeing that the authorities cited stand, without exception, upon the ground of the modern social order, the thought occurs to none that, with the aid of another social order, the causes of prostitution, and, consequently, prostitution itself, might disappear; none of them seeks to fathom the causes. Indeed, upon one and another, engaged in this question, the fact at times dawns that the sorry social conditions, which numerous women suffer under, might be the chief reason why so many women sell their bodies; but the thought does not press itself through to its conclusion, to wit, that, therefore, the necessity arises of bringing about other social conditions. Among those who recognize that the economic conditions are the chief cause of prostitution belong Th. Bade, who declares:[3] "The causes of the bottomless moral depravity, out of which the prostitute girl is born, lie in the existing social conditions. . . . *It is the bourgeois dissolution of the middle classes and of their material existence, particularly of the class of the artisans,* only a small fraction of which car-

[1] "Geschichte, Statistik und Regelung der Prostitution in Wien."

[2] "Die Bestrafung und polizeiliche Behaundlung der gewerbsmässigen Unzucht."

[3] "Ueber Gelegenheitsmacherei und öffentliches Tanzvergnügen."

ries on to-day an independent occupation as a trade." Bade closes his observations, saying: "Want for material existence, that has partly worn out the families of the middle class and will yet wear them out wholly, leads also to the moral ruin of the family, especially of the female sex." In fact, the statistical figures, gathered by the Police Department of Berlin, between 1871-1872, on the extraction of 2,224 enrolled prostitutes, show:

Number.	Per Cent.	Father's Occupation.
1,015	47.9	Artisans
467	22.0	Millhands
305	14.4	Small office-holders
222	10.4	Merchants and railroad workers
87	4.1	Farmers
26	1.2	Military service

Of 102 the father's occupation was not ascertainable.

Specialists and experts rarely take up investigations of a deeper nature; they accept the facts that lie before them, and judge in the style of the "Wiener Medizinische Wochenschrift," that writes in its No. 35, for the year 1863: "What else is there left to the large majority of willing and unwilling celibates, in order to satisfy their *natural wants*, than the forbidden fruit of the Venus Pandemos?" The paper is, accordingly, of the opinion that, for the sake of these celibates, prostitution is necessary, because what else, forsooth, are they to do in order to satisfy their sexual impulse? And it closes, saying: "Seeing that prostitution is necessary, it has the right to existence, to protection, and to immunity from the State." And Dr. Huegel declares himself in his work, mentioned above, in accord with this view. Man, accordingly, to whom celibacy is a horror and a martyrdom, is the only being considered; that there are also millions of women living in celibacy is well known; but they have to submit. What is right for man, is, accordingly, wrong for women; is in her case immorality and a crime.

The Leipsic Police Doctor, Dr. J. Kuehn, says:[4] "Prostitution is not merely an evil that must be tolerated, *it is a necessary evil*, because it protects the wives from infidelity, [which only the husbands have the right to be guilty of] and virtue also [female virtue, of course, the husbands have no need of the commodity] from being assailed [sic.] and, therefore, from falling." These few words of Dr. Kuehn typify, in all its nakedness, the crass egoism of male creation. Kuehn takes the correct stand for a Police Doctor, who, by superintending prostitution, sacrifices

Die Prostitution im 19. Jahrhundert vom sanitätspolizeilichen Standpunkt."

himself, to the end of saving the men from disagreeable diseases. In the same sense with him did his successor, Dr. Eckstein, utter himself at the twelfth convention of the German Associations of House and City Real Estate Owners, held in Magdeburg in the summer of 1890. The honorable house-owners wished to know how they could prevent the numerous instances of prostitutes occupying their houses, and how to protect themselves against fines in case prostitutes are caught living in them. Dr. Eckstein lectured them on this head to the effect that prostitution was a "necessary evil," never absent from any people or religion. Another interesting gentleman is Dr. Fock, who in a treatise, entitled "Prostitution, in Its Ethical and Sanitary Respects," in the "Deutschen Vierteljahrschrift fuer offentliche Gesundheitspflege," vol. xx, No. 1, considers prostitution "an unenviable corollary of our civilized arrangements." He fears an over-production of people if all were to marry upon reaching the age of puberty; hence he considers important to have prostitution "regulated" by the State. He considers natural that the State supervise and regulate prostitution, and thereby assume the care of providing for the supply of girls that are free from syphilis. He pronounces himself in favor of the most rigid inspection of "all women, proven to lead an abandoned life;"—also when ladies of "an abandoned life" belong to the prominent classes? It is the old story. That in all logic and justice also those men should be held under surveillance who hunt up prostitutes, maintain them and make their existence possible,— of that no one thinks. Dr. Fock also demands the taxing of the prostitutes, and their concentration in given streets. In other words, the Christian State is to procure for itself a revenue out of prostitution, and, at the same time, organize and place prostitution under its protection for the benefit of male creation. What was it that the Emperor Vespasian said at a somewhat similar juncture? *"Non olet!"*—it smells not.

Did we exaggerate when we said: Prostitution is to-day a necessary social institution just as the police, standing armies, the Church and wage-mastership?

In the German Empire, prostitution is not, like in France, organized and superintended by the State; it is only tolerated. Official public houses are forbidden by law, and procuring is severely punishable. But that does not prevent that in a large number of German cities public houses continue to exist, and are winked at by the police. This establishes an incomprehensible state of things. The defiance of the law implied in such a state of things dawned even upon our statesmen and they bestirred themselves to remove the objection by legislative enactments. The German Criminal Code makes also the lodging of a prostitute a penal offense. On the other hand, however, the police are compelled to tolerate thousands of women as prostitutes, and, in a measure, to privilege them in their trade, provided they enter themselves as prostitutes on the Police Register, and submit to the Police regulations,—for instance, periodically recurring examinations by a physician. It follows, however, that, if the Government licenses the prostitute, and thereby protects the exercise of her trade, she must also have a habitation. Aye, it is even in the interest of public health and order that they have such a place to ply their trade in. What contradictions! On the one hand, the Government officially acknowledges that prostitution is necessary; on the other, it prosecutes and punishes the prostitute and the pimp. But it is out of contradictions that bourgeois society is put together. Moreover, the attitude of the Government is an avowal that prostitution is a Sphinx to modern society, the riddle which society can not solve: it considers necessary to tolerate and superintend prostitution in order to avoid greater evils. In other words, our social system, so boastful of its morality, its religiousness, its civilization and its culture, feels compelled to tolerate that immorality and corruption spread through its body like a stealthy poison. But this state of things betrays something else, besides *the admission by the Christian State that marriage is insufficient, and that the husband has the right to demand illegitimate gratification of his sexual instincts.* Woman counts with such a State in so far only as she is willing, as a sexual being, to yield to illegitimate male desires, i. e., become a prostitute. In keeping herewith, the supervision and control, exercised by the organs of the State over the registered prostitutes, do not fall upon the men also, those who seek the prostitute. Such a provision would be a matter of course if the sanitary police control was to be of any sense, and even of partial effect,—apart from the circumstance that a sense of justice would demand an even-handed application of the law to both sexes. No; "supervision and control" fall upon woman alone.

This protection by the State of man and not woman, turns upside down the nature of things. *It looks as if men were the weaker vessel and women the stronger; as if woman were the seducer, and poor, weak man the seduced.* The seduction-myth between Adam and Eve in Paradise continues to operate in our opinions and laws, and it says to Christianity: "You are right; woman is the arch seductress, the vessel of iniquity." Men should be ashamed of such a sorry and unworthy *role;* but this *role* of the "weak" and the "seduced" suits them;—*the more they are protected, all the more may they sin.*

Wherever men assemble in large numbers, they seem unable to amuse themselves without prostitution. This was shown, among other instances of the kind, by the occurrences at the German Schuetzenfest, held in Berlin in the summer of 1890, which caused 2,300 women to express themselves as follows in a petition addressed to the Mayor of the German capital: "May it please your Honor to allow us to bring to your knowledge the matters that have reached the provinces, through the press and other means of communication, upon the German shooting matches, held at Pankow from the 6th to the 13th of July of this year. The reports of the matter, that we have seen with indignation and horror, represent the programme of that festival with the following announcements, among others: 'First German Herald, the Greatest Songstress of the World;' 'A Hundred Ladies and Forty Gentlemen:' Besides these smaller *cafes chantants* and shooting galleries, in which importunate women forced themselves upon the men. Also a 'free concert,' whose gaily-clad waitresses, seductively smiling, brazenly and shamelessly invited the gymnasium students and the fathers of families, the youths and the grown men alike, to the 'shooting retreats.' . . . The barely dressed 'lady' who invited people to the booth of 'The Secrets of Hamburg, or a Night in St. Pauli,' should have been enough to justify her removal by the police. And then the shocking announcement, almost incredible of the much boasted about Imperial capital, and hardly to be believed by plain male and female citizens in the provinces, to the effect that the managers of the festival had consented to the employment, without pay, of 'young women' in large numbers, as bar-maids, instead of the waiters who applied for work. . . . We, German women, have thousands of occasions, as wives, mothers and as sisters, to send our husbands, children, daughters and brothers to Berlin in the service of the fatherland; we, consequently, pray to your Honor in all humbleness and in the confident expectation that, with the aid of the overpowering influence, which, as the chief magistrate of the Imperial capital, lies in your hand, you may institute such investigations of those disgraceful occurrences, or adopt such other measures as to your Honor may seem fit, to the end that a recurrence of those orgies may not have to be apprehended at the pending Sedan festival, for instance. . . ." (! !)

During the session of the Reichstag, from 1892 to 1893, the united Governments made an effort to put an end to the contradiction that governmental practice, on the one hand, and the Criminal Code on the other, find themselves in with regard to prostitution. They introduced a bill that was to empower the police to designate certain habitations to prostitutes. It was admitted that prostitution could not be suppressed, and that, therefore, the most practical thing was to tolerate the thing in certain localities, and to control it. The bill—upon that all minds were agreed—would, if it became a law, have called again to life the brothels that were officially abolished in Prussia about 1845. The bill caused a great uproar, and it evoked a number of protests in which the warning was raised against the State's setting itself up as the protector of prostitution, and thereby favoring the idea that the use of prostitution was not in violation of good morals, or that the

trade of the prostitute was such that the State could allow and approve
of. The bill, which met with the strongest opposition both on the
floor of the Reichstag and in the committee, was pigeon-holed, and dared
not again come into daylight. That, nevertheless, such a bill could at
all take shape reveals the embarrassment that society is in.

The administrative regulation of prostitution raises in the minds of
men not only the belief that the State allows the use of prostitution,
but also that such control protects them against disease. Indeed, this
belief greatly promotes indulgence and recklessness on the part of men.
Brothels do not reduce sexual diseases, they promote the same:
the men grow more careless and less cautious.

Experience has taught that neither the establishment of houses of
prostitution, controlled by the police, nor the supervision and medical
inspection, ordered by the police, afford the slightest guarantee against
contagion. The nature of these diseases is frequently such that they
are not to be easily or immediately detected. If there is to be any
safety, the inspection would have to be held several times a day. That,
however, is impossible in view of the number of women concerned,
and also of the costs. Where thirty or forty prostitutes must be
"done" in an hour, inspection is hardly more than a farce; moreover,
one or two inspections a week is wholly inadequate. The success of
these measures also suffers shipwreck in the circumstance that the
men, who transmit the germs of disease from one woman to another,
remain free from all official annoyance. A prostitute, just inspected
and found healthy, may be infected that same hour by a diseased man,
and she transmits the virus to other patrons, until the next inspection day, or until she has herself become aware of the disease. The
control is not only illusory: These inspections, made at command,
and conducted by male, instead of female physicians, hurt most deeply
the sense of shame; and they contribute to its total ruination. This is
a phenomenon confirmed by many physicians. Even the official report
of the Berlin Police Department admits the fact by stating: "It may
also be granted that *registration causes the moral sense of the prostitute
to sink* still lower."[5] Accordingly, the prostitutes try their utmost to
escape this control. A further consequence of these police measures is
that they make it extraordinarily difficult, even impossible, for the
prostitute ever again to return to a decent trade. *A woman, that has
fallen under police control, is lost to society; she generally goes down
in misery within a few years.* Accurately and exhaustively did the fifth
Congress at Geneva for Combatting Immorality utter itself against the
police regulation of prostitutes, by declaring: "The compulsory medi-

[5] Zweiter Verwaltungsbericht des Königl. Polizei-Präsidiums von Berlin für
die Jahre 1881-1890 ; pp. 351-359.

cal inspection of prostitutes is an all the more cruel punishment to the woman, seeing that, by destroying the remnants of shame, still possible within even the most abandoned, such inspection drags down completely into depravity the wretched being that is subjected thereto. The State, that means to regulate prostitution with the police, forgets that it owes equal protection to both sexes; it demoralizes and degrades women. Every system for the official regulation of prostitution has police arbitrariness for its consequence, as well as the violation of civic guaranties that are safeguarded to every individual, even to the greatest criminal, against arbitrary arrest and imprisonment. Seeing this violation of right is exercised to the injury of woman only, the consequence is an inequality, shocking to nature, between her and man. Woman is degraded to the level of a mere means, and is no longer treated as a person. *She is placed outside of the pale of law.*"

Of how little use police control is, England furnishes a striking illustration. In the year 1866 a law was enacted on the subject for places in which soldiers and marines were garrisoned. Now, then, while from 1860 to 1866, without the law, the lighter cases of syphilis had declined from 32.68 to 24.73 per cent., after a six years' enforcement of the new law, the percentage of diseased in 1872 was still 24.26. In other words, it was not one-half per cent. lower in 1872 than in 1866; but the average for these six years was 1·16 per cent. higher than in 1866. In sight of this, a special Commission, appointed in 1873, to investigate the effect of that law, arrived at the unanimous conclusion that "the periodical inspection of the women who usually have sexual intercourse with the *personnel* of the army and navy, *had, at best, not occasioned the slightest diminution in the number of cases,*" and it *recommended the suspension* of periodical inspections.

The effects of the Act of Inspection on the women subjected thereto were, however, quite different from those on the troops. In 1866, there were, to every 1,000 prostitutes, 121 diseases; in 1868, after the law had been in force two years, there were 202. The number then gradually dropped, but, nevertheless, still exceeded in 1874 the figure for 1866 by 16 cases. Under the Act, deaths also increased frightfully among the prostitutes. In 1865 the proportion was 9.8 to every 1,000 prostitutes, whereas, in 1874 it had risen to 23. When, towards the close of the sixties, the English Government made the attempt to extend the Act of Inspection to all English cities, a storm of indignation arose from the women. The law was considered an affront to the whole sex. The Habeas Corpus Act,—that fundamental law, that protects the English citizen against police usurpation—would, such was the sentiment, be suspended for women: any brutal policeman, animated by revenge or any other base motive, would be free to seize any decent woman on the suspicion of her being a prostitute, whereas the licentiousness of the men would remain unmolested, aye, would be protected and fed, by just such a law.

Although this intervention in behalf of the outcasts of their sex readily exposed the English women to misrepresentation and degrading remarks from the quarter of narrow-minded men, the women did not allow themselves to be held back from energetically opposing the introduction of the law that was an insult to their sex. In newspaper articles and pamphlets the "pros" and "cons" were discussed by men and women; in Parliament, the extension of the law was, first, prevented; its repeal followed later. The German police is vested with a similar power, and cases that have forced themselves into publicity from Berlin, Leipsic and other cities, prove that its abuse—or be it "mistakes" in its exercise—is easy; nevertheless, of an energetic opposition to such regulations naught is heard. Even in middle class Norway, brothels were forbidden in 1884; in 1888 the compulsory registration of the prostitutes and the inspection connected therewith were abolished in the capital, Christiania; and in January, 1893, the enactment was made general for the whole country. Very rightly does Mrs. Guillaume-Schack remark upon the "protective" measures adopted by the State in behalf of the men: "To what end do we teach our sons to respect virtue and morality if the State pronounces immorality a necessary evil; and if, before the young man has at all reached mental maturity, the State leads woman to him stamped by the authorities as a merchandise, as a toy for his passion?"

Let a sexually diseased man, in his unbridled career of licentiousness, contaminate ever so many of these poor beings—who, to the honor of woman be it said, are mostly driven by bitter want or through seduction to ply their disgraceful trade,—the scurvy fellow remains unmolested. But woe to the woman who does not forthwith submit to inspection and treatment! The garrison cities, university towns, etc., with their congestion of vigorous, healthy men, are the chief centers of prostitution and of its dangerous diseases, that are carried thence into the remotest corners of the land, and everywhere spread infection. The same holds with the sea towns. What the moral qualifications are with a large number of our students the following utterance in a publication for the promotion of morality may give an idea of: "*With by far the larger number of students, the views entertained upon matters of morality are shockingly low, aye, they are downright unclean.*"[6] And these are the circles—boastful of their "German breed," and "German morals"—from which our administrative officers, our

[6] "Korrespondenzblatt zur Bekämpfung der öffentlichen Sittenlosigkeit," August 15, 1893.

District Attorneys and our Judges are in part recruited.

"Thy sins shall be visited upon the children unto the third and fourth generation." This Bible sentence falls upon the dissipated and sexually diseased man in the fullest sense of the word, unhappily also upon the innocent woman. "Attacks of apoplexy with young men and also women, several manifestations of spinal debility and softening of the brains, all manner of nervous diseases, affections of the eyes, cariosity, inflammation of the intestines, sterility and atrophy, *frequently proceed from nothing else than chronic and neglected, and, often for special reasons, concealed syphilis*. . . As things now are, ignorance and lightheadedness also contribute towards *turning blooming daughters of the land into anaemic, listless creatures*, who, under the burden of a chronic inflammation of the pelvis, *have to atone for the excesses committed by their husbands before and after marriage.*"[7] In the same sense does Dr. Blaschke utter himself:[8] "Epidemics like cholera and smallpox, diphtheria and typhus, whose visible effects are, by reason of their suddenness, realized by all, although hardly equal to syphilis in point of virulence, and, in point of diffusion, not to be compared therewith, yet are they the terror of the population . . . while before syphilis society stands, one feels inclined to say, with frightful indifference." The fault lies in the circumstance that it is considered "improper" to talk openly of such things. Did not even the German Reichstag stop short before a resolution to provide by law that sexual diseases, as well as all others, shall be treated by Sick-Benefit Associations?

The syphilitic virus is in its effects the most tenacious and hardest poison to stamp out. Many years after an outbreak has been overcome, and the patient believes every trace to be wiped out, the sequels frequently crop up afresh in the wife or the new-born child;[9] and a swarm of ailments among wives and children trace their causes back, respectively, to marital and parental venereal diseases. With some who are born blind, the misfortune is due to the father's sins, the consequences of which transmitted themselves to the wife, and from her to the child. Weak-minded and idiotic children may frequently ascribe their infirmity to the same cause. Finally, what dire disaster may be achieved through vaccination by an insignificant drop of syphilitic blood, our own days can furnish crass illustrations of.

In the measure that men, willingly or otherwise, renounce marriage,

[7] "Die gesundheitschädliche Tragweite der Prostitution," Dr. Oskar Lassar.
[8] "Die Behandlung der Geschlechtskrankheiten in Krankenkassen und Heilanstalten."
[9] In the English hospitals, during 1875, fully 14 per cent. of the children under treatment were suffering of inherited venereal diseases. In London, there died of these diseases 1 man out of every 190 cases of death; in all England, 1 out of every 159 cases; in the poor-houses of France, 1 out of 160.5.

and seek the gratification of natural impulses through illegitimate channels, seductive allurements increase also. The great profits yielded by
all undertakings that cater to immorality, attract numerous and un-
scrupulous business men, who spare no artifice of refinement to draw
and keep customers. Account is taken of every demand, according
to the rank and position of the custom, also of its means and readiness
to bleed. If some of these "public houses" in our large cities were to
blab out their secrets, the fact would appear that their female tenants—
mostly of low extraction, without either culture or education, often
unable to write their own names, but possessed of all the more physical
charms—stand in the most intimate relations with "leaders of society,"
with men of high intelligence and culture. There would be found
among these Cabinet Ministers, high military dignitaries, Councillors,
members of Legislatures, Judges, etc., going in and out, and side by
side with representatives of the aristocracy of birth, of finance, of commerce and of industry,—all of them, who, by day and in society, strut
about with grave and dignified mien as "representatives and guardians
of morality, of order, of marriage, and of the family," and who stand
at the head of the Christian charity societies and of societies for the
"suppression of prostitution." Modern capitalist society resembles a
huge carnival festival, at which all seek to deceive and fool one
another. Each carries his official disguise with dignity, in order later,
unofficially and with all the less restraint, to give a loose to his inclinations and passions. All the while, public life is running over
with "Morality," "Religion" and "Propriety." In no age was there
greater hypocrisy than in ours. The number of the augurs swells daily.

The supply of women for purposes of lust rises even more rapidly
than the demand. Our increasingly precarious social conditions—want,
seduction, the love for an externally brilliant and apparently easy life—
furnish the female candidates from all social strata. Quite typically
does a novel of Hans Wachenhusen[10] depict the state of things in the
capital of the German Empire. The author expresses himself on the
purpose of his work in these words: "My book deals mainly with the
victims of the female sex and its steady depreciation, due to the unnatural plight of our social and civic state, through its own fault, through
neglect of education, through the craving of luxury and the increasing
light-headed supply in the market of life. It speaks of this sex's increasing surplus, which renders daily more hopeless the new-born ones,
more prospectless those that grow up. . . . I wrote much in the
same way as the District Attorney puts together the past life of a
criminal, in order to establish therefrom the measure of his guilt.
Novels being generally considered works of fiction, permissible opposites

[10] "Was die Strasse verschlingt."

of Truth, the following is, in that sense, no novel, but a true picture of life, without coloring." In Berlin, things are no better and no worse than in other large cities. Whether Greek-Orthodox St. Petersburg or Catholic Rome, Germanic-Christian Berlin or heathen Paris, puritanic London or gay Vienna, approach nearer to Babylon of old is hard to decide. "Prostitution possesses its written and its unwritten laws, its resources, its various resorts, from the poorest cottage to the most splendid palace, its numberless grades from the lowest to the most refined and cultivated; it has its special amusements and public places of meeting, its police, its hospitals, its prisons and its literature."[11] "We no longer celebrate the festival of Osiris, the Bacchanalia and the Indian orgies of the spring month; but in Paris and other large cities, under the black cloak of night, behind the walls of 'public' and 'private' houses, people give themselves over to orgies and Bacchanalia that the boldest pen dare not describe."[12]

Under such conditions, the traffic in female flesh has assumed mammoth proportions. It is conducted on a most extensive scale, and is most admirably organized in the very midst of the seats of civilization and culture, rarely attracting the notice of the police. A swarm of brokers, agents, carriers, male and female, ply the trade with the same unconcern as if they dealt in any other merchandise. Birth certificates are forged, and bills of lading are drawn up with accurate descriptions of the qualifications of the several "articles," and are handed over to the carriers as directions for the purchasers. As with all merchandise, the price depends upon the quality, and the several catagories are assorted and consigned, according to the taste and the requirements of the customers in different places and countries. The slyest manipulations are resorted to in order to evade the snares and escape the vigilance of the police; not infrequently large sums are used to shut the eyes of the guardians of the law. A number of such cases have been established, especially in Paris.

Germany enjoys the sorry fame of being the woman market for half the world. The innate German migratory disposition seems to animate also a portion of the women. In larger numbers than those of any other people, the Austrian excepted, do they furnish their contingent to the supply of international prostitution. German women populate the harems of the Turks, as well as the public houses of central Siberia, and as far away as Bombay, Singapore, San Francisco and Chicago. In a book of travels,[13] the author, W. Joest, speaks as follows on the German trade in girls: "People so often grow warm in our moral Germany

[11] Dr. Elizabeth Blackwell, "The Moral Education."
[12] Montegazza, "L'Amour dans l'Humanite."
[13] "Aus Japan nach Deutschland durch Sibirien."

over the slave trade that some African negro Prince may be carrying
on, or over conditions in Cuba and Brazil, but they should rather keep
in mind the beam in their own eyes: *in no country is there such a trade
with white female slaves, from no country is the export of this living
merchandise as large as it is from Germany and Austria.* The road that
these girls take can be accurately followed. From Hamburg they are
shipped to South America; Bahia and Rio de Janeiro receive their
quotas; the largest part is destined for Montevideo and Buenos Ayres,
while a small rest goes through the Straits of Magellan as far as Val-
paraiso. Another stream is steered via England, or direct to North
America, where, however, it can hold its own only with difficulty against
the domestic product, and, consequently, splits up down the Mississippi
as far as New Orleans and Texas, or westward to California. Thence,
the coast is supplied as far south as Panama; while Cuba, the West
Indies and Mexico draw their supplies from New Orleans. Under the
title of "Bohemians," further droves of German girls are exported over
the Alps to Italy and thence further south to Alexandria, Suez, Bombay,
Calcutta and Singapore, aye, even to Hongkong and as far as Shanghai.
The Dutch Indies and Eastern Asia, Japan, especially, are poor markets,
seeing that Holland does not allow white girls of this kind in its colonies, while in Japan the daughters of the soil are themselves too pretty
and cheap. American competition from San Francisco also tends to
spoil the otherwise favorable chances. Russia is provided from East
Prussia, Pommerania and Poland. The first station is usually Riga.
Here the dealers from St. Petersburg and Moscow supply themselves, and
ship their goods in large quantities to Nischnij-Nowgororod and beyond
the Ural Mountains to Irbit and Krestofsky, aye as far as the interior
of Siberia. I found, for instance, a German girl in Tschita who had
been traded in this way. This wonderful trade is thoroughly organized,
it is attended to by agents and commercial travelers. *If ever the Foreign Department of the German Empire were to demand of its consuls
reports on this matter, quite interesting statistical tables could be put
together."*

This trade flourishes to this day at its fullest, as proved in the autumn
of 1893 by a Social Democratic delegate to the German Reichstag.

The number of prostitutes is hard to estimate; accurately it can not
be at all given. The police can state approximately the number of
women whose principal occupation is prostitution; but it can not do this
with regard to the much larger number of those who resort to it as a
side means of income. All the same, the figures approximately known
are frightfully high. According to v. Oettingen, the number of prostitutes in London was, as early as the close of the sixties, estimated at
80,000. In Paris the number of registered prostitutes in 1892 was 4,700,
but fully one-third escape police control. In all Paris, there were, in

1892, about sixty brothels, with 600 to 700 prostitutes, and the number of brothels is steadily on the decline. On the other hand, based upon an investigation, instituted by the Municipal Council of Paris, in 1889, the number of women who prostitute themselves is placed at the enormous figure of 120,000. In Berlin, the number of prostitutes, registered with the police, was:—

1886	3,006	1888	3,392
1887	3,063	1889	3,703
	1890	4,039	

In 1890, there were six physicians employed, whose duty it was to devote two hours a day to inspection.[14] Since then the number of physicians has been increased. The prostitutes, registered with the police, constitute, however, in Berlin also, only a very small portion of the total. Expert sources estimate it at not less than 50,000. In the year 1890 alone, there were in 9,024 liquor saloons 2,022 bar-maids, almost all of whom yield to prostitution. Furthermore, the, from year to year, rising number of girls, arrested for disorderly conduct, shows that prostitution in Berlin is steadily on the increase. The numbers of these arrests were:—

1881	10,878	1887	13,358
1884	11,157	1890	16,605

Of the 16,605 girls, arrested in 1890, there were 9,162 carried for sentence before the Judge. There were, accordingly, 30 of these at every session of the court, and 128 of them were placed under the police by judicial decree. Already in 1860, it was calculated in Hamburg that every ninth woman was a prostitute. Since then the proportion has become greatly worse.

In Germany, the number of prostitutes probably runs up to 180,000. Accordingly, we here have to do with a large female army, that considers prostitution as a means of livelihood; and the number of victims, whom disease and death claim, is in proportion.[15]

Tait calculates for Edinburg that the average life of the prostitute is 22 to 25 years. According to him, year in and year out, *every fourth aye, every third prostitute seeks to take her own life, and every twelfth actually succeeds in killing herself.* A truly shocking state of things. The majority of prostitutes are heartily tired of their way of living; aye, that they are disgusted thereat, is an experience admitted by all experts.

---

[14] "Zweiter Verwaltungsbericht des Kgl. Polizei-Präsidiums von Berlin vom Jahre 1881-1890."
[15] In the large trades union sick-benefit associations of Berlin the number of syphilitic diseases increased from 4326 in 1881 to 9420 in 1890. Dr. A. Blaschko, *ubi supra.*

But once fallen into prostitution, only to very few is the opportunity ever offered to escape.

And yet the number of prostitutes increases in the same measure that does that of the women engaged as female labor in the various branches of industry and trade, and that are paid off with wages that are too high to die, and too low to live on. Prostitution is, furthermore, promoted by the industrial crises that have become a necessity of the capitalist world, that commence to become chronic, and that carry want and misery into hundreds and thousands of families. According to a letter of the Chief Constable of Bolton, October 31, 1865, to a Factory Inspector, the number of young prostitutes had increased more during the English cotton famine, consequent upon the North American war for the emancipatiorí of the slaves, than during the previous twenty-five years.[16] But it is not only the working-women, who, through want, fall a prey to prostitution. Prostitution also finds its recruiting grounds in the higher walks of life. Lombroso and Ferrero quote Mace,[17] who says of Paris that "a governess certificate, whether of high or low degree, is not so much a draft upon bread, *as upon suicide, theft and prostitution.*"

Parent-Duchatelet made out in his time a statistical table, according to which, out of 5,000 prostitutes there were 1,440 who took to the occupation out of want and misery; 1,250 were orphaned and without support; 80 prostituted themselves in order to feed poor parents; 1,400 were concubines left by their keepers; 400 were girls whom officers and soldiers had seduced and dragged to Paris; 280 had been deserted by their lovers during pregnancy. These figures speak for themselves. They need no further explanation. Mrs. Butler, the zealous champion of the poorest and most wretched of her sex in England, says on the subject of prostitution: "Fortuitous circumstances, the death of a father, of a mother, lack of work, insufficient wages, misery, false promises, snares, have led them to sin." Instructive also is the information given by K. Schneidt[18] on the causes that lead the Berlin bar-maids so often into the arms of prostitution. Shockingly large is the number of female servants that become barmaids, and that almost always means prostitutes. The answers that Schneidt received on his schedules of questions addressed to bar-maids, ran like this: "Because I got a child from my master and had to earn my living;" or "Because my book was spoiled;" or "Because with sewing shirts and the like too little is made;" or "Because I was discharged from the factory and could get no more work;" or "Because my father died, and there were four other little ones." That, particularly, servant girls, after they fall a prey to seduction by their masters, furnish a large contingent to the prostitutes, is a known

[16] Karl Marx, "Capital," p. 461, Swan Sonnenschein & Co., 1896.
[17] *Ubi supra.*
[18] "Das Kellnerinnen-Elend in Berlin," Berlin, 1893.

fact. On the subject of the shockingly large number of seductions of servant girls by their masters or by the sons of these, Dr. Max Taude expresses himself reproachfully.[19] When, however, the upper classes furnish their quota to prostitution, it is not want but seduction and the inclination for an easy life, for dress and for pleasures. On that subject a certain work[20] utters itself this wise:

"Cold with horror and dismay, many a staid citizen, many a parson, teacher, high official, high military dignitary, etc., learns that his daughter has secretly taken to prostitution. *Were it allowable to mention all these daughters by name, either a social revolution would take place on the spot, or the popular ideas concerning honor and virtue would be seriously damaged.*"

It is especially the finer prostitutes, the *haute volee* among the prostitutes, that are recruited from these circles. Likewise do a large portion of actresses, whose wardrobe outlays alone stand in crass disproportion to their salaries, depend upon such unclean sources of revenue.[21] The same with numerous girls, engaged as sales-ladies, and in similar capacities. There are employers dishonorable enough to justify the low wages that they pay by referring their female employes to the aid of "friends." For instance: In 1889 the "Sachsische Arbeiter Zeitung" of Dresden published a notice that ran as follows: "A cultured young lady, long time out of work on account of lung troubles, looked, upon her recovery, for work of any sort. She was a governess. Nothing fit offered itself quickly, and she decided to accept the first job that came along, whatever it was. She first applied to Mr. ———. Seeing she spoke readily several languages, she was acceptable; but the 30 marks a month wages seemed to her too small to get along with. She stated to Mr. ———, and his answer was that most of his girls did not get even that much, but from 15 to 20 marks at most, and they all pulled through quite well, each having a 'good friend,' who helped along. Another gentleman, Mr. ———, expressed himself in the same sense. Of course, the lady accepted a place in neither of the two establishments."

Seamstresses, female tailors, milliners, factory girls by the hundreds of thousands find themselves in similar plight. Employers and their subalterns—merchants, mill owners, landlords, etc.,—who keep female hands and employes, frequently consider it a sort of privilege to find these women handy to administer to their lusts. Our pious and conservative folks love to represent the rural districts as truly idyllic in

---

[19] Dr. Max Taube, "Der Schutz der unehelichen Kinder," Leipsic 1893.

[20] "Die gefallenen Mädchen und die Sittenpolizei," Wilh. Issleib, Berlin, 1889.

[21] In a work, "Kapital und Presse," Berlin, 1891, Dr. F. Mehring proves that a by no means indifferent actress was engaged at a well known theater at a salary of 100 marks a month, and that her outlay for wardrobe alone ran up to 1000 marks a month. The deficit was covered by a "friend."

point of morality, compared with the large cities and industrial centers. Everyone acquainted with the actual state of things knows that it is not so; and the fact was evidenced by the address, delivered by a baronial landlord of Saxony in the fall of 1889, reported as follows in the papers of the place:

"GRIMMA.—Baron Dr. v. Waechter of Roecknitz, recently delivered an address, before a diocese meeting that took place here, upon the subject of 'Sexual Immorality in Our Rural Communities." Local conditions were not presented by him in a rosy color. The speaker admitted with great candor that *employers*, even *married* ones, are frequently in *very intimate relations* with their female domestics, the consequences of which were either cancelled with *cash*, or were removed from the eyes of the world through a *crime*. The fact could, unfortunately, not be cloaked over, that immorality was nursed in these communities, not alone by girls, who, as nurses in cities, had taken in the poison, or by fellows, who made its acquaintance in the military service, but that, sad to say, also the *cultured classes*, through the stewards of manorial estates, and through the officers on the occasions of field manoeuvres, carried lax principles of morality into the country districts. According to Dr. v. Waechter, there are *actually here in the country few girls who reach the age of seventeen* without having fallen." The open-hearted speaker's love of truth was answered with a social boycott, placed upon him by the officers who felt insulted. The *jus primae noctis* of the medieval feudal lord continues in another form in these very days of ours.

The majority of prostitutes are thrown into the arms of this occupation at a time when they can hardly be said to have arrived at the age of discretion. Of 2,582 girls, arrested in Paris for the secret practice of prostitution, 1,500 were minors; of 607 others, 487 had been deflowered under the age of twenty. In September, 1894, a scandal of first rank took the stage in Buda-Pest. It appeared that about 400 girls of from twelve to fifteen years fell prey to a band of rich rakes. The sons of our "property and cultured classes" generally consider it an attribute of their rank to seduce the daughters of the people, whom they then leave in the lurch. Only too readily do the trustful daughters of the people, untutored in life and experience, and generally joyless and friendless, fall a prey to the seduction that approaches them in brilliant and seductive guise. Disillusion, then sorrows, finally crime,—such are the sequels. Of 1,846,171 live births in Germany in 1891, 172,456 were illegitimate. Only conjure up the volume of worry and heartaches prepared for a great number of these mothers, by the birth of their illegitimate children, even if allowance is made for the many instances when the children are legitimatized by their fathers! *Suicide by women and in-*

fanticide are to a large extent traceable to the destitution and wretchedness in which the women are left when deserted. The trials for child murder cast a dark and instructive picture upon the canvas. To cite just one case, in the fall of 1894, a young girl, who, eight days after her delivery, had been turned out of the lying-in institute in Vienna and thrown upon the streets with her child and without means, and who, in her distress and desperation, killed the infant, *was sentenced to be hanged* by a jury of Krems in Lower Austria. About the scamp of a father nothing was said. And how often do not similar instances occur! The seduced and outrageously deserted woman, cast helpless into the abyss of despair and shame, resorts to extreme measures: she kills the fruit of her womb, is dragged before the tribunals, is sentenced to penitentiary or the gallows. The unconscionable, and actual murderer,—he goes off scott-free; marries, perchance, shortly after, the daughter of a "respectable and honest" family, and becomes a much honored, upright man. There is many a gentleman, floating about in honors and distinctions, who has soiled his honor and his conscience in this manner. Had women a word to say in legislation, much would be otherwise in this direction.

Most cruel of all, as already indicated, is the posture of French legislation, which forbids inquiry after the child's paternity, and, instead, sets up foundling asylums. The resolution on the subject, by the Convention of June 28, 1793, runs thus: "The nation takes charge of the physical and moral education of abandoned children. From that moment they will be designated only by the term of orphans. No other designation shall be allowed." Quite convenient for the men, who, thereby, shifted the obligation of the individual upon the collectivity, to the end of escaping exposure before the public and their wives. In all the provinces of the land, orphan and foundling asylums were set up. The number of orphans and foundlings ran up, in 1893, to 130,945, of which it was estimated that each tenth child was legitimate, but not wanted by its parents. But no particular care was taken of these children, and the mortality among them was, accordingly, great. In that year, fully 59 per cent., i. e., more than one-half died during the first year of their lives; 78 per cent. died twelve years of age and under. Accordingly, of every 100 only 22 reached the age of twelve years and over. It is claimed that matters have in the meantime improved in those establishments.

In Austria and Italy also foundling asylums were established, and their support assumed by the State. *"Ici on fait mourir les enfants"* (Here children are killed) is the inscription that a certain King is said to have recommended as fit for foundling asylums. In Austria they are gradually disappearing; there are now only eight of them left; also the treatment and care of the children has considerably improved to what it was. In 1888, there were 40,865 children cared for in Austria, including Galicia; of these 10,466 were placed in public institutions, 30,399 under private care, at a joint cost of 1,817,372 florins. Mortality was slighter among the children in the public institutions than among those placed under private care. This was especially the case in Galicia. There, 31.25 per cent. of the children died during the year 1888 in the public establishments, by far more than in the public establishments of other countries; but of those under private care, 84.21 per cent. died,—a veritable mass-assassination. It almost looks as though the Polish slaughterhouse system aimed at killing off these poor little worms as swiftly as possible. It is a generally accepted fact that the percentage of deaths among children born out of wedlock is far higher than among those born in wedlock. In Prussia there died, early in the sixties, during the first year of their lives 18.23 per cent. of children born in wedlock, and 33.11 per cent. of children born out of wedlock, accordingly twice as many of the latter. In Paris there died, 100 children born in wedlock to every 139 born out of wedlock, and in the country districts 215. Italian statistics throw up this picture: Out of every 10,000 live-births, there died—

Legitimate children:	1881.	1882.	1883.	1884.	1885.
One month old	751	741	724	698	696
Two to twelve months	1,027	1,172	986	953	1,083
Illegitimate children:					
One month old	2,092	2,045	2,139	2,107	1,813
Two to twelve months	1,387	1,386	1,437	1,437	1,353

The difference in the mortality between legitimate and illegitimate children is especially noticeable during the first month of life. During that period, the mortality of children born out of wedlock is on an average three times as large as that of those born in wedlock. Improper attention during pregnancy, weak delivery and poor care afterwards, are the very simple causes. Likewise do maltreatment and the infamous practice and superstition of "making angels" increase the victims. The number of still-births is twice as large with illegitimate than with legitimate children, due, probably, mainly to the efforts of some of the mothers to bring on the death of the child during pregnancy. The illegitimate children who survive revenge themselves upon society for the wrong done them, by furnishing *an extraordinary large percentage of criminals of all degrees.*

Yet another evil, frequently met, must also be shortly touched upon. Excessive sexual indulgence is infinitely more harmful than too little. A body, misused by excess, will go to pieces, even without venereal diseases, Impotence, barrenness, spinal affections, insanity, at least intellectual weakness, and many other diseases, are the usual consequences. *Temperance* is as necessary in sexual intercourse as in eating and drinking, and all other human wants. But temperance seems difficult to youth. Hence the large number of "young old men," in the higher walks of life especially. The number of young and old *roues* is enormous, and they require special irritants, excess having deadened and surfeited them. Many, accordingly, lapse into the unnatural practices of Greek days. The crime against nature is to-day much more general than most of us dream of: upon that subject the secret archives of many a Police Bureau could publish frightful information. But not among men only, among women also have the unnatural practices of old Greece come up again with force. Lesbian love, or Sapphism, is said to be quite general among married women in Paris; according to Taxal,[22] it is enormously in practice among the prominent ladies of that city. In Berlin, one-fourth of the prostitutes are said to practice "tribady;" but also in the circles of our leading dames there are not wanting disciples of Sappho. Still another unnatural gratification of the sexual instinct manifests itself in the violation of children, a practice that has increased greatly during the last thirty years. In France, during 1851-1875, 17,656 cases of this nature were tried. The colossal number of these crimes in France is intimately connected with the two-child system, and with the abstinence of husbands towards their wives. To the German population also we find people recommending Malthusianism, without stopping to think what the sequels will be. The so-called "liberal professions," to whom belong mainly the members of the upper classes, furnish in Germany about 5.6 per cent. of the ordinary criminals, but they furnish 13 per cent. of the criminals indicted for violation of children; and this latter percentage would be still higher were there not in those circles ample means to screen the criminals, so that, probably, the majority of cases remain undiscovered. The revelations made in the eighties by the "Pall Mall Gazette" on the violation of children in England, are still fresh in the public memory.

The moral progress of this our best of all possible worlds is recorded in the below tables for England, the "leading country in civilization." In England there were:—

Year.	Immoral Acts of Violence.	Deaths from Syphilis.	Insane.
1861	280	1,345	39,647
1871	315	1,995	56,755
1881	370	2,334	73,113
1882	466	2,478	74,842
1883	390	....	76,765
1884	510	....	.....

Increase since 1861..82 per cent. 84 per cent. 98 per cent.

[22] Lombroso and Ferrero, *ubi supra.*

A frightful increase this is of the phenomena that point to the rising physical and moral ruin of English society.

The best statistical record of venereal diseases and their increase is kept by Denmark, Copenhagen especially. Here venereal diseases, with special regard to syphilis, developed as follows:—

Year.	Population.	Venereal Diseases.	Of these, Syphilis.
1874	196,000	5,505	836
1879	227,000	6,299	934
1885	290,000	9,325	1,866

Among the personnel of the navy in Copenhagen, the number of venereal diseases increased 1224 per cent. during the period mentioned; in the army and for the same period, 227 per cent.[23] And how stands it in Paris? From the year 1872 to the year 1888, the number of persons treated for venereal diseases in the hospitals Du Midi, de Lourcine and de St. Louis was 118,223, of which 60,438 suffered of syphilis and 57,795 of other venereal affections. Besides these, of the number of outside persons, who applied to the clinics of the said three hospitals, there was a yearly average of 16,385 venereals.[24]

We have seen how, as a result of our social conditions, vice, excesses, wrongs and crimes of all sorts are bred. All society is kept in a state of unrest. Under such a state of things woman is the chief sufferer.

Numerous women realize this and seek redress. They demand, first of all, economic self-support and independence; they demand that woman be admitted, as well as man, to all pursuits that her physical and mental powers and faculties qualify her for; they demand, especially, admission to the occupations that are designated with the term "liberal professions." Are the efforts in these directions justified? Are they practical? Would they mend matters? These are questions that now crowd forward.

[23] "Die venerischen Krankheiten in Dänemark," Dr. Giesing.
[24] Report of the Sanitary Commission on the organization of sanitation relative to prostitution in Paris, addressed to the Municipal Council of Paris, 1890.

CHAPTER IV.

The endeavor of woman to secure economic self-support and personal independence has, to a certain degree, been recognized as legitimate by bourgeois society, the same as the endeavor of the workingman after greater freedom of motion. The principal reason for such acquiescence lies in the class interests of the bourgeoisie itself. The bourgeoisie, or capitalist class, requires the free and unrestricted purveyance of male and female labor-power for the fullest development of production. In even tempo with the perfection of machinery, and technique; with the subdivision of labor into single acts requiring ever less technical experience and strength; with the sharpening of the competitive warfare between industry and industry, and between whole regions—country against country, continent against continent—the labor-power of woman comes into ever greater demand.

The special causes, from which flows this ever increasing enlistment of woman in ever increasing numbers, have been detailed above *in extenso*. Woman is increasingly employed *along with man, or in his place, because her material demands are less than those of man*. A circumstance predicated upon her very nature as a sexual being, forces woman to proffer herself cheaper. More frequently, on an average, than man, woman is subject to physical derangements, that cause an interruption of work, and that, in view of the combination and organization of labor, in force to-day in large production, easily interfere with the steady course of production. Pregnancy and lying-in prolong such pauses. The employer turns the circumstance to advantage, and *recoups himself doubly for the inconveniences*, that these disturbances put him to, *with the payment of much lower wages*.

Moreover—as may be judged from the quotation on page 90, taken from Marx's "Capital"—the work of married women has a particular fascination for the employer. The married woman is, as working-woman, much more "attentive and docile" than her unmarried sister. Thought of her children drives her to the utmost exertion of her powers, in order to earn the needed livelihood; accordingly, she submits to many an imposition that the unmarried woman does not. In general, the working-woman ventures only exceptionally to join her fellow-toilers in securing better conditions of work: That raises her value in the eyes of the employer; not infrequently she is even a trump card in his hands against refractory workingmen. Moreover, she is endowed with great patience, greater dexterity of fingers, a better developed artistic sense, the latter of which renders her fitter than man for many branches of work.

These female "virtues" are fully appreciated by the virtuous capitalist, and thus, along with the development of industry, woman finds from year to year an ever wider field for her application—but, and this is the determining factor, *without tangible improvement to her social condition*. If woman labor is employed, it generally sets male labor free. The displaced male labor, however, wishes to live; it proffers itself for lower wages; and the proffer, in turn, re-acts depressingly upon the wages of the working-woman. The reduction of wages thus turns into an endless screw, that, due to the constant revolutions in the technique of the labor-process, is set rotating all the more swiftly, seeing that the said technical revolutions, through the savings of labor-power, set also female labor free,—all of which again increases the supply of hands. New industries somewhat counteract the constant supply of relatively superfluous labor-power, but is not strong enough to establish lasting improvement. Every rise of wages above a certain measure causes the employer to look to further improvements in his plant, calculated to substitute will-less, automatic mechanical devices for human hands and human brain. At the start of capitalist production, hardly any but male labor confronted male labor in the labor-market; now sex is played against sex, and, further along the line, age against age. Woman displaces man, and, in her turn, woman is displaced by younger folks and child-labor. Such is the "Moral Order" in modern industry.

The endeavor, on the part of employers, to extend the hours of work, with the end in view of pumping more surplus values out of their employes, is made easier to them, thanks to the slighter power of resistance possessed by women. Hence the phenomenon that, in the textile industries, for instance, in which women frequently constitute far more than one-half of the total labor employed, the hours of work are everywhere longest. Accustomed from home to the idea that her work is "never done," woman allows the increased demands to be placed upon her without resistance. In other branches, as in the millinery trade, the manufacture of flowers, etc., wages and hours of work deteriorate through the taking home of extra tasks, at which the women sit till midnight, and even later, without realizing that they thereby only compete against themselves, and, as a result, earn in a sixteen-hour workday what they would have made in a regular ten-hour day.[1] In what measure female labor has

[1] On this subject, the law for protection of working-women, adopted by the people of the canton of Zurich in August, 1894, with 49,909 votes against 12,531, contains an excellent provision. The law makes it a penal offence

increased in the leading industrial countries may appear from the below sets of tables. We shall start with the leading industrial country of Europe,—England. The last census furnishes this picture:

Year.	Total Persons Employed.	Males.	Females.
1871	11,593,466	8,270,186	3,323,280
1881	11,187,564	7,783,646	3,403,918
1891	12,898,484	8,883,254	4,016,230

Accordingly, within twenty years, the number of males employed increased 613,068, or 7.9 per cent.; the number of females, however, by 692,950, or 20.9 per cent. It is especially to be observed in this table that, in 1881, a year of crisis, the number of males employed fell off by 486,540, and the number of females increased by 80,638. The increase of female at the cost of male persons employed is thus emphatically brought to light. But within the increasing number of female employes itself a change is going on: *younger forces are displacing the older*. It transpired that in England, during the years 1881-1891, female labor-power of the age 10 to 45 had increased, while that above 45 had decreased.

Industries in which female exceeded considerably the number of male labor, were mainly the following:

Industries.	Females.	Males.
Manufacture of woman's clothing	415,961	4,470
Cotton industry	332,784	213,231
Manufacture of worsted goods	69,629	40,482
Manufacture of shirts	52,943	2,153
Manufacture of hosiery	30,887	18,200
Lace industry	21,716	13,030
Tobacco industry	15,880	13,090
Bookbinding	14,249	11,487
Manufacture of gloves	9,199	2,756
Teachers	144,393	50,628

Again the wages of women are, in almost all branches, considerably lower than the wages of men *for the same hours*. In the year 1883, the wages in England were for men and women as follows, per week:—

for working-women to take from the shop, where they are employed during the day, work to be done at home. This law goes further than any other known to us for the protection of working-women. It also prescribes an extra pay of 25 per cent. for the extra hours fixed by law: the most effective means to check the evil of overwork.

Industries.	Males.		Females.	
Flax and jute factories....26	Marks		10—11 Marks	
Manufacture of glass......38	"		12	"
Printing ....32—36	"		10—12	"
Carpet factories 29	"		15	"
Weaving 26	"		16	"
Shoemaking 29	"		15	"
Dyeing ....25—29	"		12—13	"

Similar differences in wages for men and women are found in the Post Office service, in school teaching, etc. Only in the cotton industry in Lancashire did both sexes earn equal wages for equal hours of work in the tending of power looms.

In the United States, according to the census of 1890, there were 2,652,-157 women, of the age of ten years and over engaged in productive occupations:—594,510 in agriculture, 631,988 in manufacture, 59,364 in trade and transportation, and 1,366,235 in personal service, of whom 938,910 were servants. Besides that, there were 46,800 female farmers and planters, 5,135 Government employes, 155,000 school teachers, 13,182 teachers of music, 2,061 artists.[2] In the city of New York, 10,961 working-women participated in strikes during the year 1890, a sign that working-women in the United States, like their European fellow-female wage slaves, understand the class distinctions that exist between Capital and Labor. In what measure women are displacing the men in a number of industries in the United States also, is indicated by the following item from the "Levest. Journ." in 1893:

"One of the *features* of the factory towns of Maine is a class of men that may be termed 'housekeepers.' In almost every town, where much factory work is done, these men are to be found in large numbers. Whoever calls shortly before noon will find them, with aprons tied in front, washing dishes. At other hours of the day they can be seen scrubbing, making the beds, washing the children, tidying up the place, or cooking. Whether any of them attend to the sewing and mending of the family

[2] The census of 1890 gives 3,914,571 women of at least 10 years of age engaged in gainful occupations in the United States; that is 17.6 per cent. of the total population engaged in gainful occupations, and 12.7 per cent. of the total female population of the country.

According to the census of 1900 there were 5,319,912 women of at least 10 years of age engaged in gainful occupations in the United States; that is 18.2 per cent. of the total population engaged in gainful occupations, and 14.3 per cent. of the total female population of the country.

Classified by kinds of occupation, the census of 1900 shows: 977,336 women engaged in agricultural pursuits; 430,576 in professional service; 2,095,449 in domestic and personal service; 503,347 in trade and transportation; 1,313,204 in manufacturing and mechanical pursuits.—THE TRANSLATOR.

we are not quite sure. These men attend to the household for the simple reason that *their wives can earn more in the factory than they,* and it means a saving of money if the wife goes to work."[3]

The closing sentence should read: "Because the women work for wages that the men can no longer work for, and the employer therefore prefers women,"—which happens in Germany also. The towns here described are the so-called "she-towns," already more fully referred to.

In France, there were, in 1893, not less than 15,958 women engaged in the railroad service (in the offices and as ticket agents) ; in the provincial Post Office there were 5,383 women employed; as telegraphists and telephonists, 9,805; and in the State Savings Banks 425. Altogether the number of women in France engaged in gainful occupations, inclusive of agriculture and personal service, was, in 1893, in round figures 4,415,000. Of 3,858 decisions, rendered by the trades courts of Paris, not less than 1,674 concerned women.

To what extent female labor was applied in the industries of Switzerland as early as 1886, is told by the following figures of the "Bund":

Industries.	Males.	Females.
Silk industry	11,771	51,352
Cotton industry	18,320	23,846
Linen and half-linen industry	5,553	5,232
Embroidery	15,724	21,000

[3] For the sake of verification, and especially with the view of avoiding any serious discrepancy that might arise from a translation back into English from a German translation of the original English, an attempt was made to secure a transcript of the original of the above interesting article. A serious difficulty was encountered. Besides the indefinite date, the abbreviated form, in which the German text gives the name of the Maine paper quoted from—"Levest. Journ."—and as reproduced in this translation, forced a recourse to guess work. The nearest that any Maine paper, given in the American Newspaper Directory, came to the abbreviation was the "Lewiston Evening Journal." The below correspondence tells its tale:

"Daily People, 2, 4 and 6 New Reade street,
New York, May 18th, 1903.
"Editor 'Lewiston Evening Journal,' Lewiston, Me.:
"Dear Sir—The within is a translation from the German of what purports to be a German translation of an article, or part of an article, that appeared in the 'Journal.' The only date given is 1893.
"I shall esteem it a favor if you will let me have an accurate transcript of the passage in the original. If the 'Journal' had such an article, the enclosed re-translation back into English may help to identify the article. Thanking you in advance,   Yours truly,   "D. DeLeon,
"Ed. 'The People.' "

"D. DeLeon, Esq., New York City:
"My Dear Sir—I regret that I can not find the article of which the enclosed is a transcript.
"I have no doubt of its correctness, for such is frequently the case in cities like these, where the woman is the six-loom weaver, and by her deftness is the better wage-earner.   "Very truly yours,
"Arthur G. Staples,
"Managing Ed. 'Lewiston Journal.' "

Altogether, there were then in the textile industries, 103,452 women engaged, besides 52,838 men; and the "Bund" expressly declares that there is hardly an occupation in Switzerland in which women are not found.

In Germany, according to the census of occupations of 1882, of the 7,340,789 persons engaged in gainful occupations, 1,506,743 were women; or 20.6 per cent. The proportions were, among others, these:—

Industries.	Males.	Females.	Per Cent.
Commercial occupations	536,221	181,286	25.2
Service and restaurants.....................	172,841	141,407	45.0
Messenger and day laborers................	9,212	3,265	26.2
Spinning	69,272	100,459	30.0
Weaving	336,400	155,396	32.0
Embroidery	42,819	31,010	42.0
Lace and crochet work....................	5,676	30,204	84.0
Lace manufacture	13,526	17,478	56.4
Bookbinding and paste-board box-making....	31,312	10,409	25.0
Paper manufacture	37,685	20,847	35.6
Tobacco working	64,477	48,919	43.1
Clothes-making, etc,.....................	279,978	440,870	61.2

To these must be added 2,248,909 women engaged in agriculture, 1,282,-400 female servants, also school teachers, artists, Government office-holders, etc.

According to the census of occupations for 1875-1882, the following was the result. There were employed in industrial occupations in the German Empire:—

Year.	Total Persons Employed.		Total Persons Employed. In the Small Trades.		In the Large Trades.	
	Males.	Females.	Males.	Females.	Males.	Females.
1875	5,463,856	1,116,095	3,453,357	705,874	2,010,499	410,221
1882	5,815,039	1,506,743	3,487,073	989,422	2,327,966	514,321
Increase in 1882	351,183 or 6.4 per cent.	390,648 or 35 per cent.	33,716 or 1 per cent.	283,548 or 40.2 per cent.	317,966 or 15.8 per cent.	107,100 or 26.1 per cent.

According to these figures, not only did female labor increase by 35 per cent. during the period of 1875-1882, while male labor increased only

Though success was not complete, the letter of the managing editor of the "Lewiston Journal" is a corroboration of the substance of the passage quoted. —THE TRANSLATOR.

by 6.4 per cent., but the great increase of female labor, especially in small industries, tells the tale that *only by dint of a strong application of female labor, with its correspondingly low wages, can small production keep itself afloat, for a while.*

In 1882, there were to every 1,000 persons engaged in industry 176 women; in commerce and transportation, 190; in agriculture, 312.

In 1892, the number of women, employed in the factories of Germany, were of the following ages:

Age.	Number Employed.
12-14	3,897
14-16	68,735
16-21	223,538
Over 21	337,499
Besides (for Reuss younger line without designation of ages)	6,197
	639,866

In the Kingdom of Saxony, notedly the most industrial portion of Germany, the number of working-women employed in the factories was:—

Year.	16 Years and Over.	12 to 16.
1883	72,716	8,477
1892	110,555	13,333
Increase	37,839	4,856
	52 per cent.	57 per cent.

As a result of the new factory regulations, which limited the hours of female labor, between the ages of 14 to 16, to 10 a day, and wholly forbade factory work to children of school age, the number of working-women between the ages of 14 to 16 sank to 6,763, and of girls between the ages of 12 to 14, sank by 6,334. The strongest increase in the number of working-women, as far as we are informed, took place in the tobacco industry of Baden. According to the reports of the Baden Factory Inspector, Dr. Woerishoffer, the number of persons engaged in the said industry and their subdivisions by sexes, was as follows:

Year.	Total Number Employed.	Males.	Females.
1882 12,192		5,193	6,999
1892 24,056		7,932	16,124
Increase 11,864		2,739 or 52.8 per cent.	9,125 or 130 per cent.

This increase in the number of female tobacco workers, denotes the sharpening competitive struggle, that has developed during the last ten years in the German tobacco as well as many other industries, and which compels the ever intenser engagement of the cheaper labor of woman.

And, as in the rest of Germany, so likewise in Baden the industrial development in general shows a larger increase of female than of male workers. Within a year, it recorded the following changes:—

Year.	Males.	Females.
1892	79,218	35,598
1893	84,470	38,557
Increase	5,252	2,959
	or 6.6 per cent.	or 8.3 per cent.

Of the working-women over 16 years of age, 28.27 were married. In the large ammunition factory at Spandau, there were, in 1893, 3,000 women out of a total of 3,700 employes.

As in England, in Germany also, female labor is paid worse than male. According to the report of the Leipsic Chamber of Commerce for the year 1888, the weekly wage for equal hours were:—

Industries.	Males. Marks.	Females. Marks.
Lace manufacture	20 —35	7 —15
Cloth glove manufacture..	12 —30	6 —25
Linen and jute weaving...	12 —27	5 —10
Wool-carding	15 —27	7.20—10.20
Sugar refinery	10.50—31	7.50—10
Leather and leather goods.	12 —28	7 —18
Chemicals	8.50—25	7.50—10
Rubber fabrics	9 —28	6 —17
One factory of paper lanterns	16 —22	7.50—10

In an investigation of the wages earned by the factory hands of Mannheim in 1893, Dr. Woerishoffer divided the weekly earnings into three classes: one, the lowest, in which the wages reached 15 marks; one from 15 to 24; and the last and highest in which wages exceeded 24 marks. According to this subdivision, wages in Mannheim presented the following picture:—

	Low.	Medium.	High.
Both sexes	29.8 per cent.	49.8 per cent.	20.4 per cent.
Males	20.9 per cent.	56.2 per cent.	22.9 per cent.
Females	99.2 per cent.	0.7 per cent.	0.1 per cent.

The working-women earned mostly veritable starvation wages. They received per week:—

Marks.	Percentage of Females.
Under 5	4.62
5— 6	5.47
6— 8	43.96
8—10	27.45
10—12	12.38
12—15	5.38
Over 15	0.74

In the Thüringer Wald district, in 1891, the workingmen engaged in the slate works received 2.10 marks a day; the women 0.70. In the spinning establishments, the men received 2 marks, the women from 0.90 to 1 mark.

Worst of all are the earnings in the tenement industry, for men as well as for women, but for the women it is still more miserable than for the men. In this branch, hours of work are unlimited; when the season is on, they transcend imagination. Furthermore, it is here that the sweating system is generally in vogue, i. e., work given out by middlemen (contractors) who, in recompense for their irksome labor of superintendence, keep to themselves a large part of the wages paid by the principal. Under this system, women are also expected to submit to indignities of other nature.

How miserably female labor is paid in the tenement industries, the following figures on Berlin conditions may indicate. Men's colored shirts, paid for in 1889 with from 2 marks to 2.50, the employer got in 1893 for 1 mark 50 pfennig. A seamstress of average skill must work from early till late if she means to make from 6 to 8 of these skirts. Her earnings for the week are 4 or 5 marks. An apron-maker earns from 2 marks 50 pfennig to 5 marks a week; a necktie-maker, 5 to 6 marks; a skilled blouse-maker, 6 marks; a very skilled female operator on boys' clothing, 8 to 9 marks; an expert jacket-maker, 5 to 6 marks. A very swift seamstress on men's shirts may, in the good season, and working from 5 in the morning to 10 at night, make as much as 12 marks. Millinery workers, who can copy patterns independently, make 30 marks a month. Quick trimmers, with years of experience, earn from 50 to 60 marks a month during the season. The season usually lasts five months. An umbrella-maker, working twelve hours a day, makes 6 to 7 marks. Such starvation wages force the working-women into prostitution: even with the very plainest wants, no working-women can live in Berlin on less than 8 or 9 marks a week.

Acording to a statistical report on wages, ordered by the Chamber of Commerce of Reichenberg for its own district, 91 per cent. of all the working-women came under the wage category of from 2 to 5 guilders a week. Upon the enforcement in Austria of the law on sick insurance, the authorities discovered that in 116 districts (21.6 per cent. of all) the working-women earned at most 30 kreuzer a day, 90 guilders a year; and in 428 districts (78.4 per cent. of the total) from 30 to 50 kreuzer, or from 90 to 150 guilders a year. The young working-women, under 16 years of age, earned in 173 districts (30.9 per cent.) 20 kreuzer a day at the most, or at the most 60 guilders a year; and in 387 districts (69.1 per cent.) from 20 to 30 kreuzer, or from 60 to 90 guilders a year.

Similar differences between the wages of male and female labor exist in all countries on earth. According to the report on Russian industry at the Chicago Exposition in 1893, a workingman made in cotton weaving 66 marks a month, a working-woman 18; a male cotton spinner 66 marks, a female 14. In the lace industry men earned up to 130 marks, women 26; in cloth manufacture, with the power loom, a working man made 90 marks, a working-women 26 a month.

These facts show that woman is increasingly torn from family life by modern developments. Marriage and the family, in the bourgeois sense, are undermined by this development, and dissolved. From the view point afforded by this fact also, it is an absurdity to direct women to a domestic life. That can be done only by such people, who thoughtlessly walk the path of life; who fail to see the facts that shape themselves all around, or do not wish to see them, because they have an interest in plying the trade of optimism. Facts furnish a very different picture from that presented by such gentlemen.

In a large number of industries women are employed exclusively; in a larger number they constitute the majority; and in most of the others women are more or less numerously found. Their number steadily increases, and they crowd into ever newer occupations, that they had not previously engaged in. Finally, the working-woman is not merely paid worse than the working man; where she does as much as a man, her hours are, on an average, longer.

The German factory ordinances of the year 1891 fixed a maximum of eleven hours for adult working-women. The same is, however, broken through by a mass of exceptions that the authorities are allowed to make. Nightwork also is forbidden for working-women in factories, but here also the Government can make exceptions in favor of factories where work is continuous, or for special seasons; in sugar refineries, for instance. German legislation has not yet been able to rise to the height of really effective measures for the protection of working-women; consequently, these are exploited by inhumanly long hours, and physically wrecked in the small factories, especially in the tenement house industry. Their exploitation is made all the easier to the employer through the circumstance that, until now, a small minority excepted, the women have not realized that, the same as the men, they must organize in their trades, and, there where also men are employed, they must organize jointly with them, in order to conquer for themselves better conditions of work. The ever stronger influx of women in industrial pursuits affects, however, not those occupations only that their correspondingly weaker physique especially fits them for, but it affects also all occupations in which the modern system of exploitation believes it can, with their aid, knock off larger profits. Under this latter head belong both the physically exhausting and the most disagreeable and dangerous occupations. Thus the fantastic pretence of seeing in woman only a tender, finely-strung being, such as poets and writers of fiction love to depict for the delectation of men, a being, that, if it exists at all exists only as an exception, is again reduced to its true value.

Facts are obstinate things, and it is only they that concern us. They alone preserve us from false conclusions, and sentimental twaddle. These facts teach us that to-day we find women engaged in the following occupations, among others:—in cotton, linen and woolen weaving; in cloth and flannel making; in mechanical spinning, calico printing and dyeing; in steel pen and pin making; in the preparation of sugar, chocolate and cocoa; in manufacturing paper and bronzes; in making glass and porcelain and in glass painting; in the manufacture of faience, majolica and earthen ware; in making ink and preparing paints; making twine and paper bags; in preparing hops and manure and chemical disinfectants; in spinning and weaving silk and ribbons; in making soap, candles and rubber goods; in wadding and mat making; in carpet weaving; portfolio and cardboard making; in making lace and trimmings, and embroidering; making wall-paper, shoes and leather goods; in refining oil and lard and preparing chemicals of all sorts; in making jewelry and galvanoplastic goods; in the preparation of rags and refuse and bast; in wood carving, xylography and stone coloring; in straw hat making and cleaning; in making crockery, cigars and tobacco products; in making lime and gelatine fabrics; in making shoes; in furriery; in hat making; in making toys; in the flax, shoddy and hair industries; in watchmaking and housepainting; in the making of spring beds, pencils and wafers; in making looking-glasses, matches and gunpowder preparations; in dipping phosphorus match-sticks and preparing arsenic; in the tinning of iron; in the delicacy trade; in book printing and composition; in the preparation of precious stones; in lithography, photogra-

phy, chromo-lithography and metachromotype, and, also in the founding
of types; in tile making, iron founding and in the preparation of metals
generally; in the construction of houses and railroads; in electrical
works; in book-binding, wood-carving and joining; in the making of
footwear and clothing; file making; the making of knives and brass
goods; in manufacturing combs, buttons, gold thread and gas implements;
in the making of tanned goods and trunks; in making starch and chicory
preparations; in metallurgy, wood-planing, umbrella making and fish
manufacturing; the preservation of fruit, vegetables and meat; in the
making of china buttons and fur goods; in mining above ground—in
Belgium also underground after the women are 21 years old; in the
natural oil and wax production; in slate making and stone breaking; in
marble and granite polishing; in making cement; the transportation
of barges and canal boats. Also in the wide field of horticulture, agriculture and cattle-breeding, and all that is therewith connected. Lastly,
in the various industries in which they have long been considered to have
the right of way: in the making of linen and woman's clothing, in the
several branches of fashion, also as saleswomen, and more recently as
clerks, teachers, kindergarten trainers, writers, artists of all sorts. Thousands upon thousands of women of the middle class are being utilized
as slaves in the shops and in the markets, and are thereby withdrawn
from all domestic functions, the training of children in particular.
Finally, there is one occupation to be mentioned, in which young, especially pretty, girls are ever more in demand, to the great injury of their
physical and moral development: it is the occupation in public resorts
of all sorts as bar-maids, singers, dancers, etc., to attract men in quest
of pleasure. This is a field in which impropriety runs riot, and the
holders of white slaves lead the wildest orgies.

Among the occupations mentioned, not a few are most dangerous.
Dangerous, for instance, are the sulphuric and alkaline gases in the
manufacturing and cleaning of straw hats; so is the inhalation of chlo-
rine gases in the bleaching of vegetable materials; the danger of poisoning is imminent in the manufacture of colored paper, colored wafers
and artificial flowers; in the preparation of metachromotype, poisons
and chemicals; in the painting of leaden soldiers and leaden toys. The
on-laying of looking-glasses with quicksilver is simply deadly to the
fruit of pregnant women. If, of the live-births in Prussia, 22 per cent.
on an average die during the first year, there die, according to Dr. Hirt,
65 per cent. of the live-births of female on-layers of quicksilver, 55 per
cent. of those of female glass-polishers, 40 per cent. of those of female
lead-makers. In 1890, out of 78 lying-in women, who had been occupied
in the type foundries of the district of Wiesbaden, only 37 had a normal
delivery. Furthermore, according to Dr. Hirt, the manufacture of col-

ored paper and artificial flowers, the so-called powdering of Brussels lace with white lead, the preparation of decalcomany pictures, the onlaying of mirrors, the manufacture of rubber goods, in short, all occupations at which the working-women are exposed to the inhalation of carbonic acid gases, are especially dangerous from the second half of pregnancy onward. Highly dangerous is also the manufacture of phosphorus matches and work in the shoddy mills. According to the report of the Baden Trades Inspector for 1893, the yearly average of premature births with women engaged in industry rose from 1,039 in the years 1882-1886, to 1,244 in the years 1887-1891. The number of births that had to be aided by an operation averaged for the period of 1882-1886 the figures of 1,118 a year, and for the period of 1886-1891 it averaged 1,385. Facts much graver than any of these would come to light if similar investigations were held also in the more industrially developed countries and provinces of Germany. As a rule the Inspectors are satisfied with stating in their reports: "No special injurious effects were discovered in the employment of women in the factories." How could they discover any, with their short visits and without drawing upon medical advice? That, moreover, there are great dangers to life and limb, especially in the textile industry, in the manufacture of explosives and in work with agricultural machinery, is an established fact. Even a glance at the above and quite incomplete list will tell every reader that a large number of these occupations are among the hardest and most exhausting even to men. Let people say as they please, this work or that is not suitable for woman; what boots the objection if no other and more suitable occupation is furnished her?

Among the branches of industry, or special occupations in the same, that Dr. Hirt[*] considers girls should not be at all employed in, by reason of the danger to health, especially with an eye to their sexual functions, are: The preparation of bronze colors, of velvet and glazed paper, hat making, glass grinding, lithography, flax combing, horsehair twisting, fustian pulling, iron tinning, and work in the flax and shoddy mill.

In the following trades, young girls should be occupied only when the necessary protective measures (ventilation, etc.) are properly provided for: The manufacture of paper matting, china ware, lead pencils, shot lead, etherial oils, alum, blood-lye, bromium, chinin, soda, paraffin and ultramarine (poisonous) colored paper, wafers that contain poison, metachromotypes, phosphorous matches, Schweinfurt green and artificial flowers. Also in the cutting and sorting of rags, sorting and coloring of tobacco leaf, cotton beating, wool and silk carding, cleaning of bed feathers, sorting pencil hairs, washing (sulphur) straw hats, vulcanizing and melting rubber, coloring and printing calico, painting

[*] "Die gewerbliche Thätigkeit der Frauen."

lead soldiers, packing snuff, wire netting, on-laying of mirrors, grinding needles and steel pens.

Truly, it is no inspiring sight to see women, and even pregnant ones, at the construction of railroads, pushing heavily laden wheelbarrows in competition with men; or to watch them as helpers, mixing mortar and cement or carrying heavy loads of stone at the construction of houses; or in the coal pits and iron works. All that is womanly is thereby rubbed off from woman, her womanliness is trodden under foot, the same as, conversely, all manly attributes are stripped from the men in hundreds of other occupations. Such are the sequels of social exploitation and of social war. Our corrupt social conditions turn things topsy-turvy.

It is, accordingly, easy to understand that, considering the extent to which female labor now prevails, and threatens to make still further inroads in all fields of productive activity, the men, highly interested in the development, look on with eyes far from friendly, and that here and there the demand is heard for the suppression of female labor and its prohibition by law. Unquestionably, with the extension of female labor, the family life of the working class goes ever more to pieces, the dissolution of marriage and the family is a natural result, and immorality, demoralization, degeneration, diseases of all natures and child mortality increase at a shocking pace. According to the statistics of population of the Kingdom of Saxony, child mortality has greatly increased in all those cities that become genuine manufacturing places during the last 25 or 30 years. During the period 1880-1885 there died in the cities of Saxony, on an average, 28.5 per cent. of the live-births during the first year of life. In the period of 1886-1890, 45.0 of the live-births died in Ernsthal during the first year of their lives, 44.5 in Stolling, 40.4 in Zschopau, 38.9 in Lichtenstein, 38.3 in Thum, 38.2 in Meerane, 37.7 in Crimmitschau, 37.2 in Burgstaedt, 37.1 in Werdau, 36.5 in Ehrenfriedersdorf, 35.8 in Chemnitz, 35.5 in Frankenberg, 35.2 in Buchholz, 35.1 in Schneeberg, 34.7 in Lunzenau, 34.6 in Hartha, 34.5 in Geithaim, etc.[5] Worse yet stood things in the majority of the large factory villages, quite a number of whom registered a mortality of 40 to 50 per cent. Yet, all this notwithstanding, the social development, productive of such sad results, is progress,—precisely such progress as the freedom to choose a trade, freedom of emigration, freedom to marry, and the removal of all other barriers, thus promoting the development of capitalism on a large scale, but thereby also giving the death-blow to the middle class and preparing its downfall.

The working class is not inclined to help the small producer, should he attempt the re-establishment of restrictions to the freedom to choose

[5] Statistisches Jahrbuch für das Königreich Sachsen auf das Jahr, 1894.

a trade and of emigration, or the restoration of the guild and corporation restrictions, contemplated with the end in view of artificially keeping dwarf-production alive for a little while longer,—more than that is beyond their power. As little is a return possible to the former state of things with regard to female labor, but that does not exclude stringent laws for the prevention of the excessive exploitation of female and child labor, and of children of school age. In this the interests of the working class coincides with the interests of the State, of humanity, in general, and of civilization. When we see the State compelled to lower the minimum requirements for military service—as happened several times during the last decades, the last time in 1893, when the army was to be further increased—and we see such lowering of the minimum requirements resorted to for the reason that, as a result of degenerating effects of our economic system, the number of young men unfit for military service becomes ever larger,—when we see that, then, forsooth, all are interested in protective measures. The ultimate aim must be to remove the ills, that progress—such as machinery, improved means of production and the whole modern system of labor—has called forth, while at the same time causing the enormous advantages, that such progress is instinct with for man, and the still greater advantages it is capable of, to accrue in full measure to all the members of society, by means of a corresponding organization of human labor.

It is an absurdity and a crying wrong that the improvements and conquests of civilization—the collective product of all—accrue to the benefit of those alone who, in virtue of their material power, are able to appropriate them to themselves, while, on the other hand, thousands of diligent workingmen are assailed with fear and worry when they learn that human genius has made yet another invention able to multiply many fold the product of manual labor, and thereby opening to them the prospect of being thrown as useless and superfluous upon the sidewalk.* Thus, that which should be greeted with universal joy becomes an object of hostility, that in former years occasioned the storming of many a factory and the demolition of many a new machine. A similar hostile feeling exists to-day between man and woman as workers. This feeling also is unnatural. The point, consequently, is to seek to establish a social condition in which *the full equality of all without distinction of sex shall be the norm of conduct.*

The feat is feasible—the moment all the means of production become

---

* Factory Inspector A. Redgrave delivered in the end of December, 1871, an address in Bradford, in the course of which he said: "I have been struck for some time past by the altered appearance of the wool factories. Formerly they were filled with women and children, now machinery seems to be doing all the work. On inquiry a manufacturer gave me the following information; 'Under the old system I employed 63 persons; after the introduc-

*the property of society; when collective labor, by the application of
all technical and scientific advantages and aids in the process of production, reaches the highest degree of fertility; and when the obligation lies
upon all, capable of work, to furnish a certain measure of labor to society,
necessary for the satisfaction of social wants, in exchange whereof society
guarantees to each and all the means requisite for the development of
his faculties and for the enjoyment of life.*

Woman shall be like man, a productive and useful member of society,
equal-righted with him. Precisely like man, she shall be placed in position to fully develop all her physical and mental faculties, to fulfil her
duties, and to exercise her rights. A free being and the peer of man,
she is safe against degradation.

We shall point out how modern developments in society run out into
such a state of things, and that it is these very crass and monstrous ills
in modern development that compel the establishment of the New Order.

Although the development of the position of woman, as above characterized, is palpable, is tangible to the sight of all who have eyes to see,
the twaddle about the "natural calling" of woman is heard daily, assign-
ing her to domestic duties and the family. The phrase is heard loudest
there where woman endeavors to penetrate into the sphere of the so-called
higher professions, as for instance, the higher departments of instruction and of the civil service, the medical or legal careers, and the pursuit
of the natural sciences. The most laughable and absurd objections are
fetched up, and are defended with the air of "learning." Gentlemen,
who pass for learned, appeal, in this as in so many other things, to
science in order to defend the most absurd and untenable propositions.
Their chief trump card is that woman is inferior to man in mental
powers and that it is folly to believe she could achieve aught of importance in the intellectual field.

These objections, raised by the "learned," fit so well with the general prejudices entertained by men on the calling and faculties of woman
that, whoever makes use of them can count upon the applause of the
majority.

New ideas will ever meet with stubborn opposition so long as general
culture and knowledge continue at so low an ebb as at present, especially
if it lies in the interest of the ruling classes to confine culture and knowledge as much as possible to their own ranks. Hence new ideas will
at the start win over but a small minority, and this will be scoffed at,
maligned and persecuted. But if these new ideas are good and sound,

tion of improved machinery I reduced my hands to 33, and, later, in consequence of new and extensive alterations, I was able to reduce them from 33
to 13.' Thus, within a few years, a reduction of labor, amounting to almost
80 per cent. took place, with an output at least as large as before." Many
interesting items of information on this subject are found in Marx's "Capital."

if they are born as the necessary consequence of existing conditions, then will they spread, and the one-time minority finally becomes a majority. So has it been with all new ideas in the course of history: the idea of establishing the complete emancipation of woman presents the same experience.

Were not one time the believers in Christianity a small minority? Did not the Protestant Reformers and modern bourgeoisdom once face overpowering adversaries? And yet they triumphed. Was the Social Democracy crippled because gagged and pinioned by exclusion laws, so that it could not budge? Never was its triumph more assured than when it was thought to have been killed. The Social Democracy overcame the exclusion laws; it will overcome quite other obstacles besides.

The claim regarding the "natural calling of woman," according whereto she should be housekeeper and nurse, is as unfounded as the claim that there will ever be kings because, since the start of history, there have been such somewhere. We know not where the first king sprang up, as little as we know where the first capitalist stepped upon the scene. This, however, we do know: Kingship has undergone material changes in the course of the centuries, and the tendency of development is to strip it ever more of its powers, until a time comes, no longer far away, when it will be found wholly superfluous. As with the kingship, so with all other social and political institutions; they are all subject to continuous changes and transformations, and to final and complete decay. We have seen, in the course of the preceding historic sketch, that the form of marriage, in force to-day, like the position of woman, was by no means such "eternally"; that, on the contrary, both were the product of a long process of development, which has by no means reached its acme, and can reach it only in the future. If 2,400 or 2,300 years ago Demosthenes could designate the "bringing forth of legitimate children and officiating as a faithful warder of the house" as the only occupation of woman, to-day we have traveled past that point. Who, to-day, would dare uphold such a position of woman as "natural" without exposing himself to the charge of belittling her? True enough, there are even to-day such sots, who share in silence the views of the old Athenian; but none dare proclaim publicly that which 2,300 years ago one of the most eminent orators dared proclaim frankly and openly as *natural*. Therein lies the great advance made.

If, on the one hand, modern development, especially in industrial life, has wrecked millions of marriages, it, on the other hand, promoted favorably the development itself of marriage. Only a few decades ago, and it was a matter of course in every citizen's or peasant's house not only that woman sewed, knitted and washed—although even this has now extensively gone out of fashion—but she also baked the bread,

spun, wove, bleached, brewed beer, boiled soap, made candles. To have
a piece of wearing apparel made out of the house was looked upon as
unutterable waste. Water-pipes, gaslight, gas and oil cooking ranges—
to say nothing of the respective electric improvements—together with
numberless others, were wholly unknown to the women of former times.
Antiquated conditions exist even to-day, but they are the exception. The
majority of women have discontinued many an occupation, formerly
considered of course, the same being attended to in factory and shop
better, more expeditiously and cheaper than the housewife could, whence,
at least in the cities, all domestic requirements for them are wanting.
Thus, in the period of a few decades, a great revolution for them has
been accomplished within our family life, and we pay so little attention
to the fact because we consider it a matter of course. Phenomena, that
develop, so to speak, under the very eyes of man, are not noticed by
him, unless they appear suddenly and disturb the even tenor of events.
He bristles up, however, against new ideas that threaten to lead him out
of the accustomed ruts.

The revolution thus accomplished in our domestic life, and that pro-
gresses ever further, has altered the position of woman in the family,
in other directions besides. Woman has become freer, more independent.
Our grandmothers, if they were honest masters' wives, would not have
dared, and, indeed the thought never crossed their minds, to keep their
working people and apprentices from the table, and visiting, instead,
the theatres, concerts and pleasure resorts, by day at that. Which
of those good old women dared think of occupying her mind with public
affairs, as is now done by many women? To-day they start societies
for all manner of objects, establish papers, call conventions. As working-women they assemble in trades unions, they attend the meetings
and join the organizations of men, and here and there—we are speaking
of Germany—they have had the right of electing boards of labor arbi-
tration, a right that the backward majority of the Reichstag took away
again from them in the year of grace one thousand eight hundred and
ninety.

What sot would seek to annul the changes just described, although
the fact is not to be gainsaid that, there are also dark sides to the bright
sides of the picture, consequent upon our seething and decaying conditions? The bright sides, however, predominate. Women themselves,
however conservative they are as a body, have no inclination to return
to the old, narrow, patriarchal conditions of former times.

In the United States society still stands, true enough, on bourgeois
foundations; but it is forced to wrestle neither with old European prejudices nor with institutions that have survived their day. As a consequence American society is far readier to adopt new ideas and institu-

tions that promise advantage. For some time the position of woman has been looked upon from a viewpoint different than ours. There, for instance, the idea has long taken hold that it is not merely troublesome and improper, but not even profitable to the purse, for the wife to bake bread and brew beer, but that it is unnecessary for her to cook in her own kitchen. The private kitchen is supplanted by co-operative cooking, with a large central kitchen and machinery. The women attend to the work by turns, and the meals generally come out cheaper, taste better, offer a greater variety, and give much less trouble. Our army officers, who are not decried as Socialists and Communists, act on a similar plan. They establish in their casinos a co-operative kitchen; appoint a steward, who attends to the supply of victuals on a large scale; the bill of fare is arranged in common; and the food is prepared in the steam kitchen of the barracks. They live much cheaper than in a hotel, and fare at least as well. Furthermore, thousands of the rich families live the whole year, or part of the year, in boarding-houses or hotels, without in any way missing the private kitchen. On the contrary, they consider it a great convenience to be rid of it. The aversion of especially well-to-do women towards all matters connected with the kitchen does not seem to indicate that this function either belongs to the category of the "natural calling" of woman. On the contrary, the circumstance that princely and other prominent families do like the hotels, and all of them engage male cooks for the preparation of their food, would rather indicate that cooking is a male occupation.—All of which is stated for the benefit of those people who are unable to picture to themselves a woman without brandishing a kitchen ladle.

It is but a step to set up, beside the central kitchen, also the central laundry and corresponding steaming arrangements for public use—as already established in all large cities by rich private persons or speculators, and found highly profitable. With the central kitchen may also be connected central heating, warm water along with cold water pipes, whereby a number of bothersome and time-consuming labors are done away with. Large hotels, many private houses, hospitals, schools, barracks, etc., have now these and many other such arrangements, such as electric light and baths. The only fault to find is that only public establishments and the well-to-do classes enjoy these advantages. Placed within the reach of all, an enormous amount of time, trouble, labor and material could be saved, and the standard of life and the well-being of all raised considerably. In the summer of 1890, the papers published a description of the progress made in the United States in the matter of centralized heating and ventilation. It was there stated:

"The recent attempts, made especially in North America, to effect the heating of whole blocks of houses or city wards from one place have

to record no slight success. From the constructive point of view, they
have been carried out so carefully and effectively that, in view of the
favorable results and the financial advantages which they offer, their
further extension may be confidently expected. More recently the attempt
is being made to furnish from central locations not heat alone, but
also fresh air, either warm or cool, to certain extensive but not too
wide areas of the city. These plans are found in execution in the
so-called Timby System, which, according to the central organ of the
Department of Buildings, gathered from a report of the technical
attaché in Washington, Government Architect Petri, has recently been
thoroughly explained in Washington by the 'National Heating and
Ventilating Company.'' The said company originally planned to supply
50,000 people from one place. The difficulties presented by the requisite
speed of transit and the size of the pneumatic machines, have, however,
caused a limitation to 0.8 kilometers, and in instances of specially
closely built business quarters, the building of a special central power
place."

What was then only projected, has since been in great part executed.
Philistine narrowness in Germany lives to shrug its shoulders at these
and such like schemes, although in Germany also we find ourselves just
now in the midst of one of those technical revolutions, that render the
private kitchen, together with a number of other occupations, hitherto
appertaining to the household, as superfluous as handicraft has been
rendered by machinery and modern technique. In the early days of the
nineteenth century, Napoleon pronounced insane the idea of construct-
ing a ship that could be set in motion by steam. The idea of building
a railroad was declared silly by many folks who passed for sensible:
nobody, it was argued, could remain alive on such a conveyance: the
rapidity of motion would deprive the passengers of breath. Identical
treatment is to-day accorded to a number of new ideas. He who sixty
years ago would have made to our women the proposition of replacing
the carrying of water with water-pipes would have been exposed to the
charge of trying to lead women and servants into idleness.

Nevertheless the great revolution in technique is in full march on all
fields; nothing can any longer hold it back; and bourgeois society, having conjured the same into life, has the historic mission of also carrying
the revolution to perfection, and to promote on all fields the budding of
the germs for radical transformations, *which a social order, built on
new foundations, would only have to generalize on a large scale, and
make common property.*

The trend, accordingly, of our social life is not to banish woman back
to the house and the hearth, as our "domestic life" fanatics prescribe,
and after which they lust, like the Jews in the Desert after the flesh-

pots of Egypt. *On the contrary, the whole trend of society is to lead woman out of the narrow sphere of strictly domestic life to a full participation in the public life of the people*—a designation that will not then cover the male sex only—and in the task of *human civilization.* Laveleye fully recognized this when he wrote:[7] "In the measure that what we are in the habit of designating as civilization advances, the sentiments of piety and the family bonds weaken, and they exercise a decreasing influence upon the actions of men. This fact is so general that a law of social development may be recognized therein." Not only has the position of woman changed, but also the relation of son and daughter to the family, who have gradually attained a degree of independence unknown in former days,—a fact noticeable especially in the United States, where the self-dependent and independent education of the individual is carried on much further than with us. The dark sides that to-day accompany also this form of development, are not necessarily connected with it; they lie in the social conditions of our times. Capitalist society evokes no benificent phenomenon unaccompanied with a dark side: as Fourier long ago pointed out with great perspicacity, capitalist society is in all its progressive steps double-faced and ambiguous.

With Laveleye, Schaeffle also detects in the changed character of the family of our days the effect of social development. He says:[8] "It is true that the tendency described in Chapter II, to reduce and limit the family to its specific functions is traceable throughout history. The family relinquishes one provisional and temporary function after the other. In so far as it officiated only in a surrogate and gap-filling capacity it makes way to independent institutions for law, order, authority, divine service, education, technique, etc., as soon as these institutions take shape."

Women are pressing even further, though as yet only in a minority, and only a fraction of these with clear aims. They aspire to measure their power with men, not on the industrial field alone; they aspire not only after a freer and more independent position in the family; they also aspire at turning their mental faculties to the higher walks of life. The favorite objection raised against them is that they are not fit for such pursuits, not being intended therefor by Nature. The question of engaging in the higher professional occupations concerns at present only a small number of women in modern society; it is, however, important in point of principle. The large majority of men believe in all seriousness that, mentally as well, woman must ever remain subordinate to them, and, hence, has no right to equality. They are, accordingly, the most determined opponents of woman's aspirations.

[7] "Original Property," chap. 20.
[8] Bau und Leben des sozialen Körpers," Tübingen, 1878.

The self-same men, who raise no objection whatever to the employment of woman in occupations, many of which are very exhausting, often dangerous, threaten the impairment of her feminine physique and violently compel her to sin against her duties as a mother,—these self-same men would exclude her from pursuits in which these obstacles and dangers are much slighter, and which are much better suited to her delicate frame.

Among the learned men, who in Germany want to hear nothing of the admission of women to the higher studies, or who will yield only a qualified assent, and express themselves publicly on the subject are Prof. L. Bischoff, Dr. Ludwig Hirt, Prof. H. Sybel, L. von Buerenbach, Dr. E. Reich, and many others. Notedly has the livelier agitation, recently set on foot, for the admission of women to the Universities, incited a strong opposition against the plan in Germany. The opposition is mainly directed against woman's qualifications for the study of medicine. Among the opponents are found Pochhammer, Fehling, S. Binder, Waldeyer, Hegar, etc. Von Buerenbach is of the opinion that both the admission to and the fitness of woman for science can be disposed of with the argument that, until now, no genius has arisen among woman, and hence woman is manifestly unfit for philosophic studies. It seems the world has had quite enough of its male philosophers: it can, without injury to itself, well afford to dispense with female. Neither does the objection that the female sex has never yet produced a genius seem to us either to hold water, or to have the weight of a demonstration. Geniuses do not drop down from the skies; they must have opportunity to form and mature. This opportunity woman has lacked until now, as amply shown by our short historic sketch. For thousands of years she has been oppressed, and she has been deprived or stunted in the opportunity and possibility to unfold her mental faculties. It is as false to reason that the female sex is bereft of genius, by denying all spark of genius to the tolerably large number of great women, as it would be to maintain that there were no geniuses among the male sex other than the few who are considered such. Every village schoolmaster knows what a mass of aptitudes among his pupils never reach full growth, because the possibilities for their development are absent. Aye, there is not one, who, in his walk through life, has not become acquainted, some with more, others with fewer persons of whom it had to be said that, had they been able to mature under more favorable circumstances, they would have been ornaments to society, and men of genius. Unquestionably the number of men of talent and of genius is by far larger among the male sex than those that, until now, have been able to reveal themselves: social conditions did not allow the others to develop. Precisely so with the faculties of the female sex, a sex that for centuries has been held under, hampered and crippled, far worse than any other subject beings. We have absolutely no measure to-day by which to gauge the fullness of mental powers and faculties that will develop among men and women so soon as they shall be able to unfold amid natural conditions.

It is with mankind as in the vegetable kingdom. Millions of valuable seeds never reach development because the ground on which they fall is unfavorable, or is taken up by weeds that rob the young and better plant of air, light and nourishment. The same laws of Nature hold good in human life. If a gardener or planter sought to maintain with regard to a given plant that it could not grow, although he made no trial, perhaps even hindered its growth by wrong treatment, such a man would be pronounced a fool by all his intelligent neighbors. Nor would he fare any better if he declined to cross one of his female domestic animal with a male of higher breed, to the end of producing a better animal.

There is no peasant in Germany to-day so ignorant as not to understand the advantage of such treatment of his trees or animals—provided always his means allow him to introduce the better method. Only with regard to human beings do even men of learning deny the force of that which with regard to all other matters, they consider an established law. And yet every one, even without being a naturalist, can make instructive observations in life. Whence comes it that the children of peasants differ from city children? It comes from the difference in their conditions of life and education.

The one-sidedness, inherent in the education for one calling, stamps man with a peculiar character. A clergyman or a schoolmaster is generally and easily recognized by his carriage and mien; likewise an officer, even when in civilian dress. A shoe maker is easily told from a tailor, a joiner from a locksmith. Twin brothers, who closely resembled each other in youth, show in later years marked differences if their occupations are different, if one had hard manual work, for instance, as a smith, the other the study of philosophy for his duty. Heredity, on one side, adaptation on the other, play in the development of man, as well as of animals, a decisive *role*. Indeed, man is the most bending and pliable of all creatures. A few years of changed life and occupation often suffice to make quite a different being out of the same man. Nowhere does rapid external change show itself more strikingly than when a person is transferred from poor and reduced to materially improved circumstances. It is in his mental make-up that such a person will be least able to deny his antecedents, but that is due to the circumstance that, with most of such people, after they have reached a certain age, the desire for intellectual improvement is rarely felt; neither do they need it. Such an upstart rarely suffers under this defect. In our days, that look to money and material means, people are far readier to bow *before the man with a large purse, than before a man of knowledge and great intellectual gifts, especially if he has the misfortunte of being poor and rankless.* Instances of this sort are furnished every day. The worship of the golden calf stood in no age higher than in this,—whence it comes that we are living "in the best possible world."

The strongest evidence of the effect exercised upon man by radically different conditions of life is furnished in our several industrial centers. In these centers employer and employe present externally such a contrast as if they belonged to different races. Although accustomed to the contrast, it struck us almost with the shock of a surprise on the occasion of a campaign mass meeting, that we addressed in the winter of 1877 in an industrial town of the Erzgebirge region. The meeting, at which a debate was to be held between a liberal professor and ourselves, was so arranged that both sides were equally represented. The front part of the hall was taken by our opponents,—almost without exception, healthy, strong, often large figures; in the rear of the hall and in the galleries stood workingmen and small tradesmen, nine-tenths of the former weavers,—mostly short, thin, shallow-chested, pale-faced figures, with whom worry and want looked out at every pore. One set represented the full-stomached virtue and solvent morality of bourgeois society; the other set, the working bees and beasts of burden, on the product of whose labor the gentlemen made so fine an appearance. *Let both be placed for one generation under equally favorable conditions, and the contrast will vanish with most; it certainly is blotted out in their descendants.*

It is also evident that, in general, it is harder to determine the social standing of women than of men. Women adapt themselves more readily to new conditions; they acquire higher manners more quickly. Their power of accommodation is greater than that of more clumsy man.

What to a plant are good soil, light and air, are to man healthy social conditions, that allow him to unfold his powers. The well known saying: "Man is what he eats," expresses the same thought, although somewhat one-sidedly: The question is not merely what man eats; it embraces his whole social posture, the social atmosphere in which he moves, that promotes or stunts his physical and mental development, that affects, favorably or unfavorably, his sense of feeling, of thought, and of action. Every day we see people, situated in favorable material conditions, going physically and morally to wreck, simply because, beyond the narrower sphere of their own domestic or personal surroundings, unfavorable circumstances of a social nature operate upon them, and gain such overpowering ascendency that they switch them on wrong tracks. The general conditions under which a man lives are even of far greater importance than those of the home and the family. If the conditions for social development are equal to both sexes, if to neither there stand any obstacles in the way, and if the social state of society is a healthy one, *then woman also will rise to a point of perfection in her being, such as we can have no full conception of, such conditions having hitherto been absent in the history of the development of the race.* That which some women are in the meantime achieving, leaves no doubt upon this head: these rise as high above the mass of their own sex as the male geniuses do above the mass of theirs. Measured with the scale usually applied to Princes, women have, on an average, displayed greater talent than men in the ruling of States. As illustrations, let Isabella and Blanche of Castile be quoted; Elizabeth of Hungary; Catharine Sforza, the Duchess of Milan and Imola; Elizabeth of England; Catharine of Russia; Maria Theresa, etc. Resting upon the fact that, in all races and all parts of the world, women have ruled with marked ability, even over the wildest and most turbulent hordes, Burbach makes the statement that, *in all probability, women are fitter for politics than men.*[*] For the rest, many a great man in history would shrink considerably, were it only known what he owes to himself, and what to others. Count Mirabeau, for instance, is described by German historians, von Sybel among them, as one of the greatest lights of the French Revolution: and now research has revealed the fact that this light was indebted for the concept of almost all of his speeches to the ready help of certain scholars, who worked for him in secret, and whom he understood to utilize. On the other hand, apparitions like those of a Sappho, a Diotima of the days of Socrates, a Hypatia of Alexander, a Madame Roland, Madame de Stael, George Sand, etc., deserve the greatest respect, and eclipse many a male star. The effect of women as mothers of great men is also known. Woman has achieved all that was possible to her under the, to her, as a whole, most unfavorable circumstances; all of which justifies the best hopes for the future. As a matter of fact, only the second half of the nineteenth century began to smooth the way for the admission of women in large numbers to the race with men on various fields; and quite satisfactory are the results attained.

But suppose that, on an average, women are not as capable of higher development as men, that they cannot grow into geniuses and great philosophers, was this a criterion for men when, at least according to the letter of the law, they were placed on a footing of equality with "geniuses" and "philosophers?" The identical men of learning, who deny higher aptitudes to woman, are quite inclined to do the same to artisans and workingmen. When the nobility appeals to its "blue" blood and to

[*] "Husband and Wife," Dr. Havelock Ellis.

its genealogical tree, these men of learning laugh in derision and shrug their shoulders; but as against the man of lower rank, they consider themselves an aristocracy, that owes what it is, not to more favorable conditions of life, but to its own talent alone. The same men who, on one field, are among the freest from prejudice, and who hold him lightly who does not think as liberally as themselves, are, on another field,—the moment the interests of their rank and class, or their vanity and self-esteem are concerned—found narrow to the point of stupidity, and hostile to the point of fanaticism. The men of the upper classes look down upon the lower; and so does almost the whole sex upon woman. The majority of men see in woman only an article of profit and pleasure; to acknowledge her an equal runs against the grain of their prejudices:—woman must be humble and modest; she must confine herself exclusively to the house and leave all else to the men, the "lords of creation," as their domain: woman must, to the utmost, bridle her own thoughts and inclinations, and quietly accept what her Providence on earth—father or husband—decrees. The nearer she approaches this standard, all the more is she praised as "sensible, modest and virtuous," even though, as the result of such constraint, she break down under the burden of physical and moral suffering. What absurdity is it not to speak of the "equality of all" and yet seek to keep one-half of the human race outside of the pale!

Woman has the same right as man to unfold her faculties and to the free exercise of the same: she is human as well as he: like him, she should be free to dispose of herself as her own master. The accident of being born a woman, makes no difference. To exclude woman from equality on the ground that she was born female and not male—an accident for which man is as little responsible as she—is as inequitable, as would be to make rights and privileges dependent upon the accident of religion or political bias; and as senseless as that two human beings must look upon each other as enemies on the ground that the accident of birth makes them of different stock and nationality. Such views are unworthy of a truly free being. The progress of humanity lies in removing everything that holds one being, one class, one sex, in dependence and in subjection to another. *No inequality is justified other than that which Nature itself establishes in the differences between one individual and another, and for the fulfillment of the purpose of Nature. The natural boundaries no sex can overstep:it would thereby destroy its own natural purpose.*

The adversaries of full equality for woman play as their trump card the claim that woman has a smaller brain than man, and that in other qualities, besides, she is behind man, hence her permanent inferiority (subordination) is demonstrated. It is certain that man and woman are beings of different sexes; that they are furnished with different organs, corresponding to the sex purpose of each; and that, owing to the functions that each sex must fill to accomplish the purpose of Nature, there are a series of other differences in their physiologic and psychic conditions. These are facts that none can deny and none will deny; nevertheless, they justify no distinction in the social and political rights of man and woman. The human race, society, consists of both sexes; both are indispensable to its existence and progress. Even the greatest male genius was born of a mother, to whom frequently he is indebted for the best part of himself. By what right can woman be refused equality with man?

Based upon information furnished us by a medical friend, we shall here sketch with a few strokes the essential differences, that, according to leading authorities, manifest themselves in the physical and mental qualities of man and woman. The bodily size of man and woman stands, on an average, in the relation of 100 to 93.2. The bones of woman are shorter and thinner, the chest smaller, wider, deeper and flatter. Other differences depend directly upon the sex purpose. The muscles of woman are not as massive. The weight of the heart is 310 grains in man, 255 in woman.

The composition of the blood in man and woman is as follows: Water, man, 77.19; woman, 79.11. Solid matter, man, 22.10; woman, 20.89. Blood corpuscles, man, 14.10; woman, 12.79. Number of blood corpuscles in a cubic millimeter of blood, man, 4½ to 5 millions; woman, 4 to 4½ millions. According to Meynert, the weight of the brain of man is from 1,018 to 1,925 grams; of woman, from 820 to 1,565; or in the relation of 100 to 90.93. LeBon and Bischoff agree that, while weight of brain corresponds with size of body, nevertheless short people have relatively larger brains. With woman, the smaller size of the heart, the narrower system of blood vessels and probably also the larger quantity of blood, has a lower degree of nourishment for its effect.[10] That, however, the larger skulls of larger persons, coupled with the quantitative

[10] Possibly the opposite is the case. We repeat what we explained above more extensively, that it is a widely diffused fact that women and girls nourish themselves worse and are worse nourished than men and boys. There was a time when the fashion prevailed for woman to eat as little as possible; she was to have as "etherial" an appearance as possible; the conception of beauty in our upper class, even to-day, is to the effect that it is "vulgar" if a young girl or young woman have a blooming complexion, red cheeks and a vigorous frame. It is also known, that with numberless women, under otherwise equal social conditions with men, the food is greatly inferior. Out of ignorance and acquired prejudices, women expect incredible things of themselves, and the men encourage them therein. Such neglect and maltreatment of physical nutrition must have the very worst consequences, if carried on through many generations by the very sex that, by reason of the heavy monthly losses of blood and of the expenditure of energies, required by pregnancy, child-birth and nursing, has its physique heavily taxed.

changes occasioned by the size of the skull promote the vigor of the several sections of the brain is a matter that *cannot be asserted*.[11]

Of 107 mentally healthy men and 148 women of the ages of 20 to 59, the weight of the brain per thousand was:

Sex.	Medulla Oblongata.	Cerebellum.	Pons.	Average Length in Centimeters.
Men	790	107.5	102	166.5
Women	787	110.0	103	156.0

The absolute and relative excess in the weight of the cerrebellum of woman has an enormous significance. With animals that run immediately upon birth, the cerebellum is much more powerfully developed than with animals that are born blind, are helpless, and that learn to walk with difficulty. Acordingly, and in consequence of its connection with the cerebrum, subcortical center and the spinal cord, the cerebellum is a station of the muscular and of the chief nervous system, by means of both of which qualities we keep our equilibrium. The more massive cerebellum with woman, together with the comparative shortness and tenderness of her bones, explains her comparative quickness and easiness of motion, her quicker and higher co-ordination of the muscles for their functions, and her knack of quickly sizing up a situation, and finding her way in the midst of a confusion of associations. Woman is furthermore aided in the latter faculty through the greater excitability of her cerebral cortex. Meynert says:—

1. All structural anomalies associated with anaemia of the blood—including also a small heart and narrow arteries—should be considered as subject structural defects. Upon this depends not only the ready exhaustibility of the cortex, but also the phenomena of irritability, named by Meynert, localized irritable weakness.

2. The branches of blood vessels, supplying the subcortical centers from the base, are short, thick, straight, palisade-like, while those on the surface of the brain, supplying the cortex, run in long tortuous lines. And it is because of that, since with the increased length of the blood vessels the resistance to the propulsive force of the heart is increased, that the subcortical centers, the moment fatigue supervenes, are better supplied with blood than the cortex, they are less readily fatigued than the more readily exhaustible cerebrum.

---

[11] "Men of genius are, as a rule, of inferior size and massive brain. These are also the leading features of the child, and the general facial expression as well as the temperament of such men recall the child."—Dr. Havelock Ellis, "Husband and Wife."

3. Because of this and because of the more watery character of woman's blood and great extent of subcortical centers in woman in comparison with cerebrum, the physical equilibrium of woman is more unstable than of man.

4. All nerves (except the optic and olfactory, which spread out directly in the cortex, save some of their filaments terminating in the subcortical centers) terminate in the subcortical center; the cortex of the cerebrum acts as a checking organ for the subcortical center; as the cerebral cortex in woman, as already stated, is at a disadvantage not only from the anatomical standpoint, but also in the quality of its blood supply, woman is not only more easily fatigued, but also more readily excitable (irritable, nervous).

These facts explain, on the one hand, what is called the superior endowment of woman, and, on the other, her inclination to sudden changes of opinion, as well as to hallucinations and illusions. This state of unstable equilibrium between the *dura mater* and the *pons* becomes particularly normal during menstruation, pregnancy, lying-in, and at her climacteric. As a result of her physical organization, woman is more inclined to melancholy than man, and likewise is the inclination to mental derangement stronger with her; on the other hand, the male sex excels her in the number of cases of megalomania.

Such, in substance, is the information furnished us by the authority whom we have been quoting.

As a matter of course, in so far as the cited differences depend upon the nature of the sex-distinctions, they can not be changed; in how far these differences in the make-up of the blood and the brain may be modified by a change of life (nourishment, mental and physical gymnastics, occupation, etc.) is a matter that, for the present, lies beyond all accurate calculation. But this seems certain: *modern woman differs more markedly from man than primitive woman, or than the women of backward peoples, and the circumstance is easily explained by the social development that the last 1,000 or 1,500 years forced upon woman among the nations of civilization.*

According to Lombroso and Ferrero, the mean capacity of the female skull, the male skull being assumed at 1,000, is as follows:—

Negro 984	Slav 903
Australian ...967	Gipsy 875
Hindoo 944	Chinese 870
Italian 921	German ....838—897
Hollander ...919 (Tiedemann)	Englishman 860
Hollander ...883 (Davis)	Parisian 858

The contradictory findings for Hollanders and Germans show that the measurements were made on very different quantitative and qualitative materials, and, consequently, are not absolutely reliable. One thing, however, is evident from the figures: Negro, Australian and Hindoo women have a considerably larger brain capacity than their German, English and Parisian sisters, and yet the latter are all more intelligent. The comparisons established in the weight of the brain of deceased men of note, reveal similar contradictions and peculiarities. According to Prof. Reclam, the brain of the naturalist Cuvier weighed 1,861 grams, of Byron 1,807, of the mathematician Dirichlet 1,520, of the celebrated mathematician Gauss 1,492, of the philologist Hermann 1,358, of the scientist Hausmann 1,226. The last of these had a brain below the average weight of that of women, which, according to Bischoff, weighs 1,250 grams. But a special irony of fate wills it that the brain of Prof. Bischoff himsel, who died a few years ago in St. Petersburg, weighed only 1,245 grams, and Bischoff it was who most obstinately grounded his claim of woman's inferiority on the fact that woman, on the average, had 100 grams less brain than man. The brain of Gambetta also weighed considerably below the average female brain, it weighed only 1,180 grams, and Dante, too, is said to have had a brain below the average weight for men. Figures of the same sort are found in Dr. Havelock Ellis' work. According thereto, an every day person, whose brain Bischoff weighed, had 2,222 grams; the poet Turgeniew 2,012; while the third heaviest brain on the list belonged to an idiot of the duchy of Hants. The brain of a common workingman, also examined by Bischoff, weighed 1,925 grams. The heaviest woman's brains weighed 1,742 and 1,580 grams, two of which were of insane women.

The conclusion is, accordingly, justified that as little as size of body justifies inferences as to strength of body, so little does the weight of the brain-mass warrant inferences as to mental powers. There are very small animals (ants, bees) that, in point of intelligence, greatly excel much larger ones (sheep, cows), just as men of large body are often found far behind others of smaller or unimposing stature. Accordingly, the important factor is not merely the quantity of brain matter, but *more especially the brain organization, and, not least of all, the exercise and use of the brain power.*

The brain, if it is to fully develop its powers, must be diligently exercised, the same as any other organ, and also correspondingly fed. Where this is not done, or where the training is turned into wrong channels, instead of the sections of the understanding being developed, those are developed in which imagination has its seat. In such cases, *not only is the organ stunted, but even crippled. One section is developed at the expense of another.*

No one, approximately familiar with the history of the development of woman, will deny that, for thousands of years, woman has been and continues to be sinned against in that direction. When Prof. Bischoff objects that woman could have trained her brain and intelligence as well as man did, he reveals unpardonable and unheard of ignorance on the subject. The sketch, drawn in this work, of the position of woman in the course of the progress of civilization, explains fully how the thousands of years of continued male supremacy over woman are mainly responsible for the great differences in the mental and physical development of the two sexes.

Our naturalists should recognize that the laws of their science are applicable to man also, and to his evolution. The laws of evolution, of heredity, of adaptation, hold good with human beings as with all other creatures of nature. Seeing that man is no exception in nature, the law of evolution must be applied to him also: forthwith light is shed upon what otherwise remains confused and dark, and, as such, becomes the fit subject for scientific mysticism, or mystic science.

The training of the brain took its course with the different sexes wholly in conformity with the difference in the education of the two—if such a term as "education" is at all allowable, with regard to woman in particular, during long stretches of the past, and the term "bringing up" is not the correcter. Physiologists are agreed that the organs of thought are located in the front part of the brain, and those especially of feeling and sentiment are to be looked for in the middle of the head. With man the front, with woman the middle of the head is more developed. *The ideal of beauty, male and female, shaped itself accordingly.* According to the Greek ideal, which is standard to this day, *woman has a narrow, man a high and, particularly, broad forehead,*—and this ideal an expression of their own degradation, is so stamped on their minds, that our women bewail a forehead that exceeds the average, as a deformity in their appearance, and seek to improve nature by art, drawing their hair over the sinning forehead, to make it look lower.

In a polemic in Nos. 39 and 40 of the "Sozialdemokrat" for 1890, which appeared in London, Sophie Nadejde had two articles in which she sought to refute the charges concerning the great inferiority of woman. She says therein that Broca, a well known Parisian physiologist, measured the cubic contents of 115 skulls from the eleventh and twelfth centuries, and got an average of 1,426 cubic centimeters. The measurements of 125 skulls from the eighteen century gave, however, an average of 1,462 cubic centimeters. According to this, the conclusion would be that, in the course of a few centuries, the brain had grown considerably. A measurement by Broca of skulls from the Stone Age resulted, however, in an average of 1,606 cubic centimeters for the skulls of men, and 1,581 for the skulls of women,—accordingly, both considerably larger than those of the eleventh, twelfth and eighteenth centuries. Mrs. Nadejde concluded therefrom that Herbert Spencer was right when he claimed in his physiology that brain weight depended upon the amount of motion and the variety of motions.

The lady furthermore emphasized the point that it depends a deal less on the brain-mass than on the proportion in the two sexes of the brain-weight to the weight of the body. Proceeding from these premises, it appeared that *the female brain was heavier than the male*. The argument on this head, Mrs. Nadejde presents in these words:

"Let us compare the average weights of the bodies, and let us take, as the difference between man and woman only 8 kilograms, although many naturalists, among them Gay, whom Delaunay quotes, takes 11 kilograms. According to the average weights of 9,157 American soldiers: 64.4 kilograms (average weight of the male body): 56 kilogrames (average weight of the female body)=1,141 or 1.14, i. e., the average weight of woman being taken as 100, that of man is represented by 114. According to the average weights of 12,740 Bavarians: 65.5 kilograms (average for males): 57.5 (average for females = 1,139 or 1.14 as above. Assuming the average weight of women as 100, that of man is found to be 114. Acording to the average weights of 617 Englishmen, 68.8 (average for males): 60.8 (average for females) = 1,131, or 1.13; the average weight of woman being assumed as 100, that of man is found to be 113.[12]

"Acordingly, it appears that, under otherwise equal conditions, women have ¼ per cent. of brain-mass in excess of men. That is to say, for every 100 grams of female brain-mass, men should have 113 or 114 grams; in reality, however, they only have from 110 to 112 grams. The fact can be put still more plastically: According to this calculation, *the male brain falls short 25 to 51 grams of brain-mass.*[13]

"But L. Manouvrier proves more. He says:[14] 'The influence of the weight of the body strikes the eye when we note the figures among the vertebrates. The influence is equally manifest with man, and it is a wonder how so many naturalists have not yet recognized this truth, even after it was illustrated and treated by others.

"'There are a number of facts that prove the influence of the size of the body upon the weight of the brain. The lower races and of high stature, not only have a larger average weight of brain than the Euro-

[12] The corporal weights are taken from Taupinard's "Anthropologie."

[13] If, with the authority quoted by Delaunay, we assume 11 kilograms as the difference in weight between men and women, we would have found 35 to 70 grams.

[14] L. Manouvrier, "Revue Scientifique," No. 23, June 3, 1882.

pean, but also is the number of large brains greater with them. We must not imagine that the intelligence of a race is determined by the number of large brains: the Patagonians, Polynesians and Indians of North America (and according to the figures given above the people of the Stone Age may be added) greatly surpass us Parisians and all races of Europe, not only in the number of large brains, but also in the large average capacity of the skull.

" 'The influence of the weight of the body upon the size of the brain is confirmed by the fact that the small skull capacities are found among races of slight stature, like the Bushmen, the Andamans, and the Hindoo pariahs.'

"All scientists who have treated the brain question in a really scientific manner, have expressed themselves with greatest caution on the difference shown by the two sexes. Other writers, on the contrary, especially during the last years, have treated the question with such levity, that it has been compromised in the public esteem. If there be any intellectual difference between man and woman, it must, at any rate, be very slight, a physiologist like Stuart Mill having declared that he failed to find the difference. Size of body, strength of muscle, mass— all of these present decided differences. Due to these differences woman has been termed the defective sex; and authors who were not able to understand these manifest differences, presumed to establish a physiologic difference; to solve a much more difficult and complex question; they raised their voices in praise of their own sex!

"It follows that the difference between the sexes in point of weight of brain and capacity of skull, considered scientifically, can not be scored to the disadvantage of woman. All the facts point to the conclusion that the difference depends upon the weight of the body. There is no anatomical reason to represent woman as a backward and, in point of intelligence, subordinate being, compared with man. I shall presently prove this.

"The proportion between the weight of the brain and the height of the body is smaller with the female than with the male sex.[15] But the fact is easily explained. The height of the body does not actually express the development, or, rather, the weight of the body.

"But when we compare the proportion of the brain-weights we find that women have more brain than men, in childhood as well as throughout life. The difference is not great, but it would be much more considerable, if we did not include in the weight of the body the fat, which is present in much larger quantity with women, and which, as an inert (inactive) mass, has no influence whatever upon the weight of the brain."

[15] Quatrefages found the proportion to be slightly larger with woman than with men. Thurman found the reverse, just as L. Manouvrier.

Later, in 1883, L. Manouvrier published in the seventh number of the "Revue Scientifique" the following results of his investigations:—

"If we designate with 100 each the weight of the brain, thighbone, skull, and lower jawbone, we find the following weights for woman:—

Brain 88.9
Skull 85.8
Lower jawbone 78.7
Thighbone 62.5

"It is, furthermore, an established fact that the weight of the skeleton (without skull) differs as with the thighbone. Hence we may compare the weight of the brain with that of the thighbone. It follows from the figures given above, that women have, relatively, 26.4 per cent. more brain-mass.

"Let us express the figures herein given somewhat more plastically.

"If a man has 100 grams of brain-mass, woman should have, instead of 100, only 62.5 grams; but she has 88.9 grams,—an excess of 26.4 grams. It follows that if we accept 1,410 grams (according to Wagner) as the average weight of the male brain, the female brain should weigh only 961.25 grams, instead of 1,262: woman, acordingly, has 301.75 grams more brain-mass than the proportion demands. If we take the figures of Huschel we find an excess of 372 grams; finally, the figures of Broca give us an excess of 383 grams. *Under otherwise equal conditions woman has between 300 and 400 grams more brain-mass than man.*"

Although it is by no means proven that, by reason of their brain-mass, women are inferior to men, it is no cause for wonder that, women are mentally such as we know them to-day. Darwin is certainly right when he says that a list of the most distinguished men in poetry, painting, sculpture, music, science and philosophy side by side with a similar list of the most distinguished women on the same fields will not bear comparison with each other. But are we to wonder at that? *Wonderful were it if it were otherwise.* For that reason Dr. Dodel-Zurich[16] says with perfect right that matters would stand otherwise if through a number of generations women and men were educated equally, and trained in the exercise of those arts and of mental discipline. On an average, woman is also weaker than man, which is by no means the case with many wild peoples.[17] What exercise and training from early youth are able to change in this matter, we may see in the circus women

[16] "Die neuere Schöpfungsgeschichte."

[17] Dr. Havelock Ellis furnishes a number of proofs of this fact in his frequently quoted book. According thereto, woman, among wild and half-wild people, is not only equal to man in physical strength and size of body, but she is partly superior. On the other side, Ellis agrees with others that, in consequence of our progress in civilization, the difference in the capacity of the skull of the two sexes has steadily become more marked.

and female acrobats, who in courage, foolhardiness, dexterity and physical strength achieve marvelous feats.

Seeing that such a development is a matter of the conditions of life and education—or, to express it in the naked language of science, of "breeding"—it may be taken for certain that the application of these laws to the physical and mental life of man would lead to the most brilliant results, *the moment man sets his hand to the work with full consciousness of his object and his aim.*

As plants and animals depend upon the conditions for existence that they live under—promoted by favorable, checked by unfavorable ones— and as forcible conditions compel them to change their appearance and character, provided such conditions are not unfavorable enough to destroy them wholly, so it is with man. The manner in which a person makes his living influences not his external appearance only, it influences also his feelings, his thoughts and his actions.[18] If, accordingly, man's unfavorable conditions of life—defective social conditions—are the cause of defective individual development, it follows that *by changing his condition of life, man is himself changed.* The question, therefore, is so to change the social conditions that every human being shall be afforded the possibility for the full and unhampered development of his being; that the laws of evolution and adaptation, designated after Darwin as "Darwinian," be consciously rendered effective to humanity. But this is possible only under Socialism.

As a thinking and intelligent being, *man must constantly, and conscious of his purpose, change, improve and perfect his social conditions, together with all that thereby hangs; and he must so proceed in this that equally favorable opportunities be open to all.* Every individual must be placed in a position to be able to develop his abilities and faculties to his own as well as to the advantage of the collectivity; but his may not be the power to injure either others or the collectivity. His own and the advantage of others must be mutual. *Harmony of interests* must be brought about; it must substitute the existing *conflict of interests* to the end that not even the thought may be conceived of ruling and injuring others.

Darwinism, as all genuine science, is eminently democratic.[19] If any of its advocates holds a contrary view, he only proves himself unable to grasp its range. Its opponents, particularly the reverend clergy, who ever display a fine nose, the moment earthly benefits or injuries are im-

[18] This is a discovery, first made by Karl Marx, and classically demonstrated by him in his works. especially in "Capital." The Communistic Manifesto, that appeared in 1848, and was composed by K. Marx and Frederick Engels, is grounded upon this fundamental principle, and must be considered, to this day, as the norm for all agitational work, and the most excellent of all.

[19] "The Hall of science is the Temple of democracy," Buckle, "History of Civilization in England."

minent, have understood this well, and, consequently denounce Darwinism as Socialistic and Anarchistic. Also Prof. Virchow agrees with his sworn enemies in this. In 1877, at the convention of naturalists in Munich, he played the following trump declaration against Prof. Haeckel:[20] "The Darwinian theory leads to Socialism." Virchow sought to discredit Darwinism and to denounce it because Haeckel demanded the adoption of the theory of evolution in the schools. To teach natural science in our schools in the sense of Darwin and of recent investigations, that is an idea against which are up in arms all those who wish to cling to the present order of things. The revolutionary effect of these theories is known, hence the demand that they be taught only in the circles of the select. We, however, are of the opinion that if, as Virchow claims, the Darwinian theories lead to Socialism, the circumstance is not an argument against Darwin's theories, but in favor of Socialism. Never may a scientist inquire whether the conclusions from his science lead to this or that political system, to this or that social system, nor seek to justify the same. His is the duty to inquire whether the theory is right. *If it is that, then it must be accepted along with all its consequences.* He who acts otherwise, be it out of personal interest, be it out of a desire to curry favor from above, or be it out of class and party interests, *is guilty of a contemptible act, and is no honor to science.* Science as a gild so very much at home in our Universities, can only in rare instances lay claim to independence and character. The fear of losing their stipends, of forfeiting the favor of the ruler, of having to renounce titles, decorations and promotions cause most of the representatives of science to duck, to conceal their own convictions, or even to utter in public the reverse of what they believe and know. If, on the occasion of the festival of declaration of allegiance at the Berlin University, in 1870, a Dubois-Reymond exclaimed: "The Universities are the training places for the life-guards of the Hohenzollern," one may judge how the majority of the others, who stand both in knowledge and importance far below Dubois-Rey-

---

[20] Ziegler, quoted above, denies that such is the meaning of Virchow's argument. His own quotation of Virchow's argument, however, confirms the interpretation. Virchow said: "Now, only picture to yourselves *how the theory of the descent of man presents itself in the head of a Socialist!* (Laughter.) Yes, gentlemen, that may seem funny to some; it is, however, a serious matter, and I hope that the theory of the descent of man *may not bring upon us all the horrors that similar theories have actually brought upon our neighboring country. At any rate, this theory, if consistently carried out, has a side of extraordinary gravity; and that Socialism has shown its sympathy therewith, will, it is to be hoped, not have escaped you. We must be perfectly clear upon that.*" Now, then, we have simply done what Virchow feared: we have drawn the conclusions from the Darwinian theories, conclusions that Darwin himself and a large portion of his followers either did not draw at all, or drew falsely. And Virchow warned against the gravity of these theories, just because he foresaw that Socialism would *and was bound to draw the conclusions that are involved in them.*

mond,[21] think regarding the purpose of science. Science is degraded to a maid-servant of the ruling powers.

We can understand how Prof. Haeckel and his disciples, such as Prof. O. Schmidt, v. Hellwald and others, defend themselves energetically against the charge that Darwinism plays into the hands of Socialism; and that they, in turn, maintain the contrary to be true: that Darwinism is aristocratic in that it teaches that everywhere in Nature the more highly developed and stronger organism dominates the lower. Seeing that, according to these gentlemen, the property and cultured classes represent these more highly developed and stronger organisms in society, they look upon the domination of these as a matter of course, being justified by nature.

This wing among our Darwinians has not the faintest notion of the economic laws that sway capitalist society, whose blind will raises, without selecting, either the best, or the ablest, or the most thorough, often the most scampish and corrupt; places him on top; and thus puts him in a position to make the conditions of life and development most favorable for his descendants, without these having as much as to turn their hands. Striking an average, under no economic system is the prospect poorer than under capitalism for individuals animated with good and noble qualities, to rise and remain above; and it may be added without exaggeration that the prospect grows darker in the measure that this economic system approaches its apogee. Recklessness and unscrupulousness in the choice and application of the means, are weapons infinitely more effective and promiseful of success than all human virtues put together. To consider a social system, built upon such a basis, a system of the "fittest and best" is a feat that only he can be capable of whose knowledge of the essence and nature of such a society equals zero; or who, swayed by dyed-in-the-wool bourgeois prejudices, has lost all power to think on the subject and to draw his conclusions. The struggle for existence is found with all organisms. Without a knowledge of the circumstances that force them thereto, the struggle is carried on unconsciously. Such a struggle for existence is found among men also, within all social systems in which the sense of solidarity has vanished, or has not yet come to the surface. This struggle changes according to the forms that the social relations of man to man assume in the course of social evolution. In the course of this evolution it takes on the form of a class struggle that is carried on upon an even higher plane. But these struggles lead—and in this human beings differ from all other creatures—to an ever clearer understanding of the situation, and finally to the recognition of the laws that

[21] Dubois-Reymond repeated this sentence in February, 1883, to the attacks directed upon him, on the occasion of the anniversary celebration of Frederick the Great.

govern and control their evolution. *Man has in the end but to apply this knowledge to his social and political development, and to adapt the latter accordingly.* The difference between man and the brute is that *man may be called a thinking animal, the brute, however, is no thinking man.* It is this that a large portion of our Darwinians can not, in their one-sidedness, understand. Hence the vicious circle in which they move.

A work from the pen of Prof. Enrico Ferri[22] proves, especially as against Haeckel, that Darwinism and Socialism are in perfect harmony, and that it is a fundamental error on the part of Haeckel to character-ize, as he has done down to latest date, Darwinism as aristocratic. We are not at all points agreed with Ferri's work, and especially do we not share his views with regard to the qualities of woman, a matter in which he is substantially at one with Lombroso and Ferrero. Ellis has shown in his "Man and Woman" that while the qualities of man and woman are very different, still they are of *equal value,*—a confirmation of the Kantian sentence that man and woman only together constitute the human being. This notwithstanding, the work of Ferri comes quite *apropos.*

Professor Haeckel and his followers, of course, also combat the claim that Darwinism leads to atheism, and we find them, after themselves having removed the Creator by all their scientific arguments and proofs, making hysterical efforts to smuggle him in again by the back door. To this particular end, they construct their own style of "Re-ligion," which is then called "higher morality," "moral principles," etc. In 1882, at the convention of naturalists at Eisenach, and in the pres-ence of the family of the Grand Duke of Weimar, Prof. Haeckel made the attempt not only to "save religion," but also to represent his master Darwin as "religious." The effort suffered shipwreck, as all will admit who read the essay and the letter of Darwin therein quoted. Darwin's letter expressed the reverse of that which Prof. Haeckel sought to make out, although in cautious words. Darwin was constrained to con-sider the "religious sentiments" of his countrymen, the English, hence he never dared to express his opinion openly upon religion. Privately, however, he did so to Dr. L. Buechner, as became known shortly after the Weimar convention, whom he frankly informed that *since his fortieth year*—that is to say, since 1849—*he believed nothing, not hav-ing been able to find any proof for his belief.* During the last years of his life Darwin supported an atheist paper published in New York.

Woman is to take up the competitive struggle with man on the intel-lectual field also. She does not propose to wait till it please man to develop her brain functions and to clear the way for her. The move-ment is well under way. Already has woman brushed aside many an

[22] "Socialism and Modern Science (Darwin-Spencer-Marx)."

obstacle, and stepped upon the intellectual arena,—and quite success-fully in more countries than one. The movement, ever more noticeable, among women for admission to the Universities and High Schools, as well as for admission to the functions that correspond to these studies, is, in the very nature of existing conditions, confined to the women of the bourgeois circles. The circles of the working-women are not di-rectly interested therein: to them, these studies, together with the posts attainable through them, are shut off. Nevertheless, the movement and its success are of general interest, partly, because the matter concerns a question of principle, affecting the position in general of woman towards man, partly also because it will show what woman is capable of achieving, even now, under conditions highly unfavorable to her de-velopment. Finally, the female sex has a special interest herein, in cases of sickness, for instance, when they may confide their ailments more freely to a physician of their own than to one of the opposite sex. To a large number of women, female practitioners, are a positive benefit. The necessity of having to resort to male doctors in cases of illness, generally connected with physical disturbances that flow from their sex peculiarities, frequently deters women from seeking timely aid, or any aid at all. Hence arise a number of troubles, not infrequently serious ones, not to the wives alone, but to their husbands as well. There is hardly a physician who has no cause to complain of this frequently criminal diffidence on the part of women, and their objection to state their complaint freely. All this is easy to understand; irrational, how-ever, is the posture of the men, and of several physicians among them, who will not admit the justice and necessity of the study of medicine, in particular, by women.

Female doctors are no new sight. Among most of the ancient peoples, the old Germans in particular, it was upon woman that the healing cares devolved. There were female physicians and operators of great repute during the ninth and tenth centuries in the Arabian Kingdom, particularly among the Arabians (Moors) in Spain, where they studied at the University of Cordova. The pursuit by women of scientific studies at several Italian Universities—Bologna and Palermo, for in-stance,—was likewise due to Moorish influence. Later, when the "heathen" influence vanished from Italy, the practice was forbidden. In 1377 the faculty of the University of Bologna decreed:

"And whereas woman is the fountain of sin, the weapon of the devil, the cause of man's banishment from Paradise and the ruin of the old laws; and whereas for these reasons all intercourse with her is to be diligently avoided; therefore do we interdict and expressly forbid that any one presume to introduce in the said college any woman whatsoever, however honorable she be. And if, this notwithstanding, any one should perpetrate such an act, he shall be severely punished by the Rector."

Indeed, down to this day, Christian clergymen, of both Protestant and Catholic confession, are among the most zealous enemies of the pursuit of scientific studies by woman. The fact was shown in the debates of the German Reichstag on the admission of women to the study of medicine; it is furthermore shown by the reports of the Evangelical convention, held in the spring of 1894 in Frankfurt-on-the-Main, where clerical mouth-pieces protested sharply against allowing women equal rights in the discussions of the convention.

The admission of women to the pursuit of University professions has, above all, the result of exercising a beneficent influence upon the industry of the male youth. As admitted from different quarters, the ambition of the male students leaves much to be wished for. That alone were a great gain. Their morals also would be greatly improved: the inclination to drunkenness and brawling, as well as habitual dissipations in taverns, so common among our students, would receive a severe blow: the institutions whence mainly proceed our political pilots, judges, district attorneys, higher police officers, clergymen and members of legislatures would acquire a tone better in keeping with the purpose for which these institutions are established and supported. According to the unanimous opinion of impartial people, qualified to judge, an improvement in this tone is a crying need of the hour.

The number of the countries that admit women to the Universities and High Schools has been greatly on the increase during the last twenty years; nor can any country, that lays claim to being a member of civilization, shut its ears in the long run to the demand. Ahead of all went the United States; Russia followed—two political systems that present in all respects the strongest contrasts; that notwithstanding, both were guided by the identical views with regard to the equal rights of woman. In the North American Union, women are to-day admitted in all the States to University studies,—in Utah since 1850, Iowa since 1860, Kansas since 1866, Wisconsin since 1868, Minnesota since 1869, California and Missouri since 1870, Ohio, Illinois and Nebraska since 1871; since then all the other States followed in rapid succession. In keeping with the extension of female studies, woman conquered her place in the United States. According to the census of 1890, there were in the country 2,348 female physicians and surgeons, 2,136 female architects, 580 female journalists, 300 female writers, 165 female ministers, 110 female lawyers.[23]

In Europe, Switzerland, principally, opened its Universities to women. There the number of female students grew, since 1887, as follows:—

[23] According to the census of 1900, the figures for these respective occupations were: 7,387 female physicians and surgeons, 1,041 female architects, designers and draftsmen, 2,193 female journalists, 5,984 female literary and scientific persons, 3,378 female ministers, 2,193 female lawyers.—THE TRANSLATOR.

Year.	Total Students.	Female Students.
1887	2,229	167
1888	2,339	206
1889	2,412	196
1890	2,552	248
1891	2,889	297
1892	3,076	318
1893	3,307	451
1893-94 (Winter course)	3,609	599

Accordingly, the participation of women in University studies increased considerably in the interval between 1887-1894. In 1887 the number of female students was 7.5 per cent. of the total number of students; in 1893-1894, however, it had risen to 16.6 per cent. In 1887, there were, among 744 medical students, 79 women, or 10.6 per cent.; in the winter course of 1893-1894, there were, of 1,073 medical students, 210 women, or 19.6 per cent. In the department of philosophy, in 1887, there were, of 530 students, 41 women, or 7.8 per cent.; in 1893-1894, there were, of 1,640 students, 381 women, or 23.2 per cent. The large majority of the female students in Switzerland are foreigners, among them many Germans, whose number increases almost yearly. The example of Switzerland was followed in the early seventies by Sweden; in 1874 by England, in so far as medical colleges for women have been established. Nevertheless, it was not until 1881 that Oxford, and 1884 that Cambridge decided to admit female students. Italy followed in 1876, then Norway, Belgium, France and Austria. In Paris, during 1891, there were 232 female students, mostly of medicine. Of these female students, 103 were Russian, 18 French, 6 English, 3 Roumanian, 2 Turk, and 1 each from America, Greece and Servia. In the department of philosophy there were 82 French female students and 15 foreigners matriculated.

As it will have been noticed, even Turkey is represented among the female students. There, more than anywhere else, are female physicians needed, due to the position that custom and religion assign to woman as against man. The same reason caused Austria also to open Universities to female students, in order that the Mohammedan women of Bosnia and Herzogovina might enjoy medical attendance. Even Germany, whose "pig-tail" was thickest, i. e., where the disfavor towards admitting women to the Universities was most bitter, has been compelled to fall in line with progress. In the spring of 1894, the first female student passed her examination in Heidelberg for the degree of Doctor of Philosophy, and a second one in the fall of the same year in Göttingen. In Karlsruhe and Berlin, High Schools were established to prepare women for the Universities; finally in the summer of 1894, the Prussian

Minister of Public Worship issued regulations for the remodelling of the higher instruction of girls, looking for their preparation for the study of medicine. Also India has furnished a small contingent of female students. Obviously, there is progress everywhere.

All medical authorities are agreed that women render the best service as nurses of the sick, aye, that they positively can not be got along without. In an address, delivered by Prof. Ziemssen a few years ago, he said:

"Above all, see to it, gentlemen, in your practice that you have thorough, well trained, kind-hearted, characterful female nurses. Without them, all your sacrifices of time and effort are idle."

In the September, 1892, issue of the "German Review", Prof. Virchow thus expressed himself in favor of female nurses:

"That the post of real responsibility at the sick-bed shall fall to woman is, in my opinion, a principle that should be enforced in all our hospitals. In the hands of a cultivated, womanly, trained person the care of even a sick man is safer than in those of a man."

If woman is fit for the extraordinarily difficult service of nurse, a service that places a heavy strain upon patience and self-sacrifice, why should she not be also fit for a physician?

Above all, the idea must be resisted that women shall be educated for physicians by separate courses of study, i. e., separated from the male students,—a plan that Frau Mathilde Weber of Tübingen has declared herself satisfied with.[24] If the purpose be to degrade the female physicians, from the start, to the level of physicians of second or third rank, and to lower them in the eyes of their male colleagues, then, indeed, that is the best method. If it is no violation of "ethics" and "morality" that female nurses assist in the presence of male physicians at the performance of all possible operations upon male and female subjects, and on such occasions render most useful service; if it is "ethically" and "morally" permissible that dozens of young men, as students and for the sake of their studies, stand as observers at the bed of a woman in travail, or assist at the performance of operations on female patients, then it is absurd and laughable to deny such rights to female students.

Such prudery in natural things is the rage, particularly in Germany, this big children's play-room. The English, discredited by reason of the same qualities, may, nevertheless, be our teachers in the treatment of natural things.

In this direction, it is the United States, in particular, that furnish the example most worthy of imitation. There, and to the utter horror of our learned and unlearned old fogies of both sexes, High Schools have existed for decades, at which both sexes are educated in common. Let us hear with what result. President White of the University of Michi-

[24] Aerztinnen für Frauenkrankheiten, eine ethische und sanitäre Nothwendigkeit," Berlin, 1893.

gan declared as early as the middle of the seventies: "The best pupil in Greek, for several years, among 1,300 students, has been a young lady; the best pupil in mathematics in one of the strongest classes of our Institute is, likewise, a young lady; and several among the best pupils in natural science and the sciences in general are likewise young ladies." Dr. Fairchild, President of Oberlin College in Ohio, where over a thousand students of both sexes are instructed in common, said at about the same time: "During my incumbency of eight years as professor of ancient languages—Latin, Greek, and Hebrew—also in the ethical and philosophic studies, and during my incumbency of eleven years in abstract and applied mathematics, I have never noticed any difference in the two sexes except in the manner of reciting." Edward H. Machill, President of Swarthmore College in Delaware County, Pa., and author of a pamphlet,[25] from which these facts are taken, says that, after an experience of four years, he had arrived at the conclusion that, with an eye to both manners and morals, the education of the two sexes in common had given the best results. Many a pig-tail has yet to be cut off in Germany before common sense shall have broken its way through here.

More recently, lively controversies have arisen in the literature of almost all countries of civilization on the question whether woman could achieve intellectually as much as man. While some, by dint of great acumen and with the aid of facts supposed to be proofs, deny that such is possible, others maintain that, on many fields, it undoubtedly is the case. It is claimed that, generally speaking, woman is endowed with qualities that man is deficient in, and *vice versa*: the male method of reasoning is reflective and vigorous, woman's, on the contrary, distinguishes itself by swiftness of perception and quickness of execution. Certain it is that woman finds her way more quickly in complicated situations, and has more tact than man. Ellis, who gathered vast materials upon this question, turned to a series of persons, who had male and female students under their guidance for many years, and questioned them on their opinion and experience. McBendrick of Glasgow answered him: "After having taught female students for twenty years, I would sum up my observations with the statement that many women accomplish as much as men in general, and that many men do not accomplish as much as the female average." Other opinions in Ellis' book are less favorable, but none is unfavorable. According to the Yearbook of Berlin for 1870, pp. 69-77, investigation showed girls to be stronger in the sense of space, boys at figures; the girls excelled in the telling of stories, the boys in the explaining of religious principles. Whatever the way these questions may be turned and twisted, the fact appears that the two sexes supplement each other; the one is superior on one, the

[25] "An Address upon the Co-education of the Sexes."

other on some other field, while on a number óf others there is no difference in point of sex, but only in point of individual.

It follows, furthermore, that there is no reason for confining one sex to a certain field ,and prescribing to it the course of development that it shall pursue, nor that, based on differences in natural bent, in advantages and in defects, which mutually equalize themselves, privileges may be deducted for one sex, hindrances for another. Consequently— equality for all, and a free field for each, with a full swing according to their capacity and ability.

Based upon the experience made during the last decades in the higher studies of woman, there is no longer any valid reason against the same. The teacher can do much, by the manner in which he teaches, to affect the attitude of his male and female pupils. Women, who devote themselves to a science, are often animated with an earnestness and willpower in which they excel most other students. The zeal of the female students is, on an average, greater than that of the male.

In reality, it is wholly different reasons that cause most professors of medicine, University teachers, in general, to take a hostile stand towards female students. They see in it a "degradation" of science, which might lose in the esteem of the narrow-minded masses, if the fact were to transpire that female brains also could grasp a science, which, until then, was confined to the select of the male sex only.

All claims to the contrary notwithstanding, our Universities, along with our whole system of education, are in poor plight. As, at the public school, the child is robbed of valuable time by filling his brain with matters that accord neither with common sense nor scientific experience; as a mass of ballast is there dumped into him that he can not utilize in life, that, rather, hampers him in his progress and development; so likewise is it done in our higher schools. In the preparatory schools for the Universities a mass of dry, useless matter is pounded into the pupils. These matters, that the pupils are made to memorize, take up most of their time and engage their most precious brain-power; whereupon, at the University, the identical process is carried on further. They are there taught a mass of antiquated, stale, superfluous lore, along with comparatively little that is valuable. The lectures, once written, are reeled off by most of the professors year after year, course after course, the interlarded witticisms included. The high ministry of education becomes with many an ordinary trade; nor need the students be endowed with great sagacity to find this out. Furthermore, tradition regarding University life sees to it that the young folks do not take their years of study too seriously, and many a youth, who would take them seriously, is repelled by the pedantic and unenjoyable style of the professors. The decline in the zeal to learn and to study is a fact generally noticed at all our Universities and higher schools, and is even cause **for serious** concern with those in authority. Intimately connected therewith is the "grafting" tendency, which, in these days of ours, so poor in character, makes great progress and grows ever ranker in the higher schools. To have "safe views" takes the place of knowledge, and the poison spreads. To be a "patriot," that is to say, a person without a mind of his own, who carefully takes his cue from above, sees how the wind blows there, and trims his sails accordingly, bends and crawls,—such a person is more considered than one of character and knowledge. When the time for examination approaches, the "grafter" crams for a few months what seems most indispensible, in order to squeeze through. When, finally, examination has been happily passed and an office or professional post is secured, most of these "ex-students" work along in a merely mechanical and journeyman style, and are then highly offended if one, who was not a "student," fails to greet them with the greatest respect, and to treat them as specimens of some other and higher race. The majority of the members of our so-called higher professions—district attorneys, judges, doctors, professors, Government officials, artists, etc.,—*are mere journeymen at their trades, who feel no need of further culture, but are happy to stand by the crib.* Only the industrious man discovers later, but only then, how much trash he has learned, often was not taught the very thing that he needed most, and has to begin to learn in good earnest. During the best time of his life he has been pestered with useless or even harmful stuff. He needs a second part of his life to rub all this off, and to work himself up to the height of his age. Only then can he become a useful member of society. Many do not arrive beyond the first stage; others are stranded in the second; only a few have the energy to reach the third.

But "decorum" requires that the mediaeval trumpery and useless curriculum be retained; and, seeing, moreover, that women, as a consequence of their sex, are from the start excluded from the preparatory schools, the circumstance furnishes a convenient pretext to shut the doors of the University lecture rooms in their faces. In Leipsic, during the seventies, one of the most celebrated professors of medicine made the undisguised confession to a lady: *"The gymnasium (college) training is not necessary to the understanding of medicine. This is true. Nevertheless, it must be made a condition precedent for admission, in order that the dignity of science may not suffer."*

Gradually is the opposition to the necessity of a "classical" education for the study of medicine being felt in Germany also. The immense progress made in the natural sciences, together with their importance to life, require an early initiation. Collegiate education, with its preference for the classic languages, Greek and Latin, looks upon the natural sciences as subordinate and neglects them. Hence, the students are frequently devoid of the necessary and preparatory knowledge in natural science that are of decided importance in certain studies, medicine, for instance. Against such a one-sided system of education opposition begins to spring up even in the circles of teachers, as proven by a declaration published in the autumn of 1894 by about 400 teachers of the German High Schools. Abroad, in Switzerland, for instance, the leading place has long since been given to the studies in natural science, and any one, even without a so-called classic education, is admissible to the study of medicine, provided otherwise sufficiently equipped in natural science and mathematics. Similarly in Russia and the United States.

In one of his writings, the late Prof. Bíschoff gave *"the rudeness of the students"* as the reason why he did not recommend the study of medicine to women. He certainly was a good judge of that. In another place, and also quite characteristically, he says: "Why should not one (as professor) now and then allow some interesting, intelligent and handsome woman to attend a lecture upon some simple subject?"—an opinion that v. Sybel evidently shares and even expresses: "Some men there are who have rarely been able to refuse their assistance and help to a female pupil, greedy of knowledge and not uncomely."

Pity the words spent in the refutal of such "reasons" and views! The time will come, when people will trouble themselves about the rudeness of the "cultured" as little as about the old fogyism and sensuous lusts of the learned, but will do what common sense and justice bid.

In Russia, after much pressure, the Czar gave his consent in 1872 to the establishment of a female faculty in medicine. The medical courses were attended in the period of 1872-1882 by 959 female students. Up to 1882 there were 281 women who had filled the medical course; up to the beginning of 1884, there were 350; about 100 came from St. Petersburg. Of the female students who visited the faculty up to 1882, there were 71 (9.0 per cent.) married and 13 (1.6 per cent.) widows; of the rest, 116 (15.9 per cent.) married during their studies. Most of the female students, 214, came from the ranks of the nobility and government officials; 138 from the merchant and privileged bourgeois class; 107 from the military, 59 from the clergy, and 54 from the lower classes of the population. Of the 281 female physicians, who, up to 1882, had finished their studies, 62 were engaged by several Semstwos; 54 found occupation in clinics; 12 worked as assistants at medical courses; and 46 took up private practice. It is noteworthy that, of these female students, more than 52 per cent. had learned neither Latin nor Greek, and yet they did as good work as the men. This notwithstanding, female study was far from being a favorite among the Russian Government circles, until the great services rendered by the female physicians on the theater of war in Turkey during the Russo-Turkish campaign of 1877-1878, broke the ice. At the beginning of the eighties, female studies took great increment in Russia: thousands of female pupils devoted themselves to several branches. Due thereto, and due especially to the fact that thereby free ideas were breaking through, threatening to endanger despotism, the female courses were suppressed by an imperial ukase of May 1, 1885, after the lives of the female students had for some time been made as hard as possible.[26] Since then, resolutions have been adopted at several Russian conventions of physicians to petition for the re-opening of the medical courses for women,—more than a German convention of physicians would do. As yet the attempt in Russia has remained unsuccessful.

In Finland, a country that, although belonging to Russia, occupies an exceptionally privileged position in the Russian system, 105 female students were at the University of Helsingfors during the winter course of 1894-1895, as against 73 in the summer course of 1894. Of these 105 female students, 47 were entered in the faculty of philosophy of history and 45 in that of mathematics; 5 studied medicine, a strikingly small figure compared with elsewhere; 7 law; and 1 theology.

Among the women who distinguished themselves in their studies, belong the late Mrs. v Kowalewska, who received in 1887 from the Academy of Sciences in Paris the first prize for the solution of a mathematical problem, and since 1884 occupied a professorship of mathematics at the University of Stockholm. In Pisa, Italy, a lady occupies a professorship in pathology. Female physicians are found active in Algiers, Persia and India. In the United States there are about 100 female professors, and more than 70 who are superintendents of female hospitals. In Germany also the ice has been broken to the extent that in several cities—Berlin, Dresden, Leipsic, Frankfurt-on-the-Main, etc.,—female physicians, especially dentists, are in successful practice.

With regard to energy and capacity in the scientific studies, England, in particular, can cite a series of handsome results. At the examinations in 1893, six women and six men held the highest marks. The examinations on art and on the theory and history of pedagogy were passed by nine women and not one man. At Cambridge, ten women sustained the severest test in mathematics. According to the sixteenth report of examinations of female students in Oxford, it appears that 62 women sustained the test of the first class, and 82 that of the second class; moreover the honorary examinations were sustained by more than one-half of the female candidates. Surely extraordinary favorable results.

Hostility to competition with women is particularly pronounced in Germany, because here the military turns out every year such a large number of mustered-out officers and under-officers as aspirants for the Civil Service, where there is little room for applicants from other sources. If, however, women are employed, and then at lower salaries, they appear to the already jealous men in a light that is doubly bad,—

[26] Neue Zeit, 1884, "Das Frauenstudium in Russland."

first, as cheap labor; then as lowerer of wages. An extensive field of activity have women gained as teachers, a field for which, on the whole, they are well fitted. This is particularly the case in the United States, where, in 1890, of 363,000 teachers, 238,000 were female.[27] In Berlin there were on January 1, 1892, along with 194 Rectors and 2,022 teachers, 1,024 pedagogically educated and 642 technical female teachers, inclusive of their helpers. In England, France and the United States there are, furthermore, since several years, women successfully engaged in the important service of Factory Inspectors, a move that, in view of the enormous proportions that female labor is assuming ever more in the trades and industries, is well justified and becomes everywhere a necessity.

At the Chicago Exposition of 1893 women, furthermore, distinguished themselves in that, not only did female architects draw the plan and superintend the execution of the magnificent building for the exhibition of female products, but that women also appeared as independent operators in a number of products of art, which provoked general applause, and even astonishment. Also on the field of invention have women distinguished themselves, a subject on which, as early as 1884, a publication in the United States imparted information to the world by producing a list of female inventors. According to the list, the following inventions were made or improved by women: an improved spinning machine; a rotary loom, that produces three times as much as the ordinary loom; a chain elevator; a winch for screw steamers; a fire-escape; an apparatus for weighing wool, one of the most sensitive machines ever invented and of priceless value in the woolen industry; a portable water-reservoir to extinguish fires; a device for the application of petroleum in lieu of wood and coal as fuel on steamers; an improved catcher of sparks and cinders on locomotives; a signal for railroad crossings; a system for heating cars without fire; a lubricating felt to reduce friction on railroad cars; a writing machine; a signal rocket for the navy; a deep-sea telescope; a system for deadening noise on railroads; a smoke-consumer; a machine to fold paper bags, etc. Many improvements in the sewing machines are due to women, as for instance: an aid for the stretching of sails and heavy stuffs; an apparatus to wind up the thread while the machine is in motion; an improvement for the sewing of leather, etc. The last of these inventions was made by a woman who for years kept a saddle and harness shop in New York. The deep-sea telescope, invented by Mrs. Mather, and improved by her daughter, is an innovation of great importance: it makes possible the inspection of the keel of the largest ship, without bringing the same on the dry-dock. With the aid of this glass, sunken

[27] The census of 1900 gives 327,614 female teachers and professors in colleges, out of a total force of 446,133, leaving, accordingly, only 118,519 men on this field.—THE TRANSLATOR.

wrecks can be inspected from the deck of a ship, and search can be made for obstructions to navigation, torpedoes, etc. Along with these practical advantages, its application in science is full of promise.

Among the machines, the extraordinary complexity and ingenuity of whose construction excited great admiration in America and Europe, is one for making paper bags. Many men, leading mechanics among them, had until then vainly sought to construct such a machine. A woman, Miss Maggie Knight, invented it. Since then, the lady invented also a machine to fold paper bags, that does the work of 30 persons. She herself superintends the construction of the machine in Amherst, Mass. That German women have made similar inventions is not yet known.

The movement among women has spread even to Japan. In the autumn of 1892, the Japanese Parliament decided that it was forbidden to women to figure as publishers or editors of newspapers, also of such papers as are devoted to fashions, cooking, education of children, etc. In Japan, even the unheard-of sight has been seen of a woman becoming the publisher of a Socialist paper. That was a little too much for the Japanese legislators, and they issued the above stated decree. It is, however, not forbidden to women to act as reporters for newspapers. The Japanese Government will succeed as little in denying their rights to women as its European rivals of equal mental make-up.

CHAPTER V.

The social dependence of a rank or a class ever finds its expression in the laws and political institutions of a country. Laws are the mirror in which is reflected a country's social condition, to the extent that the same has been brought within definite rules. *Woman, as a subject and oppressed sex, constitutes no exception to the principle.* Laws are negative or positive. Negative in so far as they ignore the oppressed in the distribution of privileges and rights, as though he did not exist; positive, in so far as they expressly assign his dependent position to the oppressed, and specify possible exceptions in his favor.

Our common law rests upon the Roman law, which recognized persons only as property-holding beings. The old German law, which treated woman more worthily, has preserved its force only partially. In the French language, the human being and the man are designated by the same word, *"l'homme"*; likewise in the English language,—*"man."* French law knows the human being only as *man;* and so was it also until recently in England, where woman found herself in slavish dependence upon man. It was similarly in Rome. There were Roman citizens, and wives of Roman citizens, but no female citizens.

Impossible were it to enumerate the numberless laws found on the motley map of German common rights. Let a few instances suffice.

According to the common law of Germany, the wife is a minor towards her husband; the husband is her master, to whom she owes obedience. If the woman is "disobedient," then, according to the law of Prussia, the husband of "low" estate has the right of "moderate castigation." Men of "high" estate also there are said to be who arrogate such a right to themselves. Seeing that nowhere is the force or number of the blows prescribed, the husband is the sovereign judge. The old city law of Hamburg declares: "For the rest, the right of *moderate castigation of the wife by her husband,* of children by their parents, of pupils by their teachers, or servants by their masters and mistresses, is hereby adjudged just and permissible."

Similar provisions are numerous in Germany. According to the law of Prussia, the husband may prescribe to the wife *how long she shall suckle her child.* In cases of disposing of the children, the father alone decides. If he dies, the wife is in most German States compelled to accept a guardian for her children: she herself is considered a minor, and is held unfit to attend to their education herself, even when she supports her children by her property or labor. As a rule, her husband administers her property, and, in cases of bankruptcy, the same is considered and disposed of as his own, unless a pre-marital contract secures the property to her. Wherever the right of primogeniture attaches to landed property, a woman, even if she be the first born, can not enter into possession if there be younger brothers. She can step in only when she has no brothers. In most German States, a married woman can contract only with the consent of her husband, unless she owns a business in her own name, such as, according to more recent law, she is allowed to start. She is shut off from all public function. The Prussian law on associations forbids pupils and apprentices under 18 years of age and women to join political organizations. Until a few decades ago, the attendance of women among the public at open trials was forbidden by several German codes of criminal procedure. If a woman gives birth to an illegitimate child, it has no claim to support from its father if its mother accepted any presents from him during her pregnancy. If a woman is divorced from her husband, she continues to carry his name as a lasting memento, unless she marry again.

In Germany, hundreds of frequently contradictory laws are met with. According to the bill for the new civil laws of Germany, the adminis- tration of the wife's property falls to the husband, unless the wife has secured her property to herself by special contract. This is a reactionary attitude, long since discarded by many other countries. On the other hand, the wife is allowed to retain what she has earned by her own personal labor, and without assistance of her husband, or by the inde- pendent conduct of a business enterprise.

In England, and down to 1870, the common law of the land gave to the husband all the personal property of the wife. Only with regard to real estate were her proprietary rights safeguarded; the husband, nevertheless, had the right of administration and of use. At the bar of law, the English woman was a zero: she could perform no legal act, not even execute a valid testament; she was a veritable serf of her husband. A crime committed by her in his presence, he was answerable for: she was at all points a minor. If she injured any one, damage was assessed as if done by a domestic animal: the husband was held. According to an address delivered in 1888 by Bishop J. N. Wood in the chapel of Westminster, as recently as a hundred years ago the wife was not allowed to eat at table or to speak before she was spoken to: above the bed hung a stout whip, that the husband was free to use when the wife displayed ill temper: only her daughters were subject to her orders: her sons saw in her merely a female servant. Since 1870 and 1882, the wife is not merely secured in the sole possession of the prop- erty that she brings with her, she is also the proprietor of all she earns, or receives by inheritance or gift. These rights can be altered only by special contract between the husband and wife. English legislation followed the example of the United States.

Particularly backward is the civil law of France, of most of the Swiss cantons, of Belgium, etc., in the matter of woman's civic rights. According to the *Code Civil*, the husband could sue for divorce upon the adultery of the wife; she, however, could institute such an action only if the husband kept his concubine at his own home (Article 230). This provision has been repealed by the divorce law of July 27, 1884, but the difference continues in force in the French criminal code,—a characteristic manoeuvre on the part of the French legislator. If the wife is convicted of adultery, *she is punished with imprisonment for not less than two months nor more than three years. The husband is punished only when, according to the spirit of the former Article 230 of the Code Civil, he keeps a concubine under the domestic roof against the wish of his wife. If found guilty, he is merely fined not less than 100 and not more than 1,000 francs.* (Arts. 337 and 339 *Code Penal.*) Such inequality before the law were impossible if but one woman sat in the French Parliament. A similar law exists in Belgium. The punishment for adultery by the wife is the same as in France; the husband is liable only if the act of adultery is committed at the home of the married couple: he may then suffer imprisonment for not less than one month, or more than one year. Slightly juster is, accordingly, the law in Belgium than in France; nevertheless, in the one place as in the other, there are two different standards of right, one for the husband, another for the wife. Similar provisions exist, under the influence of French law, in Spain and Portugal. The civil law of Italy of 1865 enables the wife to obtain a divorce from her husband only if the husband keeps his concubine at his own home, or at such other place where the concubine's presence must be considered in the light of a grave insult to the wife.

In France, Belgium and Switzerland, woman falls, as in Germany, under the guardianship of her husband, the moment she marries. According to section 215 of the *Code Civil*, she is not allowed to appear in Court without the consent of her husband and of two of her nearest male relations, not even if she conducts a public business. According to section 213 the husband must protect the wife, and she must yield obedience to him. There is a saying of Napoleon I. that typifies his idea concerning the status of woman: "One thing is utterly un-French —a woman that can do what she pleases."[1] In these countries, furthermore, woman may not appear as a witness in the execution of contracts, testaments or any notarial act. On the other hand—odd contradiction— she is allowed to act as a witness in all criminal trials, where her testimony may lead to the execution of a person. *Within the purview of the criminal code, she is on all hands considered of equal value, and she is measured for every crime or offense with the same yard-stick as man.* The contradiction, however, does not penetrate the wool of our legislators.

[1] Louis Bridel, "La Puissance Maritale," Lausanne, 1879.

As a widow, she may dispose of her property by testament; as witness to a testament, however, she is not admissible in a number of countries; all the same, according to Art. 1029 of the *Code Civil*, she may be appointed the executor of a will. In Italy, since 1877, woman is qualified to appear as a witness in civil actions also.

According to the law of the canton of Zurich, the husband is the guardian of his wife; he administers her property; and he represents her before third parties. According to the *Code Civil*, the husband administers the property that the wife brings with her, he can sell her property, alienate it, load it with mortgages without requiring her consent, or signature. Similar provisions exist in several other cantons of Switzerland besides Zurich, in France, Belgium, Luxemburg, the Netherlands, Spain, Portugal, Sweden, Denmark and also in a large part of Germany. Countries in which community of property may be excluded in marriage are, besides parts of Germany, and a large part of Switzerland, Austria, Poland and the Baltic provinces. Countries in which the absolute independence of married women exist with respect to their property are: Italy, Russia, Great Britain and Ireland. In Norway, a law of the year 1888, on the administration of the property of married persons, provides that a married woman has the same power to disposes of her property as unmarried women, only the law specifies a few exceptions. In this law the expression is used that *woman becomes un-free in marriage*. Who could blame her if, there also, as happens frequently in France, women are seen to waive formal matrimonial contracts.

According to the law of Berne, what the married woman earns belongs to her husband. Similarly with most cantons of Switzerland, also in France and Belgium. The consequence is that the wife often finds herself in a state of virtual slavery: the husband squanders with lewd women or in the grog-shop what his wife makes: he incurs debts: gambles away his wife's earnings: leaves her and her children in want. He even has the right to demand from her employer the wages due her.

By the law of December 11, 1874, Sweden secures to the married woman the right to dispose freely of that which she earns by her personal effort. Denmark has raised the same principle to the force of a law; nor can, according to Danish law, the property of the wife be seized to cover the debts of the husband. Similarly runs the law of Norway of 1888.[2] The right of educating the children and of deciding thereupon is, according to the legislation of most countries, the attribute of the father: here and there a subordinate co-operation is granted the mother. The old Roman maxim, that stood in sharp contradiction to the principles prevalent during the mother-right, and that clothed the

---

[2] In the presentation of these civil rights we have merely followed Louis Bridel's work: "Le Droit des Femmes et le Marriage," Paris, 1893.

father alone with rights and powers over the child, is to this day the key-note of legislation on the subject.

Among the continental countries, woman holds the freest position in Russia,—due to the communistic institutions there still in existence, or to reminiscences of the same. In Russia, woman is the administrator of her property: she enjoys equal rights in the administration of the community. Communism is the most favorable social condition to woman. The fact transpired from the sketch of the age of the mother-right, given on previous pages.[8] In the United States women have conquered full civil equality; they have also prevented the introduction of the English and similar laws regulating prostitution.

The civic inequality of woman has provoked among the more advanced members of the female sex demand for political rights, to the end of wielding the power of legislation in behalf of their civic equality. It is the identical thought that moved the working class everywhere to direct their agitation towards the conquest of the political powers. What is right for the working class can not be wrong for woman. Oppressed, disfranchised, relegated everywhere to the rear, woman has not the right only, she has the duty to defend herself, and to seize every means she may deem fit to conquer a more independent position for herself. Against these efforts also the reactionary mob, of course, bristles up. Let us see how.

The great French Revolution, that, as is well known, started in 1789 and threw all old institutions out of joint, conjured up a freedom of spirits such as the world had never seen before. Woman also stepped upon the stage. During the previous decades immediately preceding the outbreak of the Revolution, many of them had taken part in the great intellectual struggle that then raged throughout French society. They flocked in swarms to the great scientific discussions, attended political and scientific meetings, and did their share in preparing the Revolution, where theory was to crystalize into fact. Most historians have noted only the excesses of the Revolution,—and as always happens when the object is to cast stones at the people and arouse horror against them—

[8] How correct this view is transpires also from the comedy of Aristophanes: "The Popular Assembly of Women." In that comedy, Aristophanes depicts how the Athenian government had reached the point when everything was going at sixes and sevens. The Prytancum put the question to the popular assembly of the Athenian citizens: "How is the State to be saved?" Thereupon a woman, disguised as a man, made the proposition to entrust the helm of State to the women, and the proposition was accepted without opposition "because it was the only thing that had never before happened in Athens." The women seized the helm, and forthwith institute *communism*. Of course, Aristophanes turns this condition into ridicule, but the significant point in the play is that, the moment the women had a decisive word in public affairs, they instituted communism as the only rational political and social condition from the standpoint of their own sex. Aristophanes little dreamed how he hit the truth while meaning to joke.

have enormously exaggerated these to the end of all the more readily extenuating the shameful transgressions of the ruling class. As a rule, these historians have belittled the heroism and greatness of soul, displayed also by many women in both camps. So long as the vanquishers remain the historians of the vanquished, it will ever be thus.

In October, 1789, a number of women petitioned the National Assembly "that equality be restored between man and woman, work and occupation be given them free, places be left for them that their faculties were fit for."

When in 1793 the Convention proclaimed "*le droit de l'homme*" (the Rights of Man), the more far-seeing women perceived that these were only the rights of males. Olympe de Gouges, Louise Lecombe and others paralleled these "Rights of Man" with 17 articles on the "Rights of Woman," which, on the 28th Brumaire (November 20, 1793) they defended before the Commune of Paris upon the principle: "If woman has the right to mount the scaffold, she must also have the right to mount the tribune." Their demands remained unheeded. When, subsequently, upon the march of monarchic Europe against the Republic, the Convention declared the "Fatherland in danger," and called upon all men, able to carry arms, to defend the Fatherland and the Republic, inspired Parisian women offered to do what twenty years later inspired Prussian women likewise did against the domination of Napoleon,—defend the Fatherland, arms in hand. The radical Chaumette rose against those Parisian women and addressed them, asking: "Since when is it allowed to women to renounce their sex and become men? Since when is it usage for them to abandon the sacred cares of their households, the cradles of their children, and to appear at public places, to speak from the tribunes, to step in the files of the troops,—in short, to fill duties that Nature has devolved upon man alone? Nature said to man: 'Be thou *man!* Racing, the chase, the cultivation of the fields, politics and violent labors of all sorts are thy *privilege!*' It said to woman: 'Be thou *woman!* The care of thy children, the details of thy household, the sweet inquietudes of motherhood,—that is thy *work!*' Unwise women, why wish you to become men? Is not mankind properly divided? What more can you want? In the name of Nature, remain what you are; and, far from envying us the perils of so stormy a life, rest satisfied to make us forget them in the lap of our families, by allowing our eyes to rest upon the fascinating spectacle of our children, made happy by your tender care."

The women allowed themselves to be silenced, and went away. There can be no doubt that the radical Chaumette voiced the innermost sentiments of most of our men, who otherwise abhor him. We also hold that it is a proper division of work to leave to men the defense of the country, and to women the care of the home and the hearth. In Russia, late in the fall of the year and after they have tended the fields, the men of whole village districts move to distant factories, and leave to the women the administration of the commune and the house. For the rest, the oratorical gush of Chaumette is mere phrases. What he says concerning the labors of the men in the fields is not even correct: since time immemorial down to to-day, woman's was not the easy part in agriculture. The alleged labors of the chase and the race course are no "labors" at all: they are amusements of men; and, as to politics, it has perils for him only who swims *against* the stream, otherwise it offers the men at least as much amusement as labor. It is the egoism of man that speaks in that speech.

At about the same time when the French Revolution was under way, and engaged the attention of all Europe, a woman rose on the other side of the Channel also, in England, to labor publicly in behalf of equal rights for her sex. She was Mary Wollstoncraft, born in 1759, and who, in 1790, published a book against Edmund Burke, the most violent enemy of the French Revolution. She later, 1792, wrote a second book— "A Vindication of the Rights of Woman"—in which she took the stand for absolute equality of rights for her sex. In this book she demands the suffrage for women in the elections for the Lower House. But she met in England with even less response than did her sisters in France. Ridiculed and insulted by her contemporaries, she went under after trying ordeals. Before the Revolution it was the encyclopedist Condorcet who principally took the field for the equal rights of both sexes.

To-day, matters lie somewhat differently. Since then, conditions have changed mightily,—the position of woman along with them. Whether married or unmarried, more than ever before woman now has a deep interest in social and political conditions. It can not be a matter of indifference to her whether the Government chains every year to the army hundreds of thousands of vigorous, healthy men; whether a policy is in force that favors wars, or does not; whether the necessaries of life are made dearer by taxes, that promote, besides, the adulteration of food, and are all the harder upon a family in the measure of its size, at a time, at that, in which the means of life are most stingily measured for the large majority. Moreover, woman pays direct and indirect taxes out of her support and her income. Again, the system of education is of highest interest to her: it goes far towards determining the position of her sex: as a mother, she has a double interest therein.

Furthermore, as has been shown, there are to-day millions of women, in hundreds of pursuits, all of them with a lively personal interest in the manner that our laws are shaped. Questions concerning the hours of work; night, Sunday and child-labor; payment of wages and notice of discharge; safety appliances in factory and shop; etc.—all are political questions that concern them as well as the men. Workingmen know little or nothing about conditions in many branches of industry, where women are mainly, or exclusively, engaged. Employers have all the interest in the world to hush up evils that they are responsible for. Factory inspection frequently does not extend to branches of industry in which women are exclusively employed: such as it is, it is utterly inadequate: and yet these are the very branches in which protective measures frequently are most needed. It suffices to mention the workshops in which seamstresses, dressmakers, milliners, etc., are crowded together in our larger cities. From thence, hardly a complaint issues; thither no investigation has as yet penetrated. Finally, as a trader, woman is also interested in laws on commerce and tariffs. There can, accordingly, be no doubt that woman has an interest and a right to demand a hand in the shaping of things by legislation, as well as man. Her participation in public life would impart a strong stimulus thereto, and open manifold new vistas.

Such demands, however, are met with the curt rebuff: "Women know nothing of politics, and most of them don't want to, either; neither do they know how to use the ballot." True, and not true. True enough, until now, very few women, in Germany at least, have ventured to demand political equality also. The first woman, who, as a writer, came out in its favor in Germany was, as far as we know, Frau Hedwig Dohm. More recently, it is mainly the Socialist working-women, who are vigorously agitating for the idea; and their number is ever larger.

Nothing is proved with the argument that women have, until now, shown little interest in the political movement. The fact that, hitherto, women have troubled themselves little about politics, is no proof that they should continue in the same path. The same reasons, advanced to-day against female suffrage, were advanced during the first half of the sixties in Germany against manhood suffrage. Even as late as 1863, the author of this book himself was of those who opposed manhood suffrage; four years later he owed to it his election to the Reichstag. Thousands of others went through the same mill: from Sauls they became Pauls. Many are the men, who either do not care or do not know how to use their important political rights. And yet that fact was no reason to withhold the suffrage from them ,and can be none to now deprive them of it. At the Reichstag elections in Germany, 25 to 30 per cent. of the qualified voters do not vote at all. These non-voters are recruited from *all* classes: among them are scientists and laborers. Moreover, of the 70 to 75 per cent. of those who participate in the election, the majority, according to our judgment,· vote in a way that they would not, if they realized their true interests. That as yet they have not realized them comes from defective political training, a training, however, that these 70 to 75 per cent. possess in a higher degree than the 25 to 30 per cent., who stay away altogether. Among the latter, those must be excepted who remain away from the hustings because they cannot, without danger, vote according to their convictions.

Political education is not gained by keeping the masses from public affairs; it is gained by admitting them to the exercise of political rights. Practice makes perfect. The ruling classes have hitherto found their account in keeping the large majority of the people in political child-hood. Hence it has ever been the task of a class-conscious minority to battle with energy and enthusiasm for the collective interest of society, and to shake up and drag the large inert mass after them. Thus has it been in all great Movements: it is neither astonishing nor discouraging that the experience made with the Movement of the working class is repeated in the Movement for the emancipation of woman. Previous successes prove that pains, labor and sacrifices are rewarded; the future brings triumph.

The moment woman acquires equal rights with man, the sense of her duties will be quickened. Called upon to cast her ballot, she will ask, What for? Whom for? Immediately, emulation in many directions will set in between man and woman that, so far from injuring, will materially improve their mutual relations. The less posted woman will naturally turn to the better posted man. Interchange of ideas and mutual instruction follows,—a condition of things until now found most rarely between husband and wife: it will impart a fresh charm to life. The unhappy differences in education and view-points between the two sexes,—differences, that so frequently lead to dissensions between husband and wife, that place the husband at variance with his many-sided duties, and that injure the well-being of all, will be wiped out. Instead of a clog, the husband will gain a supporter in a compatible wife: whenever, prevented by other duties from personal participation, she will spur her husband to fulfil his own. She will find it legitimate that a fraction of his earnings be spent in a newspaper, for agitational purposes, because the paper serves to educate and entertain her also, and because she realizes the necessity of the sacrifice, a sacrifice that helps to conquer that which she, her husband and her children lack,—an existence worthy of human beings.

Thus, the joining of hands by husband and wife for the common weal, so closely connected with the weal of the individual, will exert a most ennobling influence. The very reverse is called into life of that which is claimed by near-sighted people, or by the foes of a commonwealth based upon the equality of all. Nor would it end there. The relation between the two sexes would be beautified in the measure as the social institutions will liberate husband and wife from material cares and from excessive work. Practice and education will, here as in all other cases, give further aid. If I go not in the water, I shall never learn to swim; if I study no foreign language and do not practice it, I shall never learn to speak it. Everyone finds that natural; and yet many fail, to realize that the same holds good in the affairs of government and society. Are our women unfitter than the far lower negroes, to whom full political equality was conceded in North America? And shall a highly intellectual woman be vested with lesser rights than the rudest, least cultured man,—an ignorant day-laborer of the backwoods of Pommerania, or an ultramontane canalman, for instance, and all because accident let these come into the world as men? The son has greater rights than his mother, from whom, perchance, he derives his best qualities, the very qualities that alone make him what he is. Truly wonderful!

Moreover, we in Germany would no longer be running the risk of being the first to take the leap in the dark and the unknown. The United States, England and other countries have opened the way. In the State of Wyoming in the United States, woman suffrage has been tested since 1869. On November 12, 1872, writing from Laramie City, Wyo., on the subject, Judge Kingman says in the Chicago "Women's Journal":

"Three years ago to-day women obtained the right of electing and of being elected to office in our Territory, in the same manner as the other electors. During this period they have voted and have been voted for; they have exercised the functions of jurors and arbiters; they have taken part in large numbers at our elections, and although I believe that some among us oppose the admission of women from motives of principle, no one, I think, can refuse to recognize that their influence on the elections has been an elevating one. It caused them to be conducted in a more peaceable and orderly manner, and at the same time enabled our courts of justice to discover and punish various kinds of crime that had until then remained unpunished.

"For instance, when the Territory was first organized, there was scarcely a man who did not carry a revolver and made use of it in the slightest dispute. I cannot remember a single case in which a jury composed of men brought in a verdict of guilty against one of those who had shot with a revolver, but when two or three women were among them, they have invariably attended to the instructions of the Court."

In what esteem woman suffrage was held in Wyoming twenty-five years after its introduction, may be gathered from the address issued on November 12, 1894, to the Parliaments of the world by the Legislature of that State. It says:

"The possession and exercise of suffrage by the women in Wyoming for the past quarter of a century has wrought no harm and has done great good in many ways; it has largely aided in banishing crime, pauperism, and vice from this State, and that without any violent or oppressive legislation; it has secured peaceful and orderly elections, good government, and a remarkable degree of civilization and public order;

and we point with pride to the facts that after nearly twenty-five years of Woman Suffrage not one county in Wyoming has a poorhouse, that our jails are almost empty, and crime, except that committed by strangers in the State, almost unknown; and as the result of experience we urge every civilized community on earth to enfranchise its women without delay."[4]

While giving fullest credit to the political activity of the women of Wyoming, we cannot go to the extreme, reached by the enthusiastic defenders of woman suffrage in the Legislature of that State, of ascribing exclusively to the ballot in woman's hands the enviable conditions, which, according to the account of the address, Wyoming rejoices in. A number of social causes of other nature contribute thereto. Nevertheless, the fact is unquestionable that female suffrage has been accompanied by the most beneficent results for that State, and without one disadvantage. That is the most brilliant justification of its introduction.

The example of Wyoming found followers. To-day there are a number of countries in which woman enjoys political rights to greater or less extent. In the United States, women obtained several years ago the ballot in Colorado, and in 1894 they elected a number of representatives; likewise in Arizona, and still more recently in Minnesota. In New Zealand, they took a lively part in the parliamentary elections of 1893, livelier, in fact, than the men, although they were only qualified to elect: only men were qualified to be elected. In March, 1894, the

[4] The above two paragraphs are left as they appear in the text, although they seem to be subject to corrections.

A diligent search in the libraries of this city for the original of the above "Address to the Parliaments of the World," stated to have been issued by the Legislature of Wyoming in 1894, having proved vain, the Secretary of the State of Wyoming was written to. His answer was:

The State of Wyoming,
Office of the Secretary of State.
Cheyenne, June 5, 1903.

Mr. Daniel DeLeon, New York City:

Dear Sir—Replying to your letter of June 1st, would say that the Legislature of Wyoming was not in session in 1894, and did not pass any resolutions on Woman Suffrage in 1893 or 1895.

I enclose herewith the resolutions adopted by the Legislature of 1901, and also Senate and House resolutions adopted in 1903 on the subject of Woman Suffrage.   Yours truly,

F. Chatterton,
Secretary of State.

The resolutions enclosed in the above letter were these:

[House Joint Resolution No. 8, adopted February, 1901.]

Whereas, Wyoming was the first state to adopt equal suffrage and equal suffrage has been in operation since 1869; was adopted in the constitution of the State of Wyoming in 1890, during which time women have exercised the privilege as generally as men, with the result that better candidates have been selected for office, methods of election have been purified, the character of legislation improved, civic intelligence increased and womanhood developed to greater usefulness by political responsibility;

Therefore, Resolved, by the House of Representatives, the Senate concurring, That, in view of these results, the enfranchisement of women in every state and territory of the American Union is hereby recommended as a meas-

Prime Minister declared to a deputation of women that he would advocate their qualification to be elected. In 1893, there were twenty-two States in the North American Union where women were qualified both to elect and be elected for the School Boards. In Kansas, Nebraska, Colorado, Oregon, Arizona, Dakota, Idaho, Minnesota and Montana they are fully qualified electors for municipal officers, provided they are resident citizens. In Argonia, Kas., the wife of a physician was elected Mayor;[5] the same thing happened in Onehunga, New Zealand. Since more than ten years ago, women in Sweden have the suffrage for departmental and municipal elections, under the same restrictions as men.

In England, the struggle for woman's political rights has a regular

ure tending to the advancement of a higher and better social order.

That an authenticated copy of these resolutions be forwarded by the Governor of the state to the legislature of every state and territory, and that the press be requested to call public attention to these resolutions.

Edward W. Stone,
President of Senate.

J. S. Atherly,
Speaker of House.

Approved February 13th, 1901.
DeF. Richards,
Governor.

[Senate and House Resolution, Seventh Legislature, 1903.]

Whereas, The question of equal suffrage is being seriously considered in many States of the Union; and,

Whereas, Equal suffrage has been in operation in Wyoming ever since Territorial days in 1869, during which time women have exercised the privilege of voting generally and intelligently, with the result that a higher standard of candidates have usually been selected for office; elections have been made peaceful, orderly and dignified; the general character of legislation improved; intelligence in political, civic and social matters greatly increased; and,

Whereas, Under the responsibilities incident to suffrage the women of Wyoming have not in any sense been deprived of any of their womanly qualities, but on the contrary the womanhood of Wyoming has developed to a broader usefulness; therefore, be it

Resolved by the Senate of the Wyoming Legislature, That in view of the beneficence and practical results of equal suffrage for men and women in Wyoming, the enfranchisement of women is hereby endorsed as a great national reform and a measure that will improve and advance the political and social conditions of the country at large.

Resolved, That copies of this resolution be transmitted to Mrs. Carrie Chapman Catt, President National Women Suffrage Association, 2008 American Tract Society Building, New York, and to Mrs. Harriet Taylor Upton, National Treasurer, Warren, Ohio.

G. A. Guernsey,
President of the Senate.

Approved February 19th, 1903.
DeF. Richards,
Governor.

J. S. Atherly,
Speaker of the House.

Agitational literature on woman suffrage, furnished by the Boston, Mass., "Woman's Journal," after the above note was in print, gives the address cited in the text, but not as issued by the Legislature of Wyoming, nor in 1894. The address was adopted in March, 1893, by the House of Representatives of the Wyoming Legislature, just before the final adjournment of the body, and was not acted upon by the Senate.—THE TRANSLATOR.

[5] In Colorado, Idaho, Utah and Wyoming women have full suffrage, and

history behind it. According to the old custom of the Middle Ages, women, seized of landed property, were also vested with the suffrage, and, as such also filled judicial functions. In the course of time they lost these rights. In the bill for Parliamentary Reform in 1832, the word "person" was used, a term that, according to English conceptions, includes the members of both sexes, men and women. This notwithstanding, the law was interpreted adversely to women and they were turned back wherever they made the effort to vote. In the electoral reform Act of 1867, the word "man" was substituted for the word "person." John Stuart Mill moved the re-insertion of "person" in place of "man," with the express purpose that women shall be vested with the suffrage under the same conditions as men. The motion was defeated by 196 votes against 83. Sixteen years later, 1883, the attempt was again made in the Lower House to grant women the suffrage. A motion to that effect was defeated by a majority of 16. A further attempt in 1884 was defeated in a fuller House by more than 136 votes. But the minority did not evacuate the field. In 1886 it succeeded in carrying to a second reading a motion to grant women the suffrage; but the dissolution of Parliament prevented a final vote being taken. Again, on April 27, 1892, the Lower House defeated with 175 votes against 152, the second reading of a motion on the subject presented by Sir A. Rollit, and which provided as follows:

"Every woman who in Great Britain is registered or entitled to be registered as an elector for a Town Council or County Council or who in Ireland is a rate payer entitled to vote in the election of Guardians of the Poor, shall be entitled to be registered as a Parliamentary elector, and when registered, to vote at any Parliamentary election for the county, borough, or division wherein the qualifying property is situate."

On November 29, 1888, Lord Salisbury held a speech in Edinburgh, in the course of which he said: "I earnestly hope that the day is not far distant when women also will bear their share in voting for members in the political world and in the determining the policy of the country." And Alfred Russell Wallace, celebrated as a naturalist and follower of Darwin, expressed himself upon the same question this wise: "When men and women shall have freedom to follow their best impulses, when both shall receive the best possible education, when no false restraints

vote for all officers, including Presidential electors. In Utah and Wyoming woman suffrage is a constitutional provision.

In Indiana women may hold any office under the school laws, but can not vote for any such office.

In Kansas women exercise the suffrage largely in municipal elections.

In some form, mainly as to taxation or the selection of school officers, woman suffrage exists in a limited way in Arizona, Connecticut, Delaware, Illinois, Iowa, Kentucky, Massachusetts, Michigan, Minnesota, Montana, Nebraska, New Hampshire, New Jersey, New York, North Dakota, Ohio, Oklahoma, Oregon, South Dakota, Texas, Vermont, Washington and Wisconsin.—THE TRANSLATOR.

shall be imposed upon any human being by the reason of the accident of sex, and when public opinion shall be regulated by the wisest and best and shall be systematically impressed upon youth, then shall we find that a system of human selection will arise that is bound to have a reformed humanity for its result. So long as woman is compelled to regard marriage as a means by which to escape poverty and avoid neglect, she is and remains at a disadvantage with man. Hence, the first step in the emancipation of woman is the removal of all restraints that prevent her from competing with man on all the fields of industry and in all pursuits. But we must go further, and allow woman the exercise of her *political rights*. Many of the restraints, under which woman has suffered until now, would have been spared to her, had she had direct representation in Parliament."

In most sections of England, married women have the same political rights as men in the elections for the School Boards and Guardians of the Poor, and in many places are themselves qualified for election. At the county elections, *unmarried* women have the right to vote under the same restrictions as men, but are not themselves qualified for election. Likewise did all independent tax-paying women obtain the right to vote by the Reform Act of 1869, but are not qualified for election. *Married women* are in virtue of a court decision, rendered in 1872, excluded from the suffrage, because *in English law woman loses her independence by marriage*—a decided encouragement for women to keep away from the legal formality of legitimate marriage. Seeing that also in other respects unmarried or divorced women in England and Scotland are clothed with rights denied to married women, the temptation is not slight for women to renounce legitimate unions. It is not exactly the part of wisdom for the male representatives of bourgeois society to degrade bourgeois marriage into a sort of slave status for woman.[6]

In Austria, women who are landed proprietors, or conduct a business, to which the suffrage is attached, have the right to exercise the privilege *by attorney*. This holds both for local and Reichstag elections. If the woman is proprietor of a mercantile or industrial establishment, which gives the right to vote for the Chamber of Commerce, her franchise must be exercised by a business manager. In France, on the contrary, a woman who conducts a business, has a right to vote at the election of members for the tribunals of commerce, but she cannot herself be elected. According to the law of 1891 of the old Prussian provinces, women have the suffrage, if the landed property that belongs to them conveys the right to vote, nevertheless they must exercise the privilege through

---

[6] On September 5, 1902, the Trades Union Congress of England—made up, of course, of the British style of Trades Unionism, known in America as "Pure and Simple" Trades Unionism—rejected a resolution introduced for the purpose of giving the franchise to women on the same terms as men.—THE TRANSLATOR.

a male representative, neither are they eligible themselves. Likewise according to the laws of Hanover, Brunswick, Sleswig-Holstein, Sachsen-Weimar, Hamburg and Luebeck. In Saxony, the law allows women the suffrage if they are landed proprietors and are *unmarried*. If married, the woman's vote goes to her husband. In all these cases, accordingly, the right of suffrage does not attach to persons but to property—quite a light upon existing political and legal morality: Man, thou art zero if moneyless or propertyless; knowledge, intellect are secondary matters. Property decides.

We see that the principle of denying woman the suffrage on the theory of her not being "of age" is broken through in fact; and yet objection is raised to granting her the right in full. It is said that to grant woman the suffrage is dangerous because she yields easily to religious prejudices, and is conservative. She is both only because she is ignorant. Let her be educated and taught where her interests lie. For the rest, the influence of religion on elections is exaggerated. Ultramontane agitation has hitherto been so successful in Germany only because it knew how to join *social with religious interests*. The ultramontane chaplains long vied with the Socialists in uncovering the social foulness. Hence their influence with the masses. With the close of the Kulturkampf, the influence of the Catholic clergymen upon the masses waned. The clergy is forced to discontinue its opposition to the Government; simultaneously therewith, the rising class struggle compels it to consider the Catholic capitalist class and Catholic nobility; it will, accordingly, be compelled to observe greater caution on the social field. Thus the clergy will forfeit its influence with the workingmen, especially at such critical junctures when considerations for the Government and the ruling classes drive it to approve of, or tolerate actions and laws directed against the interests of the working class. The same causes will, in the end, have their influence upon woman. When at public meetings, through newspapers and from personal observation she will have learned where her own interest lies, woman will emancipate herself from the clergy, the same as man has done. The fiercest opponent of female suffrage is the clergy, and it knows the reason why. Its rule and its domains are endangered.

That the movement for the political rights of woman has not been promptly crowned with greater success is no reason to withhold the ballot from her. What would the workingmen say if the Liberals proposed abolishing manhood suffrage—and the same is very inconvenient to them—on the ground that it benefits the Socialists in particular? A good law does not become bad by reason of him who wields it not yet having learned its right use.

Naturally, the right to be elected should go together with the right to elect. "A woman in the tribune of the Reichstag, that would be a spectacle!" we hear people exclaim. Our generation has grown accustomed to the sight of women in the speaker's tribune at their conventions and meetings; in the United States, also in the pulpit and the jury box—why not, then, also in the tribune of the Reichstag? The first woman elected to the Reichstag, would surely know how to impose respect. When the first workingmen entered the Reichstag it was also believed they could be laughed down, and it was claimed that the working class would soon realize the foolishness it had committed in electing such people. Its representatives, however, knew how to make themselves quickly respected; the fear to-day is lest there be too many of them. Frivolous witlings put in: "Just imagine a pregnant woman in the tribune of the Reichstag; how utterly unesthetic!" The identical gentlemen find it, however, quite in order that pregnant women work at the most unesthetic trades, at trades in which female dignity, health and decency are undermined. In the eyes of a Socialist, that man is a wretch who can crack jokes over a woman with child. The mere thought that his own mother once looked like that before she brought him into the world, should cause his cheeks to burn with shame; the thought that he, rude jester, expects from a similar condition on the part of his wife the fulfillment of his dearest wishes should cause him, furthermore, to hold his tongue in shame.

A woman who gives birth to children renders, at least, the same service to the commonwealth as the man who defends his country and his hearth with his life against a foe in search of conquests. Moreover, the life of a woman trembles in the scales at child-birth. All our mothers have looked death in the face at our births, and many succumbed. *The number of women who die as a result of child-birth, or who as a consequence pine away in sickness, is greater than that of the men who fall on the field of battle, or are wounded.* In Prussia, between 1816-1876, not less than 321,791 women fell a prey to child-birth fever—a yearly average of 5,363. This is by far a larger figure than that of the Prussians, who, during the same period, were killed in war or died of their wounds. Nor must, at the contemplation of this enormous number of women who died of child-birth fever, the still larger number of those be lost sight of, who, as a consequence of child-birth, are permanently crippled in health, and die prematurely.[7] These are additional reasons for woman's equal rights with man—reasons to be held up especially to those, who play man's duty to defend the Fatherland as a decisive circumstance, entitling them to superior consideration than women. For the rest, in virtue of our military institutions, most men do not even fill this duty: to the majority of them it exists upon paper only.

[7] "To every woman who to-day dies in child-bed, from 15 to 20 must be added who remain more or less seriously injured, and subject to womb troubles and general ill health, often for life."—Dr. H. B. Adams.

All these superficial objections to the public activity of woman would be unimaginable were the relations of the two sexes a natural one, and were there not an antagonism, artificially raised side by side with the relation of master and servant between the two. From early youth the two are separated in social intercourse and education. Above all, it is the antagonism, for which Christianity is responsible, that keeps the sexes steadily apart and the one in ignorance about the other, and that hinders free social intercourse, mutual confidence, a mutual supplementing of traits of character.

One of the first and most important tasks of a rationally organized society must be to end this unhallowed split, and to reinstate Nature in its rights. The violence done to Nature starts at school: First, the separation of the sexes; next, mistaken, or no instruction whatever, in matters that concern the human being as a sexual entity. True enough, natural history is taught in every tolerably good school. The child learns that birds lay eggs and hatch them out: he also learns when the mating season begins: that males and females are needed: that both jointly assume the building of the nests, the hatching and the care of the young. He also learns that mammals bring forth live young: he learns about the rutting season and about the fights of the males for the females during the same: he learns the usual number of young, perhaps also the period of pregnancy. But on the subject of the origin and development of his own stock he remains in the dark; that is veiled in mystery. When, thereupon, the child seeks to satisfy his natural curiosity with questions addressed to his parents, to his mother in particular—he seldom ventures with them to his teacher—he is saddled with the silliest stories 'that cannot satisfy him, and that are all the more injurious when he some day does ascertain the truth. There are probably few children who have not made the discovery by the twelfth year of their age. In all small towns, in the country especially, children observe from earliest years the mating of birds, the copulation of domestic animals; they see this in closest proximity, in the yard, on the street, and when the cattle are turned loose. They see that the conditions under which the heat of the cattle is gratified, as well as the act of birth of the several domestic animals are made the subject of serious, thorough and undisguised discussion on the part of their parents, elder brothers and servants. All that awakens doubts in the child's mind on the accounts given him of his own entry into life. Finally the day of knowledge does come; but it comes in a way other than it would have come under a natural and rational education. The secret that the child discovers leads to estrangement between child and parents, particularly between child and mother. The reverse is obtained of that which was aimed at in folly and shortsightedness. He

who recalls his own youth and that of his young companions knows
what the results frequently are.

An American woman says, among other things in a work written by
her, that wishing to answer the repeated questions of her eight-year-old
son on his origin, and unwilling to saddle him with nursery tales, she
disclosed the truth to him. The child listened to her with great attention, and, from the day that he learned what cares and pains he had
caused his mother, he clung to her with a tenderness and reverence
not noticed in him before, and showed the same reverence toward other
women also.[9] The authoress proceeds from the correct premises that
only by means of a natural education can any real improvement—more
respect and self-control on the part of the male toward the female sex
—be expected. He who reasons free from prejudice will arrive at no
other conclusion.

Whatever be the point of departure in the *critique* of our social conditions, the conclusion is ever the same—their *radical transformation;*
thereby a radical transformation in the position of the sexes is inevitable.
Woman, in order to arrive all the quicker at the goal, must look for
allies who, in the very nature of things, the movement of the working
class steers in her direction. Since long has the class-conscious proletariat begun the storming of the fortress, the Class-State, which also
upholds the present domination of one sex by the other. That fortress
must be surrounded on all sides with trenches, and assailed to the point
of surrender with artillery of all calibre. The besieging army finds its
officers and munitions on all sides. Social and natural science, jointly
with historical research, pedagogy, hygiene and statistics are advancing
from all directions, and furnish ammunition and weapons to the movement. Nor does philosophy lag behind. In Mainlaender's "The Philosophy of Redemption,"[9] it announces the near-at-hand realization of the
"Ideal State."

The ultimate conquest of the Class-State and its transformation is
rendered all the easier to us through the divisions in the ranks of its
defenders, who, despite the oneness of their interests against the common enemy, are perpetually at war with one another in the strife for
plunder. Further aid comes to us from the daily-growing mutiny in the
ranks of the enemies, whose forces to a great extent are bone of our
bone, and flesh of our flesh—elements that, out of misunderstanding and
misled, have hitherto fought against us and thus against themselves, but
are gradually becoming clearsighted, and pass over to us. Finally we
are aided by the desertion of the honorable elements from the ranks of
the hitherto hostile men of thought, who have perceived the truth, and
whose higher knowledge spurs them to leap their low class interests, and,

---

[9] Isabella Beecher-Hooker, "Womanhood, Its Sanctities and Fidelities."

[9] "Philosophie der Erlösung."

following their ideal aspirations after justice, join the masses that are thirsting for freedom.

Many do not yet realize the stage of dissolution that State and Society are in. Hence, and although the dark blotches have been frequently pointed out in the preceding chapters, a separate treatment of the subject is requisite.

CHAPTER VI.

During the last few decades and in all countries of civilization, the economic life of society has assumed an uncommonly rapid pace of development, a development that every progress on any field of human activity adds swing to. Our social relations have thereby been thrown into a state of unrest, fermentation and dissolution never known before. The ruling classes no longer feel the ground safe under them, nor do existing institutions any longer possess the firmness requisite to breast the storm, that is approaching from all sides. A feeling of uneasiness, of insecurity and of dissatisfaction has seized upon all circles, high and low. The paroxysmal efforts put forth by the ruling classes to end this unbearable state of things by means of tinkering at the body social prove themselves vain and inadequate. The general sense of increasing insecurity, that comes from these failures, increases their uneasiness and discomfort. Hardly have they inserted a beam in the shape of some law into the rickety structure, than they discover ten other places where shoring is still more urgent. All along they are at perpetual strife among themselves and deeply rent by differences of opinion. What one set deems necessary, in order somewhat to calm and reconcile the increasingly discontented masses, the other considers as going too far, and unpardonable weakness and pliancy, only calculated to prick the longing after greater concessions. Striking evidences thereof are the debates in the 1894-5 sessions of the Reichstag, both on the floor of the house and in committee, on the so-called "revolutionary bill," as well as numerous other discussions in all parliaments. Within the ruling classes themselves there exist unbridgeable contrasts, and they sharpen the social conflicts.

Governments—and not in Germany alone—are shaking like a reed in the wind. They must lean on something: without support they cannot exist: they now lean on this side, then on that. In no progressive country of Europe is there a Government with a lasting parliamentary majority, on which it can count with safety. Majorities are breaking up and dissolving; and the ever changing course, in Germany, especially, undermines the last vestige of confidence that the ruling class had in themselves. To-day one set is anvil, the other the hammer; to-morrow it is the other way. The one tears down what the other painfully builds up. The confusion is ever greater; the discontent ever more lasting; the causes of friction multiply and consume in a few months more energies than years did formerly. Along with all that, material sacrifices, called for by manifold taxes, swell beyond all measure.

In the midst of all this, our sapient statesmen are lulling themselves in wondrous illusions. With an eye to sparing property and the rich, forms of taxation are selected that smite the needy classes heaviest, and they are decreed with the belief that, seeing a large portion of the masses have not yet discovered their real nature, neither will they be felt. This is an error. The masses to-day understand fully the nature of indirect imports and taxes upon the necessaries of life. Their growing political education and perspicuity disclose to them the gross injustice of the same; and they are all the more sensitive to these burdens by reason of the wretchedness of their economic conditions, especially where families are large. The rise of prices in the necessaries of life—due to indirect imposts, or to causes that bring on similar results—such as the premiums on brandy and sugar that, to the amount of dozens of millions, a part of the ruling class pockets yearly at the expense of the poor of the kingdom, and that it seeks to raise still higher —are realized to be a gross injustice, a heavy burden, measures that stand in odd contradiction with the nature of the so-called Christian State, the State of Social Reform. These measures extinguish the last spark of faith in the sense of justice of the ruling classes, to a degree that is serious to these. It changes nothing in the final effect of these measures that the draining is done in pennies. The increase in the expenditure is there, and is finally sensible to the feeling and the sight of all. Hundreds upon hundreds of millions cannot be squeezed out of practically empty pockets, without the owners of the pockets becoming aware of the lifting. The strong pressure of direct taxation, directs the dissatisfaction among the poor against the State; the still stronger indirect taxation, *directs the discontent against society also, the evil being felt to be of a social as well as political character.* In that there is progress. Him whom the gods would destroy, they first make blind.

In the endeavor to do justice to the most opposed interests, laws are heaped upon laws; but no old one is thoroughly repealed, nor new one thoroughly enforced. Everything is done by halves, giving satisfaction in no direction. The requirements of civilization that spring from the life of the people, demand some attention, unless everything is to be risked; even the fractional way they are attended to, demands considerable sacrifice, all the more seeing that our public institutions are overrun by parasites. At the same time, not only are all the unproductive institutions, wholly at variance with the trend of civilization, continued in force, but, due to the existing conflicts of interests, they are rather enlarged, and thus they become all the more burdensome and oppressive in the measure that increasing popular intelligence ever more loudly pronounces them superfluous. Police, armies, courts of law, prisons, the whole administrative apparatus—all are enlarged ever more, and become ever more expensive. And yet neither external nor internal security is obtained. The reverse follows.

A wholly unnatural state of things has gradually arisen in the international relations of the several nations. The relations between nation and nation multiply in the measure that the production of goods increases; that, thanks to improved transportation, the exchange of this mass of merchandise is facilitated; and that the economic and scientific achievements of each become the public possession of all. Treaties of commerce are concluded; expensive routes of traffic—Suez Canals, St. Gotthard Tunnels—are opened with international funds. Individual countries support with heavy subsidies steamship lines that help to promote intercourse between several nations. The Postal Union—a step of first rank in civilization—is established; international conventions are convoked for all imaginable practical and scientific purposes; the literary products of genius of any nation are spread abroad by translations into the leading languages. Thus the tendency is ever more strongly marked toward the internationalizing, the fraternizing of all peoples. Nevertheless, the political, the military state of the nations of Europe stands in strange contrast to this general development. The hatred of nation against nation, Chauvinism, is artificially nourished by all. The ruling classes seek everywhere to keep green the belief that it is the peoples who are hostilely inclined toward one another, and only wait for the moment when one of them may fall upon another and destroy it. The competitive struggle between the capitalists of several countries, together with their jealousy of one another, assume upon the international field the character of a struggle between the capitalists of one country against those of another, and, backed by the political blindness of the large masses, it conjures into existence a contest of military armaments such as the world has never seen before. This contest has brought forth armies of magnitudes that never were known; it produced implements of murder and destruction for land and naval warfare of such perfection as is possible only in an age of such advanced technique as ours. The contest drives these antagonisms to a head, it incites a development of means of destruction that finally destroy themselves. The support of the armies and navies demand sacrifices that yearly become larger, and that finally ruin the richest nation. Germany, for instance, had, according to the imperial budget of 1894-95, a regular army and navy outlay of nearly 700 million marks —inclusive of pensions and of interest on the national debt, which amounts in round figures to two milliards, incurred mainly for purposes of war. Under these war expenses, the appropriations for educational and other purposes of culture suffer severely; the most pressing needs in this direction are neglected; and that side of the State, devoted to so-called external defence, acquires a preponderance that undermines the original purpose of the State itself. The increasing armies absorb the healthiest and most vigorous portion of the nation; for their improvement all mental and physical forces are enlisted in a way as if education in mass-murder were the highest mission of our times. Furthermore, implements of war as of murder are continuously improved: they have attained—in point of swiftness, range and power—a perfection that renders them fearful to friend and foe. If some day this tremendous apparatus is set in operation—when the hostile forces of Europe will take the field with twelve or fourteen million men—the fact will appear that it has become uncontrollable. There is no general who could command such masses; there is no field vast enough to collect and set them up; no administrative apparatus that could nourish them for any length of time. If battles are delivered, hospitals would be lacking to shelter the wounded: the interment of the numerous dead would be an impossibility.

When to all this is added the frightful disturbances and devastations, produced to-day by a European *war on the economic field*, there is no exaggeration in the saying: *"the next war is the last war."* The number of bankruptcies will be unparalleled; export stops—and thereby thousands of factories are condemned to idleness; the supply of food ceases—and thereby the prices of the means of life rise enormously. The number of families whose breadwinner is in the field runs up into the millions, and most of them must be supported. Whence shall the means come for all that?

The political and military state of Europe has taken a development that cannot choose but end in a catastrophe, which will drag capitalist society down to its ruin. Having reached the height of its development, it produces conditions that end with rendering its own existence impossible; it digs its own grave; it slays itself with the identical means that itself, as the most revolutionary of all previous social systems, has called into life.

Gradually a large portion of our municipalities are arriving at a desperate pass: they hardly know how to meet the increasing demands upon themselves. It is more particularly upon our rapidly growing large cities, and upon the localities situated in industrial districts, that the quickened increase of population makes a mass of demands, which the generally poor communities can come up to only by raising taxes and incurring debts. The budgets leap upward from year to year for school buildings, and street paving, for lighting, draining and water works; for sanitary, public and educational purposes; for the police and the administration. At the same time, the favorably situated minority makes the most expensive demands upon the community. It demands higher institutions of education, theatres, the opening of particularly fine city quarters with lighting, pavement, etc., to match. However justly the majority may complain of the preference, it lies in the very nature of modern affairs. The minority has the power and uses it to satisfy its social wants as much as possible at the expense of the collectivity. In and of themselves nothing can be said against these heightened social wants: they denote progress; the fault is only that their satisfaction falls mainly to the lot of the property classes, while all others should share them. A further evil lies in that often the administration is not the best, and yet is expensive. The officials often are inadequate; they are not sufficiently equipped for the many-sided demands made upon them, demands that often presuppose thorough knowledge. The members of Aldermanic Boards have generally so much to do and to attend to in their own private affairs that they are unable to make the sacrifices demanded for the full exercise of these public duties. Often are these posts used for the promotion of private interests, to the serious injury of those of the community. The results fall upon the taxpayers. Modern society cannot think of undertaking a thorough change in these conditions. It is powerless and helpless. It would have to remove itself, and that, of course, it will not. Whatever the manner in which taxes be imposed, dissatisfaction increases steadily. In a few decades, most of our municipalities will be unable to satisfy their needs under their present form of administration and of raising revenues. On the municipal as well as on the national field, the need of a radical change is manifest: it is upon the municipalities that the largest social demands are made: it is society *in nuce*: it is the kernel from which, so soon as the will and the power shall be there, the social change will radiate. How can justice be done to-day, when private interests dominate and the interests of the commonweal are made subservient?

Such, in short, is the state of things in the nation and in the municipality. They are both but the reflection of the economic life of society.

* * * *

The struggle for existence in our economic life grows daily more gigantic. The war of all against all has broken out with virulence; it is conducted pitilessly, often regardless of the weapon used. The well-known French expression: *"ote-toi de la, que je m'y mette."* (Get away, that I may step in) is carried out in practice with vigorous elbowings, cuffings, and pinchings. The weaker must yield to the stronger. Where physical strength—which here is the power of money, of property—does not suffice, the most cunning and unworthy means are resorted to. Lying, swindle, deceit, forgery, perjury—the very blackest crimes are often committed in order to reach the coveted object. As in this struggle for existence one individual transgresses against the other, the same happens with class against class, sex against sex, age against age. Profit

is the sole regulator of human feelings; all other considerations must
yield. Thousands upon thousands of workingmen and workingwomen
are, the moment profit demands it, thrown upon the sidewalk, and,
after their last savings have been spent, turned to public charity or
forced to emigrate. Workingmen travel, so to speak, in herds from place
to place, criss-cross across the country, and are regarded by "decent"
society with all the more fear and horror, seeing that the continuity of
their enforced idleness deteriorates their external appearance, and, as a
consequence, demoralizes them internally. Decent society has no inkling
of what it means to be forced, for months at a stretch, to be denied the
simplest exigencies of order and cleanliness, to wander from place to
place with a hungry stomach, and to earn, generally, nothing but ill-
concealed fear and contempt, especially from those quarters that are
the very props of this system. The families of these wretches suffer
all along utmost distress—a distress that not infrequently drives the
parents, out of desperation, to frightful crimes upon their own children
and themselves. The last years have furnished numerous shocking instances of whole families falling a prey to murder and suicide. Let one
instance do for many. The private correspondent, S——, in Berlin, 45
years of age, with a still handsome wife 39 years old, and a daughter of
12, is without work and starving. The wife decides, with the consent
of her husband, to turn prostitute. The police gets wind thereof. The
wife is placed under moral control. The family, overcome with shame
and desperate, agree, all three, to poison themselves, and carry out
their resolve on March 1, 1883.[1] A few days before, the leading circles
of Berlin celebrated great court festivities at which hundreds of thousands were squandered.

Such are the shocking contrasts of modern society—and yet we live
in "the best of all possible worlds." Berlin has since then often witnessed the holocaust of whole families due to material want. In 1894
the spectacle was frequent, to an extent that called forth general horror;
nor are the instances few, reported from large and small towns within
and without Germany. This murder and suicide of whole families is a
phenomenon peculiar to modern times, and an eloquent sign of the
sorry economic state that society is in.

This general want also drives women and girls in increasing numbers
into the arms of prostitution. Demoralization and crime are heaped up,

---

[1] Let also one American instance be cited. It occurred on April 1, 1894,
in Dolgeville, N. Y., where an employe of the "profit-sharing" concern of
Alfred Dolge—at whose annual dinners Professor, now President George
Gunton was regularly a star guest, and orator to the "dined" workingmen
on the beauties of "profit-sharing,"—one of the workingmen, driven by the
pinching poverty and incertitude inflicted upon him by the "profit-sharing"
practice, killed his wife, four children and himself, and left a letter describing
his plight. (See "The People," April 8, 1894)—THE TRANSLATOR.

and assume the most manifold forms. The only thing that prospers is the jails, penitentiaries and so-called houses of correction, no longer able to accommodate the mass that is sent to them. The crimes of all sorts and their increase are intimately connected with the economic state of society—a fact, however, that the latter will not have. Like the ostrich, it sticks its head in the sand, to avoid having to admit the incriminating state of things, and it lies to the point of deceiving itself into the belief that the fault lies with the laziness of the workingmen, with their love of pleasure, and with their irreligiousness. This is a self-deception of the most dangerous, or a hypocrisy of the most repulsive, sort. The more unfavorable the state of society is for the majority, all the more numerous and serious are the crimes committed. The struggle for existence assumes its rudest and most violent aspect: it transfers man into conditions where each sees a mortal enemy in the other. The social bonds become looser every day.[2]

The ruling classes, who do not probe matters to the bottom, or do not like to, seek to meet the evil after their own fashion. If poverty and want, and, as a result therefrom, demoralization and crime increase, the source of the evil is not searched after, so that it may be stopped; no; the products of the conditions are punished. The more gigantic the evils grow, and the numbers of evil-doers multiply in proportion, proportionately severe penalties and persecutions are deemed necessary. It is sought to drive out the devil with Beelzebub. Prof. Haeckel also considers it proper to proceed against criminals with the severest punishments possible, and that capital punishment, in particular, be stringently applied.[3] By this stand the Professor places himself in sweet accord with the re-actionists of all shades, who otherwise are mortally opposed to him. Haeckel is of the opinion that incorrigible scape-graces must be uprooted like weeds that take from plants light, air and space. Had Haeckel turned his mind slightly toward social, instead of engaging it wholly with natural science, he would know that these criminals could, in most instances, be transformed into useful members of human society, provided society offered them the requisite conditions of existence. He would also find that the annihilation of individual criminals or the rendering of them harmless, prevents as little the com-

---

[2] As early as the days of Plato were the consequences of such conditions understood. He writes: "A nation in which classes exist, is not one, but two: one class is made up of the poor, the other of the rich, both living together, yet on the watch against each other. . . . In the end, the ruling class is unable to conduct a war, because it would then have to avail itself of the masses, whom, armed, it fears more than the enemy himself"; Plato, "The Republic." Aristotle says: "Widespread poverty is an evil, inasmuch as it is hardly possible to prevent such people from becoming inciters of sedition"; Aristotle, "Politics."

[3] "Natuerliche Schoepfungsgeschichte."

mission of fresh crimes in society, as the removal of weeds on a field would prevent their returning if the roots and seeds are not likewise destroyed. Absolutely to prevent the forming of harmful organisms in Nature is a feat man never will be able to achieve but *to so improve his own social system, a system produced by himself, that it may afford favorable conditions of life for all, and furnish to each equal freedom to unfold, to the end that they no longer need suffer hunger, or be driven to satisfy their desire for property, or their ambition at the expense of others—that is possible.* Let the cause of the crimes be studied, and let that be removed; then will the crimes themselves be wiped out.[4]

Those who would remove crimes by removing the causes thereof, cannot, as a matter of course, sympathize with a plan of brutal suppression. They cannot prevent society from protecting itself after its own fashion against the criminals, whom it cannot allow a free hand; but we demand all the more urgently the radical reformation of society, i. e., the removal of the causes of crime.

The connection between social conditions, on the one hand, and evil-doing and crimes, on the other, has been frequently established by statisticians and sociologists. One of the misdemeanors nearest at hand —one that, all Christian charitable tenets to the contrary notwithstanding, modern society regards as a misdemeanor—is begging, especially during hard times. On that subject, the statistics of the Kingdom of Saxony inform us that, in the measure in which the last industrial crisis increased—a crisis that began in Germany in 1890, and whose end is not yet in sight—the number of persons also increased who were punished for begging. In 1889, there were 8,566 persons punished for this crime in the Kingdom of Saxony; in 1890, there were 8,815; in 1891, there were 10,075; and in 1892 the figures rose to 13,120—quite an increase. Mass-impoverishment on one side, swelling affluence on the other—such is the sign-manual of our age. In Austria, in 1873, there was one pauper to every 724 persons; in 1882, to every 622 persons. Crimes and misdemeanors show similar tendency. In Austria-Hungary, in 1874, there were 308,605 persons sentenced in the criminal courts; in 1892, their number was 600,000. In the German Empire, in 1882, there were 329,968 persons sentenced for crimes and misdemeanors under the laws of the land; that is to say, to every 10,000 inhabitants of twelve years and over there were 103.2 criminals; in 1892, the number of criminals was 422,327, or 143.3—an increase of 39 per cent. Among the persons punished, there were, for crimes and misdemeanors against property:—

---

[4] Similarly Plato in "The Republic": "Crimes have their roots in want of culture, in bad education and bad social institutions." Evidently, Plato understood the nature of society better than one of his learned successors twenty-three hundred years later,—not a cheering contemplation.

Year.	Total.	To Every 10,000 Inhabitants, 12 Years of Age and Over.
1882	169,334	53.0
1891	196,437	55.8

We think these figures speak volumes. They show how the deterioration of social conditions intensify and promote poverty, want, misdemeanors and crimes.

The basis of our social state is the capitalist system of production. On it modern society rests. All social, all political institutions are results and fruits of that system. It is the ground from which the whole social and political superstructure, together with its bright and dark sides, have sprung up. It influences and dominates the thoughts and feelings and actions of the people who live under it. Capital is the leading power in the State and in Society: the capitalist is the ruler of the propertyless, whose labor-power he buys for his use, and at a price, that, like all other merchandise, is governed by supply and demand and oscillates now above, then below the cost of reproduction. But the capitalist does not buy labor-power out of "sweet charity," in order to do a favor to the workingmen, although he often so pretends. He buys it for the purpose of obtaining surplus wealth from the labor of the workingmen, which he then pockets under the name of profit, interest, house and ground rent. This surplus wealth, squeezed out of the workingmen, and which in so far as the capitalist does not squander it in dissipation, crystallizes in his hands into more capital, puts him in a condition to steadily enlarge his plant, improve the process of production, and occupy increased labor forces. That, at the same time, enables him to step up before his weaker competitors, like a mailed knight before an unarmed pedestrian, and to destroy them. This unequal struggle between large and small capital spreads amain, and, as the cheapest labor-power, next to that of children and lads, woman plays therein a *role* of increasing importance. The result is the ever sharper division of a smaller minority of mighty capitalists and a mass of capitalless male and female lack-alls whose only resource is the daily sale of their labor-power. The middle class arrives hereby at a plight that grows ever graver. One field of industry after another, where small production still predominated, is seized and occupied to capitalist ends. The competition of capitalists among themselves compels them to explore ever newer fields of exploitation. Capital goes about "like a roaring lion, seeking whom it may devour." The smaller and weaker establishments are destroyed; if their owners fail to save themselves upon some new field—a feat that becomes ever harder and less possible— then they sink down into the class of the wage earners, or of Catilin-

arians. All efforts to prevent the downfall of handicraft and of the
middle class by means of institutions and laws, borrowed from the
lumber-room of the musty past, prove utterly ineffective. They may
enable one or another to deceive himself on his actual condition; but
soon the illusion vanishes under the heavy weight of facts. The process
of absorption of the small by the large takes its course with all the power
and pitilessness of a law of Nature, and the process is sensible to the
feeling and the sight of all.

In the period between 1875-1882, the number of small industries decreased in Prussia by 39,655,[5] although the population increased in this
period by about two million heads. The number of workmen employed in
small industries sank, during that time, from 57.6 per cent., to 54.9 per
cent. The industrial statistics for 1895 will furnish much more drastic
figures. The development of large production stands in close relation
to the development of steam machine and steam horse-power. And what
is the picture presented by these? Prussia had:—

	1878.	1893.
Stationary steam boilers....	32,411	53,024 + 63.6 per cent.
Stationary steam engines....	29,895	53,092 + 77.6 per cent.
Movable machines	5,536	15,725 +184 per cent.

The Kingdom of Saxony had:—

	1861.	1891.
Stationary steam engines....	1,003	8,075 +700 per cent.
Horse-power	15,633	160,772 +922 per cent.

In 1861, a steam engine in Saxony had, on an average, a 15.5 horse-
power; in 1891, it had 19. All Germany had in 1878 about three
million horse-power in operation in industry; in 1894, about five million.
Austria had in 1873 in round figures 336,000 horse-power; in 1888, about
2,150,000. Steam power spreads daily, and stronger steam machines
drive out weaker ones—large production drives out small. The fact is
shown emphatically in the industries in which steam has become the
general power, the brewery industry, for instance. In the German
brewery tax department, exclusive of Bavaria, Wuertemburg, Baden and
Alsace-Lorraine, there were:—

Year.	Breweries in Operation.	Industrially Operated.	Output.
1873 13,561		10,927	19,654,900 hl.
1891-2 8,460		7,571	33,171,100 hl.
	5,101	3,356	13,516,200 hl.
	Decrease	Decrease	Increase
	= 38 per cent.	= 31.1 per cent.	= 68.8 per cent.

[5] In the sense of German industrial statistics, every employer is placed
under the head of "small producer" who employs less than five persons.

The breweries in general, this table shows, had decreased during this period 38 per cent., the industrially operated ones 31.1 per cent.; the output, however, had increased 68.8 per cent. The giant concerns increased at the expense of the middle and small ones. The identical development is going on *in all countries of civilization, in all industries capitalistically operated.* Let us now take up the brandy distilleries. In all the eight provinces of Prussia, there were in operation:—[6]

Year.	Distilleries.	Consumed in Distillery, Brandy (Double Quintal).	
1831	13,806	1,736,458	5,418,217
1886-87	5,814	2,518,478	24,310,196
	7,992 Decrease = 38 per cent.	782,020 Decrease = 31.1 per cent.	18,891,979 Increase = 68 per cent.

Similar results are revealed in the coal and the mineral mining industries of the German Empire. In the former, the number of leading concerns—623 in number between the years 1871-1875—dropped to 406 in 1889, but the output increased simultaneously from 34,485,400 tons to 67,342,200 tons, and the average number of employees rose from 172,074 to 239,954. In the latter, the average number of leading establishments between 1871-1875, was 3,034, with an average force of 277,878 hands, that turned out 51,056,900 tons; in 1889, the number of leading establishments had *dropped to 1,962, while the average force had risen to 368,896 hands, and the output to 99,414,100 tons.*[7] We see that in the coal mine industry the number of concerns decreased during that period 35 per cent., while the number of employees rose 40 per cent., and production as much as 95.2 per cent. Similarly in the mineral mining industry. Here the number of establishments decreased 35.3 per cent., while the number of workingmen employed rose 33 per cent., and production 94.7 per cent. A smaller but much richer number of employers now confronted a greatly swollen number of proletarians. Nor does this technical revolution proceed in industry alone: it is also going on in the department of transportation and communication. German commerce had upon the seas:—

Year.	Sailing Vessels.	Tonnage.	Crews.
1871	4,372	900,361	34,739
1893	2,742	725,182	17,522
	1,630 Decrease.	175,179 Decrease.	17,217 Decrease.

[6] Clemens Heiss: "Die grossen Einkommen in Deutschland."

[7] Clemens Heiss, *ubi supra.*

Sail navigation, we see, declines perceptibly, but in so far as it continues to exist, *the tonnage of vessels increases, and the force of the crews decreases.* In 1871, there came to every one sailing vessel 205.9 tons and 7.9 crew; in 1893, however, the average tonnage per sailing vessel was 271.7 and only a crew 6.4 strong. A different picture is offered by the German ocean steamship navigation. Germany had:—

Year.	Steamers.	Tonnage.	Crews.
1871 147		81,994	4,736
1893 986		786,397	24,113
Increase 839		704,403	19,377

We see that, not only did the number of steamers rise considerably, but that their tonnage increased still more; on the other hand, the force of the crews had relatively decreased. In 1871, steamers had on an average a 558 tonnage, with a 32.1 crew; in 1893 they had a 797.5 tonnage and only a 24.5 crew. It is an economic law that the number of workingmen *decreases* everywhere with the concentration of industry, while, relatively to the whole population, wealth concentrates in ever fewer hands, and the number of employers, rendered unable to hold their own and driven into bankruptcy by the process of concentration, mounts ever higher.

In the eight old provinces of Prussia, the population increased 42 per cent. during 1853-1890. But the incomes in the several grades rose in the following rates:—[8]

Incomes.	Increased
Up to 3,000 marks	42 per cent.
3,000— 36,000 marks	333 per cent.
36,000— 60,000 marks	590 per cent.
60,000—120,000 marks	835 per cent.
Over 120,000 marks	942 per cent.

The number of incomes up to 3,000 marks increased exactly with the population; it would, however, have lagged behind it if, within the period of 1853-1890, there had not been an extraordinary increase of national, State, municipal and private officials, the large majority of whose incomes falls below 3,000 marks. On the other hand, the number of large incomes has risen beyond all proportion, although, during the period under consideration, there was not yet any provision in Prussia making the correct estimate of incomes obligatory. This was introduced in 1891. The actual increase of incomes was, accordingly, much larger than the figures indicate. As stated before, the concentration of wealth,

[8] Clemens Heiss: "Die grossen Einkommen in Deutschland."

on the one side, is paralleled with mass-proletarianization, on the other, and also with swelling figures of bankruptcy. During the period of 1880-1889, the number of bankruptcy cases, adjudicated by law, averaged, in Germany, 4,885 a year; it rose to 5,908 in 1890; to 7,234 in 1891; and to 7,358 in 1892. These figures do not include the large number of bankruptcies that did not reach the courts, the assets not being large enough to cover the costs; neither are included among them those that were settled out of court between the debtors and their creditors.

The same picture that is presented by the economic development of Germany is presented by that of all industrial countries of the world. All nations of civilization are endeavoring to become industrial States. They wish to produce, not merely for the satisfaction of their own domestic wants, but also for exportation. Hence the absolute propriety of no longer speaking of "national" but of "international" economy. It is the world's market that now regulates the price of numberless products of industry and agriculture, and that controls the social position of nations. The productive domain, that, in the near future, will dominate the world's market is that of the United States—a quarter from which is now proceeding the principal impetus toward revolutionizing the relations of the world's market, and, along therewith, all bourgeois society. According to the census of 1890, the capital invested in industry in the United States has risen to 6,524 million dollars, as against 2,790 million in 1880, an increase of 136 per cent. The value of the industrial products rose during that period from 5,369 million dollars to 9,370 million, or 75 per cent. in round figures, while the population increased only 25 per cent.[*] The United States has reached a point of development where it must export a large mass of products in order to be able to continue producing in sufficient quantities. Instead of importing articles of industry from Europe, these will henceforth be exported in large volumes, thereby upsetting commercial relations everywhere. What pass has been reached there is indicated by the mammoth struggles between Capital and Labor, by the distress of the masses that has lasted years, and by the colossal increase of bankruptcy during the last crisis. In 1879, 1880 and 1881 the sum absorbed in bankruptcies ran up to 82 million dollars in round figures; in 1890 the amount was 190 million dollars, and in 1891 it rose to 331 million dollars. An instance will illustrate the gigantic measure of the concentration of capital in that country. In 1870, there were in the United States 2,819 woolen mills, in which 96 million dollars were invested as capital; in

[*] According to the census of 1900, the capital invested in industry was 9,831 million dollars,—an increase over 1890 of 3,307 million; and the value of the industrial products was 13,010 million dollars,—an increase over 1890 of 3,640 millions.—THE TRANSLATOR.

1890 the number of these mills had sunk to 1,312, but the capital invested had risen to 136 million.   In 1870, on an average, $34,000 sufficed to establish a woolen mill; in 1890, not less than $102,000 was requisite.   The increased demands upon capital forces the building of stock corporations ,which, in turn, promote the concentration still more. Where the powers of a single capitalist do not suffice, several of them join; they appoint technical overseers, who are well paid, and they pocket, in the form of dividends, the profits which the workingmen must raise.   The restlessness of industry reaches its classic form in the stock corporation, which demonstrates how useless the person of the capitalist has become as a leader of industry.

Seeing that this process of development and concentration is proceeding equally in all leading countries, the inevitable results of the anarchic method of production is "over-production," the stoppage of trade, the crisis.

Accordingly, the crisis is a consequence of the absence of any means whatever whereby at any time the actual demand for certain goods can be gauged and controlled.   There is no power in bourgeois society able to regulate production as a whole; the customers are spread over too vast an area; then also, their purchasing power, upon which depends their power of consumption, is affected by a number of causes, beyond the control of the individual producer.   Moreover, along with each individual producer, are a number of others, whose productive powers and actual yield also are unknown to him.   Each strives, with all the means at his command—cheap prices, advertisements, long credit, drummers, also secret and crafty detraction of the quality of the goods of his competitor, the last of which is a measure that flourishes particularly at critical moments— to drive all other competitors from the field.   Production is wholly left to accident and to the judgment of individuals.   Accident often is more unfavorable than otherwise.   Every capitalist must produce a certain quantity of goods, in order that he may exist; he is, however, driven to increase his output, partly because his increase of revenues depend upon that, partly also because upon that depend his prospects of being able to overcome his competitors, and keep the field all to himself.   For a while, the output is safe; the circumstance tends to expansion and increased production.   But prosperous times do not tempt one capitalist alone; they tempt them all. Thus production rises far above demand, and suddenly the market is found overstocked.   Sales stop; prices fall; and production is curtailed. The curtailment of production in any one branch implies a diminished demand for workingmen, the lowering of wages and a retrenchment of consumption in the ranks of labor.   A further stoppage of production and business in other departments is the necessary consequence.   Small producers of all sorts—trademen, saloonkeepers, bakers, butchers, etc.;

—whose customers are chiefly workingmen, lose the profitable sale of their goods and likewise land in distress.

The way in which such a crisis works appears from a census on the unemployed which the Social Democratic Party of Hamburg undertook on February 14, 1894. Of 53,756 workingmen who were interrogated, and of whom 34,647 were married, with an aggregate family dependents of 138,851, there were 18,422 who, during the last year, had been idle a total of 191,013 weeks; 5,084 persons had been idle from 1 to 5 weeks; 8,741 from 6 to 10 weeks; 1,446 from 11 to 15 weeks; 984 from 16 to 20 weeks; 2,167 more than 20 weeks. These are workingmen, who wished to work, but who, in this best of all possible worlds, could find no work. The sorry plight of these people may be imagined.

Again, one industry furnishes its raw material to another; one depends upon the other; it follows that all must suffer and pay for the blows that fall upon any. The circle of participants and sufferers spreads ever wider. A number of obligations, assumed in the hope of a long continuance of prosperity, cannot be met, and thus new fuel is added to the conflagration of the crisis, whose flames rise higher from month to month. An enormous mass of stored-up goods, tools, machinery, becomes almost worthless. The goods are got rid of at great sacrifices. Not only their proprietor is thereby ruined, but also dozens of others who are thereby likewise forced to give up their goods under cost. During the crisis itself, the method of production is all along improved with the view of meeting future competition; but this only prepares the ground for new and still worse crises. After the crisis has lasted years, after the surplusage of goods has been gradually done away with through sales at ruinous prices, through retrenchment of production, and through the destruction of smaller concerns, society slowly begins to recover again. Demand rises, and production follows suit—slowly at first and cautious, but, with the continuance of prosperity, the old vertigo sets in anew. Everyone is anxious to recover what he lost, and expects to be under cover before the next crisis breaks in. Nevertheless, seeing that all capitalists foster the identical thought, and that each one improves his plant so as to head off the others, the catastrophe is soon brought on again and with all the more fatal effect. Innumerable establishments rise and fall like balls at a game, and out of such continuous ups and downs flows the wretched state of things that is witnessed at all crises. These crises crowd upon one another in the measure that large production increases, and the competitive struggle—not between individuals only, but between whole nations—becomes sharper. The scampering for customers, on a small scale, and for markets on a large one, gains in fierceness, and ends finally in great losses. Goods and implements are heaped mountain high, yet the masses of the people suffer hunger and want.

The autumn of the year 1890 brought new proof of the correctness of this outline. After a long series of years of business depression, during which, however, large capitalist development was steadily progressing, an improvement in our economic life set in during 1887-8, stimulated in no slight degree by the extensive changes introduced in our army and navy systems. The upward movement continued during 1889 and up into the first quarter of 1890. During this period, a number of new establishments began to crop up everywhere in several fields of industry; a large number of others were enlarged and improved to the highest point of technical perfection, and their capacity greatly increased. In the same measure that this large capitalist development progressed, a larger and ever larger number of establishments passed from the hands of individual capitalists into stock corporations—a change that ever is more or less connected with an increase of production. The new issues, that, as a result of these combinations and due also to the increase of the public debt, were contracted in the international money market, ran up in 1887 to about 4,000 million marks; in 1888, to 5,500 million; and in 1889, to even 7,000 million. On the other hand, the capitalists of all countries were endeavoring to "regulate" prices and production by means of national and international agreements. Rings and Trusts sprang up like mushrooms over night. The majority, often all the capitalists concerned in the more important branches of production, formed syndicates, by means of which prices were fixed, and production was to be regulated by the light of accurate statistical information. Over-production was thus to be prevented. A marvelous monopolization of industry, such as had never been seen, was thus achieved in the interest of the capitalists and at the expense of the workingmen, and of the consumers in general. For a while it seemed as if capital had come into possession of the means that enabled it to control the market in all directions, to the injury of the public and to its own greater glory. But appearances deceived. The laws of capitalist production proved themselves stronger than the shrewdest representatives of the system who imagined they held in their hands the power to regulate it. The crisis set in. One of the largest international business houses of England fell and involved a number of others in its fall. All exchanges and markets—of London, Paris, Vienna and Berlin, as far as St. Petersburg, New York and Calcutta—shook and trembled. It had again been shown that the profoundest calculations prove deceptive, and that capitalist society cannot escape its fate.

All this notwithstanding, capitalism proceeds on its course: it can be no other than it is. By means of the forms that its course dictates, it throws all the laws of capitalist economics overboard. "Free competition," the Alpha and Omega of bourgeois society, is to bring the fittest to the top of the enterprises; but the stock corporation removes all individuality, and places the crown upon that combination that has the longest purse and the strongest grip. The syndicates, Trusts and rings carry the point still further. Whole branches of industry are monopolized; the individual capitalist becomes but a pliant link in a chain, held by a capitalist committee. *A handful of monopolists set themselves up as lords of the world and dictate to it the price of goods, to the workingmen their wages and conditions of life* .

The whole course of this development brings out how utterly superfluous the individual capitalist has become, and that production, conducted upon a national and international scale, is the goal toward which society steers—with this difference, that, in the end, this organized production will redound to the benefit, not of a class, but of the collectivity.

The economic revolution just sketched, and which is driving bourgeois society with great swiftness to its apogee, becomes more pointed from year to year. While Europe finds itself pressed more and more in its foreign markets, and finally on its own territory, by the competition of the United States, latterly enemies have risen in the East also, rendering still more critical the plight of Europe, and at the same time threatening the United States also. This danger proceeds from the progress of English India toward becoming a great agricultural and industrial State —a progress that, in the first place, looks to the meeting of the wants of India's own two hundred million strong population, and, in the second place, develops into a mortal enemy of English and German industry in particular. And still another industrial State is beginning to rise in the East—*Japan*. According to the "Kreuzzeitung" of February 20, 1895, "during the last ten years, Japan has imported from Europe the best perfected machinery for setting up industrial plants, especially in cotton spinning. In 1889, she had only 35,000 spindles; now she has over 380,000. In 1889, Japan imported 31 million pounds of raw cotton; in 1891, she imported 67 million. She is steadily decreasing her importations of manufactured articles, and increasing her importations of raw material, which she then retransports in the shape of manufactures. During the last year Hongkong, a European colony, bought over two million marks of Japanese cotton goods. The Japanese are providing their own markets with goods that formerly were imported from Europe and the United States. They are also exporting to Oriental markets, that were formerly provided from western sources. They are exporting matches and soap; they are manufacturing clothing, felt hats and hosiery; they have glass-blowing establishments, breweries, tileries, tan-yards and rope-walks."

The further expansion of Japan's industry steadily reduces importations from Europe and the United States, and simultaneously places it in condition to turn up in the world's market as a competitor. Should

China also, as a result of the Japanese-Chinese war, be compelled to open her immense territory to European culture, then, in view of the great adaptability and marvelous unpretentiousness of the Chinese workingman, another competitive power will have risen, more dangerous than any that the world's market has yet had to reckon with. Truly, the future of bourgeois society is threatened from all sides with grave dangers, and there is no way to escape them.

Thus *the crisis becomes permanent and international.* It is a result of all the markets being overstocked with goods. And yet, still more could be produced; but the large majority of people suffer want in the necessaries of life because they have no income wherewith to satisfy their wants by purchase. They lack clothing, underwear, furniture, homes, food for the body and mind, and means of enjoyment, all of which they could consume in large quantities. But all that does not exist to them. Hundreds of thousands of workingmen are even thrown upon the sidewalk, and rendered wholly unable to consume because their labor-power has become *"superfluous"* to the capitalists. Is it not obvious that our social system suffers of serious ailments? How could there be any "over-production" when there is no lack of capacity to consume, i. e., of wants that crave satisfaction? Obviously, it is not production, in and of itself, that breeds these unhallowed conditions and contradictions: *it is the system under which production is carried on, and the product is distributed.*

* * * *

In human society, all its members are bound to one another by a thousand threads; and these threads are all the more numerous in proportion to a people's grade of culture. If disturbances set in, they are forthwith felt by all. Disturbances in production affect distribution and consumption; and *vice versa.* The feature of capitalist production is the concentration of property into ever fewer hands and into ever larger establishments. In distribution, on the contrary, an opposite current is noticeable. Whoever, due to the destructive effect of competition, is stricken from the list of independent producers, seeks, in nine cases out of ten, to squeeze himself as a dealer between the producer and the consumer, and thus to earn his livelihood.

Hence the striking phenomenon of the increase of the middleman—dealers, shopkeepers, hucksters, commissioners, brokers, agents, saloon-keepers, etc. Most of these, among whom women are strongly represented, lead a life of worries and a needy existence. Many are compelled, in order to keep their heads above water, to speculate upon the lowest passions of man and to promote them in all manner of ways. Hence the marvelous swing of the most repulsive advertisements, particularly in all matters the object of which is the gratification of sexual pleasures.

It is undeniable, and, viewed from a higher viewpoint, it is also cheering, that the current for a greater enjoyment of life runs deep in modern society. Man begins to understand that, in order to be human, a life worthy of human beings is requisite, and the feeling is expressed in such form as corresponds with the respective conceptions of the enjoyment of life. As far as the distribution of its wealth is concerned, society has become much more *aristocratic* than at any previous period. Between the richest and the poorest, the chasm is wider to-day than ever before. On the other hand, with regard to its ideas and laws, society has become more *democratic*.[10] Hence the masses strive after greater equality; and, seeing that in their ignorance they know not yet the path by which to attain their wishes, they seek equality in the imitation of the upper classes by furnishing themselves with whatever pleasures are within their reach. All possible artificial means are resorted to in order to exploit this tendency; the consequences are often serious. The gratification of a justified desire thus leads in a number of cases to wrong paths, often to crime; and society intervenes in its own way, without thereby improving matters in the least.

The increasing mass of the middlemen draws many evils in its wake. Although this class toils arduously and works under the load of heavy cares, *the majority are parasites, they are unproductively active, and they live upon the labors of others, just the same as the capitalist class.* Higher prices is the inevitable consequence of this industry. Food and other goods rise in price in such manner that they often cost twice or many times as much as the producer received for them.[11] If it is thought unadvisable or impossible to materially raise the price of the goods, lest consumption decline, they are artificially deteriorated, and recourse is had *to adulteration of food, and to false weights and measures*, in order to make the requisite profits. The chemist Chevalier reports that he knows, among the several adulterations of food, 32 for

[10] Professor Adolf Wagner expresses the same thought in his first revised edition of Raus' "Lehrbuch der politischen Oekonomie." He says, p. 361: "The social question is the consciousness gained by the people of the contradiction between the economic development and the social principle of freedom and equality, that hovers over their minds as the ideal, and is realized in political life."

[11] Dr. E. Sax says in his work "Die Housindustrie in Thüringen," among other things, that in 1869 the production of 244¼ million slate pencils had given from 122,000 to 200,000 gilders in wages to the labor, but the final price paid by the consumer rose to 1,200,000 gilders; it was, accordingly, at least six times as much as the producer received. In the summer of 1888, there were 5 marks paid at first hand for 5 hundredweights of shellfish; the retailer paid the wholesale dealer 15 marks; and the public paid 125 marks. Moreover, large quantities of foodstuffs are destroyed because the prices will not pay for transportation. For instance, in years of great herring draughts, whole boatloads are turned to manure, while inland there are hundreds of thousands of people who can buy no herrings. It was likewise in 1892 with the large potato crops in California. And yet sense is claimed for such a state of things.

coffee, 30 for wine, 28 for chocolate, 24 for meal, 23 for brandy, 20 for bread, 19 for milk, 10 for butter, 9 for olive oil, 6 for sugar, etc. The Chamber of Commerce of Wesel reported in 1870 that an extensive system of swindle was practiced in the shops in the sale of ready-weighed articles: for 1 pound, 24 or 26 pennyweights were given, and in that way twice as much was gained than the difference in the price. Workingmen and small traders who get their goods on credit and who must, accordingly, submit, even when the fraud is obvious, fare worst of all. Grave abuses are also perpetrated in bakeries. Swindling and cheating are inseparable from our modern conditions, and certain government institutions, such as high indirect taxes, are direct incentives thereto. The laws against the adulteration of food alter matters but little. The struggle for existence compels the swindlers to resort to ever shrewder means, nor is there any thorough and strict inspection. Leading and influential circles of our ruling classes are even interested in the system of swindle. Under the pretext that, in order to discover adulterations a more comprehensive and more expensive administrative apparatus is required, and that "legitimate business" would suffer thereby, almost all inspection, worthy of the name, is lamed. If, however, laws and measures of inspection do actually intervene, they affect a considerable rise in the price of the unadulterated products, seeing that the lower price was made possible only by adulteration.

With the view of avoiding these evils of trade, evils that, as ever and everywhere, are hardest on the masses, "Consumers' Associations" have been set up. In Germany, the "Consumers' Association" plan, especially among the military and civil service employees, reaches such a point that numerous business houses have been ruined, and many are not far from the same fate. These Associations demonstrate the superfluousness of trade in a differently organized society.[12] In that consists their principal merit. The material advantages are not great for the members; neither are the facilities that they offer enough to enable the members to discover any material improvement in their condition. Not infrequently is their administration poor, and the members must pay for it. In the hands of capitalist, these Associations even become an additional means to chain the workingman to the factory, and they are used as weapons to depress wages. The founding of these "Consumers' Associations" is, however, a symptom that the evils of trade and at least the superfluousness of the middlemen have been realized in wide circles. Society will reach that point of organization at which trade becomes wholly superfluous; the product will reach the consumer without the intervention of any middlemen other than those who attend

---

[12] The industrial census of June 5, 1882, gives Germany 386,157 large and 154,474 small stores, a total of 531,631. In the large shops, there were 705,906 persons employed.

to its transportation from place to place, and who are in the service of society. A natural demand, that flows from the collective procurement of food, *is its collective preparation for the table upon a large scale, whereby a further and enormous saving would be made of energy, space, material and all manner of expenditures.*

* * * *

The economic revolution in industry and transportation has spread to agriculture also, and in no slight degree. Commercial and industrial crises are felt in the country as well. Many relatives of families located in the country are partially or even wholly engaged in industrial establishments in cities, and this sort of occupation is becoming more and more common because the large farmers find it convenient *to convert on their own farms a considerable portion of their produce.* They thereby save the high cost of transporting the raw product—potatoes that are used for spirits, beets for sugar, grain for flour or brandy or beer. Furthermore, they have on their own farms cheaper and more willing labor than can be got in the city, or in industrial districts. Factories and rent are considerably cheaper, taxes and licenses lower, seeing that, to a certain extent, the landed proprietors are themselves lawgivers and law officers: from their midst numerous representatives are sent to the Reichstag: not infrequently they also control the local administration and the police department. These are ample reasons for the phenomenon of increasing numbers of funnel-pipes in the country. Agriculture and industry step into ever closer interrelation with each other —an advantage that accrues mainly to the large landed estates.

The point of capitalist development reached in Germany also by agriculture has partially called for conditions similar to those found in England and the United States. As with the small and middle class industries, so likewise with the small and middle class farms, they are swallowed up by the large. A number of circumstances render the life of the small and middle class farmer ever harder, and ripen him for absorption by the large fellow.

No longer do the one-time conditions, as they were still known a few decades ago, prevail in the country. Modern culture now pervades the country in the remotest corners. Contrary to its own purpose, militarism exercises a certain revolutionary influence. The enormous increase of the standing army weighs, in so far as the blood-tax is concerned, heaviest of all upon the country districts. The degeneration of industrial and city life compels the drawing of by far the larger portion of soldiers from the rural population. When the farmer's son, the day laborer, or the servant returns after two or three years from the atmosphere of the city and the barracks, an atmosphere not exactly impregnated with high moral principles;—when he returns as the carrier and spreader of venereal diseases, he has also become acquainted with a mass of new views and wants whose gratification he is not inclined to discontinue. Accordingly, he makes larger demands upon life, and wants higher wages; his frugality of old went to pieces in the city. Transportation, ever more extended and improved, also contributes toward the increase of wants in the country. Through intercouse with the city, the rustic becomes acquainted with the world from an entirely new and more seductive side: he is seized with new ideas: he learns of the wants of civilization, thitherto unknown to him. All that renders him discontented with his lot. On top of that, the increasing demands of the State, the province, the municipality hit both farmer and farmhand, and make them still more rebellious.

True enough, many farm products have greatly risen in value during this period, but not in even measure with the taxes and the cost of living. On the other hand, transmarine competition in food materially contributes toward reducing prices: this reduces incomes: the same can be counterbalanced only by improved management: and nine-tenths of the farmers lack the means thereto. Moreover, the farmer does not get for his product the price paid by the city: he has to deal with the middlemen: and these hold him in their clutches. The broker or dealer, who at given seasons transverses the country and, as a rule, himself sells to other middlemen, wants to make his profits: the gathering of many small quantities gives him much more trouble than a large invoice from a single large holder: the small farmer receives, as a consequence, less for his goods than the large farmer. Moreover, the quality of the products from the small farmer is inferior: the primitive methods that are there generally pursued have that effect: and that again compels the small farmer to submit to lower prices. Again, the farm owner or tenant can often not afford to wait until the price of his goods rises. He has payments to meet—rent, interest, taxes; he has loans to cancel and debts to settle with the broker and his hands. These liabilities are due on fixed dates: he must sell however unfavorable the moment. In order to improve his land, to provide for co-heirs, children, etc., the farmer has contracted a mortgage: he has no choice of creditor: thus his plight is rendered all the worse. High interest and stated payments of arrears give him hard blows. An unfavorable crop, or a false calculation on the proper crop, for which he expected a high price, carry him to the very brink of ruin. Often the purchaser of the crop and the mortgagee are one and the same person. The farmers of whole villages and districts thus find themselves at the mercy of a few creditors. The farmers of hops, wine and tobacco in Southern Germany; the truck farmers on the Rhine; the small farmers in Central Germany—all are in that plight. The mortgagee sucks them dry; he leaves them apparent owners of a field, that, in point of fact, is theirs no longer. The capitalist vampire often finds it more profitable to farm in this way than, by seizing the land itself and selling it, or himself doing the farming. Thus many thousand farmers are carried on the registers as proprietors, who, in fact, are no longer such. Thus, again, many a large farmer—unskilled in his trade, or visited by misfortune, or who came into possession under unfavorable circumstances—also falls a prey to the executioner's axe of the capitalist. The capitalist becomes lord of the land; with the view of making double gains he goes into the business of "butchering estates:" he parcels out the domain because he can thereby get a larger price than if he sold it in lump: then also he has better prospects of plying his usurious trade if the proprietors are many and small holders. It is well known that city houses with many small apartments yield the largest rent. A number of small holders join and buy a portion of the parcelled-out estate: the capitalist benefactor is ready at hand to pass larger tracts over to them on a small cash payment, securing the rest by mortgage bearing good interest. This is the milk in the cocoanut. If the small holder has luck and he succeeds, by utmost exertion, to extract a tolerable sum from the land, or to obtain an exceptionally cheap loan, then he can save himself; otherwise he fares as shown above.

If a few heads of cattle die on the hands of the farm-owner or tenant, a serious misfortune has befallen him; if he has a daughter who marries, her outfit augments his debts, besides his losing a cheap labor-power; if a son marries, the youngster wants a piece of land or its equivalent in money. Often this farmer must neglect necessary improvements: if his cattle and household do not furnish him with sufficient manure—a not unusual circumstance—then the yield of the farm declines, because its owner cannot buy fertilizers: often he lacks the means to obtain better seed. The profitable application of machinery is denied him: a rotation of crops, in keeping with the chemical composition of his farm, is often not to be thought of. As little can he turn to profit the advantages that science and experience offer him in the conduct of his domestic animals: the want of proper food, the want of proper stabling and attention, the want of all other means and appliances prevent him. Innumerable, accordingly, are the causes that bear down upon the small and middle class farmer, drive him into debt, and his head into the noose of the capitalist or the large holder.

The large landholders are generally intent upon buying up the small holdings, and thereby "rounding up" their estates. The large capitalist magnates have a predilection for investments in land, this being the safest form of property, one, moreover, that, with an increasing population, rises in value without effort on the part of the owners. England furnishes the most striking instance of this particular increase of value. Although due to international competition in agricultural products and cattle-raising, the yield of the land decreased during the last decades, nevertheless, seeing that in Scotland two millión acres were converted into hunting grounds, that in Ireland four million acres lie almost waste, that in England the area of agriculture declined from 19,153,900 acres in 1831, to 15,651,605 in 1880, a loss of 3,484,385 acres, which have been converted into meadow lands, rent increased considerably. The aggregate rent from country estates amounted, in pounds sterling, to:—

Countries.	1857.	1875.	1880.	Increase.
England and Wales	41,177,200	50,125,000	52,179,381	11,002,181
Scotland	5,932,000	7,493,000	7,776,919	1,844,919
Ireland	8,747,000	9,293,000	10,543,000	1,796,700
Total	55,856,000	68,811,000	70,500,000	14,644,000

Accordingly, an increase of 26.2 per cent. within 23 years, and that without any effort on the part of the owners. Although, since 1880, due to the ever sharper international competition in food, the agricultural conditions of England and Ireland have hardly improved, the large English landlords have not yet ventured upon such large demands upon the population as have the continental, the German large landlords in particular. England knows no agricultural tariffs; and the demand for a minimum price, fixed by government, of such nature that they have been styled "price raisers" and as the large landlords of the East Elbe region together with their train-bands in the German Reichstag are insisting on at the cost of the propertyless classes, would raise in England a storm of indignation.

According to the agricultural statistics gathered in Germany on June 2, 1882, the farms fell into the following categories according to size:—

Area.	Farms.	Percentage of Total Farms.
Under 1 hectare	2,323,316	44.03
1 to 5 hectares	1,719,922	32.54
5 to 10 hectares	554,174	10.50
10 to 20 hectares	372,431	7.06
20 to 50 hectares	239,887	4.50
50 to 100 hectares	41,623	0.80
100 to 200 hectares	11,033	0.21
200 to 500 hectares	9,814	0.18
500 to 1,000 hectares	3,629	0.07
1,000 hectares	515	0.01
Total	5,276,344	100.00

According to Koppe, a minimum of 6 hectares are requisite in Northern Germany for a farmer's family to barely beat itself through; in order to live in tolerable circumstances, 15 to 20 hectares are requisite. In the fertile districts of Southern Germany, 3 to 4 hectares are considered good ground to support a peasant family on. This minimum is reached in Germany by not four million farms, and only about 6 per cent. of the farmers have holdings large enough to enable them to get along in comfort. Not less than 3,222,270 farmers conduct industrial or commercial pursuits besides agriculture. It is a characteristic feature of the lands under cultivation that the farms of less than 50 hectares—5,200,000 in all—contained only 3,747,677 hectares of grain lands, whereas the farms of more than 50 hectares—66,000 in round figures—contained 9,636,246 hectares. One and a quarter per cent. of the farms contained 2½ times more grain land than the other 98¾ per cent. put together.

And yet the picture presented by these statistics falls by far short of the reality. It has not been ascertained among how many owners these 5,276,344 farms are divided. The number of owners is far smaller than that of the farms themselves: many are the owners of dozens of farms: it is in the instance of large farms, in particular, that many are held by one proprietor. A knowledge of the concentration of land is of the highest socio-political importance, yet on this point the agricultural statistics of 1882 leave us greatly in the lurch. A few facts are, nevertheless, ascertained from other sources, and they give an approximate picture of the reality. The percentages of large landed property—over 100 hectares—to the aggregate agricultural property was as follows:—

Provinces.	Percentage.	Provinces.	Percentage.
Pomerania	64.87	Brandenburg	42.60
Posen	61.22	Silesia	42.14
West Prussia	54.41	Saxony	30.89
East Prussia	41.79	Sleswig-Holstein	18.03

According to the memorial of the Prussian Minister of Agriculture, published in the bulletin of the Prussian Bureau of Statistics, the number of middle class farms sank, from 354,610 with 35,260,084 acres, in 1816, to 344,737 with 33,498,433 acres, in 1859. The number of these farms had, accordingly, decreased within that period by 9,873, and peasant property had been wiped out to the volume of 1,711,641 acres. The inquiry extended only to the provinces of Prussia, Posen (from 1823 on), Pomerania, exclusive of Stralsund; Bradenburg, Saxony, Silesia, and Westphalia.

What disappears as peasant property usually goes into large estates. In 1885, in the province of Pomerania, 62 proprietors held 118 estates; in 1891, however, the same number of proprietors held 203 estates with an area of 147,139 hectares. Altogether, there were in the province of

Pomerania, in 1891, 1,353 noble and bourgeois landlords, owning 2,258 estates with 1,247,201 hectares.[13] The estates averaged 551 hectares in size.

Our eastern provinces give this table of landlords for the year 1888:—

Prince of Hohenlohe-Oehringen	39,365	hectares
Prince of Sigmaringen	29,611	"
Prince of Trum and Taxis	24,482	"
Prince Bismarck	18,600	"
Prince Radziwill	16,398	"
Duke of Milzinski	13,933	"
Representative Kennemann	10,482	"
Duke Serg. v. Czarnecki	9,263	"
v. Hansemann	7,734	"
Etc., etc., etc.		

We see that we here have to do with owners of latifundia of first rank; and a portion of these gentlemen own also large estates in Southern Germany and Austria.

According to Conrad,[14] there were in the year 1888, in East Prussia, 547 entails, of which 153 were instituted before the beginning of the nineteenth century. Entailed land is property that an heir can neither mortgage, divide nor alienate. The owner may go into bankruptcy through a dissolute life, but the entail and the income that flows therefrom remain unseizable. These entails, which only the very rich can institute, are steadily increasing in number since the last decades. The 547 entails in existence in the eastern provinces of Prussia in 1888, held by 529 persons, 20 of whom were bourgeois, embraced 1,408,860 hectares, or 2,454 hectares on an average. According to the statistical figures, submitted in the spring of 1894 by the Prussian Minister of Agriculture to the Agrarian Commission, the entails of Prussia embraced at that time 1,833,754 hectares with a net income of 22,992,000 marks. Estimating the holders of entails at 550, each has an unseizable income of 41,800 marks. Assuming, however, that these entails are concentrated in one province, it would mean that the whole province of Sleswig-Holstein, with an area of 1,890,000 hectares, belonged to 550 owners. In 1888 there were in the eastern provinces of Prussia 154 persons—among them 15 ruling Princes (the Kings of Prussia, Saxony, etc.); 89 Dukes, other Princes and Counts; 40 noblemen and 10 bourgeois—who alone owned 1,830 estates aggregating 1,768,648 hectares of land. Probably, the property of these persons has in the meantime increased considerably, seeing that a good portion of the net incomes from these estates is expended in acquiring new ones. The nobility of the first and

[13] Dr. Rud. Meyer, "Das Sinken der Grundrente."

[14] "Die Fideikommisse in den westlichen Provinzen Pruessens."

second rank are the principal elements engaged in this gigantic concentration of landed property; but they are closely followed by the aristocracy of finance, who, with increasing predilection, invest their wealth in land, consisting mainly in magnificent woods, stocked with roe, deer and wild boar, that the owners may gratify their passion for the hunt. A large number of the baronial manors consist of the estates of dispossessed peasants, who were driven from their homes and reduced to day laborers. According to Neumann, in the provinces of East and West Prussia alone, there were from twelve to thirteen thousand small holdings appropriated in that way between 1825 to 1859. This process of dispossessing, proletarianizing the country population by the capitalist landlords, has the laying waste of the land as a natural consequence. The population emigrates, or moves to the cities and industrial centers. Woods and meadows gain upon cultivated lands, the remaining territories are operated with machinery, that render human labor superfluous, or that need such only for short periods during the plowing and sowing seasons, or when the crops are gathered. The rapidly increasing number of movable steam engines, already mentioned, consists mainly of engines employed in the cultivation of the land. The decrease of the rural population, resulting upon these and other causes of secondary nature, is sharply expressed in the statistics on population. Within the eight old provinces of Prussia, the proportion between the rural and the city population revealed, between 1867 and 1890, the following progression:—

Year.	City Population.	Country Population.
1867	7,452,000	16,568,000
1890	11,783,000	18,173,000
Increase	4,331,000	1,605,000
	= 58 per cent.	= 9.7 per cent.

The rapidity is obvious with which the city is surpassing the country population. But the situation is still more unfavorable to the country if the fact is considered that 148 communities, with from 5,000 to 40,000 inhabitants, and aggregating a population of 1,281,000 strong, are included in the rural but really belong to the industrial districts. They are essentially proletarian villages, located near large cities. Furthermore, 647 communities, with from 2,000 to 5,000 inhabitants, and aggregating a population of 1,884,000, are likewise included in the rural, while, to a perceptible degree, they belong to the industrial districts.

Similar conditions exist in Saxony and Southern Germany. In Baden and Wurtemberg also the population of many district is on the decline. The small farmer can no longer hold his head above water; to thousands upon thousands of them the fate of a factory hand is inevitable; they enter the field of industry; and, with the help of their families, they cultivate during leisure hours the plot of land that may still be theirs. At the same time the large landlord's hunger for land knows no bounds; his appetite increases the more peasant lands he devours.

As in Germany so are things developing in neighboring Austria where large landed property has long ruled almost unchecked. The difference there is that the Catholic Church shares the land with the nobility and the bourgeoisie. The process of smoking-out the farmer is in full swing in Austria. All manner of efforts are put forth in order to push the peasants and mountaineers of Tyrol, Salzburg, Steiermark, Upper and Lower Austria, etc., off their inherited patrimony and to drive them to relinquish their property. The spectacle, once presented to the world by England and Scotland, is now on the boards of the most beautiful and charming regions of Austria. Enormous tracts of land are bought in lump by rich men, and what cannot be bought outright is leased. Access to the valleys, manors, hamlets and even houses is thus barred by these new masters, and stubborn owners of separate small holdings are driven by all manner of chicaneries to dispose of their property at any price to these wealthy owners of the woodlands. Old farmlands, on which numerous generations have been supported for thousands of years, are being transformed into wilderness, in which the roe and the deer house, while the mountains, that the noble or bourgeois capitalist calls his own, become the abode of large herds of chamois. Whole communities are pauperized, the turning of their cattle upon the Alpine pastures being made impossible to them, or their right to do so being even disputed. And who is it that thus raises his hand against the peasant's property and independence? Princes, noblemen and rich bourgeois. Side by side with Rothschild and Baron Mayer-Melnhof are found the Dukes of Koburg and Meiningen, the Princes of Hohenlohe, the Prince of Lichenstein, the Duke of Braganza, Prince Rosenberg, Prince Pless, the Counts of Schoenfeld, Festetics, Schafgotsca, Trautmannsdorff, the hunting association of the Count of Karolysche, the hunting association of Baron Gustaedtsche, the noble hunting association of Bluehnbachér, etc.

Large landed property is everywhere on the increase in Austria. The number of large landlords rose 9.5 per cent. from 1873 to 1891, and that means a considerable decrease of small holders: land cannot be increased.

In Lower Austria, of a total area embracing 3,544,596 yokes, 521,603 were taken up by large estates (247 owners), and 94,882 yokes by the Church. Nine families alone owned, in the middle of the eighties, 157,000 yokes, among these owners was the Count of Hoyos, with 54,000 yokes. The area of Moravia is 2,222,190 hectares. Of these, the Church held

78,496, 3.53 per cent.; 145 private persons held 525,632, and one of these alone held 107,247 hectares. Of Austrian Silesia's area of 514,685 hectares, the Church owned 50,845, or 9.87 per cent.; 36 landlords owned 134,226, or 26.07 per cent. The area of Bohemia is 5,196,700 hectares: of these the clergy owned 103,459 hectares; 362 private persons owned 1,448,638. This number is distributed among Prince Colloredo-Mansfeld with 58,239 hectares; Prince Fuerstenberg with 39,814; Imperial Duke Waldstein with 37,989; Prince Lichtenstein with 37,937; the Count of Czerin with 32,277; the Count of Clam-Gallas with 31,691; Emperor Franz Joseph with 28,800; the Count von Harrach with 28,047; Prince von Lobkowitz with 27,684; Imperial Count Kinsky with 26,265; the Count of Buquoy with 25,645; the Prince of Thurn and Taxis with 24,777; Prince Schwarzenberg with 24,037; Prince Metternich-Winneburg with 20,002; Prince Auersperg with 19,960; Prince Windischgraetz with 19,920 hectares, etc.[15]

The absorption by the large landlords of the small holdings in land frequently proceeds in "alarming manner." For instance, in the judicial district of Aflenz, community of St. Ilgen, an Alpine hill of over 5,000 yokes, with pasture ground for 300 heads of cattle, and a contiguous peasant estate of 700 yokes, was all converted into a hunting ground. The same thing happened with Hoellaep, located in the community of Seewiesen, which had pasture land for 200 heads of cattle. In the same judicial district of Aflenz, 47 other pieces of land, holding 840 heads of cattle, were gradually absorbed and turned into hunting grounds. Similar doings are reported from all parts of the Alps. In Steiermark, a number of peasants find it more profitable to sell the hay to the lordly hunters as *feed for the game in winter*, than give it to their own cattle. In the neighborhood of Muerzzuschlag, some peasants no longer keep cattle, but sell all the feed for the support of the game.

In the judicial district of Schwarz, 7, and in the judicial district of Zell, 16 Alpine hills, formerly used for pasture, were "cashiered" by the new landlords and converted into hunting grounds. The whole region of the Karwendel mountain has been closed to cattle. It is generally the high nobility of Austria and Germany, together with rich bourgeois upstarts, who bought up Alpine stretches of land of 70,000 yokes and more at a clip and had them arranged for hunting parks. Whole villages, hundreds upon hundreds of holdings are thus wiped out of existence; the inhabitants are crowded off; and in the place of human beings, together with cattle meet for their sustenance, roes, deer and chamois put in their appearance. Oddest of all, more than one of the men, who thus lay whole provinces waste, is seen rising in the par-

[15] For further details see, "Das soziale Elend und die besitzenden Klassen in Oesterreich," T. W. Teisen.

liaments and declaiming on the "distress of landed property," and abuses his power to secure the protection of Government in the shape of duties on corn, wood and meat, and premiums on brandy and sugar,— all at the expense of the propertyless masses.

According to the census of the eighties, there were 8,547,285 farms in France; 2,993,450 farm owners had an average annual income of 300 francs, the aggregate income of these being 22.5 per cent. of the total income from farms; 1,095,850 farm owners had an average annual income of 1,730 francs, the aggregate income of these being 47 per cent. of the total income from farms; 65,525 large landlords, owning 109,285 farms, drew 25.4 per cent. of the total agricultural revenues:—*their possessions embraced more than one-half of the agricultural lands of France.*

Large agricultural property is becoming the standard in all countries of civilization, and, in virtue of its political influence, it sways legislation without regard to the welfare of the commonwealth. Nevertheless, the tenure of agricultural land and its cultivation is of high importance to social development. Upon land and its productivity depends first of all the population and its subsistence. Land can not be multiplied at will, hence the question is of all the greater magnitude to everyone how the land is cultivated and exploited. Germany, whose population increases yearly by from 5,600,000 heads, needs a large supply of breadstuffs and meat, if the prices of the principal necessaries of life shall remain within the reach of the people.

At this point an important antagonism arises between the industrial and the agricultural population. The industrial population, being independent of agriculture, has a vital interest in cheap food: the degree in which they are to thrive both as men and as workers depends upon that. Every rise in the price of food leads, either to further adulterations, or to a decline of exports, and thereby of wages as a consequence of increased difficulties of competition. The question is otherwise with the cultivator of the soil. As in the instance of the industrial producer, the farmer is bent upon making the largest gains possible out of his trade, whatever line that may be in. If the importation of corn and meat reduces the high prices for these articles and thereby lowers his profits, then he gives up raising corn and devotes his soil to some other product that may bring larger returns: he cultivates sugar-beet for the production of sugar, potatoes and grain for distilleries, instead of wheat and rye for bread. He devotes the most fertile tracts to tobacco instead of vegetables. In the same way, thousands of hectares are used as horse pastures because horses for soldiers and other purposes of war fetch good prices. On the other hand, extensive forests, that can be made fertile, are kept at present for the enjoyment of the hunting lords, and this often happens in neighborhoods where the dismantling of a few hectares of woodland and their conversion to agricultural purposes could be undertaken without thereby injuriously affecting the humidity of the neighborhood.

Upon this particular point, forestry to-day denies the influence of woodlands upon moisture. Woods should be allowed in large masses only at such places where the nature of the soil permits no other form of cultivation, or where the purpose is to furnish mountain regions with a profitable vegetation, or with a check to the rapid running down of water in order to prevent freshets and the washing away of the land. From this point of view, thousands of square kilometers of fertile land could be reclaimed in Germany for agriculture. But such an alteration runs counter as well to the interests of the hierarchy of office-holders—foresters—as to the private and hunting interests of the large landlords, who are not inclined to forfeit their hunting grounds and pleasures of the chase.

To what extent the process of rendering "hands" superfluous is progressing in agriculture and in the industries therewith connected has been shown in the palpable depopulation of the rural districts of Germany. It may, furthermore, be specified that in the period between 1885 and 1890, the decrease of the rural population in 74 districts east of the Elbe was above 2 per cent.; in 44 of these 74 districts it was even above 3 per cent. In western Prussia, a decrease was established of over 2 per cent. in 16 districts, in two of which the decrease exceeded 3 per cent. Especially high was the percentage of decrease in those neighborhoods where large landlords figure as special dispensations of Providence. In Wurtemberg, during the period between 1839 and 1885, the population of 22 peasant districts declined from 29,907 heads to 19,213, —not less than 35.7 per cent. In East and West Prignitz, the rural population declined during the period of 1868-1885 from 100,000 heads to 85,000,—15 per cent.

The decrease of the rural working population is marked also in England where, as well known, latifundia property reigns supreme. The progression in the decrease of agricultural workers was there as follows:—

Sexes.	1861.	1871.	Decrease.
Males	1,833,652	1,328,151	505,501
Females	376,797	186,450	193,127
Total	2,210,449	1,514,601	698,628

Since then the decrease has proceeded further. According to Dr. B.

J. Brock, in the year 1885 there was the following yield per acre in bushels:—

Countries.	Wheat.	Barley.
Great Britain	35.2	37.8
Germany	18.7	23.6
France	16.0	19.5
Austria	15.5	16.8
Hungary	11.7	16.0

The difference in productivity between Great Britain and the other countries is, we see, considerable, and it is attained through a more extensive operation of the soil. In Hungary also the number of persons engaged in agriculture has decreased considerably:—

1870	4,417,514
1880	3,669,177

a decrease of 748,457, or more than 17 per cent. in ten years. The agricultural lands passed into the hands of large magnates and capitalists, who employed machines instead of human workers, and thus rendered the latter "superfluous." These phenomena manifest themselves everywhere in agriculture,—just as in large industrial production. The productivity of labor increases, and in the same measure a portion of the working class is promoted to the sidewalk.

As a matter of course, this process has its evil consequences for woman also. Her prospects of being a proprietor and housewife decline, and the prospects increase of her becoming a servant, a cheap hand for the large landlord. As a sexual being she is more exposed even than in the city to the illicit wishes and cravings of the master or his lieutenants. More so than in industry, on the land proprietary rights in the labor-power frequently expand to proprietary rights over the whole person. Thus, in the very midst of "Christian" Europe a quasi Turkish harem system has developed. In the country, woman is isolated to a higher degree than in the city. The magistrate or a close friend of his is her employer: newspapers and a public opinion, to which she otherwise might look for protection, there are none: furthermore, male labor itself is generally in a disgraceful state of dependence. But "the heavens are away up, and the Tsar is away off."

The census of occupation of 1882 established that, out of 5,273,344 farms, only 391,746, or 7½ per cent., employ machinery. Out of the 24,999 large farms, however, containing over 100 hectares of land, machinery was in use on 20,558, or 82¼ per cent. Naturally, it is the larger farms only that can utilize machinery. The application of machinery on a large surface, all of one product, engages labor only a comparatively short time, the number of male and female hands, absolutely needed on the place and for tending the cattle, is reduced, and after the field work is done, the day laborers are discharged. Thus with us, just as in England and in a still higher degree in the United States, a rural proletariat of grave aspect springs up. If, in view of the shortness of the season, these workingmen demand correspondingly high wages when they are needed, their impudence is denounced; if, upon their discharge, they roam about in hunger and idleness, they are called vagabonds, are abused, and not infrequently dogs are set upon them to chase them from the yards as "tramps," unwilling to work, and they are handed over to the constabulary for the workhouse. A pretty social "order."

Capitalist exploitation of agriculture leads in all directions to capitalist conditions. One set of our farmers, for instance, has for years made enormous profits out of beet-root and the production of sugar therewith connected. Our system of taxation favored the exportation of sugar, and it was so framed that the tax on beets yielded but an infinitesimal revenue to the treasury of the Empire, the premium on the exportation of sugar being large enough to almost swallow the tax.

The rebate allowed the sugar manufacturers per double quintal was actually higher than the tax paid by them on beets; and this premium enabled them to sell large quantities of sugar at the expense of the domestic tax-payers, and to extend ever more the cultivation of the sugar-beet. The profit that accrued from this system of taxation to about 400 sugar factories was estimated at over 30 million marks for 1889-1890: on an average 78,000 marks per factory. Several hundreds of thousands of hectares of land, previously devoted to raising grain, were turned into beet-root fields; factories upon factories were started, and are still being started; the inevitable consequence is an eventual crash. The large returns yielded by the beet-root cultivation affected favorably the price of land. It rose. The result was the buying up of the small farms, whose owners, seduced by the high prices, allowed themselves to be inveigled into selling. While the land was thus being used for industrial speculation, the raising of potatoes and grain was being confined to narrower fields, hence the increasing need of importation of food from abroad. The demand exceeds the supply. Thereupon, the large supply of foreign farm products and their cheaper transportation from Russia, the Danubian Principalities, North and South America, India, etc., finally leads to prices on which the domestic farmers—weighed down with mortgages and taxes, and hampered by the smallness of their farms, and their often faultily organized and deficiently conducted farming—can no longer exist. High duties are then placed upon importations; but these duties accrue only to the large farmer; the small fellow profits little by them, or none at all; and they become

heavy burdens to the non-agricultural population. The advantage of
the few becomes the injury of the many; small farming retrogresses;
for it there is no balm in Gilead. That the condition of the small peasants in the tariff areas of Germany has been steadily deteriorating, will
be generally admitted. The advantages to the large farmer from high
duties, prohibitions of importations and measures of exclusion enable
him all the more easily to buy out the small holder. The large number
of those who do not produce in meat and bread what they consume
themselves—and a glance at the statistics of occupation and division of
the soil shows that these are by far the larger majority of the
farmers—even suffers a direct injury from the increased prices resulting upon higher tariffs and indirect taxes. An unfavorable crop, that
lowers still more the returns from the farm, not only aggravates the
pressure, but also increases the number of the agriculturists who are
compelled to become purchasers of farm products themselves. Tariffs
and indirect taxes can not improve the economic condition of the majority of the farmers: he who has little or nothing to sell, what, to him,
does the tariff boot, be it never so high! The incumbrance of the small
farmer and his final ruin are thereby promoted rather than checked.

For Baden—overwhelmingly a State of small farms—the increase of
mortgage indebtedness during the period of 1884-1894 is estimated at
140 to 150 million marks. The mortgage indebtedness of the Bern peasants aggregated in round figures 200 million francs in 1860; in 1890 it
aggregated 500 million francs. According to a report of the Bohemian
representative Gustave Eim, made to his constituents in 1893, the indebtedness that weighed upon the farms of Bohemia stood as follows:—

1879 ....2,716,641,754 guilders
1889 ....3,105,587,363 guilders

We see that inside of that period the burden of indebtedness increased
14.13 per cent.—that of small holdings 13.29 per cent., while that of the
large holdings increased only 3.77 per cent. The bulk of the increased
indebtedness fell to the share of middle class property.

How the cultivator of the soil operates his farm is—under the aegis
of St. Private Property—his own business. His private interest decides.
What cares he about the commonwealth and its well-being? He has to
look out for himself: so, then, stand aside! Does not the industrialist
proceed on that plan? He produces obscene pictures, turns out immoral books, sets up factories for adulterating food. These and many
other occupations are harmful to society: they undermine morality and
incite corruption. What does that matter! It brings in money, even
more money than moral pictures, scientific books, and honest dealing in
unadulterated food. The industrialist, greedy after profits, needs to con-

cern himself only about escaping the too sharp eye of the police; he can quietly pursue his shameful trade, assured that the money he will thereby rake in will earn for him the envy and esteem of society.

The Mammon character of our age is best typified by the Exchange and its doings. Land and industrial products; means of transportation; meteorologic and political conditions; scarcity and abundance; mass-misery and accidents; public debts, inventions and discoveries; the health, sickness and death of influential persons; war and rumors of war, often started for the express purpose;—all this and much more is made objects of speculation, for exploitation and mutual cheating. The matadors of capital attain decided influence upon society, and, favored by the powerful means at their disposal and their connections, they amass enormous fortunes. Cabinet ministers and whole Governments become puppets in their hands, compelled to act according as matadors of the Exchange pull the wires behind the scenes. Not the State has the Exchange, but the Exchange has the State in its power. Will he, nill he, a Minister is often forced to water the upas tree, which he might prefer to tear up by the roots, but that he now must aid in growing.

All these facts, that, seeing the evils gain by the day in magnitude, daily force themselves with increasing importunity upon the consideration of everyone, demand speedy and radical help. But modern society stands bewildered before all these phenomena, just as certain animals are said to stand before a mountain;[16] it turns like a horse in the tread-mill, constantly in a circle,—lost, helpless, the picture of distress and stupidity. Those who would bring help are yet too weak; those who should bring help still lack the necessary understanding; those who could bring help will not, they rely upon force, at best, they think with Madame Pompadour *"apres nous le deluge"* (after us the deluge). But how if the deluge were to come before their departure from life?

The flood rises and is washing out the foundations upon which our State and Social structure rests. All feel that the ground shakes and, that only the strongest props could now stead. But these demand great sacrifices on the part of the ruling classes. There is the rub. Every proposition injurious to the material interests of the ruling classes, and that threatens their privileged position, is bitterly opposed and branded as a scheme looking to the overthrow of the modern political and social order. Neither is the sick world to be cured without any danger to the privileges and immunities of the ruling classes, or without their final abolition by the abolition of the classes themselves.

"The struggle for the emancipation of the working class is no struggle

---

[16] A German idiom, expressive of dumb bewilderment, uses the simile: "Like oxen before a mountain."—THE TRANSLATOR.

for privileges, but a struggle for equal rights and equal duties; it is a struggle for the abolition of all privileges"—thus runs the programme of the Socialist Movement. It follows that half-measures and small concessions are fruitless.

Until now, the ruling classes regard their privileged position as quite natural and normal, as to the justice of which no doubt may be entertained. It is a matter of course, therefore, that they should object and resolutely oppose every attempt to shake their prerogatives. Even propositions and laws, that affect neither the fundamental principles of the existing social order nor the privileged position of the ruling classes, throw them into great commotion the moment their purses are or might be touched. Mountains of paper are filled in the parliaments full of speeches and printed matter, until the heaving mountains bring forth a ridiculous mouse. The simplest and most obvious questions regarding the protection of Labor are met by them with such a resistance as though the existence of society hinged on such concessions. After endless struggles a few concessions are finally wrung from them, and then they act as if they had sacrificed a large part of their fortunes. The same stubborn resistance do they display if the point is the formal recognition of the equality of the oppressed classes, to allow these, for instance, to have an equal voice with them in wage and other labor agreements.

This resistance to the simplest matters and the most obvious demands confirms the old principle founded in experience, that no ruling class can be convinced by *reasoning,* until the force of circumstances drives them to sense and to submission. This force of circumstances lies in the development of society, and in the increasing intelligence awakened by this very development among the oppressed. The class-antagonism—the sketch of our social conditions has pointed them out—grow more pronounced, visible and sensible. Along therewith increases the understanding of the untenableness of the existing order among the oppressed and exploited classes; their indignation mounts higher, and, as a result thereof, also the imperious demand for a change and for improved conditions. By penetrating ever wider circles, such understanding of the situation finally conquers the vast majority of society, most directly interested in the change. In the same measure, however, as the popular understanding increases regarding the untenableness of the existing order and the necessity of its radical change, the power of resistance decreases on the part of the ruling classes, whose power rests upon ignorance and lack of intelligence on the part of the oppressed and exploited. This cross effect is evident; hence, everything that promotes it must be welcome. The progress made by large capitalization, on one side, is amply compensated, on the other, by the increasing perception by the **proletariat** of the contradiction in which the social order stands with the well-being of the enormous majority. The dissolution and abolition of the social antagonisms may cost extraordinary pains, sacrifices and efforts, it may depend upon factors that lie beyond the influence of the individual, or even of a class. Nevertheless, the solution is reached the moment these antagonisms have reached their acme,—a point towards which they are rushing.

The measures to be adopted at the various phases of development depend upon the then conditions. It is impossible to foretell what measures may become necessary under given circumstances. No Government, no Minister, be he ever so powerful, can foresee what circumstances may require in the next few years. All the less is it possible to foretell measures, that will be influenced by circumstance, which elude all accurate calculation. The question of "measures" is a question of tactics in battle. These depend upon the enemy and upon the means at his disposal, and at mine. A measure that would be excellent to-day, may be harmful to-morrow, the circumstances that yesterday justified its application having changed to-day. With the goal in view, the means to attain it by depend upon time and tide; imperative is but the seizing of the most effective and thorough going ones that time and tide may allow. In forecasting the future, hypotheses alone are available: things must be supposed to exist that have not yet set in.

Accordingly, we suppose the arrival of a day when all the evils described will have reached such maturity that they will have become oppressingly sensible to the feeling as to the sight of the vast majority, to the extent of being no longer bearable; whereupon a general irresistible desire for a radical change will seize society, and then the quickest will be regarded the most effective remedy.

All social evils, without exception, have their source in that social order of things, which, as has been shown, rests upon capitalism, upon the capitalist system of production. Under this system, the capitalist class is the possessor of all instruments of labor—land, mines, quarries, raw material, tools, machines, means of transportation and communication—and it exploits and oppresses the vast majority of the people. The result of such abuses is an increased precariousness of livelihood, increased misery, oppression and degradation of the exploited classes. It is, consequently, necessary to convert this capitalist property into social property by means of a general expropriation. *Production for sale must be converted into socialist production, conducted for and by Society. Production on a large scale, and the increasing fertility of social labor,—until now a source of misery and of oppression for the exploited classes—must be turned into a source of highest well-being and of full and harmonious culture.*

CHAPTER VII.

THE SOCIALIZATION OF SOCIETY.

The soon as possible general expropriation of all the means of production furnishes society with a new foundation. The conditions of life and labor—in manufacture, agriculture, transportation and communication, education, marriage, science, art and intercourse—are radically changed for both sexes. Human existence acquires a new sense. The present political organization gradually loses ground: the State vanishes: in a measure it abolishes itself.

It was shown in the first part of this book why the State arose. It arises, as the product of a social growth, from a primitive form of society, that rested on communism and that dissolved in the measure that *private property* developed. With the rise of private property, antagonistic interests take shape within society; in the course of its development these antagonisms lead to rank and class contrasts, and these, in turn, grow into enmities between the several groups of interests, and finally into rank and class struggles, that threaten the existence of the new social order. In order to keep down these rank and class struggles, and to protect the property-holders, an organization is requisite that parries the assaults on property, and that pronounces "legal and sacred" the property obtained under certain forms. *This organization and power, that guards and upholds property, is the State.* Through the enactment of laws it secures the owner in his ownership, and it steps as judge and avenger before him who assails the established order. By reason of its innermost being, the interest of a ruling property class, and of the Government therewith connected, is ever conservative. The organization of the State changes only when the interest of property so demands. The State is, accordingly, the *inevitably necessary* organization of a social order that rests upon class rule. The moment class antagonisms fall through the abolition of private property, the State loses both the *necessity* and the *possibility* for its existence. With the removal of the conditions for rulership, the State gradually ceases to be, the same as creeds wane when the belief ceases in supernatural beings, or in transcendental powers gifted with reason. Words must have sense; if they lose that they cease to convey ideas.

"Yes," interjects at this point a capitalist-minded reader, "that is all very well, but by what 'legal principle' can society justify such a change?" The legal principle is the same that ever prevailed, whenever it was the question of changes and reforms,—*public policy*. Not the State, but society is the source of right; the State is but the committee of Society, authorized to administer and dispense right. Hitherto, "Society" has been a small minority; yet it acted in the name of the whole community (the people) by pronouncing itself "Society," much as Louis XIV. pronounced himself the "State,"—*"L'etat c'est moi"* (I am the State). When our newspapers announce: "The season begins; society is returning to the city," or "The season has closed; society is rushing to the country," they never mean the people, but only the upper ten thousand, who constitute "Society" as they constitute the "State." The masses are "plebs," "vile multitude," "canaille," "people." In keeping therewith, all that the State has done in the name of Society for the "public weal" has always been to the advantage and profit of the ruling class. It is in its interests that laws are framed. *"Salus reipublicae suprema lex esto"* (Let the public weal be the supreme law) is a well known legal principle of Old Rome. But who constituted the Roman Commonwealth? Did it consist of the subjugated peoples, the millions of slaves? No. A disproportionately small number of Roman citizens, foremost among these the Roman nobility, all of whom were supported by the subject class.

When, in the Middle Ages, noblemen and Princes stole the common property, they did so "according to law," in the "interest of the public weal," and how drastically the common property and that of the help-less peasants was treated on the occasion we have sufficiently explained. The agrarian history of the last fifteen centuries is a narration of un-interrupted robbery perpetrated upon common and peasant property by the nobility and the Church in all the leading countries of Europe. When the French Revolution expropriated the estates of the nobility and the Church, it did so "in the name of the public weal"; and a large part of the seven million of landed estates, that are to-day the prop of modern bourgeois France, owe their existence to this expropriation. "In the name of the public weal," Spain more than once embargoed Church property, and Italy wholly confiscated the same,—both with the plaudits of the zealous defenders of "sacred property." The English nobility has for centuries been robbing the Irish and English people of their property, and, during the period of 1804-1832 made itself a present of not less than 3,511,710 acres of commons "in the interest of the pub-lic welfare." When during the great North American war for the emancipation of the negro, millions of slaves, the regular property of their masters, were declared free without indemnity to the latter, the thing was done "in the name of the public weal." Our whole capitalist development is an uninterrupted process of expropriation and confisca-tion, at which the manufacturer expropriates the workingman, the large landlord expropriates the peasant, the large merchant expropriates the small dealer, and finally one capitalist expropriates another, i. e., the larger expropriates and absorbs the smaller. To hear our bourgeoisie, all that happens in the interest of the "public weal," for the "good of society." The Napoleonites "saved Society" on the 18th Brumaire and 2d of December, and "Society" congratulated them. If hereafter Society shall save itself by resuming possession of the property that itself has produced, it will enact the most notable historic event— *it is not seeking to oppress some in the interest of others, but to afford to all the prerequisite for equality of existence, to make possible to each an existence worthy of human beings.* It will be morally the cleanest and most stupendous measure that human society has ever executed.

In what manner this gigantic process of social expropriation will be achieved, and under what modality, eludes all surmise. Who can tell how general conditions will then be, and what the demands of public interest will be.

In his fourth social letter to v. Kirchmann, entitled "Capital," Rodbertus says: "The dissolution of all capitalist property in land is no chimera; on the contrary, it is easily conceivable in national economy. It would, moreover, be the most radical aid to society, that, as might be put in a few words, is suffering of rent-rising—rent of land and capital. Hence the measure would be the only manner of abolishing property in land and capital, *a measure that would not even for a moment interrupt the commerce and progress of the nation.*" What say our agrarians to this opinion of their former political co-religionist?

In the contemplation of how matters will probably shape themselves along the principal lines of human activity, upon such a measure of general expropriation, there can be no question of establishing hard and fast lines, or rigid institutions. No one is able to forecast the detailed molds in which future generations may cast their social organizations, and how they will satisfy their wants. In Society as in Nature, everything is in constant fiux and reflux; one thing rises, another wanes; what is old and sered is replaced with new and living forms. Inventions, discoveries and improvements, numerous and various, the bearing and significance of which often none can tell, are made from day to day, come into operation, and, each in its own way, they revolutionize and transform human life and all society.

We can, accordingly, be concerned only with general principles, that flow inevitably from the preceding *expose*, and whose enforcement may be supervised, up to a certain point. If even hitherto society has been no artomatic entity, leadable and guidable by an individual, much as appearances often pointed the other way; if even hitherto those who imagined they pushed were themselves pushed; if even hitherto society was an organism, that developed according to certain inherent laws;—if that was hitherto the case, in the future all guiding and leading after individual caprice is all the more out of question. Society will have discovered the secret of its own being, it will have discovered the laws of its own progress, and it will apply these consciously towards its own further development.

So soon as society is in possession of all the means of production, *the duty to work, on the part of all able to work, without distinction of sex, becomes the organic law of socialized society.* Without work society can not exist. Hence, society has the right to demand that all, who wish to satisfy their wants, shall exert themselves, according to their physical and mental faculties, in the production of the requisite wealth. The silly claim that the Socialist does not wish to work, that he seeks to abolish work, is a matchless absurdity, which fits our adversaries alone. Non-workers, idlers, exist in capitalist society *only*. Socialism agrees with the Bible that "He who will not work, neither shall he eat." But work shall not be mere activity; it shall be useful, productive activity. The new social system will demand that each and all pursue some industrial, agricultural or other useful occupation, whereby to furnish a certain amount of work towards the satisfaction of existing wants. *Without work no pleasure, no pleasure without work.*

All being obliged to work, all have an equal interest in seeing the following three conditions of work in force:—

First, that work shall be moderate, and shall overtax none;

Second, that work shall be as agreeable and varied as possible;

Third, that work shall be as productive as possible, seeing that both the hours of work and fruition hinge upon that.

These three conditions hinge, in turn, upon the nature and the number of the productive powers that are available, and also upon the aspirations of society. But Socialist society does not come into existence for the purpose of living in proletarian style; *it comes into existence in order to abolish the proletarian style of life of the large majority of humanity.* It seeks to afford to each and all the fullest possible measure of the amenities of life. The question that does rise is, How high will the aspirations of society mount?

In order to determine this, an administration is requisite that shall embrace all the fields of social activity. Our municipalities constitute an effective basis thereto: if they are too large to allow a ready supervision, they can be divided into wards. As in primitive society, all members of the community who are of age participate in the elections, *without distinction of sex,* and have a voice in the choice of the persons who are to be entrusted with the administration. At the head of all the local administrations stands the central administration—as will be noted, not a Government, with power to rule, but an executive college of administrative functions. Whether the central administration shall be chosen directly by popular vote or appointed by the local administration is immaterial. These questions will not then have the importance they have today: the question is then no longer one of filling posts that bestow special honor, or that vest the incumbent with greater power and influence, or that yield larger incomes: it is then a question of filling positions of trust, for which the fittest, whether male or female, are taken; and these may be recalled or re-elected as circumstances may demand, or the electors may deem preferable. All posts are for given terms. The incumbents are, accordingly, clothed with no special "official qualities"; the feature of continuity of office is absent, likewise a hierarchical order of promotion. Hence it is also immaterial to us whether there shall be middle stages, say provincial administrations, between the central and the local administrations. If they are deemed necessary, they are set up; if they are not deemed necessary, they are left alone. All such matters are decided by actual exigencies, as ascertained in practice. If the progress of society has rendered any old organization superfluous, it is abolished without further ado and dispute, there being no longer any personal interest in conflict; and new ones are similarly established. Obviously, *such an administration, resting upon the broadest democratic foundation, differs radically from what we have to-day.* What a battle of newspapers, what a war of tongues in our parliaments, what mountains of public documents in our bureaux, if but a trivial change is made in the administration or the Government!

The principal thing to ascertain is the number and the nature of the forces that are available, the quantity and nature of the means of production,—the factories, workshops, means of transportation and communication, land—and also their productivity. The next thing to ascertain is the quantity of the supplies that are on hand and the extent to which these can satisfy the wants of society. As to-day the State and the several municipalities yearly cast up their budgets, the thing will then be done with an eye to all the wants of society, without thereby excluding changes that increased or new wants may demand. Statistics here play the chief *role:* they become the most important subsidiary science of the new order: they furnish the measure for all social activities.

Statistics are extensively used to-day for similar purposes. The Imperial, State and municipal budgets are based upon a large amount of statistical reports, made yearly by the several administrative branches. Long experience and a certain degree of stability in the running wants facilitate their gathering. Every operator of a large factory, every merchant is, under normal conditions, able to determine accurately what he will need during the next three months, and how he should regulate his production and purchases. Unless excessive changes set in, his calculations will be found safe.

The experience that crises are caused by blind, anarchic production, i. e., that production is carried on without a knowledge of the volume of supply, of sales and of demand of and for the several goods in the world's market, has, as indicated in previous passages, caused large manufacturers in several branches of industry to join in Trusts and rings, partly with the view of steadying prices, partly also for the purpose of regulating production by the light of previous experience and of the orders received. According to the capability of each establishment and to the probable demand, the output of each is determined for the next few months. Infractions are punished with heavy conventional mulcts, and even expulsion. The capitalists do not conclude these agreements for the benefit of the public, but to its injury and to their own profit. Their purpose is to utilize the power of combination in order to secure the greatest advantages to themselves. This regulation of production has for its object to enable the capitalist to demand from the public prices that could not be got if the competitive struggle was on between the several capitalists. These enrich themselves at the expense of the consumers who are forced to pay whatever price is demanded for the goods they need. As the consumer, so is the workingman injured by the Trusts. The artificial regulation of production throws a part of the working class out of work, and, in order that these may live, they underbid their fellows at work. Thus the employer derives a double advantage: he receives higher prices, and he pays lower wages. Such a regulation of production by combinations of capitalists *is exactly the reverse of that which will be practiced in Socialist society.* While to-day the interests of the capitalists is the determining factor, the interests of all will then be the guide. Production will then be carried on for the satisfaction of human wants, and not in order to obtain, through high prices, large profits for private individuals. Nevertheless, the best planned combination in capitalist society can not take in and control all the factors needed in the calculation: competition and speculation run wild despite all combinations: finally the discovery is made that the calculation had a leak, and the scheme breaks down.

The same as production on a large scale, commerce also has extensive statistics. Every week the larger centers of commerce and the ports publish reports on the supply of petroleum, coffee, cotton, sugar, grain, etc. These statistics are frequently inaccurate, seeing that the owners of the goods frequently have a personal interest in concealing the truth. On the whole, however, the statistics are pretty safe and furnish to those interested, information on the condition of the market. But here also speculation steps in, upsets all calculations, and often renders all legitimate business impossible. Seeing how impossible is a general regulation of production in capitalist society, due to the existence of many thousands of private producers with conflicting interests, it will be obvious why the speculative nature of commerce, the number of merchants and their conflicting interests render equally impossible the regulation of distribution. Nevertheless, what is done in these directions indicates what could be done so soon as private interest were to drop out and the interests of all were alone dominant. A proof of this is furnished by the statistics of crops, that are yearly issued by the leading countries of civilization, and that enable certain general conclusions to be drawn upon the size of the crops, the extent that they will supply the demand, and the probable price.

In a socialized society matters are fully regulated; society is held in fraternal bonds. Everything is done in order; there, it is an easy matter to gauge demand. With a little experience, the thing is easy as play. If, for instance, the demand is statistically established for bread, meat, shoes, linen, etc., and, on the other hand, the productivity of the respective plants is equally known, *the average daily amount of socially necessary labor is thereby ascertained. The figures would, furthermore, point out where more plants for the production of a certain article may be needed, or where such may be discontinued as superfluous, or turned to other purposes.*

Everyone decides the pursuit he chooses: the large number of different fields of activity caters to the tastes of all. If on one field there is a surplus and on another a dearth of labor-power, the administration attends to the equalization of forces. To organize production, and to furnish the several powers with the opportunity to apply themselves at the right places will be the principal task of these functionaries. In the measure that the several forces are broken in, the wheels will move with greater smoothness. The several branches and divisions of labor choose their foremen, who superintend the work. These are no slave-drivers, like most foremen of to-day; they are fellow workers, who, instead of a productive, exercise an administrative function entrusted to them. The idea is by no means excluded that, with the attainment of higher perfection, both in point of organization and of individuals, these functions should alternate so that, within a certain time, and in certain order, they are filled by all *regardless of sex.*

A system of labor, organized upon a plan of such absolute liberty and democratic equality, where each stands for all, and all stand for each, and where the sense of solidarity reigns supreme,—such a system would generate a spirit of industry and of emulation nowhere to be found in the modern economic system. Nor could such a spirit of industry fail to react both upon the productivity of labor and the quality of labor's product.

Furthermore—seeing that all are mutually active—the interest becomes general in the best and most complete, as well as in the quickest possible production of goods, with the object of saving labor, and of gaining time for the production of further wealth, looking to the gratification of higher wants. *Such a common interest spurs all to bend their thoughts towards simplifying and quickening the process of labor. The ambition to invent and discover is stimulated to the highest pitch: each will seek to outdo the other in propositions and ideas.*[1]

Just the reverse will, accordingly, happen of which the adversaries of Socialism claim. How many are not the inventors and discoverers who go to pieces in the capitalist world! How many has it not exploited and then cast aside! If talent and intellect, instead of property, stood at the head of bourgeois society, *the larger part of the employers would have to make room for their workingmen, master mechanics, technical overseers, engineers, chemists, etc.* These are the men, who, in ninety-nine cases out of a hundred, make the inventions, discoveries and improvements, which the man with the money-bag exploits. How many thousands of discoverers and inventors have gone to pieces unable to find the man of means ready to provide the wherewithal for the execution of their thoughts; how many germs of inventions and discoveries have been and continue to be nipped by the social stress for bare existence, is a matter that eludes all calculation. Not the men of head and brain, but those of large wealth are to-day the masters of the world,—which, however, does not exclude the occasional and exceptional phenomenon of brains and wealth being united in one person. The exception only proves the rule.

Everyone in practical life knows with what suspicion the workingman to-day regards every improvement, every invention introduced in the shop. And he is right. He rarely derives any advantage therefrom; it all accrues to the employer. The workingman is assailed with the fear

---

[1] "The power of emulation, in exciting to the most strenuous exertions for the sake of the approbation and admiration of others, is borne witness to by experience in every situation in which human beings publicly compete with one another, even if it be in things frivolous, or from which the public derives no benefit. A contest, who can do most for the common good, is not the kind of competition which Socialists repudiate."—John Stuart Mill's "Principles of Political Economy." Every union, every association of people, who pursue equal aims, likewise furnishes numerous examples of greater effort with no material, but only an ideal, reward in view. The emulators are moved by the ambition to distinguish themselves, by the desire to serve the common cause. But this sort of ambition is no vice; it is a virtue; it is put forth in the interest of all; and the individual finds his satisfaction in that along with all others. Ambition is harmful and objectionable only when it is put forth to the injury of the whole, and at the expense of others.

lest the new machine, the new improvement cast him off to-morrow as superfluous. Instead of gladsome applause for an invention that does honor to man and is fraught with benefit for the race, he only has a malediction on his lips. We also know, from personal experience, how many an improvement perceived by the workingman, is not introduced: the workingman keeps silent, fearing to derive no benefit but only harm from it. Such are the natural consequences of an antagonism of interests.[2]

This antagonism of interests is removed in Socialist society. Each unfolds his faculties in his own interest, and, by so doing, simultaneously benefits the commonweal. To-day personal gratification is generally antagonistic to the common weal; the two exclude each other. In the new Order, the antagonisms are removed: *The gratification of the ego and the promotion of the common weal harmonize, they supplement each other.*[3]

The marvelous effect of such a mental and moral condition is obvious. The productivity of labor will rise mightily, and such increased productivity makes possible the satisfaction of higher wants. Especially will the productivity of labor rise through the discontinuance of the present and enormous disintegration of labor, in hundreds of thousands, even millions of petty establishments, conducted with imperfect tools. According to the industrial census of the German Empire for the year 1882, there were 3,005,457 leading establishments, exclusive of com-

---

[2] Von Thuenen says in his "Der isolirte Staat": "The reason why the proletarians, on the one hand, and property classes, on the other, face each other permanently as enemies lies in the antagonism of their interests; and they will remain unreconciled *so long as this division of interests is not removed.* Not only the well-being of his wage-giver but—through discoveries in industry, the pavement of streets and building of railroads, the forming of new business connections—the revenues of the Nation also may increase. Under our present social order, however, the workingman is touched by none of these; his condition remains what it was, and *the whole increase of revenues accrues to the employers, the capitalists and the landlords.*" This last sentence is an almost literal anticipation of the words of Gladstone in the English Parliament, when he declared in 1864 "this intoxicating increase of incomes and power" that England had experienced in the course of the previous twenty years, "has been confined exclusively to the possessing classes." Again on p. 207 of his work, v. Thuenen says: "The evil lies in the divorce of the workingman from his product."
Morelly declares in his "Principles of Legislation": "Property divides us into two classes—Rich and Poor. The former love their property and care not to defend the State; the latter can not possibly love the Fatherland, seeing that it bestows upon them naught but misery. Under the system of Communism, however, all love the Fatherland, seeing that all receive from it life and happiness."

[3] In weighing the advantages and the disadvantages of Communism, John Stuart Mill says in his "Principles of Political Economy": "No soil could be more favorable to the growth of such a feeling, than a Communist association, since all the ambition, and the bodily and mental activity, which are now exerted in the pursuit of separate and self-regarding interests, would require another sphere of employment, and would naturally find it in the pursuit of the general benefit of the community."

merce, transportation, hotels and inns, in which 6,396,465 persons were
occupied. Of these leading establishments, 61.1 per cent. employed
less than 5 persons, and 16.8 per cent. employed from 6 to 50 persons.
The former are small concerns, the latter middle class ones. Through
the concentration of the small and middle class establishments into large
ones, equipped with all the advantages of modern technique, an enormous waste in power, time, material (light, heat, etc.) space, now incurred, would be avoided, and the productivity of labor would gain proportionally. What difference th·re is in the productivity of small,
middle class and large establishments, even where modern technique is
applied, may be illustrated by the census of manufactories of the State
of Massachusetts for 1890. The establishments in ten leading industries
were divided into three classes. Those that produced less than $40,000
worth of goods were placed in the lowest class; those that produced
from $40,000 to $150,000 were placed in the middle class; and those that
produced over $150,000 worth of goods were placed in the upper class.
The result was this:—

Classes.	Number of Estab- lishments.	Percentage of All Establishments.	Produc- tivity of Each Class.	Percentage of Total Productivity
Lower	2,042	55.2	51,660,617	9.4
Middle	968	26.2	106,868,635	19.5
Upper	686	18.6	390,817,300	71.1
	3,698	100.0	549,346,552	100.0

The more than twice as large number of small establishments turned
out only 9.4 per cent. of the total product. But even the large establishments could, with hardly any exception, be conducted far more
rationally than now, so that, under a system of collective production,
aided by the most highly perfected technical process, an infinitely larger
demand could be supplied.

Upon the subject of the saving of time, possible under a system of
production planted on a rational basis, Th. Hertzka of Vienna has made
some interesting calculations.[4] He investigated the amount of labor-
power and time requisite for the satisfaction of the wants of the 22
million inhabitants of Austria by means of production on a large scale.
To this end Hertzka gathered information upon the capacity of large
establishments in several fields, and he based his calculations upon the
data thus ascertained. In Hertzka's calculation are included 10,500,000
hectares of agricultural and 3,000,000 hectares of pasture lands, that
should suffice for the production of agricultural products and of meat

4 "Die Gesetze der sozialen Entwickelung."

for the said population. Hertzka also included in his computation the
building of houses on the basis of a house of 150 square meters, 5 rooms
and strong enough to last 50 years, to each family. The result was that,
for agricultural, building, the production of flour, sugar, coal, iron,
machinery, clothing and chemicals, only 615,000 workingmen were
needed, at work the whole year and at the present average hours of daily
labor. These 615,000 workingmen are, however, *only 12.3 per cent. of
the population of Austria, capable to work, exclusive of all the women
as well as the males under 16 and over 50 years of age.* If all the
5,000,000 men, and not merely the above figure of 615,000, were engaged,
then, *each of them would need to work only 36.9 days—six weeks in
round figures*—in order to produce the necessaries of life for 22 million
people. Assuming 300 work days in the year, instead of 37, and 11 as
the present daily hours of work, it follows that, under this new organization of labor, *only 1⅜ hours a day would be needed to cover the most
pressing needs of all.*

Hertzka further computes the articles of luxury that the better situated demand, and he finds that the production of the same for 22 million
people would require an additional 315,000 workingmen. Altogether,
according to Hertzka, and making allowance for some industries that
are not properly represented in Austria, one million in round figures,
equal to 20 per cent. of the male population able to work, exclusive of
those under 16 and above 50 years of age, would suffice to cover *all the
needs of the population* in 60 days. If, again, the whole male population able to work is made the basis of the computation, these would need
to furnish but *two and a half hours work a day.*[6]

This computation will surprise none who take a comprehensive view
of things. Considering, then, that, at such moderate hours, even the
men 50 years old—all the sick and invalid excepted—are able to work;
furthermore, that also youths under 16 years of age could be partially
active, as well as a large number of women, in so far as these are not
otherwise engaged in the education of children, the preparation of food,
etc.;—considering all that, it follows that even these hours could be considerably lowered, or the demand for wealth could be considerably increased. None will venture to claim that no more and unforeseen
progress, and considerable progress, at that, is possible in the process

---

[6] What does Herr Eugene Richter say to this calculation? In his "Irr-
lehren" (False Doctrines) he makes merry over the enormous shortening of
the hours of work that we have held out in this work as the result that
would follow upon the obligation of all to work and upon the higher technical
organization of the process of production. He seeks to minimize as much as
possible the productivity of production on a large scale, and to enhance the
importance of production on a small scale. He does so in order that he
might claim that the expected increased production was not practicable. In
order to make Socialism seem impossible, these defenders of the existing
"order" are forced to discredit the merits of their own social system.

of production, thus furnishing still greater advantages. But the issue now is to satisfy a mass of wants felt by all that to-day are satisfied only by a minority. With higher culture ever newer wants arise, and these too should be met. We repeat it: *the new Social order is not to live in proletarian style; it lives as a highly developed people demand to live, and it makes the demand in all its members from the first to the last.* But such a people can not rest content with satisfying merely its material wants. All its members are to be allowed fullest leisure for their development in the arts and sciences, as well as for their recreation.

Also in other important respects will Socialist society differ from the bourgeois individualist system. The motto: "Cheap and bad"—which is and must be standard for a large portion of bourgeois production, seeing that the larger part of the customers can buy only cheap goods, that quickly wear out—likewise drops out. Only the best will be produced; it will last longer and will need replacing at only wider intervals. The follies and insanities of fashion, promoted by wastefulness and tastelessness, also cease. People will probably cloth themselves more properly and sightfully than to-day, when, be it said in passing, the fashions of the last hundred years, especially as to men, distinguish themselves by their utter tastelessness. No longer will a new fashion be introduced every three months, an act of folly that stands in intimate relation with the competitive struggle of women among themselves, with the ostentatiousness and vanity of society, and with the necessity for the display of wealth. To-day a mass of establishments and people live upon this folly of fashion, and are compelled by their own interests to stimulate and force it. Together with the folly of fashion in dress, falls the folly of fashion in the style of architecture. Eccentricity reaches here its worst expression. Styles of architecture that required centuries for their development and that sprang up among different peoples—we are no longer satisfied with European styles, we go to the Japanese, Indians and Chinese—are used up in a few decades and laid aside. Our poor professional artist no longer knows whither and whereto they should turn with and for their samples and models. Hardly have they assorted themselves with one style, and expect to recover with ease the outlays they have made, when a new style breaks in upon them, and demands new sacrifices of time and money, of mental and physical powers. The nervousness of the age is best reflected in the rush from one fashion to the other, from one style to the other. No one will dare to claim any sense for such hurrying and scurrying, or the merit of its being a symptom of social health.

Socialism alone will re-introduce a greater stability in the habits of life. It will make repose and enjoyment possible; it will be a liberator from hurry and excessive exertion. Nervousness, that scourge of our age, will disappear.

But labor is also to be made pleasant. To that end practical and tastefully contrived workshops are required; the utmost precautions against danger; the removal of disagreeable odors, gases and smoke,— in short, of all sources of injury or discomfort to health. At the start, the new social system will carry on production with the old means, inherited from the old. But these are utterly inadequate. Numerous and unsuitable workshops, disintegrated in all directions; imperfect tools and machinery, running through all the stages of usefulness;— this heap is insufficient both for the number of the workers and for their demands of comfort and of pleasure. The establishment of a large number of spacious, light, airy, fully equipped and ornamented workshops is a pressing need. Art, technique, skill of head and hand immediately find a wide field of activity. All departments in the building of machinery, in the fashioning of tools, in architecture and in the branches of work connected with the internal equipment of houses have the amplest opportunity. Whatever human genius can invent with regard to comfortable and pleasant homes, proper ventilation, lighting and heating, mechanical and technical provisions and cleanliness is brought into application. The saving of motor power, heating, lighting, time, as well as the promotion of all that tends to render work and life agreeable, demand a suitable concentration of the fields of labor on certain spots. Habitations are separated from places of work and are freed from the disagreeable features of industrial and other manual work. These disagreeable features are, in their turn, reduced the lowest measure possible by means of suitable arrangements and provisions of all sorts, until wholly removed. The present state of technique has now means enough at command to wholly free from danger the most dangerous occupations, such as mining and the preparation of chemicals, etc. But these means can not be applied in capitalist society because they are expensive, and there is no obligation to do more than what is absolutely necessary for the workingman. The discomforts attached to mining can be removed by means of a different sort of draining, of extensive ventilation, of electric lighting, of a material reduction of hours of work, and of frequent shifts. Nor does it require any particular cleverness to find such protective means as would render building accidents almost impossible, and transform work in that line into the most exhilarating of all. Ample protections against sun and rain are possible in the construction of the largest edifices. Furthermore, in a society with ample labor-power at its disposal, such as Socialist society would be, frequent shifts and the concentration of certain work upon certain seasons of the year and certain hours of day would be an easy matter.

The problem of removing dust, smoke, soot and odors could likewise be completely solved by modern chemistry and technique; it is solved only partially or not at all, simply because the private employers care not to make the necessary sacrifice of funds. The work-places of the future, wherever located, whether above or under ground, will, accordingly, distinguish themselves most favorably from those of to-day. Many contrivances are, under the existing system of private enterprise, first of all, a question of money: can the business bear the expenditure? Will it pay? If the answer is in the negative, then let the workingmen go to pieces. Capital does not operate where there is no profit. Humanity is not an "issue" on the Exchange.[6]

The question of "profit" has exhausted its *role* in Socialist society: *in Socialist society the only consideration is the welfare of its members.* Whatever is beneficent to these and protects them must be introduced; whatever injures them must stop. None is forced to join in a dangerous game. If matters are undertaken that have dangers in prospect, volunteers will be numerous, all the more so seeing that the object can never be to the injury, but only to the promotion of civilization.

The amplest application of motor powers and of the best machinery and implements, the utmost subdivision of labor, and the most efficient combinations of labor-power will, accordingly, carry production to such pitch that the hours of work can be materially reduced in the production of the necessaries of life. The capitalist lengthens the hours of labor, whenever he can, especially during crises, when the worker's power of resistance is broken, and by squeezing more surplus values out of him, prices may be lowered. In Socialist society, an increase of production accrues to the benefit of all: *The share of each rises with the productivity of labor and increased productivity again makes possible the reduction of the hours of work, socially determined as necessary.*

Among the motor powers that are coming into application, electricity

[6] "Capital is said by a Quarterly Reviewer to fly turbulence and strife, and to be timid, which is very true; but this is very incompletely stating the question. Capital eschews no profit, or very small profit, just as Nature was formerly said to abhor a vacuum. With adequate profit, capital is very bold. A certain 10 per cent. will ensure its employment anywhere; 20 per cent. certain will produce eagerness; 50 per cent. positive audacity; 100 per cent. will made it ready to trample on all human laws; 300 per cent., and there is not a crime at which it will scruple, nor a risk it will not run, even to the chance of its owner being hanged. If turbulence and strife will bring a profit, it will freely encourage both. Smuggling and the slave-trade have amply proved all that is here stated." (P. J. Dunning, l. c., p. 35.) Cited by Karl Marx in "Capital," p. 786, edition Swan-Sonnenschein & Co., London, 1896.

will, according to all appearances, take a decisive place.[7] Capitalist society is now everywhere engaged in harnessing it to its service. The more extensively this is done the better. The revolutionizing effect of this mightiest of all the powers of Nature will but all the sooner snap the bonds of bourgeois society, and open the doors to Socialism. But only in Socialist society will electricity attain its fullest and most widespread application. If the prospects now opened for its application are even but partially realized—and on that head there can be no doubt—electricity, as a motor power as well as a source of light and heat, will contribute immeasurably towards the improvement of the conditions of life. Electricity distinguishes itself from all other motor power in that, above all, its supply in Nature is abundant. Our water courses, the ebb and tide of the sea, the winds, the sun-light—all furnish innumerable horse-powers, the moment we know how to utilize them in full. Through the invention of the accumulators it has been proved that large volumes of power, which can be appropriated only periodically, from the ebbs and tides, the winds and mountain streams, can be stored up and kept for use at any given place and any given time. All these inventions and discoveries are still in embryo: their full development may be surmised, but can not be forecast in detail.

The progress expected from the application of electricity sounds like a fairy tale. Mr. Meems of Baltimore has planned an electric wagon able to travel 300 kilometers an hour—actually race with the wind. Nor does Mr. Meems stand alone. Prof. Elihu Thomson of Lynn, Mass., also believes it possible to construct electromotors of a velocity of 160 kilometers, and, with suitable strengthening of the rolling stock and improvement of the signal system, of a velocity of 260 kilometers; and he has given a plausible explanation of his system. The same scientist holds, and in this Werner Siemens, who expressed similar views at the Berlin Convention of Naturalists in 1887, agrees with him, that it is possible by means of electricity *to transform the chemical elements directly into food*—a revolution that would hoist capitalist society off its hinges. While in 1887 Werner Siemens was of the opinion that it were possible, though only in the remote future, to produce artificially a hydrate of carbon such as grape sugar and later the therewith closely related starch, whereby "bread could be made out of stone," the chemist Dr. B. Meyer claims that ligneous fibre could eventually be turned into a source of human food. Obviously, we are moving towards ever newer

[7] A competitor with electricity, applied to lighting purposes, has recently arisen in the shape of the so-called acetylene gas, which was discovered in the United States, by means of an electrolytic process, similar to that used in the preparation of aluminum. A compound is made of calcium and carbon, called calcium-carbide, which, in touch with water, produces the acetylene gas. Its lighting power is fifteen times that of the ordinary illuminating gas, besides being much cheaper.

chemical and technical revolutions. In the meantime, the physiologist E. Eiseler has actually produced grape sugar artificially, and thus made a discovery that, in 1887, Werner Siemens considered possible only in the "remote future." In the spring of 1894, the French ex-Minister of Public Worship, Prof. Berthelot, delivered an address in Paris at the banquet of the Association of Chemical Manufacturers upon the significance of chemistry in the future. The address is interesting in more respects than one. Prof. Berthelot sketched the probable state of chemistry at about the year 2000. While his sketch contains many a droll exaggeration, it does contain so much that is serious and sound that we shall present it in extract. After describing the achievements of chemistry during the last few decades, Prof. Berthelot went on to say:—

"The manufacture of sulphuric acids and of soda, bleaching and coloring, beet sugar, therapeutic alkaloides, gas, gilding and silvering, etc.; then came electro-chemistry, whereby metallurgy was radically revolutionized; thermo-chemistry and the chemistry of explosives, whereby fresh energy was imparted to mining and to war; the wonders of organic chemistry in the production of colors, of flavors, of therapeutic and antiseptic means, etc. But all that is only a start: soon much more important problems are to be solved. About the year 2000 there will be no more agriculture and no more farmers: chemistry will have done away with the former cultivation of the soil. There will be no more coal-shafts, consequently, neither will there be any more miners' strikes. Fuel is produced by chemical and physical processes. Tariffs and wars are abolished: aerial navigation, that helped itself to chemicals as motor power, pronounced the sentence of death upon those obsolete habits. The whole problem of industry then consists in discovering sources of power, that are inexhaustible and restorable with little labor. Until now we have produced steam through the chemical energy of burning mineral coal. But mineral coal is hard to get and its supply decreases daily. Attention must be turned towards utilizing the heat of the sun and of the earth's crust. The hope is justified that both sources will be drawn upon without limit. The boring of a shaft 3,000 to 4,000 meters deep does not exceed the power of modern, less yet it will exceed that of future engineers. The source of all that and of all industry would be thus thrown open. Add water to that, and all imaginable machinery may be put in perpetual operation on earth: the source of this power would experience hardly any diminution in hundreds of years.

"With the aid of the earth's heat, numerous chemical problems will become solvable, among these the greatest of all—*the chemical production of food.* In principle, the problem is solved now. The synthesis of fats and oils has been long known; likewise are sugar and hydrates of carbon known; nor will it be long before the secret of compounding azote is out. The food problem is a purely chemical one. The day when the corresponding cheap power shall have been obtained; food of all sort will be producable with carbon out of carbon oxides, and with hydrogen and acids out of water, and with nitrogen out of the atmosphere. What until now vegetation has done, industry will thenceforth perform, and more perfectly than Nature itself. The time will come when everyone will carry about him a little box of chemicals wherewith to provide his food supply of albumen, fat and hydrates of carbon, regardless of the hour of the day or the season of the year, regardless of rain or drought, of frost or hail, or insects. A revolution will then set in of which no conception is so far possible. Fields bearing fruit, wine-bearing mountain slopes and pastures for cattle will have vanished. Man will have gained in gentleness and morality seeing he no longer lives on the murder and destruction of living beings. Then also will the difference drop away between fertile and barren districts; perchance deserts may then become the favorite homes of man being healthier than the damp valleys and the swamp-infected plains. Then also will Art, together with all the beauties of human life reach full development. No longer will the face of earth be marred, so to speak, with geometrical figures, now entailed by agriculture: it will become a garden in which, at will, grass or flowers, bush or woods, can be allowed to grow, and in which the human race will live in plenty, in a Golden Age. Nor will man thereby sink into indolence and corruption. Work is requisite to happiness, and man will work as much as ever, because he will be working for himself aiming at the highest development of his mental, moral and esthetical powers."

Every reader may accept what he please of this address of Prof. Berthelot; certain, however, is the prospect that in the future and in virtue of the progress of science, wealth—the volume and variety of products—will increase enormously, and that the pleasures of life of the coming generations will take undreamed of increment.

An aspiration, deeply implanted in the nature of man, is that of freedom in the choice and change of occupation. As uninterrupted repetition renders the daintiest of dishes repulsive, so with a daily treadmill-like recurring occupation: it dulls and relaxes the senses. Man then does only mechanically what he must do; he does it without swing or enjoyment. There are latent in all men faculties and desires that need but to be awakened and developed to produce the most beautiful results. Only then does man become fully and truly man. Towards the satisfaction of this need of change, Socialist society offers, as will be shown, the fullest opportunity. The mighty increase of productive powers, coupled with an ever progressing simplification of the process of labor, not only enables a considerable lowering of hours of work, it also *facili-tates the acquisition of skill in many directions.*

The old apprentice system has survived its usefulness: it exists to-day only and is possible only in backward, old-fashioned forms of produc-tion, as represented by the small handicrafts. Seeing, however, that this vanishes from the new social Order,, all the institutions and forms peculiar thereto vanish along with it. New ones step in. Every factory shows us to-day how few are its workingmen, still engaged at a work that they have been apprenticed in. The employes are of the most varied, heterogeneous trades; a short time suffices to train them in any sub-department of work, at which, in accord with the ruling system of exploitation, they are then kept at work longer hours, without change or regard to their inclinations, and, lashed to the machine, become them-selves a machine.[8] Such a state of things has no place in a changed organization of society. There is ample time for the acquisition of dexterity of hand and the exercise of artistic skill. Spacious training schools, equipped with all necessary comforts and technical perfections will facilitate to young and old the acquisition of any trade. Chemical and physical laboratories, up to all the demands of these sciences, and furnished with ample staffs of instructors will be in existence. Only then will be appreciated to its full magnitude what a world of ambitions and faculties the capitalist system of production suppresses, or forces awry into mistaken paths.[9]

It is not merely possible to have a regard for the need of change; it is the purpose of society to realize its satisfaction: the harmonious growth of man depends upon that. The professional physiognomies that modern society brings to the surface—whether the profession be in certain occupations of some sort or other, or in gluttony and idleness, or in compulsory tramping—will gradually vanish. There are to-day precious few people with any opportunity of change in their occupa-tions, or who exercise the same. Occasionally, individuals are found

---

[8] "The generality of laborers in this and most other countries, have as little choice of occupation or freedom of locomotion, are practically as de-pendent on fixed rules, and on the will of others, as they could be on any system short of actual slavery."—John Stuart Mill's "Principles of Political Economy."

[9] "A French workman, on his return from San Francisco, writes as follows: 'I never could have believed that I was capable of working at the various oc-cupations I was employed on in California. I was firmly convinced that I was fit for nothing but letter-press printing. . . Once in the midst of this world of adventurers, who change their occupation as often as they do their shirt, egad, I did as the others. As mining did not turn out remunerative enough, I left it for the town, where in succession I became typographer, slater, plumber, etc. In consequence of this finding out that I am fit for any sort of work, I feel less of a mollusk and more of a man." (A. Courbou, "De l'Enseignement Professionnel', 2eme ed. p. 50.) Cited by Karl Marx in "Capital", p. 493, edition Swan-Sonnenschein Co., London, 1896.

who, favored by circumstances, withdraw from the routine of their daily pursuits and, after having paid their tribute to physical, recreate themselves with intellectual work; and conversely, brain workers are met off and on, who seek and find change in physical labors of some sort or other, handwork, gardening, etc. Every hygienist will confirm the invigorating effect of a pursuit that rests upon alternating physical and mental work; only such a pursuit is natural. The only qualification is that it be moderately indulged, and in proportion to the strength of the individual.

Leo Tolstoi lashes the hypertrophic and unnatural character that art and science have assumed under the unnatural conditions of modern society.[10] He severely condemns the contempt for physical labor, entertained in modern society, and he recommends a return to natural conditions. Every being, who means to live according to the laws of nature and enjoy life, should divide the day between, first, physical field labor; secondly, hand work; thirdly, mental work; fourthly, cultured and companionable intercourse. More than eight hours' physical work should not be done. Tolstoi, who practices this system of life, and who, as he says, has felt himself human only since he put it into practice, perceives only what is possible to him, a rich, independent man, but wholly impossible to the large mass of mankind, under existing conditions. The person who must do hard physical work every day ten, twelve and more hours, to gain a meager existence, and who was brought up in ignorance, can not furnish himself with the Tolstoian system of life. Neither can they, who are on the firing line of business life and are compelled to submit to its exactions. The small minority who could imitate Tolstoi have, as a rule, no need to do so. It is one of the illusions that Tolstoi yields to, the belief that social systems can be changed by preaching and example. The experiences made by Tolstoi with his system of life prove how rational the same is; in order, however, to introduce such a system of life as a social custom, a social foundation is requisite other than the present. It requires a new society.

Future society will have such a foundation; it will have scientists and artists of all sorts in abundance; but all of them will work physically a part of the day, and devote the rest, according to their liking, to study, the arts or companionable intercourse.[11]

The existing contrast between mental and manual labor—a contrast that the ruling classes seek to render as pronounced as possible with the

[10] Tolstoi's "The Significance of Science and Art."

[11] What may be made of a man under favorable circumstances is illustrated by Leonardo da Vinci, who was a distinguished painter, celebrated sculptor, favorite architect and engineer, excellent builder of fortifications, musician and improvisator. Benvenuto Cellini was a celebrated goldsmith, excellent

view of securing for themselves also the intellectual means of sovereignty—will likewise be removed.

It follows from the preceding arguments that crises and compulsory idleness are impossible phenomena in the new social order. Crises arise from the circumstance that individualist, capitalist production—incited by profit and devoid of all reliable guage with which to ascertain the actual demand—brings an overstocking of the world's market, and thus overproduction. The merchandise feature of the products under capitalism, of the products that their owners endeavor to exchange, makes the use of the product dependent upon the consumer's *capacity to buy*. The capacity to buy is, however, limited, in so far as the overwhelming majority are concerned, they being under-paid for their labor, or even wholly unable to sell the same if the capitalist does not happen to be able to squeeze a surplus value out of it. *The capacity to buy and the capacity to consume are two wholly distinct things in capitalist society.* Many millions of people are in want of clothes, shoes, furniture, linen, eatables and drinkables, but they have no money, and their wants, i. e., their capacity to consume, remains unsatisfied. The market is glutted with goods, but the masses suffer hunger; they are willing to work, but they find none to buy their labor-power because the holder of money sees nothing to "make" in the purchase. "Die, canaille; become vagabonds, criminals! I, the capitalist, can not help it. I have no use for goods that I have no purchaser to buy from me with corresponding profit." And, in a way, the man is right.

In the new social Order this contradiction is wiped out. Socialist society produces not "merchandise," in order to "buy" and to "sell;" *it produces necessaries of life, that are used, consumed, and otherwise have no object.* In Socialist society, accordingly, the capacity to consume is not bounded, as in bourgeois society, by the individual's capacity to buy; *it is bounded by the collective capacity to produce.* If labor and instruments of labor are in existence, all wants can be satisfied; the social capacity to consume is bounded only by *the satisfaction of the consumers.*

There being no "merchandise" in Socialist society, neither can there be any "money." Money is the visible contrast of merchandise; yet itself is merchandise! Money, though itself merchandise, is at the same time

molder, good sculptor, leading builder of fortifications, first-rate soldier and thorough musician. Abraham Lincoln was a splitter of rails, agriculturist, boatman, shop-assistant and lawyer, until he was placed in the Presidential chair of the United States. It may be said without exaggerating, most people are engaged in occupations that do not correspond with their faculties, simply because, not freedom of choice, but the force of necessity dictated their career. Many a bad professor would do good work as a shoemaker, and many a good shoemaker could be a good professor as well.

the social equivalent for all other articles of merchandise. But Socialist society produces no articles of merchandise, only articles of use and necessity, whose production requires a certain measure of social labor. The time, on an average requisite for the production of an article is the only standard by which it is measured for social use. Ten minutes social labor in one article are equal to ten minutes social labor in another—neither more nor less. Society is not "on the make"; it only seeks to effect among its members the exchange of articles of equal quality, equal utility. It need not even set up a standard of use value. It merely produces what it needs. If society finds that a three-hour work day is requisite for the production of all that is needed, it establishes such a term of work.[12] If the methods of production improve in such wise that the supply can be raised in two hours, the two-hour work day is established. If, on the contrary, society demands the gratification of higher wants than, despite the increase of forces and the improved productivity of the process of labor, can be satisfied with two or three hours work, then the four-hour day is introduced. Its will is law.

How much social labor will be requisite for the production of any article is easily computed.[13] The relation of the part to the whole of the working time is measured accordingly. Any voucher—a printed piece of paper, gold or tin—certifies to the time spent in work, and enables its possessor to exchange it for articles of various kinds.[14] If he finds that

[12] It should always be kept in mind that production is then organized up to the highest point of technical perfection, and all the people are at work. It may thus happen that, under given circumstances, a three-hour's day is rather longer, and not shorter, than necessary. Owen in his time—first quarter of the nineteenth century—considered two-hour's work sufficient.

[13] "It is not necessary to go a round-about way in order to ascertain the amount of social labor crystallized in a given product. Daily experience shows directly the requisite average. Society can easily calculate how many hours are contained in a steam engine, in a hectoliter of last year's wheat, in a hundred square meters of cloth of a certain quality. Society will, therefore, never dream of re-expressing these units of work,—crystallized in the products and known to it directly and absolutely—by a merely relative, varying and insufficient measure, formerly used by it as a make-shift that it could not get along without; a measure, moreover, which itself is a third product, instead of by their natural, adequate and absolute measure—time. . . Society will have to organize the plan of production according to the means of production, under which category labor-power especially belongs. The various utilities of the several articles of use, balanced with one another and with the amount of labor necessary for their production, will in the end determine the plan. People settle matters a good deal more simply without the intervention of the celebrated 'money value.' "—Fr. Engels' "Herr Eugen Duehring's Umwaelzung der Wissenschaft."

[14] Herr Eugen Richter is so astonished at the dropping away of money in Socialist society—abolished money will not be: with the abolition of the merchandise character from the products of labor, money drops away of itself—that he devotes to the subject a special chapter in his "Irrelehren."

his wants are smaller than what he receives for his labor, he then works proportionally shorter hours. If he wishes to give away what he does not consume, nothing hinders him. If he is disposed to work for another out of his own free will, so that the latter may revel in the *dolce far niente*,—if he chooses to be such a blockhead, nothing hinders him. But none can compel him to work for another; none can withhold from him a part of what is due him for labor performed. Everyone can satisfy all his legitimate desires—only not at the expense of others. He receives the equivalent of what he has rendered to society—neither more nor less, and he remains free from all exploitation by third parties.

"But what becomes of the difference between the lazy and the industrious? between the intelligent and the stupid?" That is one of the principal questions from our opponents, and the answer gives them no slight headache. That this distinction between the "lazy" and the "industrious," the "intelligent" and the "stupid" is not made in our civil service hierarchy, but that the term of service decides in the matter of salary and generally of promotion also—these are facts that occur to none of these would-be puzzlers and wiseacres. The teachers, the professors—and as a rule the latter are the silliest questioners—move into their posts, not according to their own qualities, but according to the salaries that these posts bring. That promotions in the army and in the hierarchies of the civil service and the learned professions are often made, not according to worth, but according to birth, friendship and female influence, is a matter of public notoriety. That, however, wealth also is not measured by diligence and intelligence may be judged by the Berlin inn-keepers, bakers and butchers, to whom grammar often is a mystery, and who figure in the first of the three classes of the Prussian

What is particularly hard for him to understand is the idea that it is immaterial whether the voucher for labor performance be a piece of paper, gold or tin. On this head he says: "With gold, the devil of the modern social order would re-enter the Social Democratic State"—that there could then be only a Socialist society, and not a Social Democratic State, Herr Richter stubbornly overlooks: he must, else a good portion of his polemic would fall through—"seeing that gold has an independent metal value, can be easily saved, and thus the possession of gold pieces would enable the heaping up of values wherewith to purchase escape from the obligation to work, and wherewith even to lay out money on interest."

Herr Richter must take his readers for great blockheads to dare dish up such trash to them on the subject of our gold. Herr Richter, who can not rid himself of the concept of capital, can, of course, not understand that where there is no capital, neither is there any merchandise, nor can there be any "money"; and where there is no "capital" and no "money", neither could there be any "interest." Herr Richter is nailed so fast to the concept of capital that he is unable to conceive a world without "capital." We should like to know how a member of a Socialist society could "save up" his gold certificates of labor, or even loan them out to others and thereby rake in interest, when all other members possess what that one is offering them and— *on which he lives.*

electorate, while the intellectuals of Berlin, the men of science, the
highest magistrates of the Empire and the State, vote with the second
class.   There is not now any difference between the "lazy" and the "diligent," the "intelligent" and the "stupid" for the simple reason that what
is understood by these terms exists no longer.   A "lazy" fellow society
only calls him who has been thrown out of work, is compelled to lead a
vagabond's life and finally does become a vagabond, or who, grown up
under improper training, sinks into vice.   But to style "lazy fellow" the
man who rolls in money and kills the day with idleness or debauchery,
would be an insult: he is a "worthy and good man."

How do matters stand in Socialist society?   All develop under equal
conditions, and each is active in that to which inclination and skill point
him, whence differences in work will be but insignificant.[15]   The intellectual and moral atmosphere of society, which stimulates all to excel
one another, likewise aids in equalizing such differences.   If any person
finds that he cannot do as much as others on a certain field, he chooses
another that corresponds with his strength and faculties.   Whoever has
worked with a large number of people in one establishment knows that
men who prove themselves unfit and useless in a certain line, do excellent
work in another.   There is no normally constructed being who fails to
meet the highest demands in one line or another, the moment he finds
himself in the right place.   By what right does any claim precedence
over another?   If any one has been treated so step-motherly by Nature
that with the best will he can not do what others can, *Society has no
right to punish him for the shortcomings of Nature*.   If, on the contrary, a person has received from Nature gifts that raise him above
others, *Society is not obliged to reward what is not his personal desert*.
In Socialist society all enjoy equal conditions of life and opportunities
for education; all are furnished the same opportunities to develop their
knowledge and powers according to their respective capacities and inclinations.   In this lies a further guarantee that not only will the standard of culture and powers be higher in Socialist than in bourgeois society, but also that both will be more equally distributed and yet be
much more manifold.

When, on a journey up the Rhine, Goethe studied the Cathedral of
Cologne, he discovered in the archives that the old master-builders paid
their workmen equal wages for equal time.   They did so because they

---

[15] "All people of average healthy build *are born with almost equal intellectual powers, but education, laws and circumstances alter them relatively.*
The correctly understood interest of the individual is blended into one with
the common or public interest."—Helvetius' "On Man and His Education."
Helvetius is right with regard to the large majority of people; but that does
not take away that the natural faculties of each are different for different
occupations.

wished to get good and conscientious work. This looks like an anomaly to modern bourgeois society. It introduced the system of piece-work, that drives the workingmen to out-work one another, and thus aids the employer in underpaying and in reducing wages.

As with manual, so with mental work. Man is the product of the time and circumstances that he lives in. A Goethe, born under equally favorable conditions in the fourth, instead of the eighteenth, century may have become, instead of a distinguished poet and naturalist, a great Father of the Church, who might have thrown St. Augustine into the shade. If, on the other hand, instead of being the son of a rich Frankfurt patrician, Goethe had been born the son of a poor shoemaker of the same town, he never would have become the Minister of the Grand Duke of Weimar, but would probably have remained a shoemaker, and died an honorable member of the craft. Goethe himself recognized the advantage he had in being born in a materially and socially favorable station in order to reach his stage of development. It so appears in his "Wilhelm Meister." Were Napoleon I. born ten years later, he never would have been Emperor of France. Without the war of 1870-1871, Gambetta had never become what he did become. Place the naturally gifted child of intelligent parents among savages, and he becomes a savage. *Whatever a man is, society has made him.* Ideas are not creations that spring from the head of the individual out of nothing, or through inspiration from above; they are products of social life, of the *Spirit of the Age,* raised in the head of the individual. An Aristotle could not possible have the ideas of a Darwin, and a Darwin could not choose but think otherwise than an Aristotle. Man thinks according as the Spirit of the Age, i. e., his surroundings and the phenomena that they present to him drive him to think. Hence the experience of different people often thinking simultaneously the same thing, of the same inventions and discoveries being made simultaneously in places far apart from each other. Hence also the fact that an idea, uttered fifty years too early, leaves the world cold; fifty years later, sets it ablaze. Emperor Sigismund could risk breaking his word to Huss in 1415 and order him burned in Constance; Charles V., although a more violent fanatic, was compelled to allow Luther to depart in peace from the Reichstag at Worms in 1521. Ideas are, accordingly, the product of combined social causes and social life. What is true of society in general, is true in particular of the several classes that, at given historic epochs, constitute society. As each class has its special interests, it also has its special ideas and views, that lead to those class struggles of which recorded history is full, and that reach their climax in the class antagonisms and class struggles of modern days. Hence, it depends not merely upon the age in which a man lives, but also upon the social stratum of a certain age in which he lived or lives, and whereby his feelings, thoughts and actions are determined.

Without modern society, no modern ideas. That is obvious. With regard to the future social Order, it must be furthermore added that the means whereby the individual develops are the property of society. Society can, accordingly, not be bound to render special homage to what itself made possible and is its own product.

So much on the qualification of manual and brain work. It follows that there can be no real distinction between "higher" and "lower" manual work, such as not infrequently a mechanic to-day affects towards the day-laborer, who performs work on the street, or the like. Society demands only socially necessary work; hence all work is of equal value to society. If work that is disagreeable and repulsive can not be performed mechanically or chemically and by some process converted into work that is agreeable—a prospect that may not be put in doubt, seeing the progress made on the fields of technique and chemistry—and if the necessary volunteer forces can not be raised, then the obligation lies upon each, as soon as is his turn, to do his part. False ideas of shame, absurd contempt for useful work, become obsolete conceptions. These exist only in our society of drones, where to do nothing is regarded as an enviable lot, and the worker is despised in proportion to the hardness and disagreeableness of his work, and in proportion to its social usefulness. To-day work is badly paid in proportion as it is disagreeable. The reason is that, due to the constant revolutionizing of the process of production, a permanent mass of superfluous labor lies on the street, and, in order to live, sells itself for such vile work, and at such prices that the introduction of machinery in these departments of labor does not "pay." Stone-breaking, for instance, is proverbially one of the worst paid and most disagreeable kinds of work. It were a trifling matter to have the stone-breaking done by machinery, as in the United States; but we have such a mass of cheap labor-power that the machine would not "pay."[16] Street

[16] "If, therefore, the choice were to be made between Communism with all its chances, and the present state of society with all its sufferings and injustices; if the institution of private property necessarily carried with it as a consequence, that the produce of labor should be apportioned as we now see it, almost in an inverse ratio to the labor—the largest portions to those who have never worked at all, the next largest to those whose work is almost nominal, and so in a descending scale, the remuneration dwindling as the work grows harder and more disagreeable, until the most fatiguing and exhausting bodily labor cannot count with certainty on being able to earn even the necessaries of life; if this or Communism, were the alternative, all the difficulties, great or small, of Communism would be but as dust in the balance."—John Stuart Mill, "Principles of Political Economy." Mill strove diligently to "reform" the bourgeois world, and to "bring it to reason." Of course, in vain. And so it came about that he, like all clear-sighted men, became a

and sewer cleaning, the carting away of refuse, underground work of all sorts, etc., could, with the aid of machinery and technical contrivances, even at our present state of development, be all done in such manner that no longer would any trace of disagreeableness attach to the work. Carefully considered, the workingman who cleans out a sewer and thereby protects people from miasmas, is a very useful member of society; whereas a professor who teaches falsified history in the interest of the ruling classes, or a theologian who seeks to befog the mind with supernatural and transcendental doctrines are highly injurious beings.

The learned fraternity of to-day, clad in offices and dignities, to a large extent represents a guild intended and paid to defend and justify the rule of the leading classes with the authority of science; to make them appear good and necessary; and to prop up existing superstitions. In point of fact this guild is largely engaged in the trade of quackery and brain-poisoning—a work injurious to civilization, intellectual wage-labor in the interest of the capitalist class and its clients.[17] A social condition, that should make impossible the existence of such elements, would perform an act towards the liberation of humanity.

Genuine science, on the other hand, is often connected with highly disagreeable and repulsive work, such, for instance, as when a physician examines a corpse in a state of decomposition, or operates on supurating wounds, or when a chemist makes experiments. These often are labors more repulsive than the most repulsive ones ever performed by day-laborers and untutored workingmen. Few recognize the fact. The difference lies in that the one requires extensive studies in order to perform it, whereas the other can be performed by anyone without preparatory studies. Hence the radical difference in the estimation of the two. But in a society where, in virtue of the amplest opportunities of education afforded to all, the present distinction between "cultured" and "uncultured" ceases to exist, the contrast is likewise bound to vanish between learned and unlearned work, all the more seeing that technical development knows no limits and manual labor may be likewise performed by machinery or technical contrivances. We need but look at the development of our art handicrafts—xylography and copper-etching, for instance. As it turns out that the most disagreeable kinds of work

---

Socialist. He dared not, however, admit the fact in his life time, but ordered that, after his death, his auto-biography be published, containing his Socialist confession of faith. It happened to him as with Darwin, who cared not to be known in his life as an atheist. The bourgeoisie affects loyalty, religion and faith in authority because through the acceptance of these "virtues" by the masses its own rule is safeguarded; in its own sleeves, however, it laughs at them.

[17] "Scholarship is as often the hand-maid of ignorance as of progress."—Buckle's "History of Civilization in England."

often are the most useful, so also is our conception regarding agreeable
and disagreeable work, like so many other modern conceptions, utterly
superficial; it is a conception that has an eye to externals only.

*   *   *   *   *

The moment production is carried on in Socialist society upon the
lines traced above, it no longer produces "merchandise," but only articles
of use for the direct demand of society. Commerce, accordingly, ceases,
having its sense and reason for being only in a social system that rests
upon the production of goods for sale. A large army of persons of both
sexes is thus set free for productive work.[18] This large army, set free
for production, not only increases the volume of wealth produced, but
makes possible a reduction of the hours of work. These people are to-
day more or less parasites: they are supported by the work of others:
in many instances they must toil diligently in return for a meagre existence. In Socialist society they are superfluous as merchants, hosts,
brokers and agents. In lieu of the dozens, hundreds and thousands of
stores and commercial establishments of all sorts, that to-day every
community holds in proportion to its size, large municipal stores step in,
elegant bazaars, actual exhibitions, requiring a relatively small administrative personnel. This change in itself represents a revolution in all
previous institutions. The tangled mass of modern commerce is transformed in a centralized and purely administrative department, with only
the simplest of functions, that can not choose but grow still simpler
through the progressive centralization of all social institutions. Likewise does the whole system of transportation and communication undergo
a complete change.

[18] According to the census of 1882 there were in Germany engaged in trade
and transportation 1,570,318 persons, inclusive of those occupied in hotels
and inns, and exclusive of 295,451 domestics.
[Some opinion may be formed of the volume of useless labor, parasitism, in
the United States, from the census figures for 1900. Under this head of "Trade
and Transportation" alone come 4,766,964 persons. Among them, substantially useless, are the 241,162 agents, the 73,277 brokers, the 92,919 commercial travelers, the 76,649 hucksters and peddlers, the 790,886 merchants
and dealers (except wholesale), the 42,293 merchants and dealers (wholesale), the 74,072 officials of banks and companies, the 33,656 livery stable
keepers, the 71,622 messengers and errand and office boys, and the 59,54￫
packers and shippers—in all 1,556,081. Of the remaining 3,210,883—among
whom are 254,880 bookkeepers and accountants, 632,127 clerks and copyists,
611,139 salesmen and women—fully two-thirds could be spared to-day under
a rational social system. The proportion of wasteful forces, and even parasitism, is still larger under the heads of "Professional Service" and "Domestic and Personal Service," among which—to pick up only a few of the
worst items—are 111,638 clergymen, 114,460 lawyers, 86,607 government officials, including officers of the United States army and navy, 33,844 saloon
keepers, 1,560,721 servants and waiters, 43,235 soldiers, sailors and marines
(U. S.), etc., etc.—THE TRANSLATOR.]

The telegraph, railroads, Post Office, river and ocean vessels, street railways—whatever the names of the vehicles and institutions may be that attend to the transportation and communication of capitalist society—now become *social* property. Many of these institutions—Post Offices, telegraph and railroads generally—are now State institutions in Germany. Their transformation into social property presents no difficulties: there no private interests are left to hurt: if the State continues to develop in that direction, all the better. But these institutions, administered by the State, are no Socialist institutions, as they are mistakenly taken for. They are business plants, that are exploited as capitalistically as if they were in private hands. Neither the officers nor the workingmen have any special benefit from them. The State treats them just as any private capitalist. When, for instance, orders were issued not to engage any workingman over 40 years of age in the railway or marine service of the Empire, the measure carries on its brows the class stamp of the State of the exploiters, and is bound to raise the indignation of the working class. Such and similar measures that proceed from the State as an employer of labor are even worse than if they proceed from private employers. As against the State, the latter is but a small employer, and the occupation that this one denies another might grant. The State, on the contrary, being a monopolistic employer, can, at one stroke, cast thousands of people into misery with its regulations. That is not Socialist, it is capitalist conduct; and the Socialist guards against allowing the present State ownership being regarded as Socialism, or the realization of Socialist aspirations. In a Socialist institution there are no employers. The leader, chosen for the purpose, can only carry out the orders and superintend the execution of the disciplinary and other measures prescribed by the collectivity itself.

As in the instance of the millions of private producers, dealers and middlemen of all sorts, large centralized establishments take their place, so does the whole system of transportation and communication assume new shape. The myriads of small shipments to as many consignees that consume a mass of powers and of time, now grow into large shipments to the municipal depots and the central places of production. Here also labor is simplified. The transportation of raw material to an establishment of a thousand workers is an infinitely simpler matter than to a thousand small and scattered establishments. Thus centralized localities of production and of transportation for whole communities, or divisions of the same, will introduce a great saving of time, of labor, of material, and of means both of production and distribution. The benefit accrues to the whole community, and to each individual therein. The physiognomy of our productive establishments, of our system of transportation and communication, especially also of our habitations, will be completely altered for the better. The nerve-racking noise, crowding and rushing of our large cities with their thousands of vehicles of all sorts ceases substantially: society assumes an aspect of greater repose. The opening of streets and their cleaning, the whole system of life and of intercourse acquires new character. Hygienic measures—possible to-day only at great cost and then only partially, not infrequently only in the quarters of the rich—can be introduced with ease everywhere. To-day "the common people" do not need them; they can wait till the funds are ready; and these never are.

Such a system of communication and transportation can not then choose but reach a high grade of perfection. Who knows but aerial navigation may then become a chief means of travel. The lines of transportation and communication are the arteries that carry the exchange of products—circulation of the blood—throughout the whole body social, that effect personal and mental intercourse between man and man. They are, consequently, highly calculated to establish an equal level of well-being and culture throughout society. The extension and ramification of the most perfect means of transportation and communication into the remotest corners of the land is, accordingly, *a necessity and a matter of general social interest.* On this field there arise before the new social system tasks that go far beyond any that modern society can put to itself. Finally, such a perfected system of transportation and communication, will promote the decentralization of the mass of humanity that is to-day heaped up in the large cities. It will distribute the same over the country, and thus—in point of sanitation as well as of mental and material progress—it will assume a significance of inestimable value.

* * * * *

Among the means of production in industry and transportation, land holds a leading place, being the source of all human effort and the foundation of all human existence, hence, of Society itself. Society resumes at its advanced stage of civilization, what it originally possessed. Among all races on earth that reached a certain minimum degree of culture, we find community in land, and the system continues in force with such people wherever they are still in existence. Community in land constituted the foundation of all primitive association: the latter was impossible without the former. Not until the rise and development of private property and of the forms of rulership therewith connected, and then only under a running struggle, that extends deep into our own times, was the system of common ownership in land ended, and the land usurped as private property. The robbery of the land and its transformation into private property furnished, as we have seen, the first source of that bondage that, extending from chattel slavery to the "freedom" of the wage-earner of our own century, has run through all imaginable stages, until finally the enslaved, after a development of thousands of years re-convert the land into common property.

The importance of land to human existence is such that in all social struggles the world has ever known—whether in India, China, Egypt, Greece (Cleaomenes), Rome (the Gracchi), Christian Middle Ages (religious sects, Munzer, the Peasants War), in the empires of the Aztecs and of the Incas, or in the several upheavals of latter days—the possession of land is the principal aim of the combatants. And even to-day, the public ownership of land finds its justifiers in such men as Adolf Samter, Adolf Wagner, Dr. Schaeffle, who on other domains of the Social Question are ready to rest content with half-measures.[19]

The well-being of the population depends first of all upon the proper cultivation of the land. To raise the same to the highest degree of per-

---

[19] Even the Fathers of the Church, Bishops and Popes could not refrain from preaching in a communistic vein during those early centuries when community of property still prevailed, but its theft was assuming larger proportions. The Syllabus and the encyclicals of the nineteenth century have lost all recollection of this tone, and even the Roman Popes have been compelled to become subjects of capitalist society, and now pose as its zealous defenders against the Socialists.

In contrast therewith Bishop Clemens I. (deceased 102 of our reckoning) said: "The use of all things in this world is to be common to all. It is an injustice to say: 'This is my property, this belongs to me, that belongs to another.' Hence the origin of contentions among men."

Bishop Ambrose of Milan, who lived about 347, exclaimed: "Nature bestows all things on all men in common, for God has created all things that their enjoyment might be common to all, and that the earth might become the common possession of all. Common possession is, therefore, a right established by Nature, and only unjust usurpation (usurpatio) has created the right of private property."

St. John Chrysostomus (deceased 407) declared in his homilies directed against the immorality and corruption of the population of Constantinople: "Let none call aught his own; we have received everything from God for enjoyment in common, and 'mine' and 'thine' are words of falsehood."

St. Augustine (deceased 430) expressed himself thus: "Because private property exists there exists also law suits, enmities, dissensions, wars, rebellions, sins, injustice, murder. Whence proceed all these scourges? From property only. Let us then, my brothers, refrain from possessing anything as our property; at least let us refrain from loving it."

Pope Gregory the Great declares about 600: "Let them know that the earth from which they spring and of which they are formed belongs to all men in common, and that therefore the fruits which the earth brings forth must belong to all without distinction."

And one of the moderns, Zacharia, says in his "Forty Books on the State": "All the evils with which civilized nations have to contend, can be traced back to private property in land."

All these authorities have recognized more or less accurately the nature of private property, which, since its existence, as St. Augustin correctly puts it, brought law suits, enmities, dissensions, wars, rebellions, injustice and murder into the world,—all of them evils that will disappear with its abolition.

fection is eminently a matter of public concern. That the cultivation of
the land can reach the necessary high degree of perfection neither under
the large, nor the middle, least of all under the small landlord system,
has been previously shown. The most profitable cultivation of land depends not merely upon the special care bestowed upon it. Elements
come here into consideration that neither the largest private holder, nor
the mightiest association of these is equal to cope with. These are elements that lap over, even beyond the reach of the State and require international treatment.

Society must first of all consider the land as a whole—its topographi-
cal qualities, its mountains, plains, woods, lakes, rivers, ponds, heaths,
swamps, moors, etc. The topography together with the geographical
location of land both of which are unchangeable, exercises certain influences upon climate and the qualities of the soil. Here is an immense
field on which a mass of experience is to be gathered and a mass of experiments to be made. What the State has done until now in this line
is meager. What with the small means that it applies to these purposes, and what with the limitations imposed upon it by the large landlords, who even if the State were willing, would check it, little or nothing has been done. The State could do nothing on this field without
greatly encroaching upon private property. Seeing, however, that its
very existence is conditioned upon the safe-keeping and "sacredness" of
private property, the large landlords are vital to it, and it is stripped of
the power, even if it otherwise had the will, to move in that direction.
Socialist society will have the task of undertaking vast improvements
of the soil,—raising woods here, and dismantling others yonder, draining
and irrigating, mixing and changing of soil, planting, etc., in order to
raise the land to the highest point of productivity that it is capable of.

An important question, connected with the improvement of the land,
is the contrivance of an ample and systematically planned network of
rivers and canals, conducted upon scientific principles. The question of
"cheaper" transportation on the waterways—a question of such gravity
to modern society—loses all importance in Socialist society, seeing that
the conceptions "cheap" and "dear" are unknown to it. On the other
hand, waterways, as comfortable means of transportation, that
can, moreover, be utilized with but slight expenditure of strength and
matter, deserve attention. Moreover river and canal systems play important *roles* in the matter of climate, draining and irrigation, and the
supply of fertilizers and other materials needed in the improvement of
agricultural land.

Experience teaches that poorly-watered regions suffer more severely
from cold winters and hot summers than well-watered lands, whence

coast regions are exempt from the extremes of temperature, or rarely undergo them. Extremes of temperature are favorable neither to plants nor man. An extensive system of canalization, in connection with the proper forestry regulations, would unquestionably exercise beneficent influences. Such a system of canalization, along with the building of large reservoirs, that will collect the water in cases of freshets through thaws or heavy rainfalls, would be of great usefulness. Freshets and their devastating results would be impossible. Wide expanses of water, together with their proportional evaporations, would also, in all probability, bring about a more regular rain-fall. Finally such institutions would facilitate the erection of works for an extensive system of irrigation whenever needed.

Large tracts of land, until now wholly barren or almost so, could be transformed into fertile regions by means of artificial irrigation. Where now sheep can barely graze, and at best consumptive-looking pine trees raise their thin arms heavenward, rich crops could grow and a dense population find ample nutriment. It is merely a question of labor whether the vast sand tracts of the Mark, the "holy dust-box of the German Empire," shall be turned into an Eden. The fact was pointed out in an address delivered in the spring of 1894 on the occasion of the agricultural exposition in Berlin.[20] The requisite improvements, canals, provisions for irrigation, mixing of soil, etc., are matters, however, that can be undertaken neither by small nor the large landlords of the Mark. Hence those vast tracts, lying at the very gates of the capital of the Empire, remain in a state of such backward cultivation that it will seem incredible to future generations. Again, a proper canalization would, by draining, reclaim for cultivation vast swamps and marshes in North as well as South Germany. These waterways could be furthermore utilized in raising fish; they could thus be vast sources of food; in neighborhoods where there are no rivers, they would furnish opportunity for commodious bath-houses.

Let a few examples illustrate the effectiveness of irrigation. In the neighborhood of Weissensfels, 7½ hectares of well-watered meadows produced 480 cwts. of after-grass; 5 contiguous hectares of meadow land of the same quality, but not watered, yielded only 32 cwts. The former had, accordingly, a crop ten times as large as the latter. Near Reisa in Saxony, the irrigation of 65 acres of meadow lands raised their revenue from 5,850 marks to 11,100 marks. The expensive outlays paid. Besides the Mark there are in Germany other vast tracts, whose soil,

---

[20] "The employment of water in the cultivation of fruit as well as of vegetables is highly desirable; water associations with these ends in view could turn with us also deserts into paradises." Official report on the Chicago Exposition of 1893, rendered by the Imperial Commissioner, Berlin, 1894.

consisting mainly of sand, yields but poor returns, even when the summer is wet. Crossed and irrigated by canals, and their soil improved,
these lands would within a short time yield five and ten times as much.
There are examples in Spain of the yield of well-irrigated lands exceed-
ing thirty-seven fold that of others that are not irrigated. Let there
but be water, and increased volumes of food are conjured into existence.

Where are the private individuals, where the States, able to operate
upon the requisite scale? When, after long decades of bitter experience,
the State finally yields to the stormy demands of a population that has
suffered from all manner of calamities, and only after millions of values
have been destroyed, how slow, with what circumspection, how cautious
does it proceed! It is so easy to do too much, and the State might by
its precipitancy lose the means with which to build some new barracks
for the accommodation of a few regiments. Then also, if one is helped
"too much," others come along, and also want help. "Man, help yourself and God will help you," thus runs the bourgeois creed. Each for
himself, none for all. And thus, hardly a year goes by without once,
twice and oftener more or less serious freshets from brooks, rivers or
streams occurring in several provinces and States: vast tracts of fertile
lands are then devastated by the violence of the floods, and others are
covered with sand, stone and all manner of debris; whole orchard planta-
tions, that demanded tens of years for their growth, are uprooted;
houses, bridges, dams are washed away; railroad tracks torn up; cattle,
not infrequently human beings also, are drowned; soil improvements are
carried off; crops ruined. Vast tracts, exposed to frequent inundations,
are cultivated but slightly, lest the loss be double.

On the other hand, unskilful corrections of the channels of large rivers
and streams,—undertaken in one-sided interests, to which the State ever
yields readily in the service of "trade and transportation"—increase the
dangers of freshets. Extensive cutting down of forests, especially on
highlands and for private profit, adds more grist to the flood mill. The
marked deterioration of the climate and decreased productivity of the
soil, noticeable in the provinces of Prussia, Pomerania, the Steuermark,
Italy, France, Spain, etc., is imputed to this vandalic devastation of the
woods, done in the interest of private parties.

Frequent freshets are the consequence of the dismantling of mountain
woodlands. The inundations of the Rhine, the Oder and the Vistula are
ascribed mainly to the devastation of the woods in Switzerland, Galicia
and Poland; and likewise in Italy with regard to the Po. Due to the
baring of the Carnian Alps, the climate of Triest and Venice has materially deteriorated. Madeira, a large part of Spain, vast and once
luxurious fields of Asia Minor have in a great measure forfeited their
fertility through the same causes.

It goes without saying that Socialist society will not be able to accomplish all these great tasks out-of-hand. But it can and will undertake them, with all possible promptness and with all the powers at its command, seeing that its sole mission is to solve problems of civilization and to tolerate no hindrance. Thus it will in the course of time solve problems and accomplish feats that modern society can give no thought to, and the very thought of which gives it the vertigo.

The cultivation of the soil will, accordingly, be mightily improved in Socialist society, through these and similar measures. But other considerations, looking to the proper exploitation of the soil, are added to these. To-day, many square miles are planted with potatoes, which are to be applied mainly to the distilling of brandy, an article consumed almost exclusively by the poor classes of the population. Liquor is the only stimulant and "care-dispeller" that they are able to procure. The population of Socialist society needs none of that, hence the raising of potatoes and corn for that purpose, together with the labor therein expended, are set free for the production of healthy food.[21] The speculative purposes that our most fertile fields are put to in the matter of the sugar beet for the exportation of sugar, has been pointed out in a previous chapter. About 400,000 hectares of the best wheat fields are yearly devoted to the cultivation of sugar beet, in order to supply England, the United States and Northern Europe with sugar. The countries whose climate favors the growth of sugar cane succumb to this competition. Furthermore, our system of a standing army, the disintegration of production, the disintegration of the means of transportation and communication, the disintegration of agriculture, etc.,—all these demand hundreds of thousands of horses, with the corresponding fields to feed them and to raise colts. The completely transformed social and political conditions frees the bulk of the lands that are now given up to these various purposes; and again large areas and rich labor-power are reclaimed for purposes of civilization. Latterly, extensixe fields, covering many square kilometers, have been withdrawn from cultivation, being needed for the manoeuvering and exercising of army corps in the new

[21] This prospect seems nearer realization and in a quite different manner than the most far-sighted could have imagined. The discovery of acetylene gas is the point of departure for a long line of products of organic chemistry, that, with proper treatment, can be drawn from it. Among the articles of enjoyment, that may be expected to be gained first of all on this path, is alcohol, the production of which promises to be the easiest of all and very cheap, and is expected in but few years. If this succeeds, a large part of the agriculture of the East Elbian district, which depends upon the production of alcohol, will be put in jeopardy. The circumstance will bring on a revolution in the respective agricultural interests that will play mightily into the hands of Socialism. Evidently, what Werner, Siemens and Berthelot held out, is approaching reality.

methods of warfare and long distance firearms. All this falls away.

The vast field of agriculture, forestry and irrigation has become the subject of an extensive scientific literature. No special branch has been left untouched: irrigation and drainage, forestry, the cultivation of cereals, of leguminous and tuberous plants, of vegetables, of fruit trees, of berries, of flowers and ornamental plants; fodder for cattle raising; meadows; rational methods of breeding cattle, fish and poultry and bees, and the utilization of their excrements; utilization of manure and refuse in agriculture and manufacture; chemical examinations of seeds and of the soil, to ascertain its fitness for this or that crop; investigations in th rotations of crops and in agricultural machinery and implements; the profitable construction of agricultural buildings of all nature; the weather;—all have been drawn within the circle of scientific treatment. Hardly a day goes by without some new discovery, some new experience being made towards improving and ennobling one or other of these several branches. With the work of J. v. Liebig, the cultivation of the soil has become a science, indeed, one of the foremost and most important of all, a science that since then has attained a vastness and significance unique in the domain of activity in material production. And yet, if we compare the fullness of the progress made in this direction with the actual conditions prevailing in agriculture to-day, *it must be admitted that, until now, only a small fraction of the private owners have been able to turn the progress to advantage,* and among these there naturally is none who did not proceed from the view point of his own private interests, acted accordingly, kept only that in mind, and gave no thought to the public weal. The large majority of our farmers and gardeners, we may say 98 per cent. of them, are in no wise in condition to utilize all the advances made and advantages that are possible: they lack either the means or the knowledge thereto, if not both: as to the others, they simply do as they please. Socialist society finds herein a theoretically and practically well prepared field of activity. It need but to fall to and organize in order to attain wonderful results.

The highest possible concentration of productions affords, of itself, mighty advantages. Hedges, making boundary lines, wagon roads and footpaths between the broken-up holdings are removed, and yield some more available soil. The application of machinery is possible only on large fields: agricultural machinery of fullest development, backed by chemistry and physics could to-day transform unprofitable lands, of which there are not a few, into fertile ones. The application of accumulated electric power to agricultural machinery—plows, harrows, rollers, sowers, mowers, threshers, seed-assorters, chaff-cutters, etc.—is only a question of time. Likewise will the day come when electricity will move from the fields the wagons laden with the crops: draught cattle can be spared. A scientific system of fertilizing the fields, hand in hand with thorough management, irrigation and draining will materially increase the productivity of the land. A careful selection of seeds, proper protection against weeds—in itself a head much sinned against to-day—sends up the yield still higher.

According to Ruhland, a successful war upon cereal diseases would of itself suffice to render superfluous the present importation of grain into Germany.[22] Seeding, planting and rotation of crops, being conducted with the sole end in view of raising the largest possible volume of food, the object is then obtainable.

What may be possible even under present conditions is shown by the management of the Schnistenberg farm in the Rhenish Palatinate. In 1884 the same fell into the hand of a new tenant, who, in the course of eight years, raised three or four times as much as his predecessor.[23] The said property is situated 320 meters above the level of the sea, 286 acres in size, of which 18 are meadows, and has generally unfavorable soil, 30 acres being sandy, 60 stony, 55 sand loam and 123 hard loam. The new method of cultivation had astonishing results. The crops rose from year to year. The increase during the period of 1884-1892 was as follows per acre:

Product.	1884.	1892.
Rye	7.75 cwts.	19.50 cwts.
Wheat	3.50 "	15.30 "
Barley	12.00 "	18.85 "
Oats	7.00 "	18.85 "

The neighboring community of Kiegsfeld, the witness of this marvelous development, followed the example and reached similar results on its own ground. The yield per acre was on an average this:

Product.	1884.	1892.
Wheat	10 to 12 cwts.	13 to 18 cwts.
Rye	12 to 15 "	15 to 20 "
Oats	7 to 9 "	14 to 22 and even 24
Barley	9 to 11 "	18 to 22 cwts.

Such results are eloquent enough.

The cultivation of fruits, berries and garden will reach a development hardly thought possible. How unpardonably is being sinned at present in these respects, a look at our orchards will show. They are generally marked by a total absence of proper care. This is true of the

[22] Dr. G. Ruhland, "Die Grundprinzipien aktueller Agrarpolitik."
[23] A petition by Julius Zuns, which finally was not sent to the Reichstag, on the subject of an agrarian investigation.

cultivation of fruit trees even in countries that have a reputation for the excellence of these; Wurtemberg, for instance. The concentration of stables, depots for implements and manure and methods of feeding— towards which wonderful progress has been made, but which can to-day be applied only slightly—will, when generally introduced, materially increase the returns in raising cattle, and thereby facilitate the procurement of manure. Machinery and implements of all sorts will be there in abundance, very differently from the experience of ninety-nine one hundredths of our modern farmers. Animal products, such as milk, eggs, meat, honey, hair, wool, will be obtained and utilized scientifically. The improvements and advantages in the dairy industry reached by the large dairy associations is known to all experts, and ever new inventions and improvements are daily made. Many are the branches of agriculture in which the same and even better can be done. The preparation of the fields and the gathering of the crops are then attended to by large bodies of men, under skilful use of the weather, such as is to-day impossible. Large drying houses and sheds allow crops being gathered even in unfavorable weather, and save losses that are to-day unavoidable, and which, according to v. d. Goltz, often are so severe that, during a particularly rainy year, from eight to nine million marks worth of crops were ruined in Mecklenburg, and from twelve to fifteen in the district of Koenigsberg.

Through the skilful application of artificial heat and moisture on a large scale in structures protected from bad weather, the raising of vegetables and all manner of fruit is possible at all seasons in large quantities. The flower stores of our large cities have in mid-winter floral exhibitions that vie with those of the summer. One of the most remarkable advances made in the artificial raising of fruit is exemplified by the artificial vineyard of Garden-Director Haupt in Brieg, Silesia, which has found a number of imitators, and was itself preceded long before by a number of others in other countries, England among them. The arrangements and the results obtained in this vineyard were so enticingly described in the "Vossische Zeitung" of September 27, 1890, that we have reproduced the account in extracts:

"The glass-house is situated upon an approximately square field of 500 square meters, i. e., one-fifth of an acre. It is 4.5 to 5 meters high, and its walls face north, south, east and west. Twelve rows of double fruit walls run inside due north and south. They are 1.8 meters apart from each other and serve at the same time as supports to the flat roof. In a bed 1.25 meters deep, resting on a bank of earth 25 centimeters strong and which contains a net of drain and ventilation pipes,—a bed 'whose hard ground is rendered loose, permeable and fruitful through chalk, rubbish, sand, manure in a state of decomposition, bonedust and potash'—Herr Haupt planted against the walls three hundred and sixty grape vines of the kind which yields the noblest grape juice in the Rhinegau:—white and red Reissling and Tramine, white and blue Moscatelle and Burgundy.

"The ventilation of the place is effected by means of large fans, twenty meters long, attached to the roof, besides several openings on the side-walls. The fans can be opened and shut by means of a lever, fastened on the roof provided with a spindle and winch, and they can be made safe against all weather. For the watering of the vines 26 sprinklers are used, which are fastened to rubber pipes 1.25 meters long, and that hang down from a water tank. Herr Haupt introduced, however, another and ingenuous contrivance for quickly and thoroughly watering his 'wine-hall' and his 'vineyard', to wit, an artificial rain producer. On high, under the roof, lie four long copper tubes, perforated at distances of one-half meter. The streams of water that spout upward through these openings strike small round sieves made of window gauze and, filtered through these, are scattered in fine spray. To thoroughly water the vines by means of the rubber pipes requires several hours. But only one faucet needs to be turned by this second contrivance and a gentle refreshing rain trickles down over the whole place upon the grape vines, the beds and the granite flags of the walks. The temperature can be raised from 8 to 10 degrees R. above the outside air without any artificial contrivance, and simply through the natural qualities of the glass-house. In order to protect the vines from that dangerous and destructive foe, the vine louse, should it show itself, it is enough to close the drain and open all the water pipes. The inundation of the vines, thus achieved, the enemy can not withstand. The glass roof and walls protect the vineyard from storms, cold, frost and superfluous rain; in cases of hail, a fine wire-netting is spread over the same; against drought the artificial rain system affords all the protection needed. The vine-dresser of such a vineyard is his own weather-maker, and he can laugh at all the dangers from the incalculable whims and caprices of indifferent and cruel Nature,—dangers that ever threaten with ruin the fruit of the vine cultivator.

"What Herr Haupt expected happened. The vines thrived remarkably under the uniformly warm climate. The grapes ripened to their fullest, and as early as the fall of 1885 they yielded a juice not inferior to that generally obtained in the Rhinegau in point of richness of sugar and slightness of sourness. The grapes thrived equally the next year and even during the unfavorable year of 1887. On this space, when the vines have reached their full height of 5 meters, and are loaded with their burden of swollen grapes, 20 hectoliters of wine can be produced yearly, and the cost of a bottle of noble wine will not exceed 40 pennies.

"There is no reason imaginable why this process should not be conducted upon a large scale like any other industry. Glass-houses of the nature of this one on one-fifth of an acre can be undoubtedly raised upon a whole acre with equal facilities of ventilation, watering, draining and rain-making. Vegetation will start there several weeks sooner than in the open, and the vine-shoots remain safe from May frosts, rain and cold while they blossom; from drought during the growth of the grapes; from pilfering birds and grape thieves and from dampness while they ripen; finally from the vine-louse during the whole year and can hang safely deep into November and December. In his address, held in 1888 to the Society for the Promotion of Horticulture, and from which I have taken many a technical expression in this description of the 'Vineyard', the inventor and founder of the same closed his words with this alluring perspective of the future: 'Seeing that this vine culture can be carried on all over Germany, especially on otherwise barren, sandy or stony ground, such as, for instance, the worst of the Mark, that can be made arable and watered, it follows that the great interests in the cultivation of the soil receive fresh vigor from 'vineyards under glass'. I would like to call this industry 'the vineyard of the future.'

"Just as Herr Haupt has furnished the practical proof that on this path an abundance of fine and healthy grapes can be drawn from the vine, he has also proved by his own pressing of the same what excellent wine they can yield. More thorough, more experienced, better experts and tried wine-drinkers and connoisseurs than myself have, after a severe test, bestowed enthusiastic praise upon the Riessling of the vintage of '88, upon the Tramine and Moscatelle of the vintage of '89, and upon the Burgundy of the vintage of '88, pressed from the grapes of this 'vineyard'. It should also be mentioned that this 'vineyard' also affords sufficient space for the cultivation of other side and twin plants. Herr Haupt raises between every two vines one rose bush, that blossoms richly in April and May; against the east and west walls he raises peaches, whose beauty of blossom must impart in April an appearance of truly fairy charm to this wine palace."

The enthusiasm with which the reporter describes this artificial 'vineyard' in a serious paper testifies to the deep impression made upon him by this extraordinary artificial cultivation. There is nothing to prevent similar establishments, on a much more stupendous scale and for other branches of vegetation. The luxury of a double crop is obtainable in many agricultural products. To-day all such undertakings are a question of money, and their products are accessible only to the privileged classes. A Socialist society knows no other question than that of sufficient labor-power. If that is in existence, the work is done in the interest of all.

Another new invention on the field of food is that of Dr. Johann Hundhausen of Hamm in Westphalia, who succeeded in extracting the albumen of wheat—the secret of whose utilization in the legume was not yet known—in the shape of a thoroughly nutritive flour. This is a far-reaching invention. It is now possible to render the albumen of plants useful in substantial form for human food.

The inventor erected a large factory which produces vegetal albumen or aleurone meal from 80 to 83 per cent. of albumen, and a second quality of about 50 per cent. That the so-called aleurone meal represents a very concentrated albuminous food appears from the following comparison with our best elements of nourishment:

	Water	Albumen	Fat	Carbon-hydrate	Celulose	Salt
Aleurone meal	8.83	82.67	0.27	7.01	0.45	0.78
Hen's eggs	73.67	12.55	12.11	0.55	0.55	1.12
Beef	55.42	17.19	26.58	....	....	1.08

Aleurone meal is not only eaten directly, it is also used as a condiment in all sorts of bakery products, as well as soups and vegetables. Aleurone meal substitutes in a high degree meat preserves in point of nutrition; moreover, it is by far the cheapest albumen obtainable to-day. One kilogram of albumen costs:

In aleurone meal...................... 1.45 marks
In white bread or white flour......... 4 to 4.5 "
In hen's eggs, according to the season... 8 to 16 "
In beef ....12 to 13 "

Beef, accordingly, is about eight times dearer, as albuminous food, than aleurone meal; eggs five times as dear; white bread or common white flour about three times as dear. Aleurone meal also has the advantage that, with the addition of about one-eighth of the weight of a potato, it not only furnishes a considerable quantity of albumen to the body, but produces a complete digestion of the starch contained in the potato. Dogs, that have a nose for albumen, eat aleurone meal with the same avidity as meat, even if they otherwise refuse bread, and they are then better able to stand hardships.

Aleurone meal, as a dry vegetal albumen, is of great use as food on ships, in fortresses and in military hospitals during war. It renders large supplies of meat unnecessary. At present aleurone meal is a side product in starch factories. Within short, starch will become a side product of aleurone meal. A further result will be that the cultivation of cereals will crowd out that of potatoes and other less productive food plants; the volume of nutrition of a given field of wheat or rye is tripled or quadrupled at one stroke.

Dr. Rudolf Meyer of Vienna, whose attention was called by us to the aleurone meal says[24] that he furnished himself with a quantity of it and had it examined on June 19, 1893, by the bureau of experiments of the Board of Soil Cultivation of the Kingdom of Bohemia. The examination fully confirmed our statements. For further details Meyer's work should be read. Meyer also calls attention to a discovery made by Otto Redemann of Bockenheim near Frankfort-on-the-Main. After granulating the peanut and removing its oil, he analyzed its component elements of nutrition. The analysis showed 47 per cent. of albumen, 19 of fat and 19 of starch—altogether 2,135 units of nutritious matter in one kilo. According to this analysis the peanut is one of the most nutrious vegetal products. The pharmacist Rud. Simpson of Mohrungen discovered a process by which to remove the bitterness from the lupine, which, as may be known, thrives best on sandy soil, and is used both as fodder and as a fertilizer; and he then produced from it a meal, which, according to expert authority, baked as bread tastes very good, is solid, is said to be more nutritious than rye-bread, and, besides all that, much cheaper.

Even under present conditions a regular revolution is plowing its way in the matter of human food. *The utilization of all these discoveries is, however, slow, for the reason that mighty classes—the farmer element together with its social and political props—have the liveliest interest in suppressing them.* To our agrarians, a good crop is to-day a horror—although the same is prayed for in all the churches—because it lowers prices. Consequently, they are no wise anxious for a double and threefold nutritive power of their cereals; it would likewise tend to lower prices. Present society is everywhere at fisticuffs with its own development.

The preservation of the soil in a state of fertility depends primarily upon fertilization. The obtaining of fertilizers is, accordingly, for future society also one of the principal tasks.[25] Manure is to the soil what food is to man, and just as every kind of food is not equally nour-

---

[24] Dr. Rudolf Meyer, "Der Kapitalismus fin de siecle."

[25] "There is a prescription for securing the fertility of the fields and perpetual repetition of their produce. If this prescription be consistently carried out it will prove more remunerative than any which has ever been applied in agriculture. It is this: Let every farmer, like the Chinese coolie, who carries a sack of corn or a hundred weight of rape, or carrots or potatoes, etc., to town, bring back with him as much if possible or more of the ingredients of his field products as he took with him, and restore it to the field whence it came. He must not despise a potato paring or a straw, but re-

ishing to man, neither is every kind of manure of equal benefit to the soil. The soil must receive back exactly the same chemical substances that it gave up through a crop; and the chemical substances especially needed by a certain vegetal must be given to the soil in larger quantities. Hence the study of chemistry and its practical application will experience a development unknown to-day.

Animal and human excrements are particularly rich in the chemical elements that are fittest for the reproduction of human food. Hence the endeavor must be to secure the same in the fullest quantity and cause its proper distribution. On this head too modern society sins grievously. Cities and industrial centers, that receive large masses of foodstuffs, return to the soil but a slight part of their valuable offal.[26] The consequence is that the fields, situated at great distances from the cities and industrial centers, and which yearly send their products to the same, suffer greatly from a dearth of manure; the offal that these farms themselves yield is often not enough, because the men and beasts who live on them consume but a small part of the product. Thus frequently a soil-vandalism is practiced, that cripples the land and decreases the crops. All countries that export agricultural products mainly, but receive no manure back, inevitably go to ruin through the gradual impoverishment of the soil. This is the case with Hungary, Russia, the Danubian Principalities, North America, etc. Artificial fertilizers, guano in particular, indeed substitute the offal of men and beasts; but many farmers can not obtain the same in sufficient quan-

member that one of his potatoes still needs a skin, and one of his ears of corn a stalk. The expense for this importation is slight, the outlay secure; a savings bank is not securer, and no investment brings in a higher rate of interest. The returns of his fields will be doubled in ten years: he will produce more corn, more meat and more cheese without expending more time or labor, and he will not be driven by constant anxiety to seek for new and unknown means, which do not exist, to make his ground fertile in another manner. . . Old bones, soot, ashes, whether washed out or not, and blood of animals and refuse of all kinds ought to be collected in storehouses, and prepared for distribution. . . Governments and town police should take precautions for preventing the loss of these materials by a suitable arrangement of drains and closets."—Liebig's "Chemical Letters."

[26] "Every coolie (in China) who carries his produce to market in the morning, brings home two buckets full of manure on a bamboo rod in the evening. The appreciation of manure goes so far that every one knows how much a man secretes in a day, a month and a year, and the Chinaman considers it more than rude if his guest leaves his house carrying with him a benefit to which his host thinks himself justly entitled as a return for his hospitality. Every substance derived from plants or animals is carefully collected and used as manure by the Chinese. . . To complete the idea of the importance attached to animal refuse, it will suffice to mention the fact that the barbers carefully collect and trade with the hairs cut from the heads and beards of the hundred millions of customers whom they daily shave. The Chinese are acquainted with the use of gypsum and chalk, and it not infrequently occurs that they renew the plaster in their kitchens merely for the purpose of using the old plaster as manure."—Liebig's "Chemical Letters."

tity; it is too dear; at any rate, it is an inversion of nature to import manure from great distances, while it is allowed to go to waste nearby.

Several years since has the Thomas-slag been recognized as an eminently fit manure for certain soils. The manufacturers, however, who grind the Thomas-slag into flour and carry it to market, have built a ring, and, to the injury of the farming interests who make bitter complaints on that score, they keep the prices high. Thus every progress is crippled by greed in bourgeois society. Another and at present inexhaustable source of fertilizers is offered by the deposits of potash in the province of Saxony and contiguous regions. The Prussian State owns a number of potash works and it also made the attempt to monopolize the industry, to the end of raising the largest possible revenues for the Treasury.

If the opinion of Julius Hensel on the subject of fertilizers proves correct, it will mean a revolution in the theory of fertilization, and a complete saving of the expenses now made for the importation of fertilizers, amounting for guano and Chile saltpeter to 80 to 100 million marks a year.[27] Hensel makes the emphatic claim, and produces numerous proofs of the correctness of his views, that the mineral of our mountains contain an inexhaustible supply of the best fertilizing stuffs. Granite, porphory, basalt, broken and ground up, spread upon the fields or vineyards and furnished with a sufficiency of water, furnished a fertilizer that excelled all others, even animal and human refuse.[28] These minerals, he claims, contain all the elements for the cultivation of plants: potash, chalk, magnesia, phosphoric, sulphuric and silicic acids, and also hydrochlorides. According to Hensel, the Sudeton, Riesen, Erz, Tichtel, Hartz, Rhone, Vogel, Taunus, Eisel and Weser mountains, the woods of Thuringen, Spessart and Oden had an inexhaustible supply of fertilizers. It will be literally possible to "make bread out of stones." The dust and dirt of our highways also are, according to Hensel, inexhaustible sources of the same blessing. In this matter we are laymen and can not test the correctness of Hensel's theories; a part of them, however, sound most plausible. Hensel charges the manufacturers of and dealers in artificial fertilizers with hostility to his discovery and with systematic opposition, because they would suffer great loss.

According to Heider, a healthy adult secretes on an average 48.8 kilograms of solid and 438 of liquid matter a year. Estimated by the present standard of the prices of manure, and if utilized without loss by evaporation, etc., this offal represents a money value of 11.8 marks.

[27] Karl Schober, Address delivered on the agricultural, municipal and national economic significance of city refuse; Berlin, 1877.
[28] "Life, Its Elements and the Means of Its Conservation."

Calculating the population of Germany to be 50,000,000 in round figures, and estimating the average value of the human offal at 8 marks, the sum of 400,000,000 marks is obtained, which now is almost totally lost to agriculture, owing to the present imperfect methods for utilizing it. The great difficulty in the way of a full utilization of these stuffs lies in the establishment of proper and extensive provisions for their collection, and in the cost of transportation. Relatively, this cost is now higher than the importation of guano from far-away transmarine deposits, which, however, decline in mass in the measure that the demand increases. Every living being, however, casts off regularly an annual supply of manure about enough for a field that yields food for one person. The enormous loss is obvious. A large portion of the city excrement runs out into our rivers and streams, and pollutes them. Likewise is the refuse from kitchens and factories, also serviceable as manure, recklessly squandered.

Future society will find means and ways to stop this waste. What is done to-day in this direction is mere patchwork, and utterly inadequate. As an illustration of what could be done to-day, may be cited the canalization and the laying out of vast fields in the capital of the Empire, on whose value, however, experts are of divided opinion. Socialist society will solve the question more easily, due, in a great measure, to the fact that *large cities will gradually cease to exist, and population will decentralize.*

No one will regard our modern rise of metropoles as a healthy phenomenon. The modern system of manufacture and production in general, steadily draws large masses of the population to the large cities.[29] There is the seat of manufacture and commerce; there the avenues of communication converge; there the owners of large wealth have their headquarters, the central authorities, the military staffs, the higher tribunals. There large institutions rear their heads—the academies of

[29] According to the census of 1890, Germany had 26 large cities of over 100,000 inhabitants each. In 1871 it had only 8 of them. In 1871, Berlin had, in round figures, 826,000 inhabitants; in 1890 it had 1,578,794—it had almost doubled. A number of these large cities were compelled to take within their municipalities the contiguous industrial towns, that in themselves had populations large enough for cities. Through the process, the population of the former rose immediately. Thus, within the period of 1885 to 1890, Leipsic rose from 170,000 to 353,000; Cologne from 161,000 to 282,000; Madgeburg from 114,000 to 201,000; Munich from 270,000 to 345,000 inhabitants, etc. At the same time, most of the other cities that incorporated no contiguous towns increased considerably during that period. Breslau grew from 299,000 to 335,000; Dresden from 246,000 to 276,000; Frankfurt-on-Main from 154,000 to 180,000; Hanover from 140,000 to 163,000; Dusseldorf from 115,000 to 146,000; Nuerenberg from 115,000 to 142,000; Chemnitz from 111,000 to 139,000 inhabitants. Similar growths were also registered by many middle-sized cities of 50,000 to 100,000 inhabitants.

[In the United States, the concentration of population in large cities has

art, large pleasure resorts, exhibitions, museums, theaters, concert halls, etc. Hundreds are drawn thither by their professions, thousands by pleasure, and many more thousands by the hope of easier work and an agreeable life.

But, speaking figuratively, the rise of metropolitan cities makes the impression of a person whose girth gains steadily in size, while his legs as steadily become thinner, and finally will be unable to carry the burden. All around, in the immediate vicinity of the cities, the villages also assume a city aspect, in which the proletariat is heaped up in large masses. The municipalities, generally out of funds, are forcel to lay on taxes to the utmost, and still remain unable to meet the demand made upon them. When finally they have grown up to the large city and it up to them, they rush into and are absorbed by it, as happens with planets that have swung too close to the sun. But the fact does not improve the conditions of life. On the contrary, they grow worse through the crowding of people in already overcrowded spaces. These gatherings of masses—inevitable under modern development, and, to a certain extent, the raisers of revolutionary centers,—will have fulfilled their mission in Socialist society. Their gradual dissolution then becomes necessary: *the current will then run the other way: population will migrate from the cities to the country: it will there raise new municipalities corresponding with the altered conditions, and they will join their industrial with their agricultural activities.*

So soon as—due to the complete remodeling and equipment of the means of communication and transportation, and of the productive establishments, etc., etc.—the city populations will be enabled to transfer to the country all their acquired habits of culture, to find there their museums, theaters, concert halls, reading rooms, libraries, etc.—just so soon will the migration thither set in. Life will then enjoy all the comforts of large cities, without their disadvantages. The population will be housed more comfortably and sanitarily. The rural population will join in manufacturing, the manufacturing population in agricultural pursuits,—a change of occupation enjoyed to-day by but few, and then often under conditions of excessive exertion.

been marked. In 1790 only 3.4 per cent. of the total population lived in cities. The proportion of urban to the total population then grew from census year to census year (decade to decade) as follows: 4.0 in 1800; 4.9 in 1810; 4.9 in 1820; 6.7 in 1830; 8.5 in 1840; 12.5 in 1850; 16.1 in 1860; 20.9 in 1870; 22.6 in 1880; 29.2 in 1890; and 33.1 in 1900. According to the census of 1900 there live 14,208,347 of the population in cities of at least 100,000 inhabitants; 5,549,271 in cities of 25,000 to 100,000 inhabitants; 5,286,375 in cities of 8,000 to 25,000 inhabitants; 3,380,193 in cities of 4,000 to 8,000 inhabitants; and 2,214,136 in cities of 2,500 to 4,000 inhabitants. In country districts there live 45,573,846 of a total population of 76,212,168, including Alaska and Hawaii,—THE TRANSLATOR.]

As on all other fields, bourgeois society is promoting this development also: every year new industrial undertakings are transferred to the country. The unfavorable conditions of large cities—high rents and high wages—drive many employers to this migration. At the same time, the large landlords are steadily becoming industrialists—manufacturers of sugar, distillers of liquor, beer brewers, manufacturers of cement, earthen wares, tiles, woodwork, paper goods, etc. In the new social order offal of all sorts will then be easily furnished to agriculture, especially through the concentration of production and the public kitchens. Each community will, in a way, constitute a zone of culture; it will, to a large extent, itself raise its necessaries of life. Horticulture, perhaps the most agreeable of all practical occupations, will then reach fullest bloom. The cultivation of vegetables, fruit trees and bushes of all nature, ornamental flowers and shrubs—all offer an inexhaustible field for human activity in a field, moreover, whose nature excludes machinery almost wholly.

Thanks to the decentralization of the population, the existing contrast and antagonism between the country and the city will also vanish.
The peasant, this Helot of modern times, hitherto cut off from all cultural development through his isolation in the country, now becomes a free being because he has fully become a limb of civilization.[30] The wish, once expressed by Prince Bismarck, that he might see the large cities destroyed, will be verified, but in a sense wholly different from that which he had in mind.[31]

If the preceding arguments are rapidly passed in review, it will be seen that, with the abolition of private property in the means of production and their conversion into social property, the mass evils, that modern society reveals at every turn and which grow ever greater and

[30] Prof. Adolf Wagner says in his work "Lehrbuch der politischen Oekonomie von Rau": "Small private holdings in land constitute an economic basis, that can be substituted by no other institution for a most important part of the population—an independent, self-sustaining peasantry, together with its peculiar socio-political position and function." Where, for the sake of his conservative friends, the author does not enthuse *a tout prix* for the small farmer, he is bound to regard this class as one of the poorest. Under existing circumstances, the small farmer is downright inaccessible to higher culture: he toils at hard labor from early dawn till late, and lives often worse than a dog. Meat, butter, eggs, milk, which he produces, he does not enjoy: he produces them for others: under present circumstances he can not raise himself into better conditions: he thus becomes an element that clogs civilization. He who loves retrogression, seeing he finds his account therein, may also find satisfaction in the continuance of such a social stratum. Human progress demands its disappearance.

[31] At the Erfurt "Union Parliament" of 1850, Prince Bismarck thundered against the large cities as "the hot-beds of revolution," that should be razed with the ground. He was quite right: capitalist society produces its own "grave-diggers" in the modern proletariat.

more intolerable under its sway, will gradually disappear. The over-lordship of one class and its representatives ceases. Society applies its forces planfully and controls itself. As, with the abolition of the wage system the ground will be taken from under the exploitation of man by man, likewise will it be taken from under swindle and cheating—the adulteration of food, the stock exchange, etc.,—with the abolition of private capitalism. The halls in the Temples of Mammon will stand vacant; national bonds of indebtedness, stocks, pawn-tickets, mortgages, deeds, etc., will have become so much waste paper. The words of Schiller: "Let our book of indebtedness be annihilated, and the whole world reconciled" will have become reality, and the Biblical maxim: "In the sweat of thy brow shalt thou eat bread" will now come into force for the heroes of the stock exchange and the drones of capitalism as well. Yet the labor that, as equal members of society they will have to perform, will not oppress them: their bodily health will be materially improved. The worry of property—said to be, judging from the pathetic assurances of our employers and capitalists in general, harder to bear than the uncertain and needy lot of the workingman—will be forever removed from those gentlemen. The excitements of speculation, that breed so many diseases of the heart and bring on so many strokes of apoplexy among our exchange jobbers, and that render them nervous wrecks, will all be saved to them. A life free from mental worry will be their lot and that of our descendents; and in the end they will gladly accommodate themselves thereto.

With the abolition of private property and of class antagonism, the State also gradually vanishes away;—it vanishes without being missed.

"By converting the large majority of the population more and more into proletarians, the capitalist mode of production creates the power, that, under penalty of its own destruction, is forced to accomplish this revolution. By urging more and more the conversion of the large, al-ready socialized means of production into State property, it points the path for the accomplishment of this revolution. . . . The State was the official representative of the whole society; it was the constitution of the latter into a visible body; but it was so only in so far as it was the State of that class which itself, at its time, represented the whole society; in antiquity, the State of slave-holding citizens; in the middle ages, the State of the feudal nobility; in our own days, the State of the capitalist class. By at last becoming actually the representative of the whole social body, it renders itself superfluous. As soon as there is no longer any social class to be kept down; as soon as, together with class rule and the individual struggle for life, founded in the pre-vious anarchy of production, the conflicts and excesses that issued therefrom have been removed, there is nothing more to be repressed, and the State or Government. as a special power of repression, is no longer necessary. The first act, wherein the State appears as the real representative of the whole body social—the seizure of the means of production in the name of society—is also its last independent act as State. The interference of the State in social relations becomes superfluous in one domain after another, and falls of itself into desuetude. The place of a government over persons is taken by the administration of things and the conduct of the processes of production. The State is not "abolished" —*it dies out!*[32]

Along with the State, die out its representatives—cabinet ministers, parliaments, standing armies, police and constables, courts, district attorneys, prison officials, tariff and tax collectors, in short, the whole political apparatus. Barracks, and such other military structures, palaces of law and of administration, prisons—all will now await better use. Ten thousand laws, decrees and regulations become so much rubbish; they have only historic value. The great and yet so petty parliamentary struggles, with which the men of tongue. imagine they rule and guide the world, are no more, they will have made room for administrative colleges and delegations whose attention will be engaged in the best means of production and distribution, in ascertaining the volume of supplies needed, in introducing and applying effective improvements in art, in architecture, in intercourse, in the process of production, etc. These are all practical matters, visible and tangible, towards which everyone stands objectively, there being no personal interests hostile to society to affect their judgment. None has any interest other than the collectivity, and that interest consists in instituting and providing everything in the best, most effective and most profitable manner.

The hundreds of thousands of former representatives of the State pass over into the various trades, and help with their intelligence and strength to increase the wealth and comforts of society. Henceforth there are known neither political crimes nor common ones. There are no more thieves, seeing that private property has ceased to be in the means of production, and everyone can now satisfy his wants with ease and comfort by work. Tramps and vagabonds likewise cease to be; they are the product of a social system based on private property; the former cease to be with the latter. And murder? Why? None can grow rich at the expense of another. Even murder out of hatred and revenge flows directly or indirectly from the modern social system. Perjury,

[32] Frederick Engels, "The Development of Socialism from Utopia to Science."

false testimony, cheating, thefts of inheritance, fraudulent failures?
There is no private property on and against which to commit these
crimes. Arson? Who is to derive pleasure or satisfaction therefrom,
seeing that society removes from him all sources of hatred? Counter-
feiting? Why, money has become a chimera, love's labor would be lost.
Contempt for religion? Nonsense. It is left to the "omnipotent and good
God" to punish him who should offend Him—provided there be still
controversies on the existence of God.

Thus all the cornerstones of the present "order" become myths.
Parents will tell their children stories on those heads, like legends from
olden days. The narrations of the persecutions, that men with new
ideas are to-day overwhelmed with, will sound to them just as the
stories of the burning of heretics and witches sound to us to-day. The
names of all the great men, who to-day distinguish themselves by their
persecutions of the new ideas, and who are applauded by their narrow-
minded contemporaries, are forgotten and blown over, and they are run
across only by the historian who may happen to dive into the past.
What remarks may escape him, we care not to tell, seeing that, unhappily, we do not yet live in an age where man is free to breathe.

As with the State, so with "Religion."[33] It is not "abolished." God
will not be "dethroned"; religion will not be "torn out of the hearts of
people"; nor will any of the silly charges against the Socialists ma-
terialize. Such mistaken policies the Socialists leave to the Bourgeois
idologists, who resorted to such means in the French Revolution and,
of course, suffered miserable shipwreck. Without any violence whatever, and without any manner of oppression of thought, religion will
gradually vanish.

Religion is the transcendental reflection of the social conditions of
given epochs. In the measure that human development advances and
society is transformed, religion is transformed along with it. It is, as
Marx puts it, a popular striving after the illusory happiness that corre-

---

[33] ["Religion" in English is not quite the same as "Die Religion" in German.
For all their etymology is identical, custom and social institutions have imparted to the German term a meaning, or a shade of a meaning, that it lacks
in English. "Die Religion" is in Germany a State institution; it is part of
the curriculum of colleges; and it is there so utterly creedy, churchianic, and
dogmatic that it is a positive abomination even to the students who mean to
devote themselves to theology. That, however, even in the German language
the word has a varying meaning may be gathered from the epigram of Schiller: "To what religion I belong? To none. Why? Out of religiousness"—literally in German, "out of religion." The reproduction in this
translation of the idea conveyed by the term "Die Religion" presented
its difficulties. As none could be found in English to convey its varying sense, the word "religion" has been preserved throughout as the nearest
equivalent.—THE TRANSLATOR.]

sponds with a social condition which needs such an illusion.[34] The illusion wanes so soon as real happiness is descried, and the possibility of its realization penetrates the masses. The ruling classes endeavor, in their own interest, to prevent this popular conception. Hence they seek to turn religion into a means to preserve their domination. The purpose appears fully in their maxim: "The people must be held to religion." This particular business becomes an official function in a society that rests upon class rule. A caste is formed that assumes this function and that turns the whole acumen of their minds towards preserving, and enlarging such a social structure, seeing that thereby their own power and importance are increased.

Starting in fetishism at low stages of civilization and primitive social conditions, religion becomes polytheism at a higher, and monotheism at a still higher stage. It is not the gods that create men, it is man who turns the gods into God. "In the image of himself (man) he created Him" (God), not the opposite way. Monotheism has also suffered changes. It has dissolved into a pantheism that embraces and permeates the universe—and it volatizes day by day. Natural science reduced to myth the dogma of the creation of the earth in six days; astronomy, mathematics, physics have converted heaven into a structure of air, and the stars, once fastened to the roof of heaven in which angels had their abodes, into fixed stars and planets whose very composition excludes all angelic life.

The ruling class, finding itself threatened in its existence, clings to religion as a prop of all authority, just as every ruling class has done heretofore.[35] The bourgeoisie or capitalist class itself believes in nothing. Itself, at every stage of its development and through the modern science that sprang from none but its own lap, has destroyed all faith in religion and authority. Its faith is only a pretence; and the Church

---

[34] Karl Marx: "Zur Kritik der Hegelschen Rechts-Philosophie."

[35] How the ancients thought upon the subject appears from the following utterance of Aristotle: "A tyrant (the term applied to autocrats in Old Greece) must put on the appearance of uncommon devotion to religion. Subjects are less apprehensive of illegal treatment from a ruler whom they consider god-fearing and pious. On the other hand, they do not easily move against him, believing that he has the gods on his side."—Aristotle's "Politics." Aristotle was born 384 P. C. at Stagira, whence he is frequently called "the Stagirite."

"A prince, then, is to have particular care that nothing falls from his mouth but what is full of the five qualities aforesaid, and that to see and to hear him, he appears all goodness, integrity, humanity and religion, which last he ought to pretend to more than ordinarily because more men do judge by the eye than by the touch; for everybody sees, but few understand: everybody sees how you appear, but few know what in reality you are, and those few dare not oppose the opinion of the multitude who have the majesty of their prince to defend them; and in the actions of all men, especially princes, where no man has power to judge, every one looks to the end. Let

accepts the help of this false friend because itself is in need of help. "Religion is ncessary for the people."

No such considerations animate Socialistic Society. Human progress and unadulterated science are its device. If any there be who has religious needs, he is free to please himself in the company of those who feel like him. It is a matter that does not concern society. Seeing that the clergyman's own mind will be improved by work, the day will dawn to him also when he will realize that *the highest aim is to be man.*

Ethics and morality exist without organized religion. The contrary is asserted only by weak-minded people or hypocrits. Ethics and morality are the expression of conceptions that regulate the relations of man to man, and their mutual conduct. Religion embraces the relations of man with supernal beings. And, just as with religion, moral conceptions also are born of existing social conditions at given times. Cannibals regard the eating of human beings as highly moral; Greeks and Romans regarded slavery as moral; the feudal lord of the Middle Ages regarded serfdom as moral; and to-day the modern capitalist considers highly moral the institution of wage-slavery, the flaying of women with night work and the demoralization of children by factory labor.36 Here we have four different social stages, and as many different conceptions of morality, and yet in none does the highest moral sense prevail. Undoubtedly the highest moral stage is that in which men stand to one another free and equal; that in which the principle: "What you do not wish to be done unto you, do not unto others" is observed inviolate throughout the relations of man to man. In the Middle Ages, the genealogical tree was standard; to-day it is property; in future society, the standard of man is man. And the future is Socialism in practice.

*   *   *   *   *   *

The late Reichstag delegate, Dr. Lasker, delivered, in the seventies, an address in Berlin, in which he arrived at the conclusion that an equal level of education for all members of society was possible. Dr. Lasker was an anti-Socialist a rigid upholder of private property and of the

---

a prince, therefore, do what he can to preserve his life, and continue his supremacy, the means which he uses shall be thought honorable, and be commended by everybody ; because the people are always taken with the appearance and event of things, and the greatest part of the world consists of the people ; those few who are wise taking place when the multitude has nothing else to rely upon."—Macchiavelli in his celebrated work, "The Prince." Macchiavelli was born in Florence, 1469.

36 Whenever the modern bourgeois is at a loss for reasons to justify some enormity with, a thousand to one he falls back upon "morality." In the spring of 1894, it went so far that, at a meeting of the Evangelical Synod, a "liberal" member of the Berlin Chamber of the Exchequer pronounced it "moral" that only taxpayers should have the right to vote at Church meetings (!)

capitalist system of production. The question of education is to-day, however, a question of money. Under such conditions, an equal level of education for all is an impossibility. Exceptional persons, situated in relatively favorable conditions, may, by dint of overcoming all difficulties and by the exertion of great energy, not given to everybody, succeed in acquiring a higher education. The masses never, so long as they live in a state of social oppression.[37]

In the new social order, the conditions of existence are equal for all. Wants and inclinations differ, and, differences being grounded in the very nature of man, will continue so to be. Each member, however, can live and develop under the same favorable conditions that obtain for all. The uniformity, generally imputed to Socialism, is, as so many other things, false and nonsensical. Even if Socialism did so wish it, the wish were absurd; it would come in conflict with the nature of man; Socialism would have to give up the idea of seeing society develop according to its principles.[38] Aye even if Socialism were to succeed in overpowering society and to force upon it unnatural conditions, it would not be long before such conditions, felt to be shackles, would be

---

[37] "A certain degree of well-being and culture is a necessary external condition for the development of the philosophic spirit. . . Thence we find that people began to philosophize only in those nations, that had raised themselves to a considerable height of well-being and culture."—Tennemann, quoted by Buckle in a foot note, *ubi supra.*

"Material and intellectual interests go hand in hand. The one can not exist without the other. Between the two there is the same connection as between body and soul: to separate them is to bring on death."—v. Thuenen's "Der isoliste Staat."

"The best life, as well for the individual in particular, as for the State in general, is that life in which virtue is decked out with *external* goods also, sufficient to make possible an active indulgence in beautiful and good actions." —Aristotle's "Politics."

[38] When Eugen Richter in his "Irrelehren" (False Doctrines) repeats the old wornout phrase about the Socialists aiming at a "Penitentiary State"— that the question is no longer about a "State" will have by this time become clear to our readers—he presupposes the existence of a "State" or social order *that will violate its own interests.* A new State or social order radically different from the preceding one can not possibly be produced at will; to imagine such a thing would be to ignore and deny all the laws of development, obedient to which State and Society have hitherto risen and developed. Eugen Richter and those who share his views may take comfort: if Socialism really implies the silly and unnatural aims imputed to it by them, it will go to pieces, and without the aid of the "Irrelehren" of Richter. But it happens that there is no political party that stands as squarely and logically upon the evolutionary field as the Social Democratic.

Quite as unfounded as all the other objections are the remarks of Eugen Richter: "For a social condition, such as the Socialists want, the people must be angels." As is well known, there are no angels, nor do we need any. Partly are men influenced by conditions, and partly are conditions influenced by men, and the latter will be increasingly the case in the measure that men learn to know the nature of the social system that they themselves rear, and in the measure that the experience thus gathered is consciously applied by them by corresponding changes in their social organization,—and that is

snapped, and Socialism would be done for. Society develops out of itself, according to laws latent in it, and it acts accordingly.[39]

One of the principal tasks of the new social system will be the
education of the rising generation in keeping with its improved opportunities. Every child that is born, be it male or female, is a welcome
addition to society. Society sees therein the prospect of its own per-
petuity, of its own further development. It, therefore, also realizes the
duty of providing for the new being according to its best powers. The
first object of its attention must, consequently, be the one that gives
birth to the new being—the mother. A comfortable home; agreeable
surroundings and provisions of all sorts, requisite to this stage of
maternity; a careful nursing—such are the first requirements. The
mother's breast must be preserved for the child as long as possible and
necessary. This is obvious. Moleschott, Sonderegger, all hygienists
and physicians are agreed that nothing can fully substitute the mother's
nourishment.

People who, like Eugen Richter, indignate at the idea of a young
mother being placed in a lying-in establishment, where she is surrounded by al that to-day is possible only to the very wealthiest, and
which even these cannot furnish in the fullness attainable at institutions
especially equipped for the purpose—such people we wish to remind of
the fact that, to-day, at least four-fifths of the population are born
under the most primitive circumstances and conditions, that are a dis-
grace to our civilization. Of the remaining one-fifth of our mothers,
only a minority is able to enjoy the nursing and comforts that should
be bestowed upon a woman in that state. *The fact is that in cities with
excellent provisions for child-birth—Berlin for instance, and all University cities—even to-day not a few women resort to such institutions
as soon as they feel their time approaching, and await their delivery.
Unfortunately, however, the expenses at such institutions are so high,
that but few women can use them, while others are held back by
prejudice.* Here again we have an instance of how everywhere bourgeois
society carries in its own lap the germ of the future order.

For the rest, maternity among the rich has a unique taste; the
maternal duties are transferred as soon as possible to a *proletarian*

Socialism. What we need is not other people, but wiser and more intelligent
people than most of them are to-day. It is with the end in view of making
people wiser and more intelligent that we agitate, Herr Richter, and that we
publish works like this one.

[39] It is surprising that, considering the fathomless blockishness of our adversaries, none has yet claimed that in Socialist society everyone would receive an equal portion of food and an equal quantity of linen and clothing so
as to "crown the work of uniformity. Such a claim is quite stupid enough
to expect its being made by our opponents.

nurse. As is well known, the Wendt Lausitz (Spreewald) is the region that the women of the Berlin bourgeoisie, who are unwilling or unable to nurse their own babies, draw their wet-nurses from. The "cultivation of nurses" is there carried on as a peculiar trade. It consists in the girls of the district causing themselves to be impregnated, with the end in view of being able, after the birth of their own children, to hire themselves out as nurses to rich Berlin families. Girls who give birth to three or four illegitimate children, so as to be able to go out as nurses, are no rarity; and they are sought after by the males of the Spreewald according to their earnings in this business. Such a system is utterly repellant from the view-point of bourgeois morality; from the view-point of the family interests of the bourgeoisie it is considered praiseworthy and desirable.

So soon as in the society of the future the child has grown up, it falls in with the other children of its own age for play, and under common surveillance. All that can be furnished for its mental and physical culture is at hand, according to the measure of general intelligence. Whosoever has watched children knows that they are brought up best in the company of their equals, their sense of gregariousness and instinct of imitation being generally strong. The smaller are strongly inclined to take the older ones as example, and rather follow them than their own parents. These qualities can be turned to advantage in education.[40] The playgrounds and kindergartens are followed by a playful introduction into the preliminaries of knowledge and of the various manual occupations. This is followed up by agreeable mental and physical work, connected with gymnastic exercises and free play in the skating rink and swimming establishments; drills, wrestling, and exercises for both sexes follow and supplement one another. The aim is to raise a healthy, hardy, physically and mentally developed race. Step by step follow the induction of the youth in the various practical pursuits—manufacturing, horticulture, agriculture, the technique of the process of production, etc.; nor is the development of the mind neglected in the several branches of science.

The same process of "dusting" and improvement observed in the system of production, is pursued in that of education; obsolete, superfluous and harmful methods and subjects are dropped. The knowledge of natural things, introduced in a natural way, will spur the desire for knowledge infinitely more than a system of education in which one subject is at odds with another, and each cancels the other, as, for instance, when "religion" is taught on one hand, and on the other natural sciences

---

[40] Fourier made this the subject of a brilliant argument, although he ran into utopianism in the elaboration of his ideas.

and natural history. The equipment of the school rooms and educational establishments is in keeping with the high degree of culture of the new social order. All the means of education and of study, clothing and support are furnished by society; no pupil is at a disadvantage with another.[41] That is another chapter at which our "men of law and order" bristle up indignantly.[42] "The school-house is to be turned into barracks; parents are to be deprived of all influence upon their children!" is the cry of our adversaries. All false! Seeing that in the future society parents will have infinitely more time at their disposal than is the case to-day with the large majority—we need but to call attention to the ten to fifteen hour day of many workingmen in the post office, the railroads, the prisons, the police department, and to the demands made upon the time of the industrial workers, the small farmers, merchants, soldiers, many physicians, etc.—it follows that they will be able to devote themselves to their children in a measure that is impossible to-day. *Moreover, the parents themselves have the regulation of education in their hands; it is they who determine the measures that shall be adopted and introduced. We are then living in a thorough-going democratic society. The Boards of Education, which will exist, of course, are made up of the parents themselves—men and women— and of those following the educational profession.* Does any one imagine they will act against their own interests? That happens only to-day when the State seeks but to enforce its own exclusive interests.

Our opponents furthermore demean themselves as though to-day one of the greatest pleasures of parents was to have their children about them all day long, and to educate them. It is just the reverse in reality. What hardships and cares are to-day caused by the education of a child, even when a family has but one of them, those parents are best able to judge who are themselves so situated. Several children, in a manner, facilitate education, but then again they give rise to so much more trouble that their father and especially the mother, who is the one to bear the heaviest burden, is happy when the school hour arrives, and thus the house is rid of the children for a portion of the day. Most parents can afford but a very imperfect education to their children.

---

[41] Condorcet demands in his plan of education: "Education must be free, equal, general, bodily, mental, industrial and political, and it must aim at real and actual equality."

Likewise Rousseau in his "Political Economy": "Above all, education must be public, equal and mixed, for the purpose of raising men and citizens."

Aristotle also demands: "Seeing the State has but one object, it must also provide one and the same education for all its members. The care hereof must be the concern of the State and not a private affair."

[42] Eugen Richter among them in his "Irrelehren,"

The large majority of fathers and mothers lack time; the former have their business, the latter their household to attend to, and their time is furthermore taken up with social duties. Even when they actually have time, in innumerable instances they lack the ability. How many parents are able to follow the course of their children's education at school, and to take them under the arm in their schoolwork at home? Only few. The mother, who in most such cases has greater leisure at her disposal, lacks capacity; she has not herself received sufficient training. Moreover, the method and the courses of education change so frequently that these are strange to the parents.

Again, the home facilities are generally so poor that the children enjoy neither the necessary comfort, nor order, nor quiet to do their schoolwork at home, or to find there the needed aid. Everything necessary is generally wanting. The home is narrow and overcrowded; small and grown-up brothers and sisters move about over that narrow space; the furniture is not what it should be, and furnishes no facilities to the child for study. Not infrequently light also, air and heat are wanting; the materials for study and work, if there be any of them, are poor; frequently even hunger gnaws at the stomach of the child and robs it of mind and pleasure for its work. As a supplement to this picture, the fact must be added that hundreds of thousands of children are put to all manner of work, domestic and industrial, that embitters their youth and disables them from fulfilling their educational task. Again, often do children have to overcome the resistance of narrow-minded parents when they try to take time for their schoolwork or for play. In short, the obstacles are so numerous that, if they are all taken into account, the wonder is the youth of the land is as well educated. It is an evidence of the health of human nature, and of its inherent ambition after progress and perfection.

Bourgeois society itself recognizes some of these evils by the introduction of public education and by facilitating the same still more through the free supply, here and there, of school material—two things that, as late as about the year 1885 the then Minister of Education of Saxony designated as a "Social Democratic demand," and as such flung the designation in the face of the Socialist Representative in the Landtag. In France, where, after long neglect, popular education advanced so much more rapidly, progress has gone still further. At least in Paris, the school children are fed at public expense. The poor obtain food free, and the children of parents who are better circumstanced contribute thereto a slight tax toward the common treasury—a communistic arrangement that has proved satisfactory to parents and children alike.

An evidence of the inadequacy of the present school system—it is unable to fulfil even the moderate demands made upon it—is the fact that thousands upon thousands of children *are unable to fulfil their school duties by reason of insufficient food.* In the winter of 1893-94, it was ascertained in Berlin that *in one school district alone 3,600 children went to school without breakfast.* In such shocking conditions there are hundreds of thousands of children in Germany to-day at certain seasons of the year. With millions of others the nourishment is utterly insufficient. For all these children public alimentation and clothing also would be a godsend. A commonwealth that pursued such a policy and thus, by the systematic nourishing and clothing of the children, would bring humanity home to them, is not likely to see the sight of "penitentiaries." Bourgeois society cannot deny the existence of such misery, which itself has called forth. Hence we see compassionate souls foregathering in the establishment of breakfast and soup houses, to the end of partially filling by means of charity what it were the duty of society to fill in full. Our conditions are wretched—*but still more wretched is the mental make-up of those who shut their eyes to such facts.*

The system of reducing so-called home school work, and of having the same done at school under the supervision of a teacher is progressing; the inadequacy of home facilities is realized. Not only is the richer pupil at an advantage over the poorer by reason of his position, but also by reason of his having private teachers and such other assistance at his command. On the other hand, however, laziness and shiftlessness are promoted with the rich pupil by reason of the effects of wealth, luxury and superfluity; these make knowledge appear superflous to him, and often they place before him such immoral sights that he easily slides into temptation. He who everv day and every hour hears the praises sung of rank, position, money, property, and that they are all-essential, acquires abnormal conceptions regarding man and his duties, and regarding State and social institutions.

Closely looked into, bourgeois society has no reason to feel indignant at the communistic education, which Socialists aim at. Bourgeois society has itself partly introduced such a system for the privileged classes, but only as a caricature of the original. Look at the cadet and alumni establishments, at the seminaries, at the schools for clergymen, and at the homes for military orphans. In them many thousands of children, partly from the so-called upper classes, are educated in a one-sided and wrongful manner, and in strict cloister seclusion; they are trained for certain specific occupations. And again, many members of the better situated classes, who live in the country or in small places as physicians, clergymen, government employes, factory owners, landlords, large farmers, etc., send their children to boarding schools in the large cities and barely get a glimpse of them, except possibly during vacations.

There is, accordingly, an obvious contradiction between the indignation expressed by our adversaries at a communistic system of education and at "the estrangement of children from their parents," on the one hand, and their own conduct, on the other, in *introducing the identical system for their own children—only in a bungling, absolutely false and inadequate style.*

In equal tempo with the increased opportunities for education must the number of teachers increase. In the matter of the education of the rising generations the new social order must proceed in a way similar to that which prevails in the army, in the drilling of soldiers. There is one "under-officer" to each eight or ten men. With one teacher to every eight or ten pupils, the future may expect the results that should be aimed at.

The introduction of mechanical activities in the best equipped workshops, in garden and field work, will constitute a good part of the education of the youth. It will all be done with the proper change and without excessive exertion, to the end of reaching the most perfectly developed beings.

Education must also be equal and in common for both sexes. Their separation is justifiable only in the cases where the difference in sex makes such separation absolutely necessary. In this manner of education the United States is far ahead of us. There education of the two sexes is in common from the primary schools up to the universities. Not only is education free, but also school materials, inclusive of the instruments needed in manual training and in cooking, as also in chemistry, physics, and the articles needed for experimenting and at bench-work. To many schools are attached gymnastic halls, bath houses, swimming basins and playgrounds. In the higher schools, the female sex is trained in gymnastics, swimming, rowing and marching.[43]

The Socialist system of education, properly regulated and ordered and placed under the direction of a sufficient force, continues up to the age when society shall determine that its youth shall enter upon their majority. Both sexes are fully qualified to exercise all the rights and fill all the duties that society demands from its adult members. Society now enjoys the certainty of having brought up only thorough, fully developed members, human beings to whom nothing natural is strange,

[43] "America's Bildungswesen," by Prof. Emil Hausknecht.

as familiar with their nature as with the nature and conditions of society which they join full-righted.

The daily increasing excesses of our modern youth—all of them the inevitable consequences of the present tainted and decomposing state of society—will have vanished. Impropriety of conduct, disobedience, immorality and rude pleasure-seeking, such as is especially noticeable among the youth of our higher educationl institutions—the gymnasia, polytechnics, universities, etc.—vices that are incited and promoted by the existing demoralization and unrest of domestic life, by the poisonous influence of social life such as the immoral literature that wealth procures—all these will likewise have vanished. In equal measure will disappear the evil effects of the modern factory system and of improper housing, that dissoluteness and self-assurance of youths at an age when the human being is most in need of reining and education in self-control. All these evils future society will escape without the need of coercive measures. The nature of the social institutions and of the mental atmosphere, that will spring from them and that will rule society itself, rendering impossible the breaking out of such evils; as in Nature disease and the destruction of organisms can appear only when there is a state of decay that invites disease; so likewise in society.

No one will deny that our present system of instruction and of education suffers of serious defects—the higher schools and educational establishments even more so than the lower. The village school is a paragon of moral health compared with the college; common schools for the manual training of poor girls are paragons of morality compared with many leading boarding schools for girls. The reason is not far to seek. In the upper classes of society, every aspiration after higher human aims is smothered; *those classes no longer have any ideal.* As a consequence of the absence of ideals and of noble endeavor, an unbounded passion for physical indulgence and hankering after excesses spread their physical and moral gangrene in all directions. How else can the youth be that is brought up in such an atmosphere? Purely material indulgence, without stint and without bounds, is the only aim that it sees or knows of. Why exert themselves, if the wealth of their parents makes all effort seem superfluous? The maximum of education with a large majority of the sons of our bourgeoisie consists in passing the examinations for the one year's service in the army. Is this goal reached, then they imagine to have climbed Pelion and Ossa, and regard themselves at least as demi-gods. Have they a reserve officer's certificate in their pocket, then their pride and arrogance knows no limit. The influence exercised by this generation—a generation it has become by its numbers—weak in the character and knowledge of its members, but strong in their designs and the spirit of graft, characterizes the present period as the "Age of Reserve Officers." Its peculiarities are: Character-lessness and ignorance, but a strong will; servility upward, arrogance and brutality downward.

The daughters of our bourgeoisie are trained as show-dolls, fools of fashion and drawingroom-ladies, on the chase after one enjoyment after another, until, finally, surfeited with *ennui*, they fall a prey to all imaginable real and supposed diseases. Grown old, they become devotees and beads-women, who turn up their eyes at the corruption of the world and preach asceticism. As regards the lower classes, the effort is on foot to lower still more the level of their education. The proletariat might become too knowing, it might get tired of its vassalage, and might rebel against its earthly gods. The more stupid the mass, all the easier is it to control and rule.

And thus modern society stands before the question of instruction and education as bewildered as it stands before all other social questions. What does it? It calls for the rod; preaches "religion," that is, submission and contentment to those who are now but too submissive; teaches abstinence where, due to poverty, abstinence has become compulsory in the utmost necessaries of life. Those who in the rudeness of their nature rear up brutally are taken to "reformatories," that usually are controlled by pietistic influences;—and the pedagogic wisdom of modern society has about reached the end of its tether.

From the moment that the rising generation in future society shall have reached its majority, all further growth is left to the individual: society will feel sure that each will seize the opportunity to unfold the germs that have been so far developed in him. Each does according as inclination and faculties serve him. Some choose one branch of the ever more brilliant natural sciences: anthropology, zoology, botany, mineralogy, geology, physics, chemistry, prehistoric sciences, etc.; others take to the science of history, philologic researches, art; others yet become musicians from special gifts, or painters, or sculptors, or actors. The future will have "guild artists" as little as "guild scientists" or "guild artisans." Thousands of brilliant talents, hitherto kept down, unfold and assert themselves and display their knowledge and ability wherever opportunity offers. No longer are there any musicians, actors, artists and scientists by profession; they will exist only by inspiration, talent and genius; and the achievements of these bid fair to excel modern achievements on these fields as vastly as the industrial, technical and agricultural achievements of future society are certain to excel those of to-day. An era of art and sciences will spring up such as the world never saw before; nor will its creations fail to correspond to such a renaissance.

What transformation and new-birth science will experience when conditions shall have become worthy of the human race, no less a man than the late Richard Wagner foresaw and expressed as early as 1850 in his work "Art and Revolution." This work is all the more significant seeing that it made its appearance immediately after a revolution that had just been beaten down, that Wagner took part in, and by reason of which he had to flee from Dresden. In this book Wagner foretells what the future will bring on. He turns directly to the working class as the one called upon to emancipate true art. Among other things he says:

"When, with the free human race of the future, the earning of a living shall no longer be the object of life; when, on the contrary, thanks to the rise of a new faith, or of higher knowledge, the gaining of a livelihood by means of compatible work shall be raised above all uncertainty;—in short, when industry shall no longer be our master but our servant, then will we place the object of life in the pleasure of life, and seek to make our children fit and worthy through education. An education that starts from the exercise of strength, from the care of the beauty of the body will, due to the undisturbed love for the child and to the joy experienced at the thriving of its charms, become purely artistic; and thus in some sense or another every being will be an artist in truth. The diversity of natural inclinations will develop the most manifold aptitudes into an unprecedented wealth of beauty!"—at all points a Socialist line of thought, and fully in keeping with the arguments herein made.

* * * * *

Social life in future will be ever more public. What the trend is may be gathered from the wholly changed position of woman, compared with former times. Domestic life will be confined to what is absolutely necessary, while the widest field will be opened to the gratification of the social instincts. Large gathering places for the holding of addresses and discussions, and for conferring upon all social questions, over which the collectivity has the sovereign word; play, meals and reading rooms; libraries, concert halls and theaters; museums and gymnastic institutions; parks, promenades, public baths, educational institutions of all sorts; laboratories, etc.;—all of these, erected in the best and equipped in the fittest manner possible, will afford richest opportunity for all manner of intercourse, of art and of science to achieve the highest. Likewise will the institutions for the nursing of the sick, the weak, the infirm through old age, meet the highest demands.

How little will then our much boasted about age seem in comparison.

This fawning for favor and sunshine from above; this cringing and dog-like frame of mind; this mutual struggle of enviousness, with the aid of the most hateful and vilest means, for the privileged place. All along the suppression of convictions; the veiling of good qualities, that might otherwise give offence; the emasculation of character; the affectation of opinions and feelings;—in short, all those qualities that may be summed up in words "cowardice and characterlessness" are now every day more pronounced. Whatever elevates and ennobles man—self-esteem, independence and incorruptibility of opinion and convictions, freedom of utterance—modern conditions generally turn into defects and crimes. Often do these qualities work the ruin of their owners, unless he suppresses them. Many do not even realize their degradation; they have grown accustomed thereto. The dog regards it a matter of course that he has a master, who, when out of temper, visits him with the whip.

Such altered conditions in social life will impart a radically different aspect to literary productions. Theological literature, whose entries are at present most numerous in the yearly catalogues of literary works, drops out in company with its juridic cousin,—there is no more interest in the former, and no more use for the latter. All the literary productions that refer to the struggle over political institutions will be seen no more,—their subject-matter has ceased to be. The study of all such matters will belong to the history of civilization. The vast mass of inane productions—the evidences of a spoiled taste, often possible only through sacrifices at the altar of the author's vanity—are gone. Even speaking from the view-point of present conditions, it may be said without exaggeration that four-fifths of all literary productions could disappear from the market without loss to a single interest of civilization. Such is the vastness of the mass of superficial or harmful books, palpable trash, extant to-day on the field of literature.

Belles-lettres and the press will be equally hit. There is nothing sorrier, more spiritless or superficial than the large majority of our newspaper literature. If our stage in civilization and scientific attainments were to be gauged by the contents of that set of papers, it would be low indeed. The actions of men and the condition of things are judged from a view-point that corresponds with centuries gone by, and that has been long since proved laughable and untenable by science. A considerable portion of our journalists are people who, as Bismarck once put it, "missed their calling," but whose education and standard of wages fit with bourgeois interests. Furthermore, these newspapers, as well as the majority of the belles-lettric magazines, have the mission of circulating impure advertisements; the interests of their purses are on this field the same as on the former: the material interests of their owners determine their contents.

On an average, belles-lettric literature is not much superior to newspaper literature. Its forte is to cultivate sex excesses: it renders homage either to shallow enlightenment or to stale prejudices and superstitions. Its general purpose is to represent the capitalist order of society, all its shortcomings notwithstanding, which are conceded in trifles, as the best of all possible worlds.

On this extensive and important field, future society will institute some thorough-going housecleaning. Science, truth, beauty, the contest of the intellect after the best will rule supreme. Everyone who achieves what is worthy will enjoy the opportunity to exercise his faculties. He no longer depends upon the favor of a publisher, moneyed considerations or prejudice, but only upon the impartial judgment of experts whom he himself joins in electing, and from whose unfavorable decision he can always appeal to the general vote of the whole community,—all of which is to-day against him or impossible. The childish notion that all contest of intellect would be held down in a Socialist society they alone can maintain who hold the bourgeois world to be the most perfect social system, and who, out of enmity to Socialism seek to slander and to belittle it. A society, that rests upon full democratic equality, neither knows nor tolerates oppression. Only the fullest freedom of thought makes uninterrupted progress possible, and this is the principle of life with society. Moreover, it is an act of deception to represent bourgeois society as the paladin of true freedom of thought. Parties that represent class interests will publish in the press only that which does not injure their class' own interests, and woe to him who would attempt the contrary. His social ruin would be sealed, as every one knows. In what manner publishers handle literary work that does not suit them, every writer almost could tell a tale of woe on. Finally, the German press and criminal laws betray the spirit that animates our ruling and leading classes. Actual freedom of thought is looked upon by them as the most dangerous of evils.

*　*　*　*　*

The individual is to develop himself fully. That must be the law of human association. Accordingly, the individual may not remain fettered to the soil on which the accident of birth first placed him. Men and the world should be known, not from books and papers only: personal observation, practical experience are also needed. Accordingly, future society must enable everyone to do what is now done by many, although in most instances it happens to-day under the whip that want cracks.

The wish for change in all the relations of life is a craving strongly stamped in man. It springs from the instinct after perfection, inherent in all organic beings. The plant that stands in a dark room, stretches and strains, as though endowed with consciousness, towards the light that falls from some crevice. Just so with man. An instinct implanted in man, consequently a natural instinct, must be rationally gratified. The conditions of future society will not balk the instinct after change; on the contrary, they promote its gratification with all: it is facilitated by the highly developed system of intercommunication; it is demanded by international relations. In future days, infinitely more people will travel through the world, and for the most varied of purposes, than happens to-day.

In order to meet all demands, society furthermore requires an ample provision of all the necessaries of life. Society regulates its hours of work accordingly. It makes them longer or shorter, according as its needs or the season of the year may suggest. It may turn its strength at one season mainly to agriculture, at another mainly to industrial and similar production. It directs its labor forces as occasion may require. Through the combination of numerous forces, equipped with the best technical provisions, it can carry through with swiftness, aye, playingly, undertakings that to-day seem impossible.

As society assumes the care of its youth, so it does of its aged, sick or invalid members. It guards whoever, by whatever circumstance, has become unable to work. There is in this no question of *charity*, but of *duty;* not of an alms morsel, but of an assistance born of every possible consideration due him, who, during the time of his strength and ability to work, fulfilled his duties to the commonwealth. The setting sun of old age is beautiful with all that society can offer: everyone being buoyed up with the confidence that he will some day himself enjoy what now he affords to others. No longer are the aged now disturbed with the thought that others are awaiting their death in order to "inherit;" likewise has the fear vanished from the mind of man that, grown old and helpless, he will be cast off like a squeezed lemon. Man now feels himself left neither to the benevolence of his children, nor to the alms of the community. What the condition is in which most parents find themselves, who depend in old age upon the support of their children, is notorious. How demoralizing is not the effect of the hope of inheriting upon the children, and, in a still greater degree, upon relatives! What vile qualities are not awakened; and how many are not the crimes that such hopes have led to!—murder, forgery, perjury, extortion, etc. Capitalist society has no reason to be proud of its laws of inheritance; to them are ascribable part of the crimes that are committed every year; and yet the large majority of people have nothing to bequeath or to inherit.[44]

The moral and physical condition of future society; the nature of its work, homes, food, clothing, its social life—everything will greatly contribute to avoid accidents, sickness, debility. Natural death by the decline of the vigor of life will become the rule. The conviction that "heaven" is on earth, and that to be dead means to be ended, will cause people to lead rational lives.[45] He enjoys most who enjoys longest. None know how to appreciate a long life better than the very clergy who prepare people for the "after world;" a life free from care makes it possible for these gentlemen to reach the highest age average.[46]

Life requires, first of all, food and drink. Friends of the so-called "natural way of living" often ask why is Socialism indifferent to vegetarianism. The question causes us to take up the subject in a few lines. Vegetarianism, that is, the doctrine that prescribes an exclusive vegetal diet, found its first supporters in such circles as are in the agreeable position of being able to choose between a vegetal and an animal diet. To the large majority of people there is no such choice: they are forced to live according to their means, the meagerness of which in many instances keeps them almost exclusively to a vegetal diet, and to the least nutritive, at that. With our working class population in Silesia, Saxony, Thuringen, etc., the potato is the principal

[44] "The person who has led an honorable and active life until old age should not then have to live either on the charity of his children or of bourgeois society. An independent old age, free from cares or toil, is the natural reward for continuous exertions in the days of strength and health."—v. Thuenen's "Der isolate Staat." But how is it to-day in this bourgeois society? Millions look with dread towards the time when, having grown old, they are thrown upon the street. And our industrial system causes people to age prematurely. The very much boasted about old-age and invalid pensions in the German Empire afford but a very scanty substitute: even its most zealous defenders admit that. Their aids are still more inadequate than the pensions which the municipalities allow to the large majority of the officials whom they provide with pensions.

[45] [It is a feature of theology to be positive, precise and emphatic in descriptions of what the describer knows nothing about. No less theologic, in this sense of the term, are negative assertions concerning matters that science has not yet illumined. Whether "to be dead means to be ended" or not, is no part either of the general question of Socialism, or the specific question of Woman. Nevertheless, while respecting the author's private opinion in the matter, and leaving his sentence untouched, the following phrasing would seem preferable, as free from the taint of what may be called the "theologic method," and also more in keeping with the mental posture of positive knowledge: "Whether to be dead means to be ended or not, is a matter on which man awaits the fiat of Science."—THE TRANSLATOR.]

[46] [It is otherwise in the United States, where, as a rule, clergymen have to "hustle"—both to curry favor with their parishioners and to countermine the mines laid by their competitors for fatter "calls," or by their numerous unemployed "brothers of the cloth." According to the census of 1900, clergy-

nourishment; even bread comes in only secondarily; meat, and then only of poor quality, is hardly ever seen on the table. Even the largest part of the rural population, although they are the raisers of cattle, rarely partake of meat: they must sell the cattle in order to satisfy other pressing wants with the money obtained therefor.

For the innumerable people, who are compelled to live as vegetarians, an occasional solid beefsteak, or good leg of mutton, would be a decided improvement in the diet. When vegetarianism directs itself against the overrating of the nutrition contained in meat, it is right; it is wrong, however, when it combats the partaking of meat as harmful and fatal, mainly on sentimental grounds—such as "the nature of man forbids the killing of animals and to partake of a corpse." In order to live comfortably and undisturbed, we are compelled to declare war upon and destroy a large number of living beings in the shape of all manner of vermin; in order not to be ourselves eaten up, we must undertake the killing and extirpating of wild animals. The quiet toleration of those "good friends of man," the domestic animals, would increase the number of these "good friends" in a few decades so immensely that they would "devour" us by robbing us of food. Neither is the claim true that a vegetarian diet produces mildness of temperament. The "beast" was awakened even in the mild, vegetarian Hindoo when the severity of the Englishmen drove him to mutiny.

In our opinion Sonderegger hits the nail on the head when he says: "There is no order of rank in the matter of the different kinds of food; but there is an unalterable law in the matter of combining their several nutritious qualities." It is true that no one can nourish himself on an exclusively meat diet, but that he can on an exclusively vegetal diet, provided always he can select to suit; but neither would any one be satisfied with one vegetable, let it be the most nutritive. Beans, for instance, peas, lentils, in short, the leguminosae, are the most nutritive of all food. Nevertheless, to be forced to feed exclusively on them— which is said to be possible—were a torture. Karl Marx mentions in "Capital" that the Chilian mine-owners compel their workingmen to eat beans year in and year out, because the food imparts to them great strength and enables them to carry burdens that they could not carry with any other diet. Despite its nutrition, the workingmen turn against

men had the very highest death rate (23.5) among the professional occupations for the registration area,—and it was among the highest altogether. It was excelled only by the death rate of the coopers (23.8); of the millers, flour and grist, (26.6); of the sailors, pilots, fishermen and oystermen (27.7); and of the stock raisers, herders and drovers (32.1). The census also shows that the death rate of clergymen is on the increase—18.2 in 1890; now 23.5. —THE TRANSLATOR.]

such food, but get none other, and are thus obliged to rest content therewith. Under no circumstances do the happiness and well-being of people depend upon a certain diet, as is claimed by the fanatics among the vegetarians. Climate, custom, individual tastes are the determining factors.

In the measure that civilization advances, a vegetal diet progressively takes the place of the exclusive meat diet, such as is indulged in by hunting and pastoral peoples. A many-sided agriculture is a sign of higher culture. On a given field, vegetal nutritive matter can be raised in larger quantities than could meat be obtained through cattle raising. This development imparts to vegetal nutrition an ever greater preponderance. The transportation of meat, that the modern vandalic economic system furnishes us with from foreign lands, especially from South America and Australia, has been very nearly exhausted within few decades. On the other hand, animals are raised, not merely for the sake of meat, but also for that of wool, hair, bristles, skin and hides, milk, eggs, etc., upon which many industries and human wants are dependent. Again offal of several kinds can be turned in no way to better advantage than through cattle raising. The seas will also in future be made to yield to man their wealth of animal food to a much larger extent than now. It will be in future a rare occurrence to see, as we do to-day, whole loads of fish turned to manure, because the facilities and costs of transportation, or the facilities of preservation prevent their being otherwise used. It follows that a purely vegetal diet is neither probable nor necessary in the future.

In the matter of food, *quality* rather than *quantity* is to be considered. Quantity is of little use if not good. Quality is greatly improved by the manner of preparation. The preparation of food must be conducted as scientifically as any other function, if it is to reach the highest point of utility possible. Knowledge and equipment are thereto requisite. That our women, upon whom to-day mainly devolves the preparation of food, do not and can not possess this knowledge, needs no proof. They lack all the necessary equipments therefor. As every well equipped hotel kitchen, the steam kitchen of barracks or of hospitals and especially the cooking expositions teach us, the cooking apparatuses, together with many technical arrangements for all manner of food preparation, have reached a high degree of perfection and have been contrived upon scientific principles. That will in the future be the rule. The object aimed at must be to obtain the best results with the smallest expenditure of power, time and material. *The small private kitchen is, just like the workshop of the small master mechanic, a transition stage, an arrangement by which time, power and material are sense-*

lessly squandered and wasted. The preparation of food also will in future society be a social establishment, conducted on the most improved plane, in proper and advantageous manner. The private kitchen disappears, as it has now disappeared in the instance of those families who, although they generally provide themselves through their own kitchen, always resort to hotel kitchens, or to those of caterers the moment the question is to provide for banquets or to procure dishes a knowledge of which both they and their domestics lack.[47]

The Chicago Exposition of 1893 brought out a mass of interesting facts on the revolution that has taken place in the kitchen also, and in the preparation of food;—among other things a kitchen in which the heating and cooking was done wholly through electricity. Electricity not only furnished the light, but was also active in the washing of dishes, which thereupon required the aid of the human hand only in finishing up. In this kitchen of the future there was no hot air, no smoke, no vapors. Numberless apparatuses and subsidiary machinery performed a number of operations that until then had to be performed by human hands. This kitchen of the future resembled more a parlor than a kitchen that everyone who has nothing to do in, likes to stay away from. Work therein at the Chicago Exposition was pleasurable and free from all the unpleasantness that are features of the modern kitchen. Can a private kitchen be imagined even approximately equipped like that? And then, what a saving in all directions through such a central kitchen! Our women would seize the opportunity with both hands to exchange the present for the kitchen of the future.

The nutritive value of food is heightened by its facility of assimilation. This is a determining factor.[48] A natural system of nourishment for all can be reached only by future society. Cato praises the Rome of before his days for having had experts in the art of healing, but, down to the sixth century of the city, no occupation for exclusive physicians. People lived so frugally and simply, that disease was rare, and death from old age was the usual form of disease. Not until gourmandizing and idleness—in short, license with some, want and excessive work with others—had permeated society, did matters change, and

---

[47] Herr Eugen Richter in his "Irrelehren" is also raving mad over the idea of abolishing the private kitchen. As far as we know, Herr Richter is a bachelor. Obviously he does not miss his own kitchen: to judge from the rotundity of his body, he does not fare ill. If Herr Richter were a married man and possessed a wife, who had herself to administer the kitchen department and to perform in it the needed work, instead of leaving all that to servants, as is the fashion with the women of the property classes, then, a hundred to one, his wife would nicely prove to him how happy she would be if she only could be freed from the bondage of the kitchen through the large and thoroughly equipped communal institute for meals.

[48] Niemeyer, "Gesundheitslehre."

radically so. In future, gluttony and license will be impossible, and likewise want, misery and privation. There is enough, and an abundance, for all. More than fifty years ago Henrich Heine sang:

> Why, there grows down here abundance
> And a plentitude for all;
> Roses, myrtles, beauty and joy;
> Yes, and sugar beans withal—
>
> Aye, sugar beans in bursting pods
> For everyone are here,
> But they're left to heaven's angels
> And the sparrows of the air.

"He who eats little lives well"—that is, long, said the Italian Cornaro in the sixteenth century, as quoted by Niemeyer. In the end chemistry will be active in the preparation and improvement of nourishment to a degree thitherto unknown. To-day the science is greatly abused in the interest of adulterations and fraud. It is obvious that a chemically prepared food that has all the qualities of the natural product will accomplish the same purpose. The form of the preparation is of secondary importance, provided the product otherwise meets all requirements.

As in the kitchen, the revolution will be accomplished throughout domestic life: it will remove numberless details of work that must be attended to to-day. As in the future the domestic kitchen is rendered wholly superfluous by the central institutions for the preparation of food, so likewise are all the former troubles of keeping ranges, lamps, etc., in working order, removed by the central heating and electric apparatuses for lighting. Warm and cold water supplies place bathing within the reach of all at pleasure, and without the aid of any person. The central laundries assume the washing, drying, etc., of clothes; the central cleaning establishments see to the dusting, etc., of clothing and carpets. In Chicago, carpet-cleaning machines were exhibited that did the work in so short a time as to call forth the admiration of the ladies who visited the Exposition. The electric door opens at a slight pressure of the finger, and shuts of itself. Electric contrivances deliver letters and newspapers on all the floors of the houses; electric elevators save the climbing of stairs. The inside arrangement of the houses—floorings, garnishing of the walls, furnitures—will be contrived with an eye to the facility of cleaning and to the prevention of the gathering of dust and bacteria. Dust, sweepings and offal of all sorts will be car-

ried by pipes out of the houses like water, that has been used, is carried off to-day. In the United States, in many a European city—
Zurich, for instance—there are to-day tenements, exquisitely equipped,
in which numerous affluent families—others could not bear the expense—live and enjoy a large part of the conveniences just sketched.

Here again we have an illustration of how capitalist society breaks
the way in revolutionizing human affairs, in this instance in domestic
life,—but only for its elect. Domestic life being thus radically transformed, the servant, this "slave of all the whims of the mistress," is no
more,—and the mistress neither. "No servants, no culture!" cries the
horrified Herr v. Treitschke with comic pathos. He can as little imagine society without servants as Aristotle could without slaves. The
matter of surprise is that Herr v. Treitschke looks upon our servants
as the "carriers of civilization." Treitschke, like Eugen Richter, is
furthermore greatly worried by the shoe-polishing and clothes-dusting
question, which neither is able to attend to personally. It so happens,
however, that with nine-tenths of the people everyone sees to that himself, or the wife does for her husband, or a daughter or son for the
family. We might answer that what the nine-tenths have hitherto
done, the remnant tenth may also do. But there is another way out.
Why should not in future society the youth of the land, without distinction of sex, be enlisted for such necessary work? Work does not
dishonor, even if it consist in polishing boots. Many a member of
the old nobility, and officers of the army at that, learned the lesson
when, to escape their debts, they ran off to the United States, and there
became servants, or shoe-polishers. Eugen Richter, in his pamphlets,
goes even so far as to cause the downfall of the "Socialist Imperial
Chancellor" on the "Shoe-polishing Question," and the consequent falling to pieces of the "Socialist State." The "Socialist Imperial Chancellor" refuses to polish his own shoes; hence his troubles. The bourgeoisie has hugely enjoyed this description of Richter, and it has thereby furnished evidence of the modesty of its demands upon a criticism of
Socialism. But Eugen Richter lived to experience the sorrow of not
only seeing one of his own party members in Nuerenberg invent a shoe-
polishing machine soon after the appearance of that pamphlet, but of
also learning that at the Chicago Exposition of 1893 an electric shoe-
polishing machine was exhibited that did the work perfectly. Thus the
principal objection, raised by Richter and Treitschke against Socialist
society, has been practically thrown overboard by an invention made
under the bourgeois social system itself.

The revolutionary transformation, that radically changes all the relations of man, especially the position of woman, is, as we see, going on

now under our own eyes. It is only a question of time when society will take the process into its own hands and upon a large scale, thus quickening and perfecting the change and affording to all, without exception, the opportunity to share its innumerable advantages.

PART III

WOMAN IN THE FUTURE

WOMAN IN THE FUTURE.

This chapter can be condensed in few words. It only contains the conclusions that flow from what has been said, conclusions that the reader may draw for himself.

The woman of future society is socially and economically independent; she is no longer subject to even a vestige of dominion and exploitation; she is free, the peer of man, mistress of her lot. Her education is the same as that of man, with such exceptions as the difference of sex and sexual functions demand. Living under natural conditions, she is able to unfold and exercise her mental powers and faculties. She chooses her occupation on such field as corresponds with her wishes, inclinations and natural abilities, and she works under conditions identical with man's. Even if engaged as a practical working-woman on some field or other, at other times of the day she may be educator, teacher or nurse, at yet others she may exercise herself in art, or cultivate some branch of science, and at yet others may be filling some administrative function. She joins in studies, enjoyments or social intercourse with either her sisters or with men,—as she may please or occasion may serve.

In the choice of love, she is, like man, free and unhampered. She woos or is wooed, and closes the bond from no considerations other than her own inclinations. This bond is a private contract, celebrated without the intervention of any functionary—just as marriage was a private contract until deep in the Middle Ages. Socialism creates in this nothing new: it merely restores, at a higher level of civilization and under new social forms, that which prevailed at a more primitive social stage, and before private property began to rule society.

Under the proviso that he inflict injury upon none, the individual shall himself oversee the satisfaction of his own instincts. *The satisfaction of the sexual instinct is as much a private concern as the satisfaction of any other natural instinct.* None is therefor accountable to others, and no unsolicited judge may interfere. How I shall eat, how I shall drink, how I shall sleep, how I shall clothe myself, is my private affair,—exactly so my intercourse with a person of the opposite sex. Intelligence and culture, perfect individual freedom—qualities that become normal through the education and the conditions of future society—will guard everyone against the commission of acts that will redound to his injury. Self-training and the knowledge of their own being are possessions of the men and the women of future society to a degree much above the present. The simple circumstance that all bashful prudery and affectation of secrecy regarding natural matters will have vanished is a guarantee of a more natural intercourse of the sexes than that which prevails to-day. If incompatibility, disenchantment, or repulsion set in between two persons that have come together, morality commands that the unnatural, and therefore immoral, bond be dissolved. Seeing, moreover, that all the circumstances and conditions, which until then condemned large numbers of women to celibacy and to prostitution, will have vanished, man can no longer superimpose himself. On the other hand, the completely changed social conditions will have removed the numerous inconveniences that to-day affect married life, that often prevent its favorable unfolding, or that even render it wholly impossible.

The contradictions in and the unnatural features of the present position of woman are realized with ever increasing force in wide social circles. The sentiment finds lively utterance in the literature of the Social Question as well as in works of fiction,—often, it must be confessed, in wrongful manner. That the present form of marriage corresponds ever less with its purpose, no thinking person any longer denies. Thus is seen the phenomenon of the demand for freedom in the choice of love, and for the untrammeled dissolution of the marriage bond, when necessary, made by people who refuse to draw the requisite conclusions for the change of the present social system. They believe that the freedom of sexual intercourse must be asserted only in behalf of the privileged classes. In a polemic against Fanny Lewalt's efforts in behalf of the emancipation of woman, Mathilde Reichhardt-Stromberg expresses herself this wise:

"If you (Fanny Lewald) claim the complete equality of woman with man in social and political life, George Sand also must be right in her struggles for emancipation, which aim no further than at what man has long been in undisputed possession of. Indeed, there is no reasonable ground for admitting the head and not the heart of woman to this equality, to give and to take as freely as man. On the contrary, if woman has by nature the right, and, consequently, also the duty—for we should not bury the talent bestowed upon us—of exerting her brain tissue to the utmost in the race with the intellectual Titans of the opposite sex, she must then have precisely the same right to preserve her equilibrium by quickening the circulation of her heart's blood in whatever way it may seem good to her. Do we not all read without the slightest moral indignation how Goethe—to begin with the greatest as an illustration—again and again wasted the warmth of his heart and the enthusiasm of his great soul on a different woman? Reasonable people regard this as perfectly natural by the very reason of the greatness of his soul, and the difficulty of satisfying it. Only the narrow-minded moralist stops to condemn his conduct. Why, then, deride the 'great souls' among women! . . . Let us suppose that the whole female sex consisted of great souls like George Sand, that every woman were a Lucretia Floriani, whose children are all children of love and who brought up all these children with true motherly love and devotion, as well as with intelligence and good sense. What would become of the world? There can be no doubt that it could continue to exist and to progress, just as it does now; it might even feel exceptionally comfortable under the arrangement."[1]

Accordingly, Mathilde Reichhardt-Stromberg is of the opinion that, if every woman were a Lucretia Floriani, that is, a great soul like George Sand, who draws her own picture in Lucretia Floriani, they should be free for the "preservation of their equilibrium to quicken the circulation of their heart's blood in whatever way it may seem good to them." But why should that be the privilege of the "great souls" only, and not of the others also, who are no "great souls," and can be none? No such difference exists to us. If a Goethe and a George Sand—to take these two from the many who have acted and are acting like them— live according to the inclinations of their hearts—and about Goethe's love affairs whole libraries are published that are devoured by his male and female admirers in wrapt ecstasy—why condemn in others that, which done by a Goethe or a George Sand, becomes the subject of ecstatic admiration?

Indeed, such freedom in the choice of love is an impossibility in bourgeois society. This fact was the objective point in our preceding array of evidence. But place the whole community under social conditions similar to those enjoyed by the material and intellectual elect, and forthwith the opportunity is there of equal rights and freedom for all. In "Jacques," George Sand depicts a husband who judges the adulterous relations of his wife with another man in these words: "No human being can command love; and none is guilty if he feels, or goes without it. What degrades the woman is the lie: what constitutes her adultery is not the hour that she grants to her lover, but the night that she thereupon spends with her husband." Thanks to this view of the matter, Jacques feels obliged to yield the place to his rival, Borel, and he proceeds to philosophize: "Borel, in my place, would have quietly beaten his wife, and perhaps would not have blushed to receive her afterwards into his bed, debased by his blows and his kisses. There are men

[1] "Fraunnenrecht und Frauenpflicht. Eine Antwort auf Fanny Lewald's Briefe 'Fuer und wider die Frauen.' "

who cut the throat of an unfaithful wife without ceremony, after the fashion of the Orientals, because they consider her as legal property. Others fight with their rival, kill him or drive him away, and again seek the kisses of the woman they pretend to love, and who shrinks from them with horror, or resigns herself in despair. These, in cases of conjugal love, are the most common ways of acting, and I say that the love of the hogs is less vile and less gross than that of these men." Commenting on these passages, Brandes observes: "These truths, which are considered elemental with our cultured classes, were 'sophisms that cried to heaven' only fifty years ago." But the "property and cultured world" dare not to this day openly avow the principles of George Sand, although, in point of fact, it lives up to them in the main. As in morality and religion, the bourgeois is a hypocrite in marriage also.

What Goethe and George Sand did, has been done and continues to be done by thousands of others, who are not to be compared with Goethe, yet without in the least losing the esteem and respect of society. All that is needed is a respectable position, the rest comes of itself. All this notwithstanding, the liberties of a Goethe and a George Sand are improper, judged from the standpoint of bourgeois morality, and stand in contradiction with the nature of its social principles. Compulsory marriage is the normal marriage of bourgeois society: it is the only "moral" union of the sexes: all other sexual union, by whomsoever entered into, is immoral. Bourgeois marriage—we have proved the point beyond cavil—is the result of bourgeois property relations. This marriage, which is intimately related with private property and the right of inheritance—demands "legitimate" children as heirs: it is entered into for the purpose of acquiring these: under the pressure of social conditions, it is forced even upon those who have nothing to bequeath:[2] it becomes a social law, the violation of which the State punishes by imprisoning for a term of years the men or women who live in adultery and have been divorced.

In future society there is nothing to bequeath, unless the domestic equipment and personal inventory be regarded as inheritance: the modern form of marriage is thus devoid of foundation and collapses. The question of inheritance is thereby solved, and Socialism need not concern

[2] In his work "Bau und Leben des sozialen Koerpers" (The Structure and Life of the Social Body), Dr. Schaeffle says: "A loosening of the bonds of matrimony by the facilitation of divorce is certainly undesirable. It flies in the face of the moral objects of human pairing, and would be injurious to the preservation of the population as well as the education of the children." After what has been said herein it follows that we not only consider this view wrong, but are inclined to regard it as "immoral." Nevertheless, Dr. Schaeffle will allow that the idea of introducing and maintaining institutions that do violence to its own conceptions of morality, is simply unimaginable in a society of much higher culture than the present.

itself about abolishing the same. No right of inheritance can arise where there is no private property.

Woman is, accordingly, free, and her children, where she has any, do not impair her freedom: they can only fill all the fuller the cup of her enjoyments and her pleasure in life. Nurses, teachers, female friends, the rising female generations—all these are ready at hand to help the mother when she needs help.

It is possible that there may be men in the future who will say with Alexander von Humboldt: "I am not built for the father of a family. Moreover, I consider marriage a sin, and the begetting of children a crime." What of it? The power of natural instincts will restore the equilibrium. We are alarmed neither by a Humboldt's hostility to marriage nor by the philosophic pessimism of a Schopenhauer, a Mainlaender or a v. Hartmann, who raise to man the prospect of self-destruction in the "ideal State," In this matter we hold with Fr. Ratzel, who justly says:

"Man may no longer look upon himself as an exception to the laws of Nature; he should rather begin at last to ascertain the law that underlies his own acts and thoughts, and to endeavor to live his life according to the laws of Nature. He will arrive at the point when he will arrange his social life with his fellows, that is, his family and the State, not after the precepts of far-back centuries, but after the rational principles of natural sense. Politics, morals, principles of justice—all of which are at present fed from all possible sources—will be determined according to the laws of Nature alone. An existence worthy of human beings, dreamed of for thousands of years, will finally become reality."[3]

That day is approaching with giant strides. Human society has traversed, in the course of thousands of years, all the various phases of development, to arrive in the end where it started from,—communistic property and complete equality and fraternity, but no longer among congeners alone, but among the whole human race. In that does the great progress consist. What bourgeois society has vainly striven for, and at which it suffers and is bound to suffer shipwreck—the restoration of freedom, equality and fraternity among men—Socialism will accomplish. Bourgeois society could only set up the theory; here, as in so many other respects, their practice was at odds with their theories. It is for Socialism to harmonize the theory with the practice.

Nevertheless, while man returns to the starting point in his development, the return is effected upon an infinitely higher social plane than that from which he started. Primitive society held property in

* Quoted in Haeckel's "Natuerliche Schoepfungsgeschichte."

common in the gens and clan, but only in the rawest and most undeveloped stage. The process of development that took place since, reduced, it is true, the common property to a small and insignificant vestige, broke up the gentes, and finally atomized the whole of society; but, simultaneously, it raised mightily the productivity of that society in its various phases and the manifoldness of social necessities, and it created out of the gentes and tribes nations and great States, although again it produced a condition of things that stood in violent contradiction with social requirements. The task of the future is to end the contradiction by the re-transformation upon the broadest basis, of property and productive powers into collective property.

Society re-takes what once was its own, but, in accord with the newly created conditions of production, it places its whole mode of life upon the highest stage of culture, which enables all to enjoy what under more primitive circumstances was the privilege of individuals or of individual classes only.

Now woman again fills the active *role* that once was hers in primitive society. She does not become the mistress, she is the equal of man.

"The end of social development resembles the beginning of human existence. The original equality returns. The mother-web of existence starts and rounds up the cycle of human affairs"—thus writes Bachofen, in his frequently quoted work "Das Mutterrecht," forecasting coming events. Like Bachofen, Morgan also passes judgment upon bourgeois society, a judgment that, without his having any particular information on Socialism, coincides essentially with our own. He says:

"Since the advent of civilization, the outgrowth of property has been so immense, its forms so diversified, its uses so expanding and its *management so intelligent in the interests of its owners, that it has become, on the part of the people, an unmanageable power.* The human mind stands bewildered in the presence of its own creation. The time will come, nevertheless, when human intelligence will rise to the mastery over property, and define the relations of the State to the property it protects, as well as the obligations and the limits of the rights of its owners. *The interests of society are paramount to individual interests, and the two must be brought into just and harmonious relations.* A mere property career is not the final destiny of mankind, if progress is to be the law of the future as it has been of the past. The time which has passed away since civilization began is but a fragment of the past duration of man's existence; and but a fragment of the ages yet to come. *The dissolution of society bids fair to become the termination of a career of which property is the end and aim; because such a career contains the elements of self-destruction. Democracy in government, brotherhood*

*in society, equality in rights and privileges, and universal education,
foreshadow the next higher plane of society to which experience, intelligence and knowledge are steadily tending. It will be a revival, in a
higher form, of the liberty, equality and fraternity of the ancient gentes.*[4]

Thus we see how men, proceeding from different starting-points, are
guided by their scientific investigations to the identical conclusions.
The complete emancipation of woman, and her equality with man is the
final goal of our social development, whose realization no power on
earth can prevent;—and this realization is possible only by a social
change that shall abolish the rule of man over man—hence also of capitalists over workingmen. Only then will the human race reach its
highest development. The "Golden Age" that man has been dreaming
of for thousands of years, and after which they have been longing, will
have come at last. Class rule will have reached its end for all time,
and, along with it, the rule of man over woman.

[4] Morgan's "Ancient Society."

PART IV

INTERNATIONALITY

INTERNATIONALITY.

In the very nature of things, an existence worthy of human beings can never be the exclusive possession of a single privileged people. Isolated from all others, no nation could either raise or keep up such an establishment. The development that we have reached is the product of the co-operation of national and international forces and relations. Although with many the national idea still wholly sways the mind, and subserves the purpose of maintaining political and social dominations, possible only within national boundaries, the human race has reached far into internationalism.

Treaties of commerce, of tariffs and of shipping, postal unions, international expositions, conventions on international law and on international systems of measurement, international scientific congresses and associations, international expeditions of discovery, our trade and intercommunication, especially the international congresses of workingmen, who are the carriers of the new social order and to whose moral influence was mainly due the international congress for factory legislation in the interest of the workingmen, assembled in Berlin in the spring of 1890 upon the invitation of the German Empire,—these and many other phenomena testify to the international character that, despite national demarcations, the relations between the various civilized nations have assumed. National boundary lines are being broken through. The term "world's economy" is taking the place of "national economy": an increasing significance is attaching to it, seeing that upon it depends the well-being and prosperity of individual nations. A large part of our own products is exchanged for those of foreign nations, without which we could no longer exist. As one branch of industry is injured when another suffers, so likewise does the production of one nation suffer materially when that of another is paralyzed. Despite all such transitory disturbances as wars and race persecutions, the relations of the several nations draw ever closer, because material interests, the strongest of all, dominate them. Each new highway, every improvement in the means of intercommunication, every invention or improvement in the process of production, whereby goods are made cheaper, strengthens these relations. The ease with which personal contact can be established between distantly located countries and peoples is a new and powerful link in the chain that draws and holds the nations together.

Emigrations and colonizations are additional and powerful levers. One people learns from the other. Each seeks to excel. Along with the interchange of material products, the interchange of the products of the mind is going on, in the original tongue as well as in translations. To millions the learning of foreign living languages becomes a necessity. Next to material advantages, nothing contributes more towards removing antipathies than to penetrate into the language and the intellectual products of a foreign people.

The effect of this process of drawing together, that is going on upon an international scale, is that the several nations are resembling one another ever more in their social conditions. With the most advanced, and therefore pace-setting nations, the resemblance is now such that he who has learned to understand the social structure of one, likewise knows that of all the others in essentials. It happens similarly as in Nature where, among animals of the same species the skeleton formation and organization is the same, and, if in possession of a part of such a skeleton, one can theoretically construct the whole animal.

A further result is this, that where the same social foundations are found, their effects must be the same—the accumulation of vast wealth, and its opposite pole of mass-poverty, wage-slavery, dependence of the masses upon the machinery of production, their domination by the property-holding minority, and the rest of the long train of consequences.

Indeed, we see that the class antagonisms and the class struggles, that rage throughout Germany, equally keep all Europe, the United States, Australia, etc., in commotion. In Europe, from Russia across to Portugal, from the Balkans, Hungary and Italy across to England and Ireland, the same spirit of discontent is prevalent, the identical symptoms of social fermentation, of general apprehension and of decomposition are noticeable. Externally unlike, according to the degree of development, the character of the people and their political organization, these movements are all essentially alike. Deep-reaching social antagonisms are their cause. Every year these antagonisms become more pronounced, the fermentation and discontent sinks deeper and spreads wider, until finally some provocation, possibly insignificant in seeming, brings on the explosion, that then spreads like lightning throughout the cilivized world, and calls upon the people to take sides— pro or con.

The battle is then on between New and Old Society. Masses of people step upon the stage; an abundance of intelligence is enlisted, such as the world never before saw engaged in any contest, and never again will see gathered for such a purpose. *It is the last social struggle of all.* Standing at the elevation of this century, the sight is obvious of the steady coming to a head of the forces for the struggle in which the New Ideas will triumph.

The new social system will then rear itself upon an international basis. The peoples will fraternize; they will reach one another the hand, and they will endeavor to gradually extend the new conditions over all the races of the earth.[1] No people any longer approaches another as an enemy, bent upon oppression and exploitation; or as the representative of a strange creed that it seeks to impose upon others;—they well meet one another as friends, who seek to raise all human beings to the height of civilization. The labors of the new social order in its work of colonization and civilization will differ as essentially in both purpose and method from the present, as the two social orders are essentially different from each other. Neither powder nor lead, neither "firewater" (liquor) nor Bible will be used. The task of civilization is entered upon with the instruments of peace, which will present the' civilizers to the savages, not as enemies, but as benefactors. Intelligent travelers and investigators have long learned to know how successful is that path.

When the civilized peoples shall have reached the point of joining in a large federation, the time will have come when for evermore the storms of war shall have been lain. Perpetual peace is no dream, as the gentlemen who strut about in uniforms seek to make people believe. That day shall have come the moment the peoples shall have understood their true interests: these are not promoted by war and dissension: by armaments that bear down whole nations; they are promoted by peaceful, mutual understandings, and jointly laboring in the path of civilization. Moreover, as was shown on page 238, the ruling classes and their Governments are seeing to it that the military armaments and wars break their own backs by their own immensity. Thus the last weapons will wander into the museums of antiquity, as so many of their predecessors have done before, and serve as witnesses to future generations of the manner in which the generations gone by have for thousands of years frequently torn up one another like wild animals—until finally the human in them triumphed over the beast.

National peculiarities are everywhere nourished by the ruling classes in order that, at a given conjuncture, a great war may furnish a drainage for dangerous tendencies at home. As a proof of the extent to which these national peculiarities engender wars, an utterance of the late General Fieldmarshal Moltke may here be quoted. In the last

[1] "National and human interests stand to-day opposed to each other. At a higher stage of civilization these interests will coincide and become one."— V. Thuenen, "Der Isolirte Staat."

volume of his posthumous work, which deals with the German-French war of 1870-71, this passage occurs among others in the introductory observations:

"So long as nations lead separate existences there will be dissensions that only strokes can arbitrate. In the interest of humanity, however, it is to be hoped that wars may become as much rarer as they have become more fearful."

Now then, this national separate existence, that is, the hostile shutting off of one nation from another, will vanish. Thus future generations will be able to achieve without trouble tasks that gifted heads have long conceived, and unsuccessfully attempt to accomplish. Condorcet, among others, conceived the idea of an international language. The late Ulysses S. Grant, ex-President of the United States, uttered himself this wise on a public occasion: "Seeing that commerce, education and the rapid exchange of thought and of goods by telegraphy and steam have altered everything, I believe that God is preparing the world to become one nation, to speak one language and to reach such a state of perfection in which armies and navies will no longer be needed." It is natural that with a full-blooded Yankee the leading *role* be played by the "dear God," who, after all, is but the product of historic development. Hypocrisy, or perhaps also ignorance in matters that concern religion, is nowhere as stupendous as in the United States. The less the power of the State presses upon the masses, all the more must religion do the work. Hence the phenomenon that the bourgeoisie is most pious wherever the power of the State is laxest. Next to the United States, come England, Belgium and Switzerland in this matter. Even the revolutionary Robespierre, who played with the heads of aristocrats and priests as with nine-pin balls, was, as is known, very religious, whence he ceremoniously introduced the "Supreme Being," which shortly before had, with equal bad taste, been dethroned by the Convention. And seeing that the frivolous and idle aristocrats of France had been greatly bragging about their atheism, Robespierre regarded atheism as aristocratic, and denounced it in his speech to the Convention on the "Supreme Being" with these words: "Atheism is aristocratic. The idea of a Supreme Being, that watches over oppressed innocence and punishes triumphant crime, comes from the people. If there were no God, one would have to be invented." The virtuous Robespierre had his misgivings concerning the power of his virtuous republic to cancel the existing social antagonisms, hence his belief in a Supreme Being that wreaks vengeance and seeks to smooth the difficulties that the people of his time were unable to smooth. Hence also was such a belief a necessity to the first republic.

One step in progress will bring another. Mankind will ever set new tasks to itself, and the accomplishment of the same will lead it to such a degree of social development that wars, religious quarrels and similar manifestations of barbarism will be unknown.

PART V

POPULATION *and* OVER-POPULATION

POPULATION AND OVER-POPULATION.

It has become quite fashionable with people who occupy themselves with the social question to consider the question of population as the most important and burning of all. They claim that we are threatened with "over-population;" aye, that the danger is upon us. This, more than any other division of the Social Question, must be treated from an international standpoint. The feeding and the distribution of the people have pre-eminently become international issues of fact. Since Malthus, the law underlying the increase of population has been the subject of extensive dispute. In his celebrated and now notorious "Essay on the Principles of Population," which Marx has characterized as a "school-boyish, superficial and pulpiteer piece of declamatory plagiarism on Sir James Stewart, Townsend, Franklin, Wallace and others" and which "contains not one original sentence," Malthus lays down the proposition that mankind has the tendency to increase in geometric progression (1, 2, 4, 8, 16, 32, etc.), while food could increase only in arithmetic progression (1, 2, 3, 4, 5, etc.); and that the consequence is a rapid disproportion between the numbers of the population and the supply of food, that inevitably leads to want and starvation. The final conclusion was the necessity of "abstinence" in the procreation of children, and abstinence from marriage without sufficient means for the support of a family, contrariwise there would be no place at "the banquet table of Nature" for the descendants.

The fear of over-population is very old. It was touched upon in this work in connection with the social conditions of the Greeks and Romans, and at the close of the Middle Ages. Plato and Aristotle, the Romans, the small bourgeois of the Middle Ages were all swayed by it, and it even swayed Voltaire, who, in the first quarter of the eighteenth century, published a treatise on the subject. The fear ever turns up again—this circumstance must be emphasized—*at periods when the existing social conditions are disintegrating and breaking down.* Seeing on all sides privation and discontent at such periods, the privation and discontent are forthwith ascribed to the shortness of the supply of food, instead of to the manner in which the existing supply is distributed.

All advanced social stages have hitherto rested upon class-rule, and the principal means of class-rule was the appropriation of the land. The land gradually slips from the hands of a large number of proprietors into those of a small number that utilize and cultivate it only partially. The large majority are rendered propertyless and are stripped of the means of existence; their share of food then depends upon the good will of their masters, for whom they now have to work. According to the social condition of things, the struggle for the land takes its form from period to period; the end, however, was that the land continued steadily to concentrate in the hands of the ruling class. If undeveloped means of transportation or political isolation impede the intercourse abroad of a community and interfere with the importation of food when the crops fail and provisions are dear, forthwith the belief springs up that there are too many people. Under such circumstances, every increase in the family is felt as a burden; the specter of over-population rises; and the terror that it spreads is in direct proportion to the concentration of the land in few hands, together with its train of evils—the partial cultivation of the soil, and its being turned to purposes of pleasure for its owners. Rome and Italy were poorest off for food at the time when the whole soil of Italy was held by about 3,000 latifundia owners. Hence the cry: "The latifundia are ruining Rome!" The soil was converted into vast hunting-grounds and wonderful pleasure-gardens; not infrequently it was allowed to be idle, seeing that its cultivation, even by slaves, came out dearer to the magnates than the grain imported from Sicily and Africa. It was a state of things that opened wide the doors for usury in grain, a practice in which the rich nobility likewise led. In consideration of this usury of grain the domestic soil was kept from cultivation. Thereupon the impoverished Roman citizen and the impoverished aristocracy resolved to renounce marriage and the begetting of children; hence the laws placing premiums on marriage and children in order to check the steady decrease of the ruling classes.

The same phenomenon appeared towards the close of the Middle Ages, after the nobility and clergy had, in the course of centuries and with the aid of all the crafty and violent means at their command, robbed unnumbered peasants of their property and appropriated the common lands to themselves. When, thereupon, the peasants revolted and were beaten down, the robber-trade gained new impetus, and it was then also practiced upon the Church estates by the Princes of the Reformation. The number of thieves, beggars and vagabonds was never larger than immediately before and after the Reformation. The expropriated rural population rushed to the cities; but there, due to causes that have been described in previous pages, the conditions of life were likewise deteriorating,—hence "over-population" was felt all around.

The appearance of Malthus coincides with that period of English industry when, due to the inventions of Hargreaves, Arkwright and Watt, powerful changes set in both in mechanism and technique, changes that affected, first of all, the cotton and linen industries, and rendered breadless the workingmen engaged in them. The concentration of capital and land assumed at the time large proportions in England: along with the rapid increase of wealth, on the one hand, there went the deepening misery of the masses, on the other. At such a juncture, the ruling classes, who have every reason to consider the existing world the "best of all possible worlds," were bound to seek an explanation for so contradictory a phenomenon as the pauperization of the masses in the midst of swelling wealth and flourishing industry. Nothing was easier than to throw the blame upon the too-rapid procreation of the workingmen, and not upon their having been rendered superfluous through the capitalist process of production, and the accumulation of the soil in the hands of landlords. With such circumstances for its setting, the "schoolboyish, superficial and pulpiteer piece of declamatory plagiarism," that Malthus published, was a work that gave drastic utterance to the secret thoughts and wishes of the ruling class, and justified their misdeeds to the world. Hence the loud applause that it met from one side, and violent opposition from another. Malthus had spoken the right word at the right time for the English bourgeoisie; hence, although his essay "contained not one original sentence," he became a great and celebrated man, and his name a synonym for the doctrine.[1]

Now, then, the conditions that caused Malthus thus to give his signal of alarm and proclaim his brutal doctrine—he addressed it to the working class, thus adding insult to injury—have since grown worse from decade to decade. They have grown worse, not alone in the fatherland of Malthus, Great Britain, but in all the countries of the world run by the capitalist system of production, whose consequences ever are the robbery of the soil and the dependence and subjugation of the masses through machinery and the factory. This system consists, as has been shown, in the separation of the workingman from his means of production—be these land or tools—and in the transfer of the latter to the capitalist class. That system produces ever new branches of industry, develops and concentrates them, and thereby throws ever larger masses of the people upon the street as "superfluous." On the field of agriculture it promotes, as the Rome of old, the latifundia ownership with all its sequences. Ireland, in this respect the classic land of Europe, and afflicted worst of all by the English system of land-grabbing, had in 1887 an area of 884.4 square miles of meadow and pasture land, but only 263.3 square miles of agricultural fields and the conversion of agri-

---

[1] That Darwin and others also became devotees of Malthus only proves how the lack of economic knowledge leads to one-sided views.

cultural fields into meadows and pastures for sheep and cattle and into hunting grounds for the landlords makes every year further strides.[2]

Moreover the agricultural fields of Ireland are, in great measure, in the hands of a large number of small tenants, who are not able to cultivate the land in the most profitable manner. Thus Ireland presents the aspect of a country that is retrogressing from an agricultural into a pastoral condition. The population, that at the beginning of the nineteenth century was over eight million strong, has declined to about five million, and still several millions are "in excess." Ireland's normal state of rebellion against England is thus easily explained; and yet the struggle of the "Home Ruler" aims only at the creation of an Irish landlord class and no wise carries the wished-for deliverance to the mass of the Irish people. The Irish people will perceive that so soon as the Home Ruler shall carry out his plans. Scotland presents a picture similar to that of Ireland with regard to the ownership and cultivation of its soil.[3]

A similar development reappears in Hungary, a country that entered upon the modern field of development only recently. Hungary, a land in point of the fertility of her soil, as rich as few in Europe, is overloaded with debt, and her population, pauperized and in the hands of usurers, emigrates in large numbers. Hungary's soil is now concentrated in the hands of modern capitalist magnates, who carry on a ruinous system of cultivation in forest and field

[2] Fred. Freiligrath sings in his fervid poem "Ireland":

> Thus naught the Irish landlord cares,
>   While hart and ox by peasant's toil
> For him are raised—he leaves undried
>   Great bogs and swamps on Erin's soil—
>
> Extensive mirelands unreclaimed,
>   Where sheaf by sheaf rich crops could wave;
> He vilely leaves—a wanton waste—
>   Where water-fowl and wild ducks lave.
>
> Four million acres feels his rod;
>   A wilderness accursed of God.

[3] "Two millions of acres . . totally laid waste, embracing within their area some of the most fertile lands of Scotland. The natural grass of Glen Tilt was among the most nutritive in the county of Perth. The deer forest of Ben Aulder was by far the best grazing ground in the wide district of Badenoch; a part of the Black Mount forest was the best pasture for black-faced sheep in Scotland. Some idea of the ground laid waste for purely sporting purposes in Scotland may be formed from the fact that it embraced an area larger than the whole county of Perth. The resources of the forest of Ben Aulder might give some idea of the loss sustained from the forced desolations. The ground would pasture 15,000 sheep, and as it was not more than one-thirtieth part of the old forest ground in Scotland . . It might, &c. . . All that forest land is as totally unproductive . . . It might thus as well have been submerged under the waters of the German Ocean."—From the London "Economist," July 2, 1866, cited by Karl Marx in "Capital," p. 757, edition Swan-Sonnenschein & Co., London, 1896.

so that Hungary is not far from the time when it will have ceased to be a grain exporting country. It is quite similarly with Italy. In Italy, just as in Germany, the political unity of the nation has taken capitalist development powerfully under the arm; but the thrifty peasants of Piedmont and Lombardy, of Tuscany, Romagna and Sicily are ever more impoverished and go to ruin. Swamps and moors are reappearing on the sites occupied but recently by the well cultivated gardens and fields of small peasants. Before the very gates of Rome, in the so-called Campagna, a hundred thousand hectares of land lie fallow in a region that once was the "garden of Rome." Swamps cover the ground, and exhale their poisonous miasmas. If, with the application of the proper means the Campagna were thoroughly drained and properly irrigated, the population of Rome would have a fertile source of food. But Italy suffers of the ambition to become a "leading power:" she is ruining herself with military and naval armaments and with African colonization plans, and, consequently, has no funds left for such tasks as the reclaiming of the Campagna for cultivation. And as the Campagna, so are South Italy and particularly Sicily. The latter, once the granary of Rome, sinks ever more into deepening poverty. There is no more sucked-out, poverty-stricken and maltreated people in all Europe than the Sicilian. The easily-contented sons of the most beautiful region of all Europe overrun half Europe and the United States as lowerers of wages because they care not to starve to death upon the native soil that has ceased to be their property. Malaria, that frightful fever, is spreading over Italy to an extent that, frightened at the prospect, the government instituted in 1882 an investigation, which brought to light the deplorable fact that, of the 69 provinces of the country, 32 were severely afflicted by the disease, 32 were infected, and only 5 had so far remained free. The disease, once known only in the rural districts, penetrated the cities, where the urban, increased by the rural proletariat, constitutes a center of infection.

These facts, together with what has been said touching the effects and results of the capitalist system of production, teach us that want and misery with the masses are not the results of insufficiency in the means of existence, but of an unequal distribution, that furnishes some with a superfluity and condemns others to privation. It causes the destruction and squandering of supplies, and, along with that, negligence in producing these. The Malthusian assertions have sense only from the standpoint of the system of capitalist production. Whoever stands on that principle has every reason to defend it, otherwise the ground would slip from under him.

On the other side, however, the capitalist system itself favors the production of children, in so far as it needs cheap "hands" in the shape of such in its factories. The begetting of children, moreover, often becomes a matter of calculation with the proletariat. They cost the parents little or nothing: they soon earn their own support. In the house industries the proletarian is even obliged to have many children: they equip him all the better for the competitive struggle. It certainly is an abominable system: it conceals the pauperization of the workingman and it provokes his own rendering of himself superfluous through the children who work for the most miserable of wages. The immorality and harmfulness of this system are obvious, and they spread with the extension of capitalism. It is precisely for that reason that the bourgeois ideologists—and all bourgeois economists are that—defend the Malthusian theories. Hence in Germany also and in particular the notion of "over-production" ever finds support among the bourgeoisie. Capital is the innocent defendant, the workingman is the criminal.

Unfortunately, however, for this theory Germany has "superfluity," not of proletarians only, but also of "intellectuals." Capital brings about not only an over-production of soil, goods, workingmen, women and children, but also of "officials and learning"—as we shall show. There is only one thing that is not "superfluous" in this capitalist world—capital and its owner, the capitalist.

If the capitalist economists are Malthusians they are simply what their capitalist interests compel them to be. Only, they should not shift their bourgeois whims to the shoulders of Socialist society. John Stuart Mill says among other things: "But Communism is precisely the state of things in which opinion might be expected to declare itself with greatest intensity against this kind of selfish intemperance. An augmentation of numbers which diminished the comfort or increased the toil of the mass, would then cause (which now it does not) immediate and unmistakable inconvenience to every individual in the association; inconvenience which could not then be imputed to the avarice of employers, or the unjust privileges of the rich. In such altered circumstances, opinion could not fail to reprobate, and if reprobation did not suffice, to repress by penalties of some description, this or any other culpable self-indulgence at the expense of the community. The Communistic scheme, instead of being peculiarly open to the objection drawn from danger of over-population, has the recommendation of tending in an especial degree to the prevention of that evil." And Prof. Ad. Wagner says: "Least of all could freedom of marriage or freedom of procreation be tolerated in a Socialist community."[4] These authors proceed from the theory that the

[4] Rau's "Lehrbuch der Politischen Oekonomie," p. 367.

tendency towards over-population is one common to all social conditions, but both allow that Socialism is better able than any other social system to establish the equilibrium between population and food. The latter is true, not so the former.

True enough, there were one time Socialists, who, tainted by the Malthusian theories, perceived the "imminent danger" of over-population. But these Socialist Malthusians have disappeared. A clearer insight into the nature of bourgeois society, together with the fact that, judging from the plaintive songs of our Agrarians, we produce not too little but too much food, and that the resulting low prices render the production of foodstuffs unprofitable, has enlightened them on the subject.

A part of our Malthusians imagine—and the chorus of the mouthpieces of the bourgeoisie parrot-like echo their utterances—that a Socialist society, in which there is freedom in the choice of love and ample provision for a livelihood worthy of human beings, must soon degenerate into a rabbit warren: it would succumb to excessive sexual indulgence and to excessive procreation. Exactly the reverse is most likely to happen, as certain observations go to prove. Until now the largest number of children were had, not by the best, but by the worst situated. It may even be said without being guilty of exaggeration: the poorer the condition of a proletarian stratum, the more numerous also is its average blessing of children, conceding exceptions here and there. Even Virchow confirms this. He says: "As the English workingman in his deepest degradation, in the utter vacancy of the mind, finally knows but two sources of enjoyment, drunkenness and coition, so did the population of Upper Silesia, until recent years, concentrate all its wishes, all its desires upon these two things. Liquor and the gratification of sexual cravings had become sovereign with it. Hence it is easy to understand that its population gained as rapidly in numbers as it lost in physical vigor and moral fibre." Karl Marx expresses himself similarly when he says in "Capital:" "As a matter of fact, not only the number of births and deaths but the absolute size of families is in reverse ratio to the height of wages, i. e., to the means of subsistence which the various categories of workmen have at their disposal. *This law of capitalist society would sound absurd among savages, or even civilized colonists.* It reminds us of the enormous power of reproduction among animals that are individually weak and much hunted down;" and Marx furthermore quotes Laing, who says: "If all the world were in comfortable circumstances, the earth would soon be depopulated." We see Laing's views are opposed to Malthus: he is of the opinion that a good living is not conducive to the increase but to the decrease of births. In the same vein says Herbert Spencer: "Always and everywhere progress and pro•creative capacity are opposed to each other. It follows that the higher development, that mankind looks forward to, will probably have as a result a decline in procreation."

Thus we see men, who otherwise differ, absolutely at one on this head, and their views coincide wholly with ours.

The whole question of population could be practically disposed of off hand with the observation that there is no danger of over-population within sight: we find ourselves in front of such a superabundance of food, which even threatens to increase, that the greatest worry, now afflicting the producers of means of subsistence, is to furnish this wealth of food at tolerable prices. A rapid increase of consumers would even be the most desirable thing for producers. But our Malthusians are tireless in the raising of objections: thus we are forced to meet these, lest they have the excuse that they can not be refuted.

They claim that the danger of an over-population in a not-distant future lies in the law of a "decreasing yield of the soil." Our fields become "tired of cultivation;" increasing crops are no longer to be looked for; seeing that fields, fit for cultivation, become daily rarer, the danger of a scarcity of food is imminent, if the population continue to increase. We believe to have proved beyond doubt, in the passages on the agricultural utilization of the soil, what enormous progress mankind can make with respect to the acquisition of new masses of nutriment. But we shall give further illustrations. A very able landlord of wide acres and economist of acknowledged worth, a man, accordingly who excelled Malthus in both respects, said as early as 1850—a time when chemical agriculture was still in its swaddling clothes—on the subject of agricultural production: "The productivity of raw products, especially foodstuffs, will in future no longer lag behind the productivity of the factory and of transportation. . . Chemical agriculture has only started in our days to open to agriculture prospects that will no doubt lead to many false roads, but that in the end will place the production of foodstuffs as fully in the power of society, as it lies now in its power to furnish yards of cloth, if but the requisite supply of wool is at hand.[5]

Justus v. Liebig, the founder of chemical agriculture, holds that "if human labor and manure are available in sufficient quantity, the soil is inexhaustible, and can yield uninterruptedly the richest harvests." The "law of a decreasing yield of the soil" is a Malthusian notion, that had its justification at a time when agriculture was in an undeveloped state; the notion has long since been refuted by science and experience.

[5] Rodbertus: "Zur Beleuchtung der sozialen Frage."

The law is rather this: "The yield of a soil stands in direct ratio to the human labor expended (science and technique being included), and to the proper fertilizers applied to it." If it was possible for small-peasant France to more than quadruple the yield of her soil during the last ninety years, without the population even doubling, much better results are to be expected from a Socialist society. Our Malthusians, furthermore, overlook the fact that, under our existing conditions, not our soil merely is to be taken into account, but the soil of the whole earth, that is, to a great extent, territories whose fertility yields twenty, thirty and many more times as much as our corresponding fields of the same size. The earth is now extensively appropriated by man; nevertheless, a small fraction excepted, it is nowhere cultivated and utilized as it could be cultivated and utilized. Not Great Britain alone could, as has been shown, produce a much larger quantity of food than she does to-day, but France, Germany, Austria and to a still much greater extent the other countries of Europe also could do the same. In little Wurtemberg, with her 879,970 hectares of grain soil, the mere application of the steam plow would raise the average crop of 6,410,000 to 9,000,000 cwts.

European Russia—measured by the present standard of the population of Germany—would be able to nourish, instead of her present population of 90,000,000, one of 475,000,000 souls. To-day European Russia has about 1,000 inhabitants to the square mile, Saxony over 12,000.

The objection that Russia contains vast stretches of territory, whose climate renders impossible any higher degree of cultivation, is true; on the other hand, however, she has to the south a climate and fertility of soil by far unknown in Germany. Then, again, due to the denseness of population and the improved cultivation of soil therewith connected, such as clearings of woods, draining, etc., changes, wholly unmeasureable to-day, will be brought on in climate. Wherever man aggregates in large numbers climatic changes are perceived. To-day we attach too little importance to this phenomenon; we are even unable to realize the same to its full extent, seeing that we have no occasion therefor, and, as things are to-day, lack the means to undertake the needed experiments on an adequate scale. Furthermore, all travelers are agreed that in the high latitudes of Northern Siberia, where spring, summer and autumn crowd together in rapid succession within a few months, an astonishing luxuriance of vegetation suddenly springs forth. Thus Sweden and Norway to-day, so sparsely populated, would, with their mammoth woods and positively inexhaustible mineral wealth, their numerous rivers and long stretch of coast lines, furnish rich sources of food for a dense population. The requisite means and appliances are not obtainable under present circumstances, and thus even that sparse population casts off its shoals of emigrants.

What may be said of the north applies with still more force to the south of Europe—Portugal, Spain, Italy, Greece, the Danubian States, Hungary, Turkey, etc. A climate of surpassing quality, a soil of so luxuriant and fertile as is hardly found in the best regions of the United States, will some day furnish an abundance of food to unnumbered people. The decrepid political and social conditions of those countries cause hundreds of thousands of our own people to prefer crossing the ocean rather than to settle in those much nearer and more comfortably located States. Soon as rational social conditions and international relations will prevail there, new millions of people will be needed to raise those large and fertile lands to a higher grade of civilization.

In order to be able to reach materially higher rungs on the ladder of civilization we shall, for a long time to come, have in Europe, not a superfluity, but a dearth of people. Under such circumstances, it is an absurdity to yield to the fear of over-population. It must ever be kept in mind that the utilization of existing sources of food, by the application of science and labor, knows no limit: every day brings new discoveries and inventions which increase the yield of the sources of food.

If we pass from Europe to the other parts of the earth, the lack of people and the excess of soil is still more glaring. The most luxuriant and fruitful lands of the earth still lie wholly or almost wholly idle: the work of bringing them under cultivation and turning them to use can not be undertaken with a few hundred or thousand people: it demands mass colonizations of many millions in order to be able to bring the but-too-luxuriant Nature under human control. Under this head belong, among others, Central and South America—a territory of hundreds of thousands of square miles. Argentina, for instance, had in 1892 about 5,000,000 hectares under cultivation, the country has, however, 96,000,000 hectares at its disposal. The soil of South America, fit for the cultivation of corn and lying fallow, is estimated at 200,000,000 hectares, at least. The United States, Austria-Hungary, Great Britain and Ireland, Germany and France have all togethor only about 105,000,000 hectares devoted to cereals. Carey maintains that the 360-mile long valley of the Orinoco alone could furnish enough food to supply the whole present human race. Let us halve the estimate, and there is still an abundance. At any rate, South America alone could feed the majority of the population now extant on earth. The nutritive value of a field planted with banana trees and one of equal size planted with wheat stands as 133 to 1. While our wheat yields in favorable soil 12 to 20 times its seed, rice in its home yields 80 to 100, maize 250 to

300 times as much. In many regions, the Philippine Islands among them, the productivity of rice is estimated at 400 times as much. The question with all these articles of food is to render them as nourishing as possible by the manner in which they are prepared. Chemistry has in this a boundless field for development.

Central and South America, especially Brazil, which alone is almost as large as all Europe—Brazil has 152,000 square miles with about 15,000,000 inhabitants, as against Europe's 178,000 square miles and about 340,000,000 inhabitants—are big with a luxuriance and fertility, that stir the astonishment and wonderment of all travelers, besides being inexhaustibly rich in minerals. Nevertheless, until now they are almost closed to the world because their population is indolent and stands, both in point of numbers and of culture, too low to overmaster the power of Nature. How matters look in Africa we have been enlightened on by the discoveries of recent years. Even if a good part of Central Africa never be fit for European agriculture, there are other regions of vast size that can be put to good use the moment rational principles of colonization are applied. On the other hand, there are in Asia not only vast and fertile territories, able to feed thousands of millions of people, but the past has also shown how in places that are there now sterile and almost desert, the mild climate once conjured up an abundance of food from the soil, provided only man knows how to lead to it the blessing-bestowing water. What with the destruction of the marvelous aqueducts and contrivances for irrigation in Asia Minor and in the regions of the Tigris and the Euphrates, with vandalic wars of conquest and the insane oppression of the people by the conquerors, fields, thousands of square miles wide, have been transformed into sandy deserts. Likewise in Northern Africa, Spain, Mexico and Peru. Let there be produced millions of civilized human beings, and inexhaustible sources of food will be unlocked. The fruit of the date tree thrives marvelously in Asia and Africa, and it takes up so little room that 200 trees can go on one acre of land. The durrha bears in Egypt more than 3,000 fold, and yet the country is poor—not by reason of excessive population ,but as the result of a robber system that accomplishes the feat of spreading the desert ever further from decade to decade. The marvelous results attainable in all these countries by the agriculture and horticulture of middle Europe is a matter that eludes all calculation.

With the present state of agriculture, the United States could easily feed fifteen and twenty times its present population (63,000,000)—that is, 1,200,000,000 people. Under the same conditions, Canada could feed, instead of 5,000,000 people, 100,000,000 people. Then there are Australia, the numerous and in some instances large and extraordinarily fertile islands of the great Indian Ocean, etc. "Multiply!"—such, and not "Reduce your numbers!"—is the call that in the name of civilization reaches the human race.

Everywhere, it is the social conditions—the existing method of production and distribution—that bring on privation and misery, not the number of people. A few rich crops in succession lower the prices of food in such manner that a considerable number of our cultivators of the soil are ruined. Instead of the condition of the cultivator being improved, it declines. A large number of farmers to-day look upon a good crop as a misfortune: it lowers prices so that the cost of production is barely covered. And this is called a rational state of things! With the view of keeping far away from us the abundance of the harvests of other countries, high duties are placed on grain: thus the entry of foreign grain is made difficult and the price of the domestic article is raised. We have no scarcity but a superabundance of food, the same as of industrial products. The same as millions of people need the yield of the factories, but can not satisfy their wants under the existing system of property and production, so are millions in want of food, being unable to pay for it, although the prices are low and the necessaries of life abundant. We ask again, Can this be called a rational state of things? The craziness and insanity of it all is obvious. Our speculators in corn often, when the crops are good, deliberately allow a large part to perish: they know the prices rise in the measure that the products are scarce. And yet we are told to look out for overpopulation! In Russia, southern Europe and many other countries of the world, hundreds of thousands of loads of grain perish yearly for want of proper storage and transportation. Many millions of hundredweights of food are yearly squandered because the provisions for gathering in the crops are inadequate, or there is a scarcity of hands at the right time. Many a corn field, many a filled barn, whole agricultural establishments are burned down, because the insurance fetches higher gains. Food and goods are destroyed for the same reason that ships are caused to go to the bottom with their whole crews.[6] A large part of the

---

[6] Similar conditions must have existed at the time of St. Basil. He calls out to the rich: "Wretches that you are, what answer will you make to the divine Judge? You cover the nakedness of your walls with carpets, but do not cover the nakedness of human beings! You ornament your horses with costly and smooth coverlets, and you despise your brother who is covered with rags. You allow your corn to rot and be devoured in your barns and your fields, and you do not spare even a look for those who have no bread." Moral homeletics have since old done precious little good with the ruling class, and they will do no better in the future. Let the social conditions be changed so that none can act unjustly towards his fellowman; the world will then get along easy enough.

crops is yearly ruined by our military manoeuvres; the costs of manoeuvres that last only a few days run up to hundreds of thousands of marks; and there are many of them every year. Moreover, as stated before, large fields are taken from cultivation for these purposes.

Nor must it be forgotten that there is the sea yet to be added to the means for increasing the volume of food. The area of water is as 18 to 7 to that of land,—two and a half times as large. Its enormous wealth of food still awaits a rational system of exploitation. The future opens a prospect to mankind, wholly different from the gloomy picture drawn by our Malthusians.

Who can say where the line is to be drawn to our chemical, physical, physiologic knowledge? Who would venture to predict what giant undertakings—so considered from our modern standpoint—the people of future centuries will execute with the object in view of introducing material changes in the climates of the nations and in the methods of exploiting their soil?

We see to-day, under the capitalist social system, undertakings executed that were thought impossible or insane a century ago. Wide isthmuses are cut through; tunnels, miles long and bored into the bowels of the earth, join peoples whom towering mountains separate; others are dug under the beds of seas to shorten distances, and avoid disturbances and dangers that otherwise the countries thus separated are exposed to. Where is the spot at which could be said: "So far and no farther?"

If all these improvements were to be undertaken simultaneously, we would be found to have, not too many but too few people. The race must multiply considerably if it is to do justice to all the tasks that are waiting for it. Neither is the soil under cultivation utilized as it should be, nor are there people enough to cultivate three-fourths of its face. Our relative over-production, continuously produced by the capitalist system to the injury of the workingman and of society, will, at a higher grade of civilization, prove itself a benefit. Moreover, a population as large as possible is, even to-day, not an impediment to but a promoter of progress—on the same principle that the existing over-production of goods and food, the destruction of the family by the enlisting of women and children in the factories, and the expropriation of the handicrafts and the peasantry by capital have all shown themselves to be conditions precedent for a higher state of civilization.

We now come to the other side of the question: Do people multiply indefinitely, and is that a necessity of their being?

With the view of proving this great reproductive power of man, the Malthusians usually refer to the abnormal instances of exceptional families and peoples. Nothing is proven by that. As against these instances there are others where, under favorable conditions, complete sterility shortly sets in. The quickness with which often well situated families die out is surprising. Although the United States offer more favorable conditions than any other country for the increase of population, and yearly hundreds of thousands of people immigrate at the most vigorous age, its population doubles only every thirty years. There are nowhere instances on a large scale of the assertion concerning a doubling period of twelve or twenty years.

As indicated by the quotations from Marx and Virchow, which may be considered to state the rule, population increases fastest where it is poorest because, as Virchow justly claims, next to drunkenness, sexual intercourse is their only enjoyment. When Gregory VII. forced celibacy upon the clergy, the priests of lower rank in the diocese of Mainz complained, as stated before, that differently from the upper prelates, they did not have all possible pleasures, and the only enjoyment left them was their wives. A lack of varying occupation may be the reason why the marriages of the rural clergy are, as a rule, so fruitful of children. It is also undeniable that our poorest districts in Germany—the Silesian Eulengebirge, the Lausitz, the Erzgebirge and Fichtelgebirge, the Thuringian Forest, the Harz, etc.,—are the centers of densest population, whose chief food are potatoes. It is also certain that sexual cravings are strong with consumptives, and these often beget children at a state of physical decline when such a thing would seem impossible.

It is a law of Nature—hinted at in the quotations made from Herbert Spencer and Laing—that she supplies in quantity what she loses in quality. The animals of highest grade and strength—lions, elephants, camels, etc., our domestic animals such as mares, asses, cows,—bring few young ones into the world; while animals of lower organization increase in inverse ratio—all insects, most fishes, etc., the smaller mammals, such as hares, rats, mice, etc. Furthermore, Darwin established that certain wild animals, so soon as tamed, forfeit their fecundity. The elephant is an illustration. This proves that altered conditions of life, together with the consequent change in the mode of life, are the determining factors in reproductive powers.

It happens, however, that it is the Darwinians who lead in the fear of over-population, and upon whom our modern Malthusians bank. Our Darwinians are everywhere infelicitous the moment they apply their theories to human conditions: their method then becomes roughly empirical, and they forget that, while man is the highest organic animal, he, being in contradistinction to animals acquainted with the laws of nature, is able to direct and utilize these.

The theory of the struggle for existence, the doctrine that the germs of new life exist in much larger numbers than are maintainable with the existing means of existence, would be wholly applicable to man if man, instead of straining his brains and enlisting the services of technical arts for exploiting air, land and water, grazed like cattle, or like monkeys indulged his sexual impulses with cynic shamelessness,—in short, if he reverted to the monkey order. In passing be it observed that the fact that, besides man, monkeys are the only beings with whom the sexual impulse is not fixed to certain periods, is a striking proof of the relationship between the two. But though closely related, they are not identical, and are not to be placed on one level and measured by one standard,—a fact that we commend to Ziegler, who, in his book herein frequently referred to, holds up the two together.

The circumstance that, under the conditions of ownership and production that have hitherto prevailed, the struggle for existence existed and continues to exist for man also and many fail to find the conditions for life, is perfectly true. But these failed, not because of the scarcity of the means of existence, but because, due to social conditions, the means of existence, though in greatest abundance, were kept from them. False also is the conclusion that, because such has hitherto been the state of things, it is unchangeable and will ever be so. It is here that the Darwinians slide and fall: they study natural science and anthropology, but not sociology, and thoughtlessly fall in line with our bourgeois ideologists. Hence they drop into their false conclusions.

The sexual instinct is perennial in man; it is his strongest instinct and demands satisfaction, lest his health suffer. Moreover, as a rule, this instinct is strong in proportion to man's health and normal development—just as a good appetite and a good digestion bespeak a healthy stomach, and are the first prerequisites for a healthy body. But gratification of the sexual instinct and begetting and conceiving are not the same thing. The most varied theories have been set up on the fecundity of the human race. On the whole, we are still groping in the dark on this important field, mainly because for a couple of thousand years a senseless shyness has stood in the way of man's occupying himself freely and naturally with the laws of his own origin, and to study thoroughly the laws of human procreation. That is gradually changing and must change much more.

On one side the theory is set up that higher mental development and strenuous mental exertion, in short, higher nervous activity, exert a repressing influence upon the sexual impulse and weaken the procreative power. This is disputed by the other side. The fact is pointed to that the better situated classes have, on an average, fewer children and

that this is not to be ascribed solely to preventive measures. Undoubtedly, intense mental occupation has a depressing influence upon the
sexual impulse, but that such occupation is indulged in by the majority
of our property classes is not so certain. On the other hand, an excess
of physical labor also has a repressing influence. But all excessive
effort is harmful, and therefore objectionable.

Others, again, claim that the manner of life, especially the food
eaten, coupled with certain physical conditions on the part of the woman,
determine the power to beget and to conceive. The nature of food more
than any other cause, this side argues, determines, as experience shows
in the instance of animals also, the effectiveness of the act of procreation. Possibly, this is in fact, the determining factor. The influence
of the nature of nourishment on the organism of certain animals manifests itself surprisingly with bees: they produce at will a queen by the
administering of special food. Bees, accordingly, are further advanced
in the knowledge of sexual development than men. They have not,
probably, been sermonized for two thousand years that it is "indecent"
and "immoral" to concern themselves with sexual matters.

It is also known that plants raised on good soil and well manured,
thrive luxuriantly, but yield no seed. That the nature of the food has
its influence upon the composition of the male sperm, and upon the
fecundity of the female egg with human beings also, is hardly to be
doubted. Thus mayhap that the procreative power of the population
depends in a high degree upon the nature of the food it lives on. Other
factors, whose nature is still but little understood, also play a *role*. It
is a striking circumstance that a young couple, who, having no children
after long years of married life, yet, having separated, and each having
mated again, both new marriages are followed by healthy children.

One factor is of leading importance in the question of population in
the future—*the higher, freer position which all women will then occupy.*
Leaving exceptions aside, intelligent and energetic women are not as a
rule inclined to give life to a large number of children as "the gift of
God," and to spend the best years of their own lives in pregnancy, or
with a child at their breasts. This disinclination for numerous children, which even now is entertained by most women, may—all the
solicitude notwithstanding that a Socialist society will bestow upon
pregnant women and mothers—be rather strengthened than weakened.
In our opinion, there lies in this the great probability that the increase
of population will proceed slower than in bourgeois society.

Our Malthusians need really not break their heads on the future of
the human race. Until now nations have gone down through the decline, never through the increase of their population. In the last analy-

sis, the number of population is regulated without harmful abstinence and without unnatural preventives, in a society that lives according to the laws of Nature. On this head also the future will vindicate Karl Marx. His theory also that every period of economic development carries with it its own law of population will prove true under the rule of Socialism.

The author of the work "Die kuenstliche Beschraenkung der Kinderzahl" (The Artificial Limitation of Progeny)[7] claims that Socialism is playing a tricky manoeuvre by its opposition to Malthusianism: a rapid increase of population promotes mass proletarianization, and this, in turn, promotes discontent: if over-population is successfully checked, the spread of Socialism would be done for, and its Socialist State, together with all its glory, buried for all time. Thus we see one more weapon added to the arsenal to kill Socialism with—Malthusianism. The grandiose ignorance of the Socialist-killer Ferdy on Socialism, transpires strongest from the following sentence, which he perpetrates on page 40 of his work:

"Socialism will go further than the Neo-Malthusians in its demands. It will demand that the minimum wage be so fixed that every workingman shall be able to produce as many children as possible under given social facilities for the acquisition of food. . . The moment the ultimate deductions of Socialism are drawn, and private property is abolished, even the dullest will then say to himself: 'Why should I have to work long and hard for the simple reason that it pleases my neighbors to shove a dozen new members into society?'" It should seem that a critic should first acquaint himself with the A B C of Socialism before presuming to write upon the subject, and such preposterous stuff at that!

In Socialist society, where alone mankind will be truly free and planted on its natural basis, it will direct its own development knowingly along the line of natural law. In all epochs hitherto, society handled the questions of production and distribution, as well as of the increase of population without the knowledge of the laws that underlie them,—hence, unconsciously. In the new social order, equipped with the knowledge of the laws of its own development, society will proceed consciously and planfully.

SOCIALISM IS SCIENCE, APPLIED WITH FULL UNDERSTANDING
TO ALL THE FIELDS OF HUMAN ACTIVITY.

[7] Hans Ferdy.

PART VI

CONCLUSION

CONCLUSION.

Our arguments have shown that, with Socialism, the issue is not an arbitrary tearing down and raising up, but a natural process of development. All the factors active in the process of destruction, on the one hand, and of construction, on the other, *are factors that operate in the manner that they are bound to operate.* Neither "statesmen of genius" nor "inflammatory demagogues" can direct events at will. They may imagine they push; but are themselves pushed. But we are near the time when "the hour has sounded."

Due to her own peculiar development, Germany, more than any other country, seems designated as that which is to assume the leading *role* in the pending revolution.[1]

[1] [Aside from the contradiction implied between this sentence and that other, on page 247, in which the internationally overshadowing economic development of the United States is admitted, the forecast, though cautiously advanced, that Germany may take the lead in the accomplishment of the pending Social Revolution, is justified neither by her economic nor her social development, least of all by her geographic location.

As to her economic development, Germany has made rapid and long strides during the last twenty years; so rapid and so long that the progress has caused the Socialists of Germany, in more instances than one, to realize—and to say so—that, what with her own progress, and with outside circumstances, Germany was distancing England economically. This is true. But the same reason that argues, and correctly argues, the economic scepter off the hands of England places it, not in those of Germany, but in the hands of the United States.

As to her social development, Germany is almost half a revolutionary cycle behind. Her own bourgeois revolution was but half achieved. Without entering upon a long list of specifications, it is enough to indicate the fact that Germany is still quite extensively feudal in order to suggest to the mind robust feudal boulders, left untouched by the capitalist revolution, and strewing, aye, obstructing the path of the Socialist Movement in that country. The social phenomenon has been seen of an oppressed class skipping an intermediary stage of vassalage, and entering, at one bound, upon one higher up. It happened, for instance, with our negroes here in America. Without first stepping off at serfdom, they leaped from chattel slavery to wage slavery. What happened once may happen again. But in the instance cited and all the others that we can call to mind, it happened through outside intervention. Can Germany perform the same feat alone, unaided? Do events point in that direction? Or do they rather point in the direction that the work, now being realized there as demanding immediate attention, and alone possible and practicable, is the completion of the capitalist revolution, first of all?

But even discounting both these objections—granting that both in point of economic and of social development Germany were ripe for the Socialist Revolution—her geographic location prevents her leadership. No one single State of the forty-four of the Union, not even the Empire State of New York, however ripe herself, could lead in the overthrow of capitalist rule in America unless the bulk of her sister States were themselves up to a certain minimum of ripeness. Contrariwise, any attempt by even such a State would be promptly smothered. What is true of any single State of the Union is true of any one country of Europe. It is, therefore, true of Germany. Whatever doubt there be as to Germany's ripeness, there can be none as to the utter un-

In the course of this work we often spoke of an over-production of goods, which brings on the crises. This is a phenomenon peculiar to the capitalist world only; it was seen at no previous period of human development.

But the capitalist world yields not merely an over-production of goods and of men, it also yields *an over-production of intelligence*. Germany is the classic land in which this over-production of intelligence, which the bourgeois world no longer knows what to do with, is yielded on a large scale. A circumstance, that for centuries was a misfortune to Germany development, has largely contributed to this state of things. It consisted in the multiplicity of small States and the check exercised by these political formations upon the development of upper capitalism. The multiplicity of small States decentralized the intellectual life of the nation: it raised numerous small centers of culture, and these exercised their influence upon the whole. In comparison with a large central government, the numerous small ones required an extraordinarily large administrative apparatus, whose members needed a certain degree of higher culture. Thus high schools and universities sprung up more numerous than in any other country of Europe. The jealousy and ambition of the several governments played in this no small *role*. The same thing repeated itself when some governments began introducing compulsory education for the people. The passion not to be left behind a neighboring State had here its good effect. The demand for intelligence rose when increasing culture, hand in hand with the material progress of the bourgeoisie, quickened the longing for political activity, popular representation and self-government on the part of municipalities. These were small governmental bodies for small countries and circles, nevertheless they contributed towards the general schooling, and caused the sons of the bourgeoisie to covet seats in them and to adapt their education accordingly.

ripeness of all the other European countries with the single exceptions of France and Belgium,—and surely none as to Russia, that ominous cloud to the East, well styled the modern Macedon to the modern Greek States of the nations of Western Europe. Though there is no "District of Columbia" in Europe, the masses would be mobilized from the surrounding hives of the Cimmerian Darkness of feudo-capitalism, and they would be marched convergently with as much precision and despatch upon the venturesome leader. And what is true as to Germany on this head is true of any other European country. Facts and their relations to one another must be ever kept in sight. 'Tis the only way to escape illusions—and their train of troubles.

For the rest, not the sordid competitive spirit of the bourgeois world, but that noble and ennobling emulation, cited by the Author in a quotation from John Stuart Mill, animates the nations of the world that are now racing towards the overthrow of capitalist domination. Surely none will begrudge the laurels due that one shall be the first to scale the ramparts of the international burg of capitalism, strike the first blow, and give the signal for the final emancipation of the human race.—THE TRANSLATOR.]

As science, so did art fare. No country of Europe has, relatively speaking, so many painting and other art academies, technical schools, museums and art collections, as Germany. Other countries may be able to make better showings in their capitals, but none has such a distribution over its whole territory as Germany. In point of art, Italy is the only exception.

While the bourgeoisie of England had conquered a controlling power over the State as early as the middle of the seventeenth, and the bourgeoisie of France towards the end of the eighteenth century, the bourgeoisie of Germany did not succeed until 1848 to secure for itself a comparatively moderate influence over the government. That was the birth year of the German bourgeoisie as a self-conscious class: it now stepped upon the stage as an independent political party, in the trappings of "liberalism." The peculiar development that Germany had undergone now manifested itself. It was not manufacturers, merchants, men of commerce and finance who came forward as leaders, but chiefly professors, squires of liberal proclivities, writers, jurists and doctors of all academic faculties. It was the German ideologists: And so was their work. After 1848 the German bourgeoisie was temporarily consigned to political silence; but they utilized the period of the sepulchral silence of the fifties in the promotion of their task. The breaking-out of the Austro-Italian war and the commencement of the Regency of Prussia, stirred the bourgeoisie anew to reach after political power. The "National Verein" (National Union) movement began. The bourgeoisie was now too far developed to tolerate within the numerous separate States the many political barriers, that were at the same time economic—barriers of taxation, barriers of communication. It assumed a revolutionary air. Herr von Bismarck understood the situation and turned it to account in his own manner so as to reconcile the interests of the bourgeoisie with those of the Prussian Kingdom, towards which the bourgeoisie never had been hostile, seeing it feared the revolution and the masses. The barriers finally came down that had hampered its material progress. Thanks to Germany's great wealth in coal and minerals, together with an intelligent and easily satisfied working class, the bourgeoisie made within few decades such gigantic progress as was made by the bourgeoisie of no other country, the United States excepted, within the same period. Thus did Germany reach the position of the second industrial and commercial State in Europe; and she covets the first.

This rapid material development had its obverse. The system of mutual exclusion, that existed between the German States up to the establishment of German unity, had until then furnished a living to an uncommonly numerous class of artisans and small peasants. With the precipitous tearing down of all the protective barriers, these people suddenly found themselves face to face with an unbridled process of capitalist production and development. At first, the prosperity epoch of the early seventies caused the danger to seem slighter, but it raged all the moré fearful when the crisis set in. The bourgeoisie had used the prosperity period to make marvelous progress, and thus now caused the distress to be felt ten-fold. From now on the chasm between the property-holding and the propertyless classes widened rapidly. This process of decomposition and of absorption, which—promoted by the growth of material power on the one hand, and the declining power of resistance on the other—proceeds with ever increasing rapidity, throws whole classes of the population into ever more straightened circumstances. They find themselves from day to day more powerfully threatened in their position and their condition of life; and they see themselves doomed with mathematical certainty.

In this desperate struggle many seek possible safety in a change of profession. The old men can no longer make the change: only in the rarest instances are they able to bequeath an independence to their children: the last efforts are made, the last means applied towards placing sons and daughters in positions with fixed salaries, which require no capital to carry on. These are mainly the civil service offices in the Empire, States or municipalities—teacherships, the Post Office and railroad positions, and also the higher places in the service of the bourgeoisie in the counting rooms, stores and factories as managers, chemists, technical overseers, engineers, constructors, etc.; finally the so-called liberal professions: law, medicine, theology, journalism, art, architecture and lastly pedagogy.

Thousands upon thousands, who had previously taken up a trade, now—the possibility of independence and of a tolerable livelihood having vanished—seek for any position in the said offices. The pressure is towards higher education and learning. High schools, gymnasiums, polytechnics, etc., spring up like mushrooms, and those in existence are filled to overflowing. In the same measure the number of students at the universities, at the chemical and physical laboratories, at the art schools, trade and commercial schools and the higher schools of all sorts for women are on the increase. In all departments, without exception, there is a tremendous overcrowding, and the stream still swells: fresh demands are constantly raised for the establishment of more gymnasiums and high schools to accommodate the large number of pupils and students.[2] From official and private sources warnings upon warnings are issued, now against the choice of one then against that of another career. Even theology, that a few decades ago threatened to dry up for want of candidates, now receives its spray from the super-abundance, and again sees its livings filled. "I am ready to preach belief in ten thousand gods and devils, if required, only procure me a position that may support me"—that is the song that re-echoes from all corners. Occasionally, the corresponding Cabinet Minister refuses his consent to the establishment of new institutions of higher education "because those in existence amply supply the demand for candidates of all professions."

This state of things is rendered all the more intolerable by the cir-cumstance that the competitive and mutually destructive struggle of the bourgeoisie compels its own sons to seek for public places. Fur-thermore, the ever increasing standing army with its swarms of officers, whose promotion is seriously paralyzed after a long peace, leads to the placing of large numbers of men in the best years of their lives upon the pension lists, who thereupon, favored by the State, seek all manner of appointments. Another swarm of lower grade in the army, takes the bread from the mouths of the other stratas. Lastly, the still larger

[2] The number of students at the German universities averaged as follows per six months:

Quarter.	Protestant Theology.	Catholic Theology.	Law.	Medicine.	Philosophy.	Total.
1841-42—1846	2117	1027	3467	1943	3072	11626
1846-47—1851	1798	1297	4061	1827	3046	12029
1851-52—1856	1751	1300	4169	2291	2840	12351
1861-62—1866	2437	1153	2867	2435	4392	13284
1866-67—1871	2154	982	3011	2838	4626	13611
1871-72—1876	1780	836	4121	3491	5896	16124
1876-77—1881	1961	682	5134	3734	8057	19568
1881-82—1886	3880	952	5034	6869	9123	25838
1886-87	4546	1178	5239	8450	8666	27828
1887	4803	1232	5505	8685	8424	28455
1887-88	4632	1137	4810	8435	8450	28480
1888	4835	1174	6106	8915	8204	29275
1888-89	4642	1207	6304	8886	8255	29294

During the summer six months of 1893—notably the weaker of the two seasons—the total number of students, exclusive of the University of Bruns-wick, of which we had no returns, had risen to 31,976. Unfortunately we had no like classification of the students, and are hence prevented from insert-ing it in the above table.

The table shows that from 1841-2 to 1871 the number of students increased little, and less than the population. From that date on the increase was by leaps and bounds, until 1886-7; from this date on the increase is again slow. From 1871 to 1888-9 the number of students increased more than 116 per cent. It is an interesting fact that the study of theology decreased steadily until 1881, but increased thereupon all the quicker until it reached high-water mark in 1888. The reason was that the excess of the supply for all the other posts increased in such measure that it was difficult to secure a place. People then turned to theology which had been neglected during the previous ten years.

swarm of children of the Imperial, State and municipal officials of all degrees are and can not choose but be trained especially for such positions in the civil service. Social standing, culture and pretensions—all combine to keep the children of these classes away from the so-called low occupations, which, however, as a result of the capitalist system, are themselves overcrowded.

The system of One Year Volunteers, which allows the reduction of the compulsory military service to one instead of two or three years for those who have obtained a certain degree of education and can make the material sacrifice, is another source from which the candidates for public office is swollen. Many sons of well-to-do peasants, who do not fancy a return to the village and to the pursuit of their fathers, come under this category.

As a result of all these circumstances, Germany has an infinitely more numerous proletariat of scholars and artists than any other country, as also a strong proletariat in the so-called liberal professions. This proletariat is steadily on the increase, and carries the fermentation and discontent with existing conditions into the higher strata of society. This youth are roused and spurred to the criticism of the existing order, and they materially aid in hastening the general work of dissolution. Thus the existing condition of things is attacked and undermined from all sides.

All these circumstances have contributed to cause the German Social Democratic party to take a hand in the leadership of the giant struggle of the future. It was German Socialists who discovered the motor laws of modern society, and who scientifically demonstrated Socialism to be the social form of the future. First of all Karl Marx and Frederick Engels; next to them and firing the masses with his agitation, Ferdinand Lasselle. Finally German Socialists are the chief pioneers of Socialist thought among the workingmen of all nations.

Almost half a century ago—grounded on his studies of the German mind and culture—Buckle could say that, although Germany had a large number of the greatest thinkers, there was no country in which the chasm between the class of the scholars and the mass of the population was as wide. This is no longer true. It was so only so long as knowledge was confined to learned circles that stood aloof from practical life. Since Germany has been economically revolutionized, science was compelled to render itself useful to practical life. Science itself became practical. It was felt that science attained its full worth only when it became applicable to human life; and the development of large capitalist production compelled it thereto. All the branches of science have been, accordingly, strongly democratized during the last decades. The large number of young men, educated for the higher professions, contributed to carry science among the people; then also the general schooling, higher to-day in Germany than in most European countries, facilitated the popular reception of a mass of intellectual products. But above all, the Socialist Movement—with its literature, its press, its unions and meetings, its parliamentary representation, and finally the incessant criticism thereby promoted on all the fields of public life—materially raised the mental level of the masses.

The exclusion law against the Social Democratic party did not check this current. It somewhat hemmed in the Movement, and slightly reduced its tempo. But, on the other hand, it caused the roots of the Movement to sink deeper, and aroused an intense bitterness against the ruling classes and the government. The final abandonment of the exclusion law was but the consequence of the progress made by the Social Democratic party under that very law, together with the economic development of the nation. And thus the Movement goes marching onward, as march it must under existing conditions.

As in Germany, the Socialist Movement has made unexpected progress in all European civilized nations, a fact eloquently attested to by the International Congresses of Labor, which, with intervals of two or three years, gather with ever increased representations.

Thus with the close of the nineteenth century the great battle of minds is on in all the countries of civilization, and is conducted with fiery enthusiasm. Along with social science, the wide field of the natural sciences, hygiene, the history of civilization and even philosophy are the arsenals from which the weapons are drawn. The foundations of existing society are being assailed from all sides; heavy blows are being dealt to its props. Revolutionary ideas penetrate conservative circles and throw the ranks of our enemies into disorder. Artisans and scholars, farmers, and artists, merchants and government employes, here and there, even manufacturers and bankers, in short, men of all conditions, are joining the ranks of the workingmen, who constitute the bulk of the army, who combat for victory, and who will win it. All support and mutually supplement one another.

To woman also in general, and as a female proletarian in particular, the summons goes out not to remain behind in this struggle in which her redemption and emancipation are at stake. It is for her to prove that she has comprehended her true place in the Movement and in the struggles of the present for a better future; and that she is resolved to join. It is the part of the men to aid her in ridding herself of all superstitions, and to step forward in their ranks. Let none underrate his own powers, and imagine that the issue does not depend upon him. None, be he the weakest, can be spared in the struggle for the progress of the human race. The unremitting dropping of little drops hollows in the end the hardest stone. Many drops make a brook, brooks make rivers, many rivers a stream, until finally no obstacle is strong enough to check it in its majestic flow. Just so with the career of mankind. Everywhere Nature is our instructress. If all who feel the call put their whole strength in this struggle, ultimate victory can not fail.

And this victory will be all the greater the more zealously and self-sacrificing each pursues the marked-out path. None may allow himself to be troubled with misgivings whether, despite all sacrifices, labor and pains he will live to see the beginning of the new and fairer period of civilization, whether he will yet taste the fruit of victory; least of all may such misgivings hold him back. We can foresee neither the duration nor the nature of the several phases of development that this struggle for the highest aims may traverse until final victory,—any more than we have any certainty on the duration of our own lives. Nevertheless, just as the pleasure in life rules us, so may we foster the hope of witnessing this victory. Are we not in an age that rushes forward, so to speak, with seven-mile boots, and therefore causes all the foes of a new and better world to tremble?

Every day furnishes fresh proof of the rapid growth and spread of the ideas that we represent. On all fields there is tumult and push. The dawn of a fair day is drawing nigh with mighty stride. Let us then ever battle and strive forward, unconcerned as to "where" and "when" the boundary-posts of the new and better day for mankind will be raised. And if, in the course of this great battle for the emancipation of the human race, we should fall, those now in the rear will step forward; we shall fall with the consciousness of having done our duty as human beings, and with the conviction that the goal will be reached, however the powers hostile to humanity may struggle or strain in resistence.

OURS IS THE WORLD, DESPITE ALL;—THAT IS, FOR THE
WORKER AND FOR WOMAN.

FINIS.